AF413378

# The Pleasure of Rope

Kahboom

First published in the United Kingdom in 2017  by Kahboom Ltd.

office@kahboom.com

©Kahboom Ltd.

ISBN 97809576275-3-6



Printed in Lithuania

# The Pleasure of Rope

## EXPLORING THE JAPANESE ART OF KINBAKU

BOB BENTLEY

Kahboom

# Credits and Acknowledgements

**The following contributors are featured in this book in order of appearance:**

Esinem

Gestalta

Nawashi Murakawa

Aizen Kaguya

Kinoko Hajime

Midori

Yukkie

Osada Steve

Mayura

Chika

Ichinawa-Kai

Kitty Mooschief

Kazami Ranki

Susie-Wong

Clover

WykD Dave

Yui Namiko

JTK

Ichigo

Hedwig

Dangerous Dolly

Simona Martini

Siân Williams

Tuppy Owens

Maria

Xue Wang

Boy Kitten

Rod MacDonald

Rebecca Tun

Vlada

Falco

Nina Russ

Gorgone

Andrea Ropes

Amy Morgan

Scarlet Rose

Dutch Dame

Rope Marks

Saki Kamijoo

Skinny Redhead

Nancy Wing

Jon Jonze

Naka Akira

Iroha Shizuki

Tom Frackrell

Bianca Zahara

Miumi-U

Maya Homerton

Fuoco

Bliss

**Special Thanks to:**

Garry Vanderhorne

Resistance Gallery

Toubaku Festival

The Flying Dutchman

Coco De Mer

Outsiders

Candid Arts Centre

Sh! Women's Erotic Emporium

Exodus

Jayne & Toby ( Tortoise )

Nana ( Translator )

Ad Meskens (archive page 33)

**Production**

Matchframe ( camera & technical services )

**Production Assistance**

Camille Saint-Pierre

Aizen Kaguya

**Still Photographers**

Ben Hooper,  page 67

Nan Zhang,  pages 82, 83

Rod MacDonald,   pages 93, 94

Mike Lee,  page 143

Clover,   pages 156, 157, 158, 159

**Additional Cinematographers**

Daniel Saul

Ricardo Sleiman

Hebari

Christopher Dengh

**Colourist**

Patrick Siboni

**Film Editors**

Daniel Saul

Ricardo Sleiman

**Book Editor**

Philip Blakeley

**Original movie:**

**filmed, directed and produced by**

Bob Bentley

# Contents

Kinbaku, or Shibari as it's also called, is a Japanese performance art form that has grown from historical obscurity to become a popular passion for men, women and couples in the worldwide BDSM scene. I discovered this community of passionate people in 2010 and as a documentary film maker wanted to make an honest film about them.  Four years later this resulted in a feature documentary which eventually led to the publication of this book.

### THE FILM

As a director I usually shoot with crews but on 'The Pleasure of Rope' I filmed mostly by myself (apart from stage performances) which gave wonderful opportunities to get to know people. I shot in Japan and then the UK, completing post production in 2015. The end result is a film about my personal experience - in which I try to understand the world of Japanese rope bondage.

In both countries I filmed performances and went back stage at Kinbaku bondage festivals to meet people who make rope a significant part of their lives. They allowed me to film them at workshop events, their homes and in some unusual locations.

I asked many of the World's top Kinbaku artists to contribute. Some did the tying, others are bound and suspended, a few explore both experiences.

By getting up close and personal, I attempted to capture the Japanese eroticism of rope play, recording intimate thoughts and emotions. Such insights reveal what I believe is the true story of Japanese rope bondage, in narratives that are sometimes surprising - and occasionally disturbing!

Together with my colleagues, we produced three versions: a 90 min television film, a 120 min theatrical film and a series of three parts, totalling 156 minutes. The different versions have been

The more comprehensive three part series has been released as a DVD - with many extras. It acquired an 18 certificate from the British Board of Film Classification even though it is less censored than the broadcast versions.

### THE BOOK

This book celebrates the three part series with extras - using image screen grabs and transcripts from the soundtrack. We have structured it in a similar way to the film - in three chapters:

JAPAN AND BACK - This describes what Shibari/Kinbaku is and takes the viewer on a journey to experience the real thing in Japan. A return visit to London by Japanese rope practitioners inspires enthusiastic responses.

CREATIVE TIES - We show how rope has been incorporated into various art forms, including painting, dance, film, photography and performance art. It is seen as part of the erotic landscape, being a therapeutic experience, enhancing understanding of mind and body.

INTIMATE BONDS - By going deeper into more extreme aspects of rope bondage, we show the passion and pain with the people who are most involved. I wanted to explore psychological desires and motivations.

Our book of 'The Pleasure of Rope' is designed to be the perfect companion to what I hope is a very collectable DVD. By going hand in hand the intention is to provide an experience you will wish to visit again and again.

Bob Bentley

www.thepleasureofrope.com

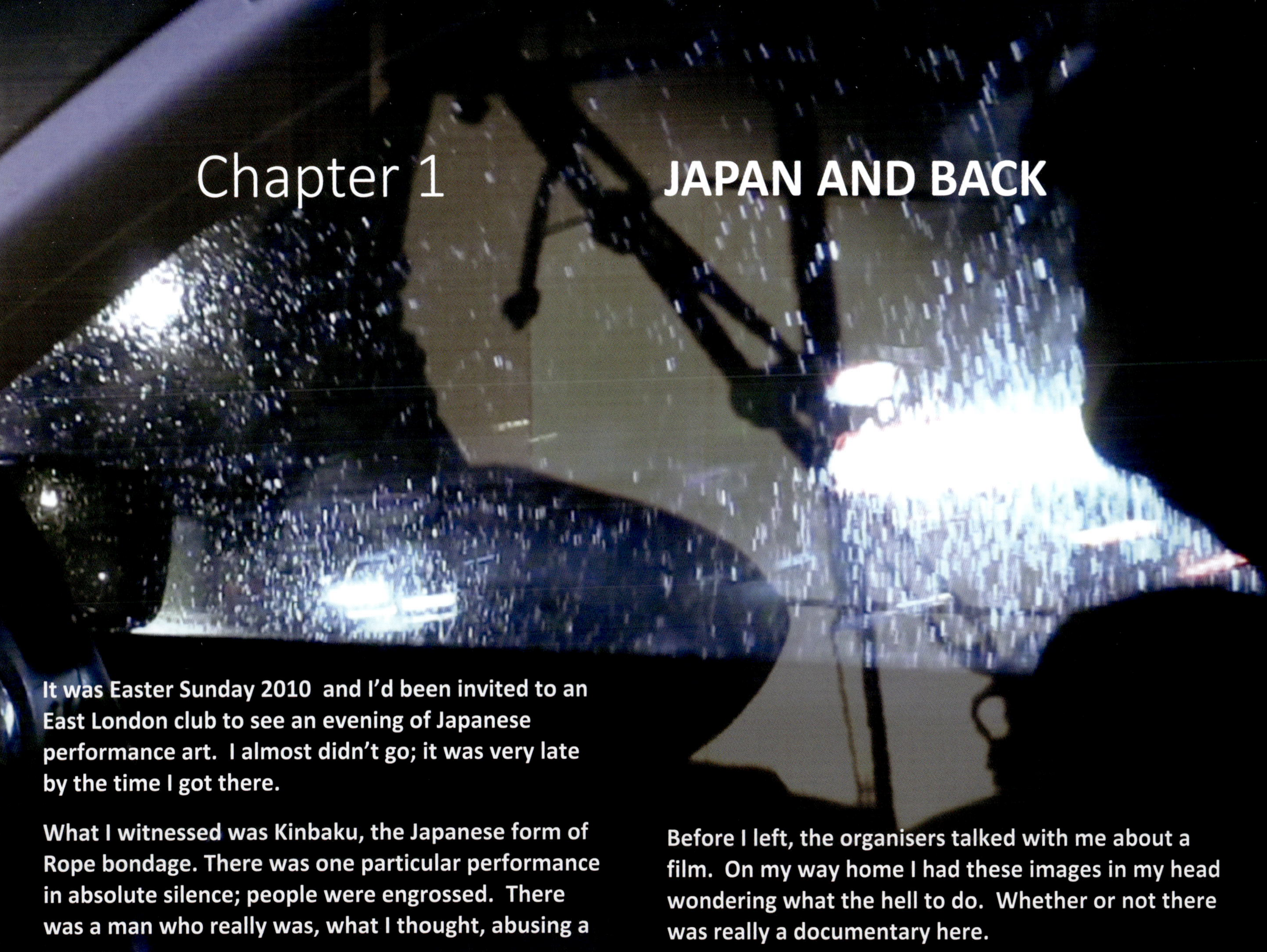

# Chapter 1     JAPAN AND BACK

It was Easter Sunday 2010 and I'd been invited to an East London club to see an evening of Japanese performance art. I almost didn't go; it was very late by the time I got there.

What I witnessed was Kinbaku, the Japanese form of Rope bondage. There was one particular performance in absolute silence; people were engrossed. There was a man who really was, what I thought, abusing a woman.

I couldn't believe the audience, particularly the women in the audience were not objecting to this.

A little while later, the couple who had been performing were in the bar and everyone seemed very happy with the show.

Before I left, the organisers talked with me about a film. On my way home I had these images in my head wondering what the hell to do. Whether or not there was really a documentary here.

I decided there was. This was really intriguing.

So this was the beginning of over four years in bondage attempting to understand rope. I wanted to meet the people who would take me on this journey…..

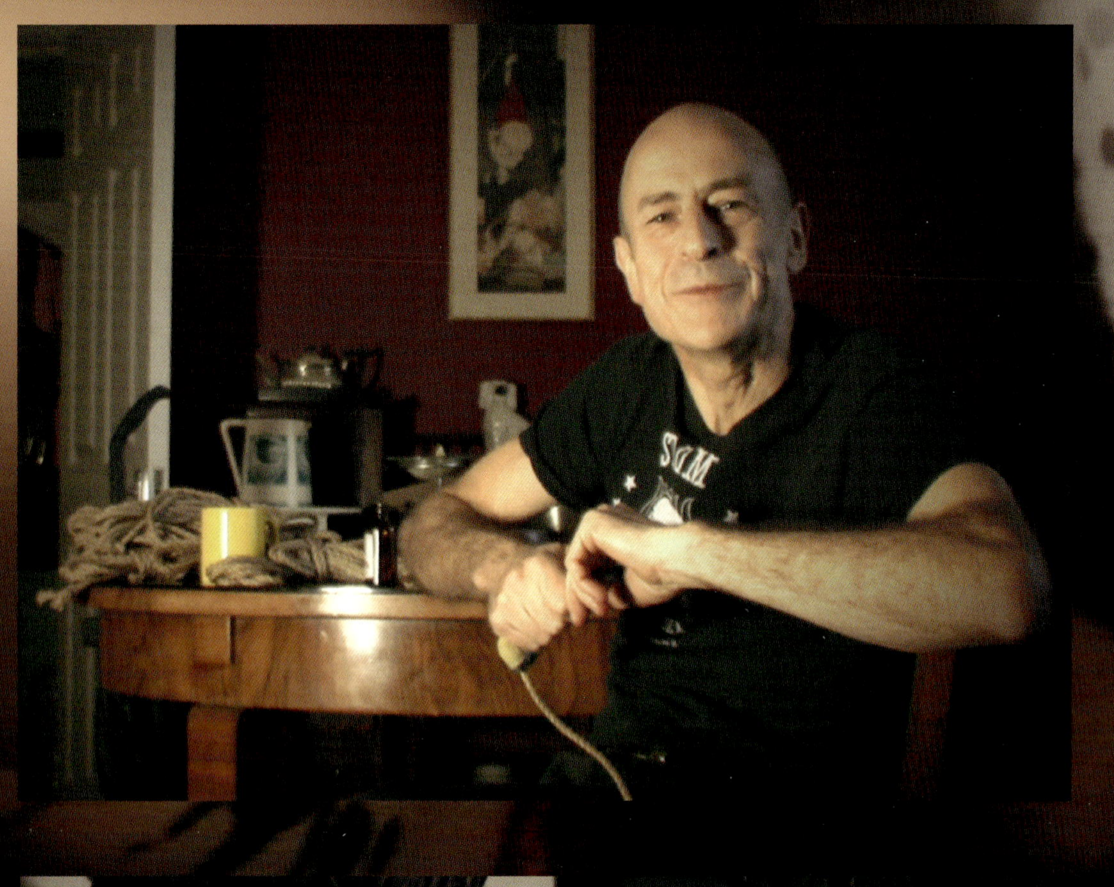

**The main organisers of the first London rope bondage event I attended included Bruce, otherwise known as Esinem.**

Esinem: I can think back to when I was a kid of about six or seven years old enjoying games that involved capturing people and taking people prisoner, with the girl across the road from me.  I am sure I had no idea of the connotations of it, but I just know that I enjoyed those sorts of games.

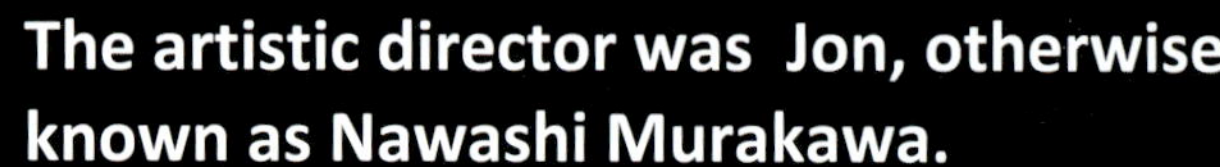

**The artistic director was  Jon, otherwise known as Nawashi Murakawa.**

Nawashi Murakawa: I describe Japanese rope bondage as an art form.  That's how I see it.  But others see it differently.  For myself I don't see it as a thing to control people.  I'm a facilitator - bringing something to the person I'm working with.

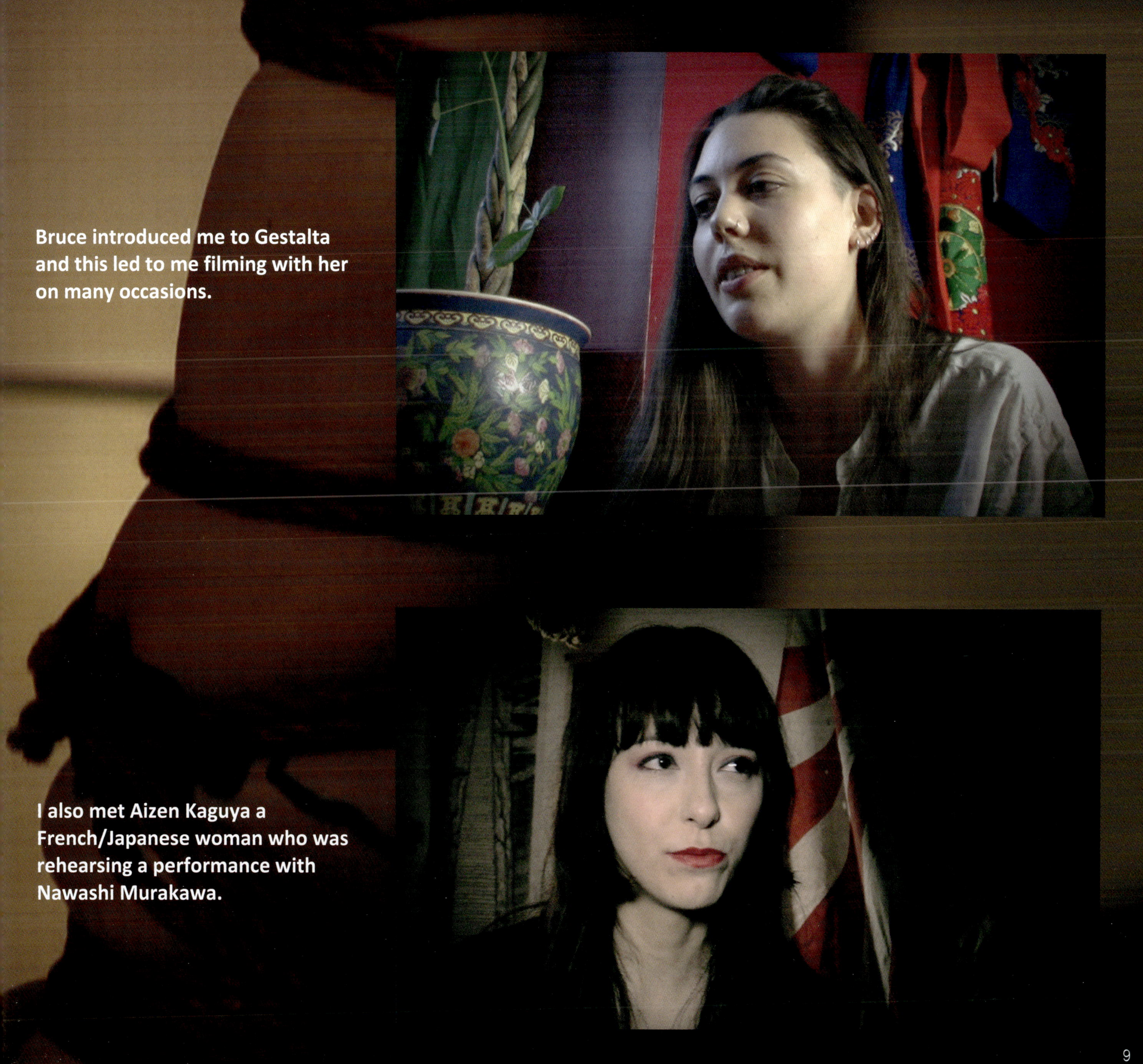

Bruce introduced me to Gestalta
and this led to me filming with her
on many occasions.

I also met Aizen Kaguya a
French/Japanese woman who was
rehearsing a performance with
Nawashi Murakawa.

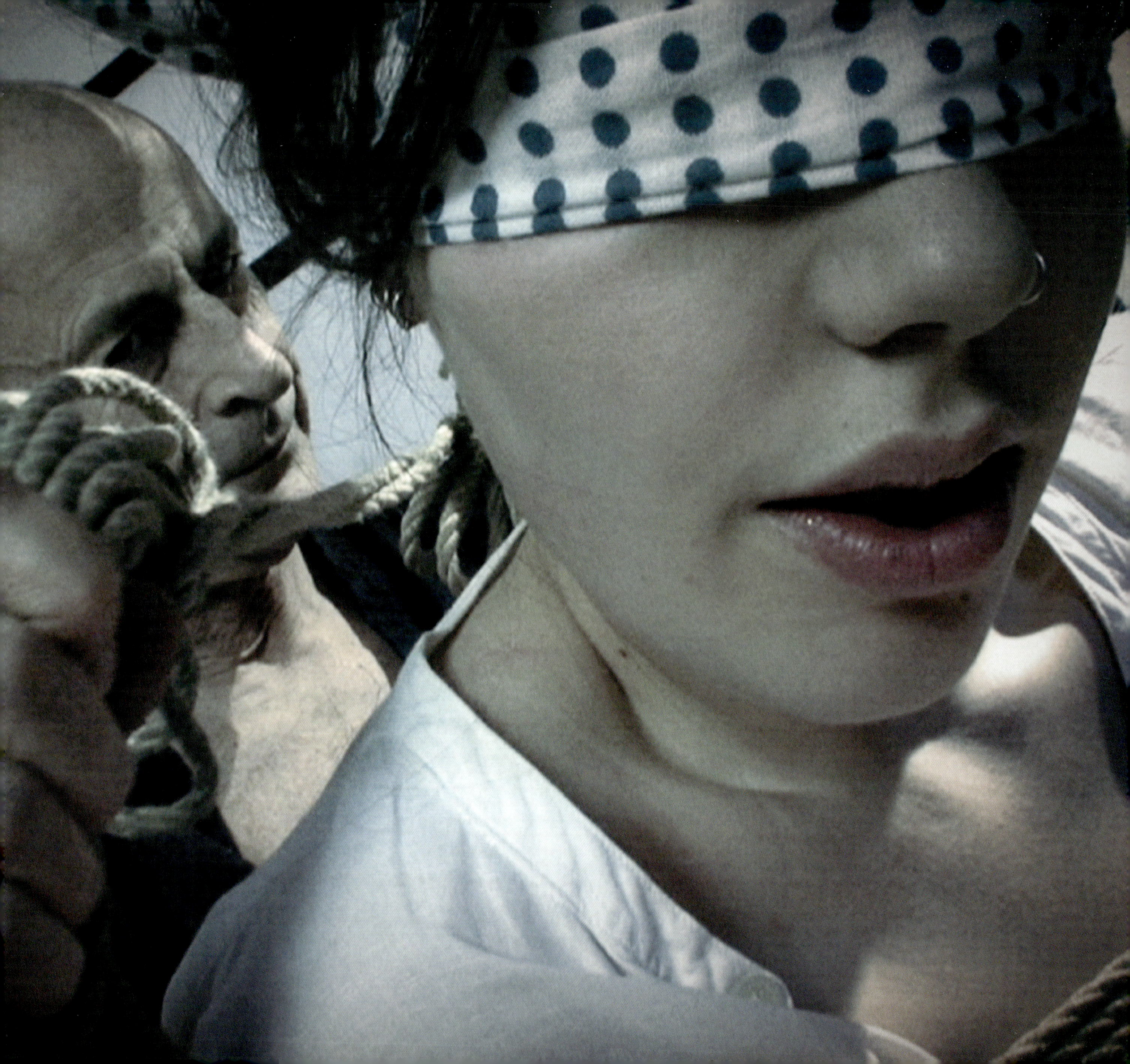

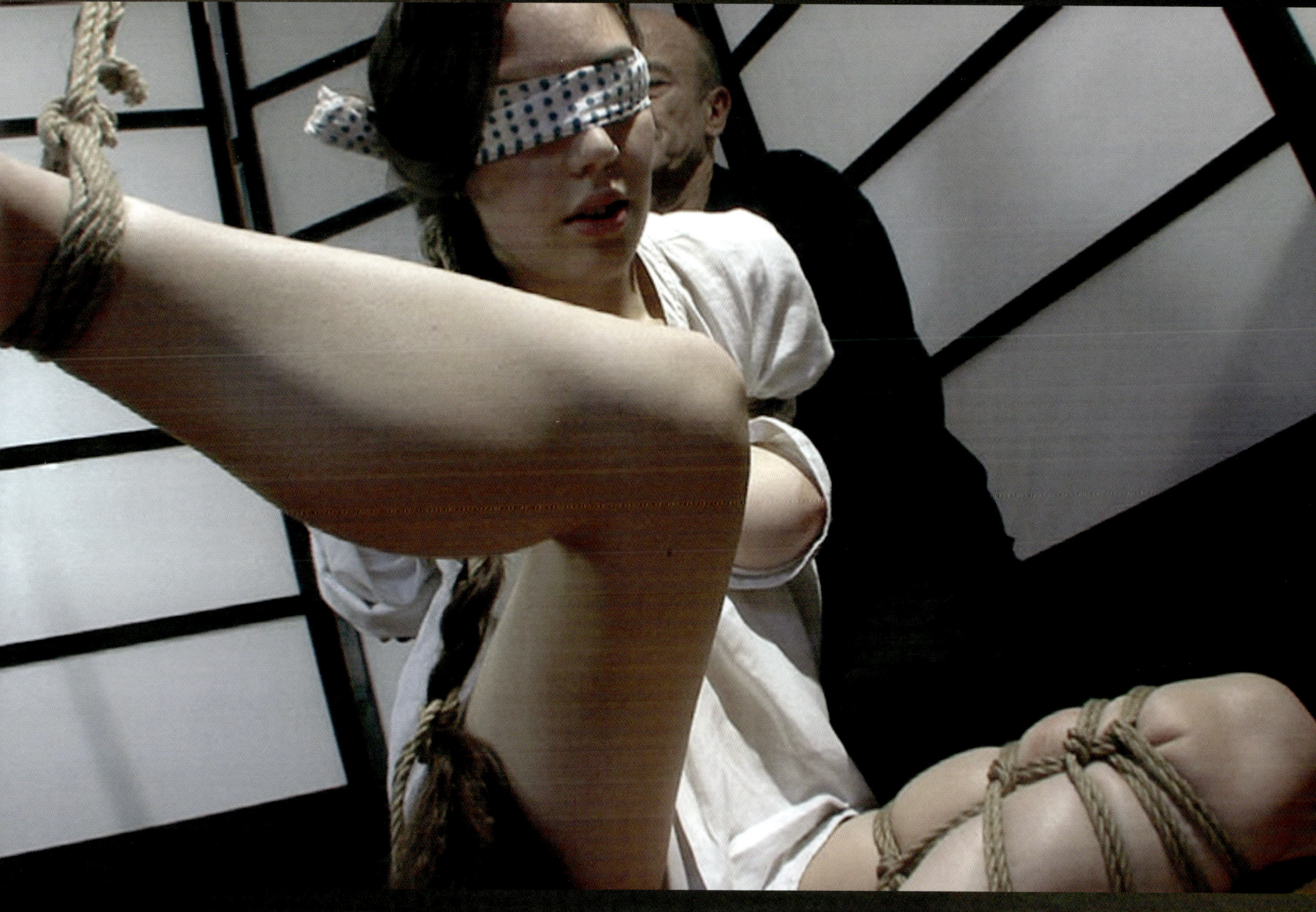

Gestalta:  I suppose I'm a bit masochistic, and got into the whole fetish scene and into other sorts of pain before I ever did any ties that were even vaguely painful.  Once I discovered it, it was a bit of a revelation in that it suddenly made so much sense.  Prior to that I'd been a bit confused as to why I was never hugely excited about ….  well, sex in general actually.  Once I sort of discovered the pain side of it, suddenly … but of course that's what I should have been doing all the time.

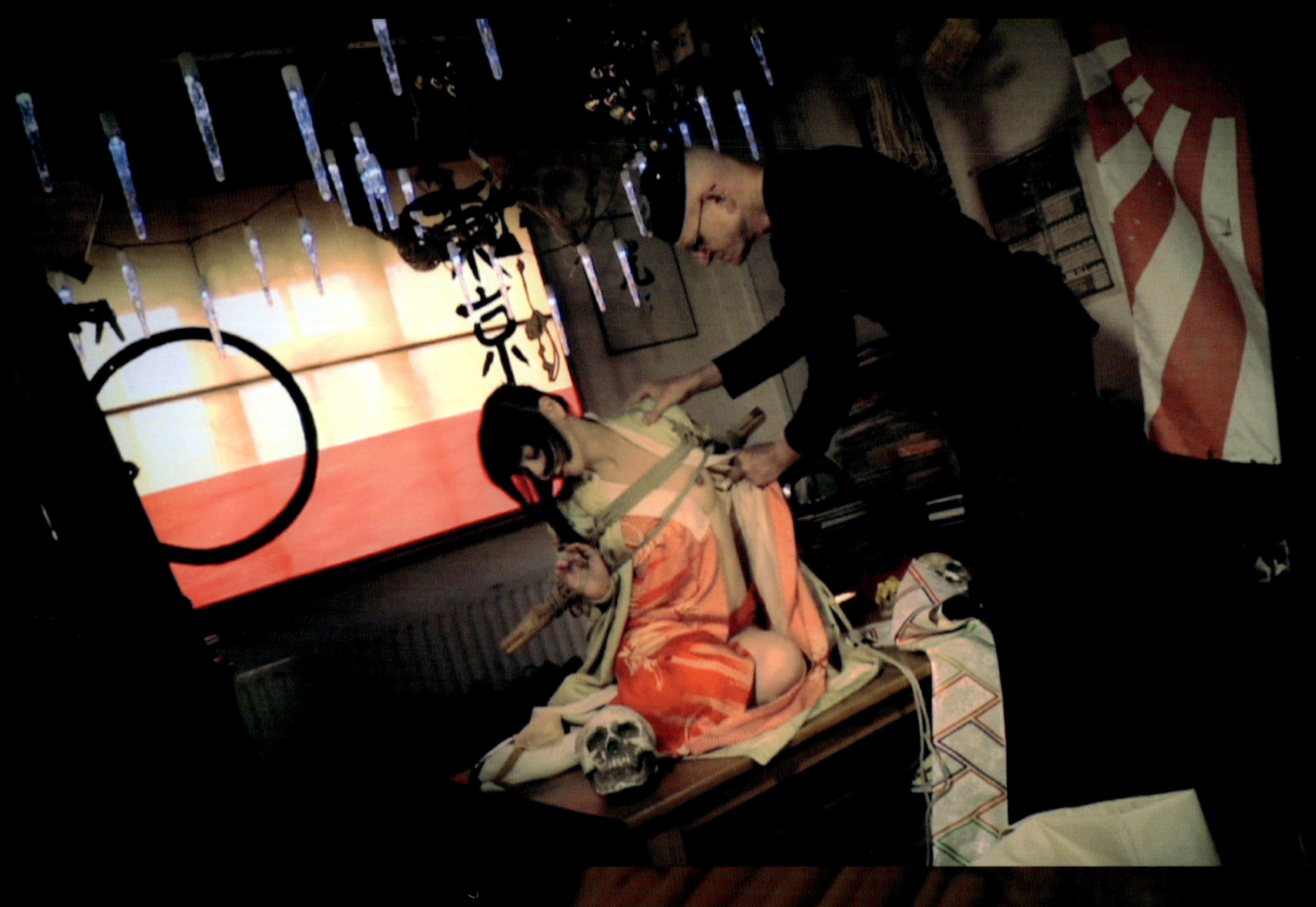

Esinem: I really started watching a lot of people whose style I liked. One of those was Nawashi Murakawa, English guy, living in London who's got a very, very nice style.

Aizen: He is very creative - he has his own style - very Japanese - very traditional.

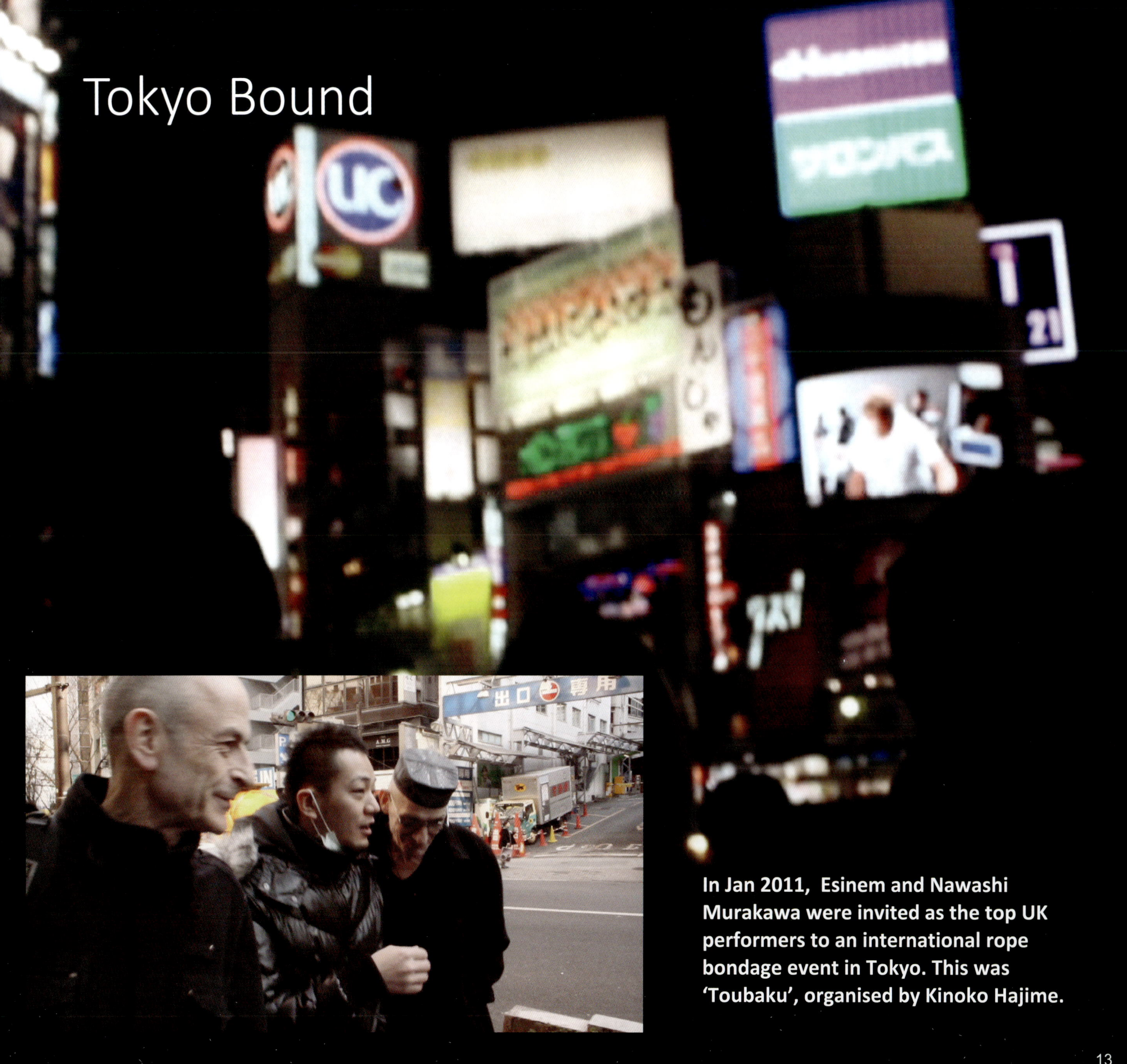

# Tokyo Bound

In Jan 2011,  Esinem and Nawashi Murakawa were invited as the top UK performers to an international rope bondage event in Tokyo. This was 'Toubaku', organised by Kinoko Hajime.

# Midori

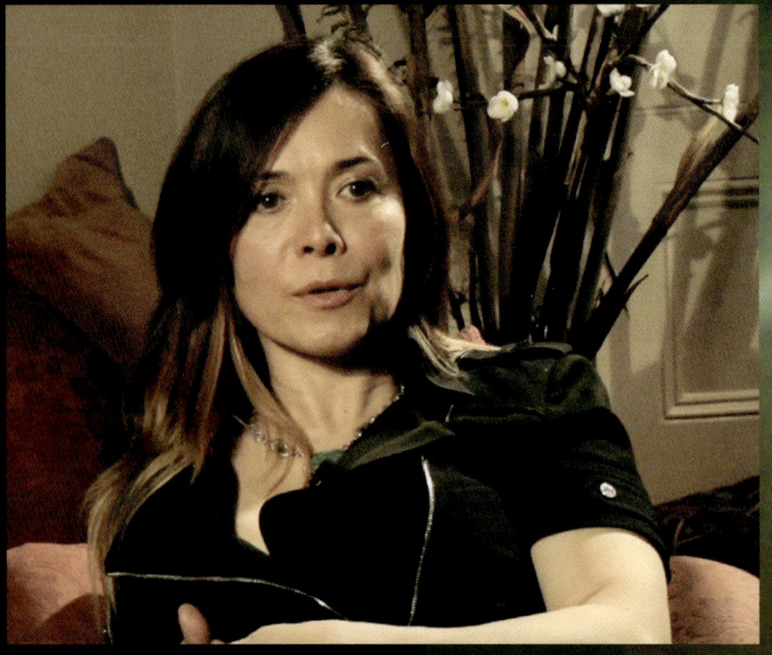

**Midori, a Japanese/American was also performing at the bondage festival.**

Midori:  Toubaku was this fabulous festival of rope bondage performances that Kinoko and his crew put on in a multi-story building in Tokyo.  I was invited there as the American performer, which is kind of funny because for me it's going home because I'm originally from Tokyo.

In my performance I took on the role of the female Ninja, the Kunoichi who captured men, tied them up, and decorated them with red roses.  That is a cue for the Barazoku; Japanese reference to gay men.

And then, with cherry blossom falling down, I cut the rope holding the men so that the lovers crumble into an embrace.

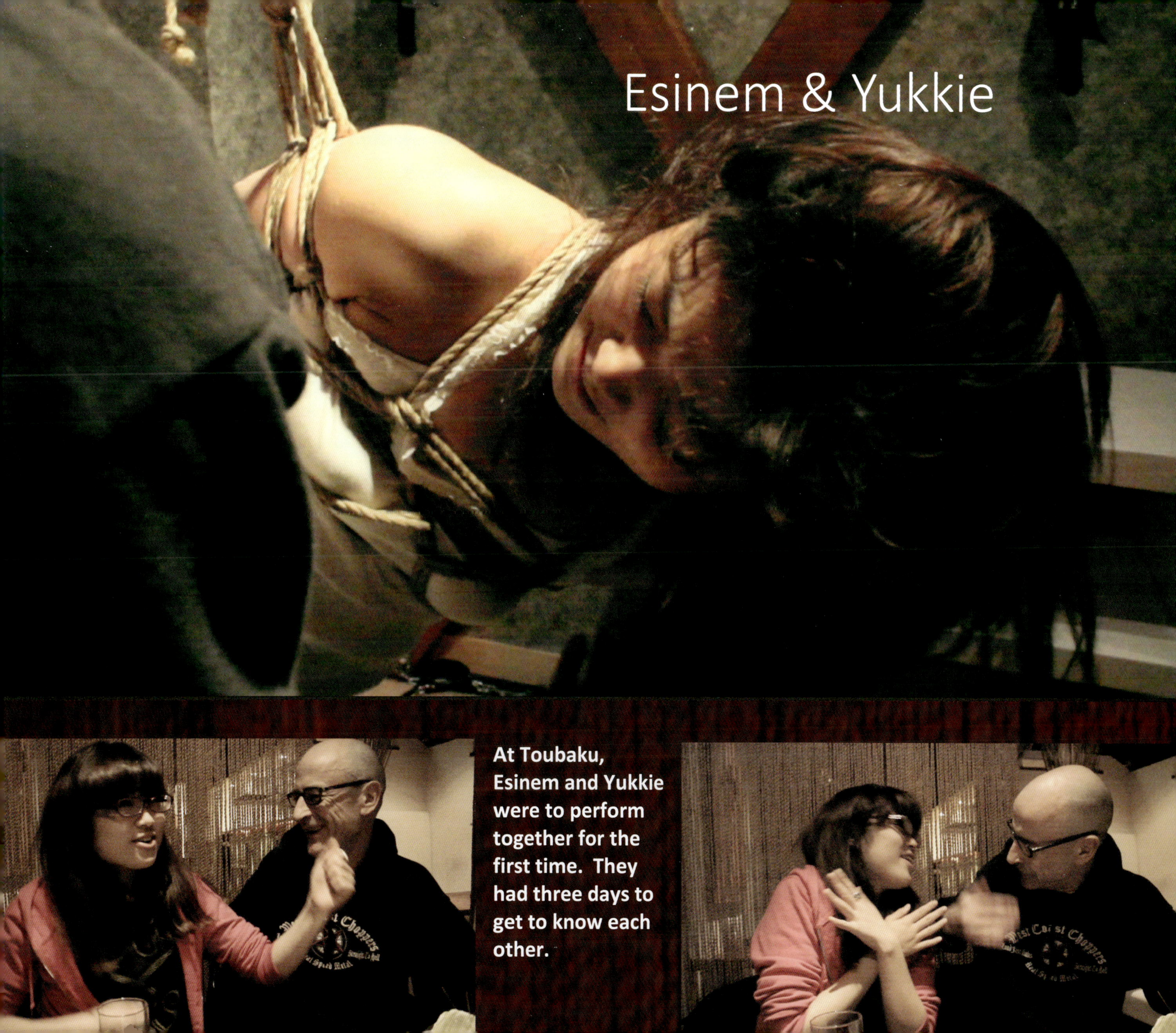

Esinem & Yukkie
At Toubaku, Esinem and Yukkie were to perform together for the first time. They had three days to get to know each other.

Esinem:  OK, here we are in Kinoko's apartment.  It's gonna be my home for the next week

**Yukkie also moved into the apartment for the run up to the performance on the Sunday.**

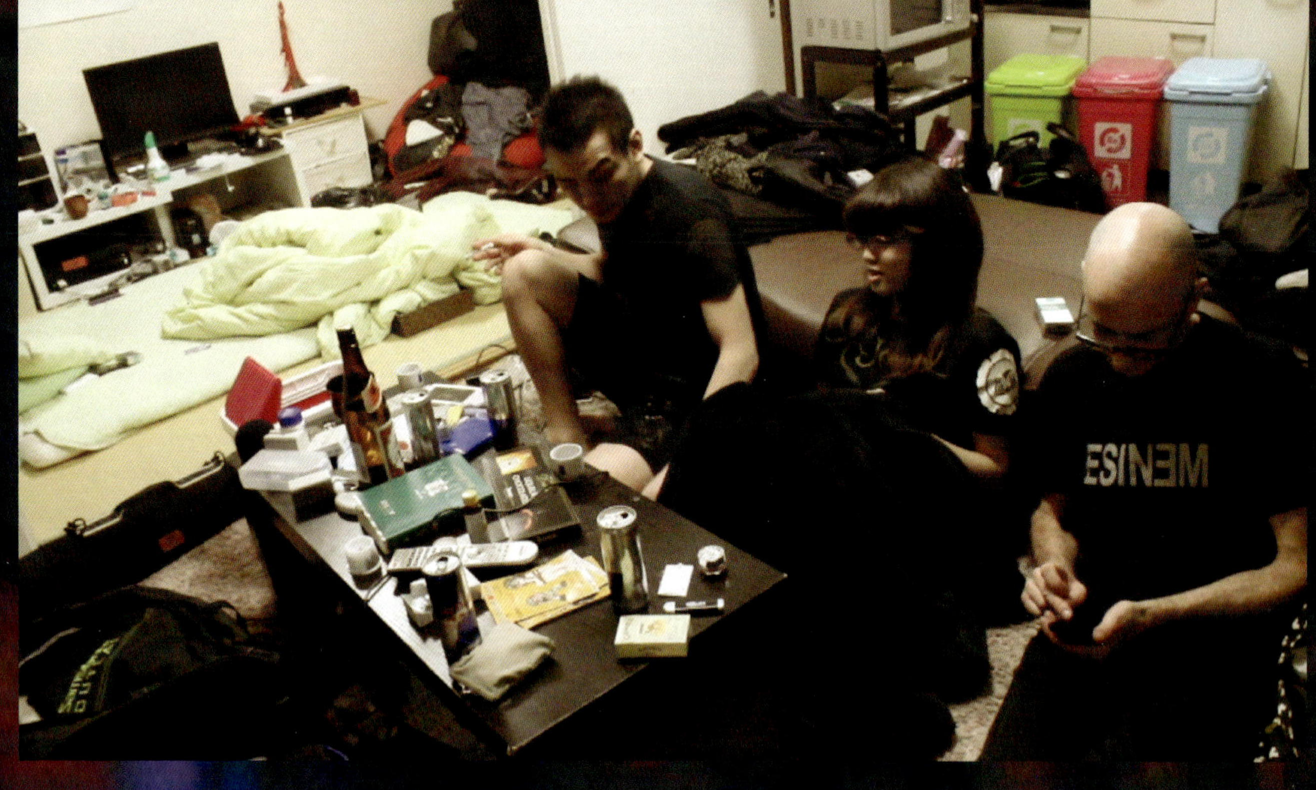

Yukkie: I want to have some normal time with Esinem , not Kinbaku time.  I want to have normal time like wake up and have breakfast. I would like to build some familiarity before the performance and would like to stay with him in a more relaxing place.

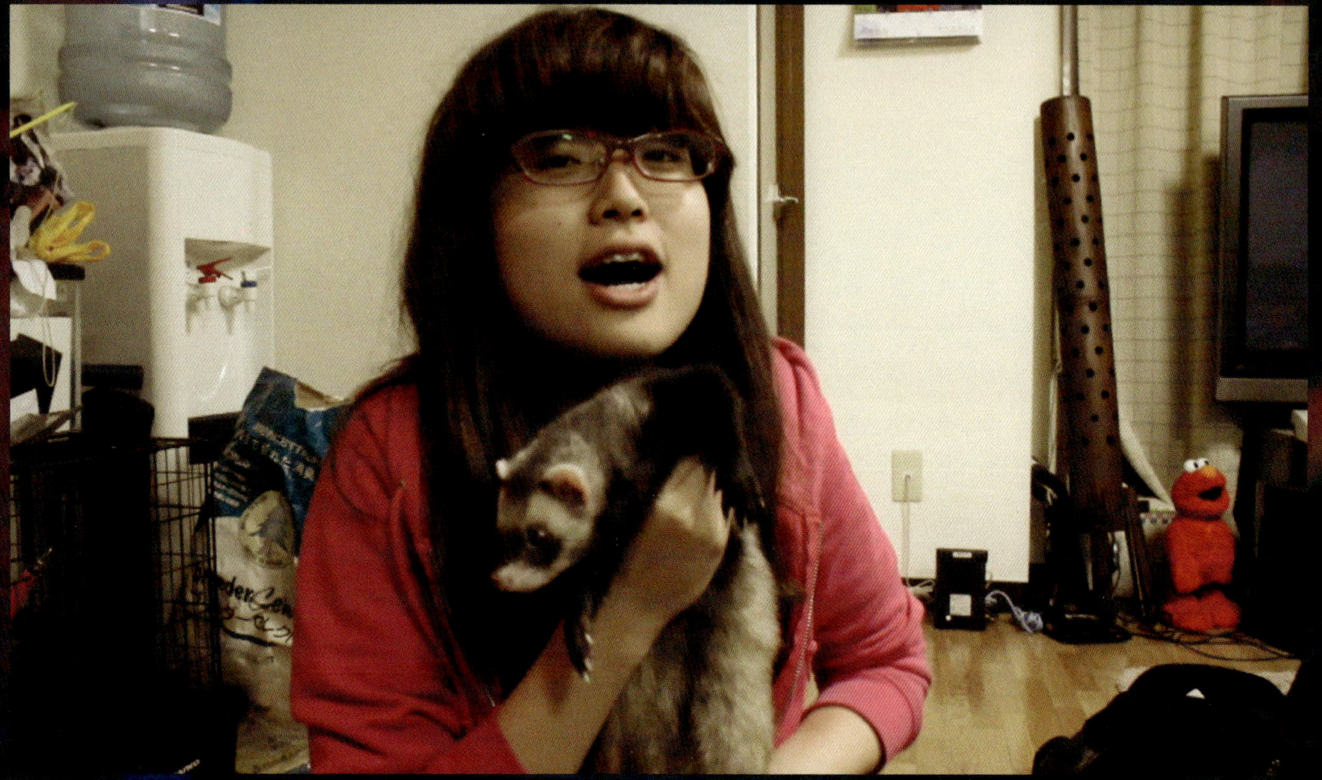

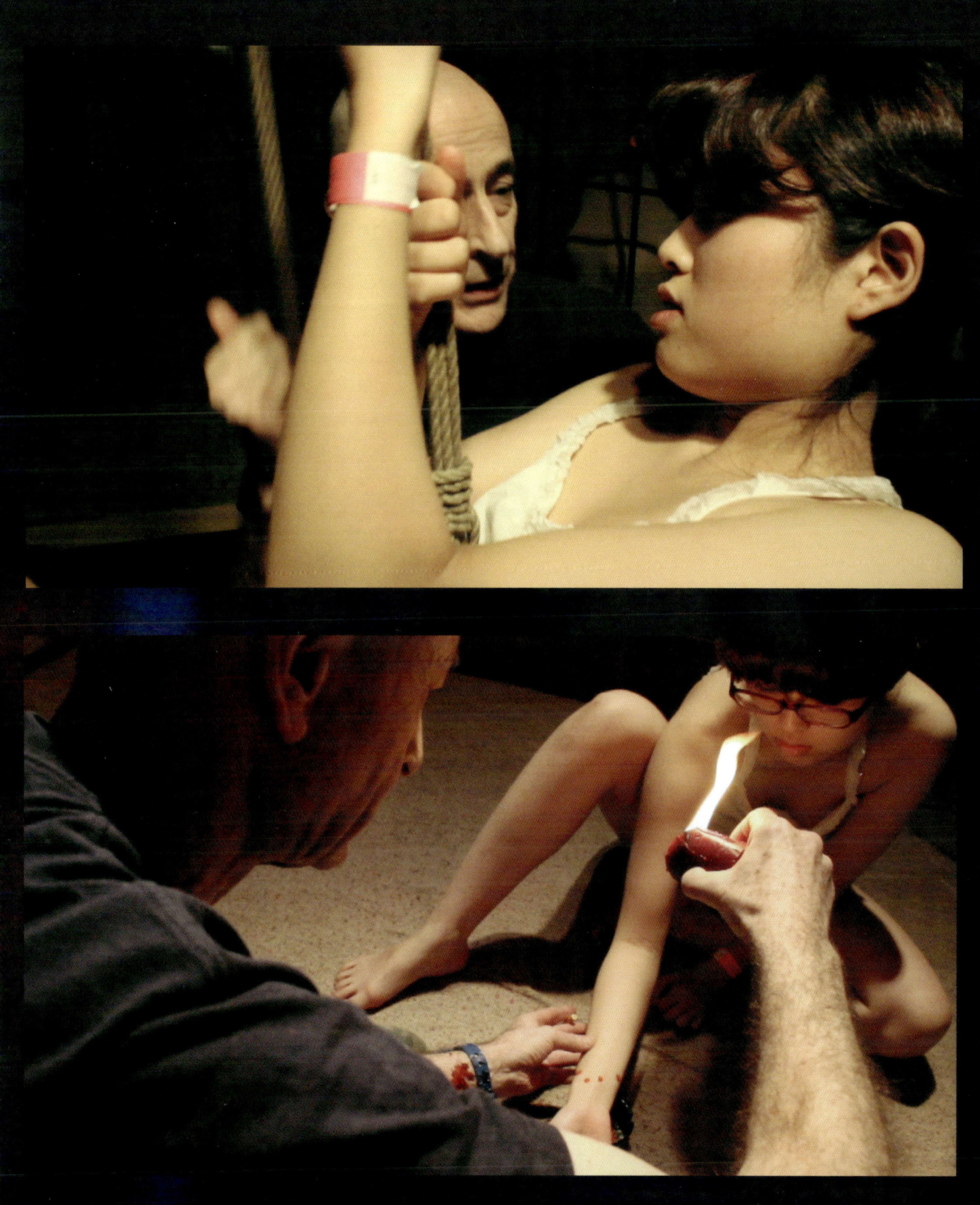

Esinem:  It's kind of surprising given – what appears to be in many ways a repressive culture – this very mysterious veneer that is a stereotype of the oriental.  There's a certain truth in that but you won't necessarily see what's going on inside from the outside.

There is a concept of beautiful suffering in Japanese culture.

And there is a comparison made between the expressions from pain and the expressions from an orgasm.

You see that the wrist is a very sensitive place for the hot wax - other parts are less sensitive.

After many rehearsals,
they are ready.

On the day of the event
they buy flowers.
Yukkie is to be tied with
them so they can be
whipped from her while
she is suspended.

This is her first public
Kinbaku performance.

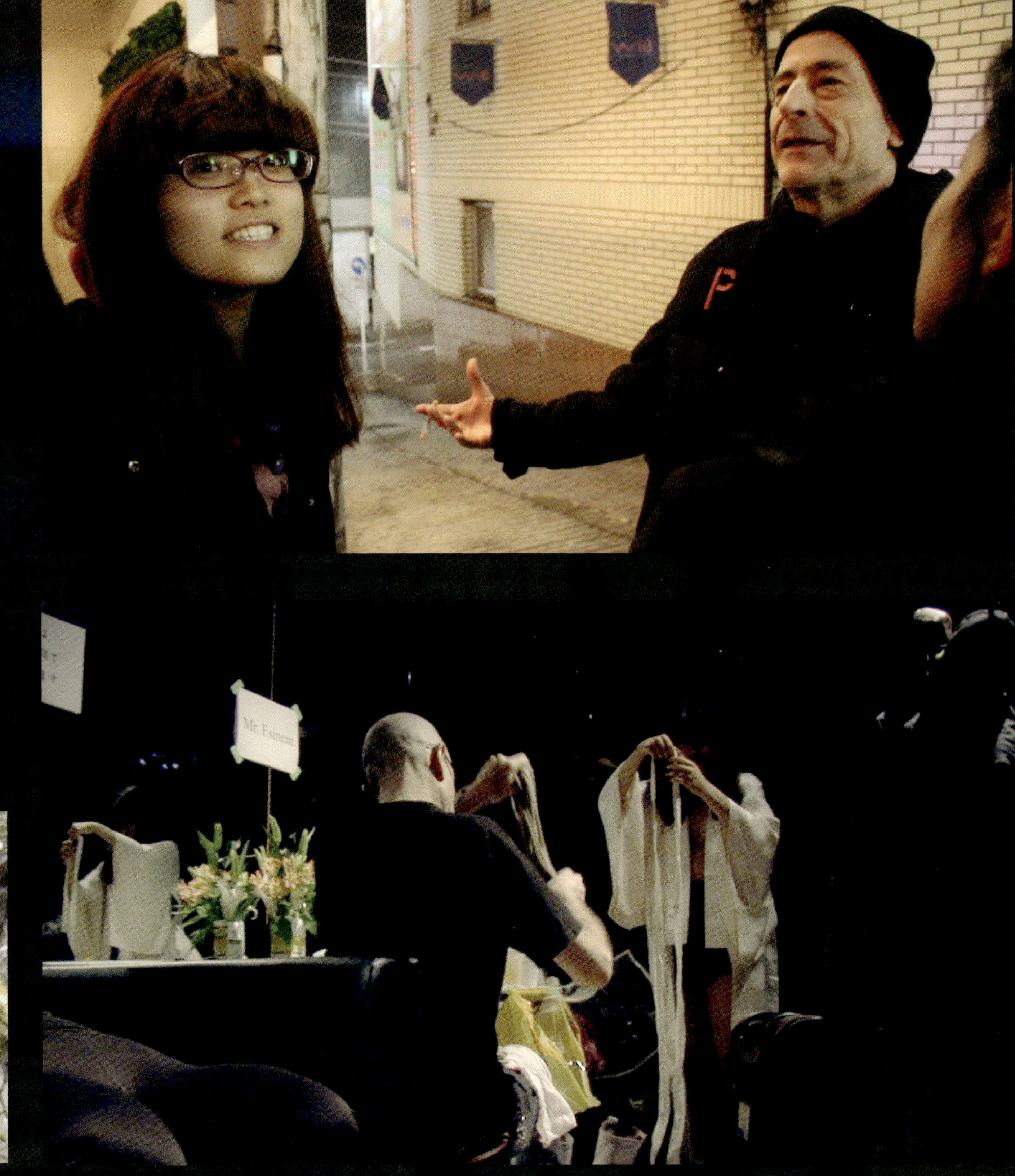

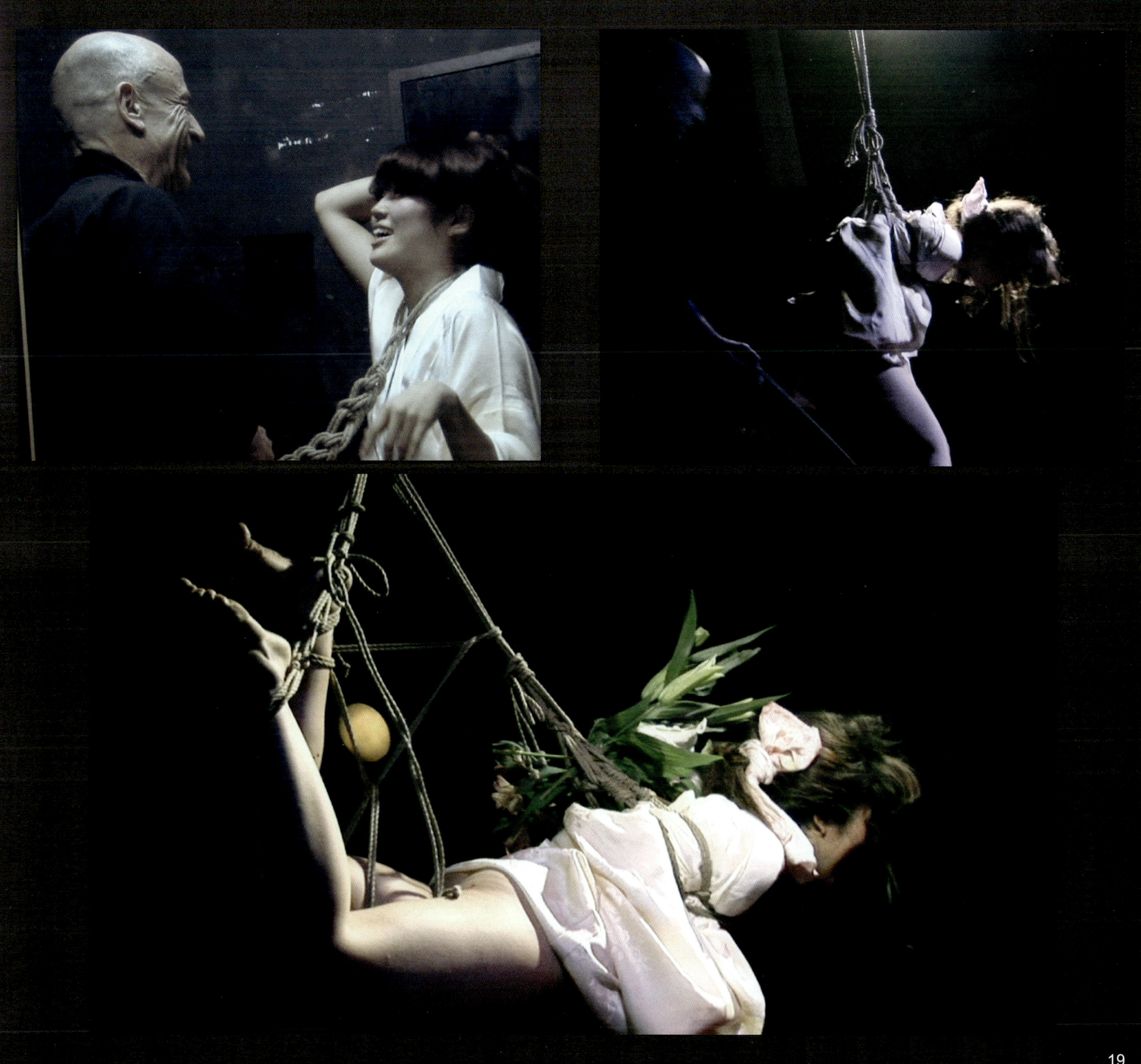

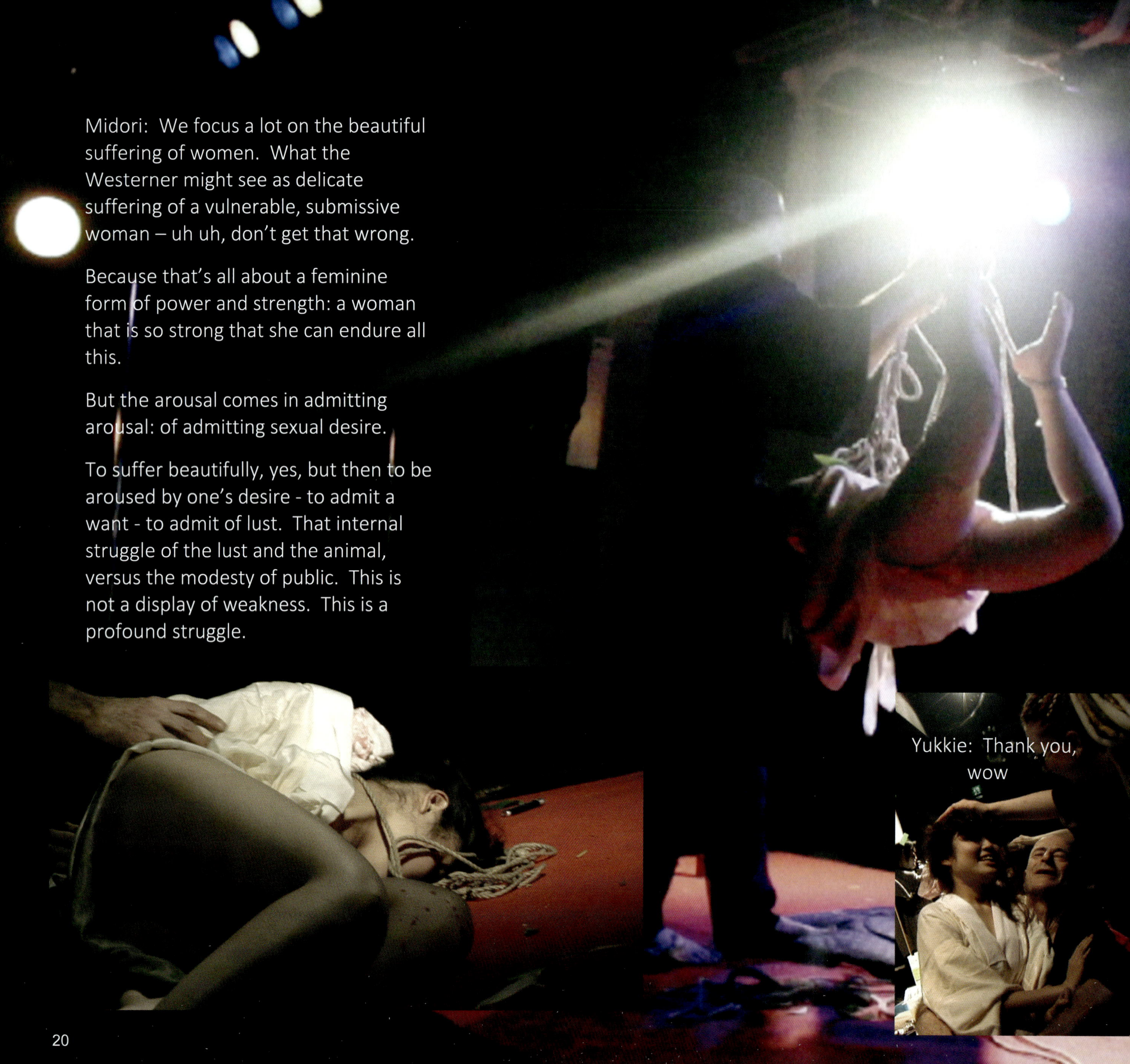

Midori:  We focus a lot on the beautiful suffering of women.  What the Westerner might see as delicate suffering of a vulnerable, submissive woman – uh uh, don't get that wrong.

Because that's all about a feminine form of power and strength: a woman that is so strong that she can endure all this.

But the arousal comes in admitting arousal: of admitting sexual desire.

To suffer beautifully, yes, but then to be aroused by one's desire - to admit a want - to admit of lust.  That internal struggle of the lust and the animal, versus the modesty of public.  This is not a display of weakness.  This is a profound struggle.

Yukkie:  Thank you, wow

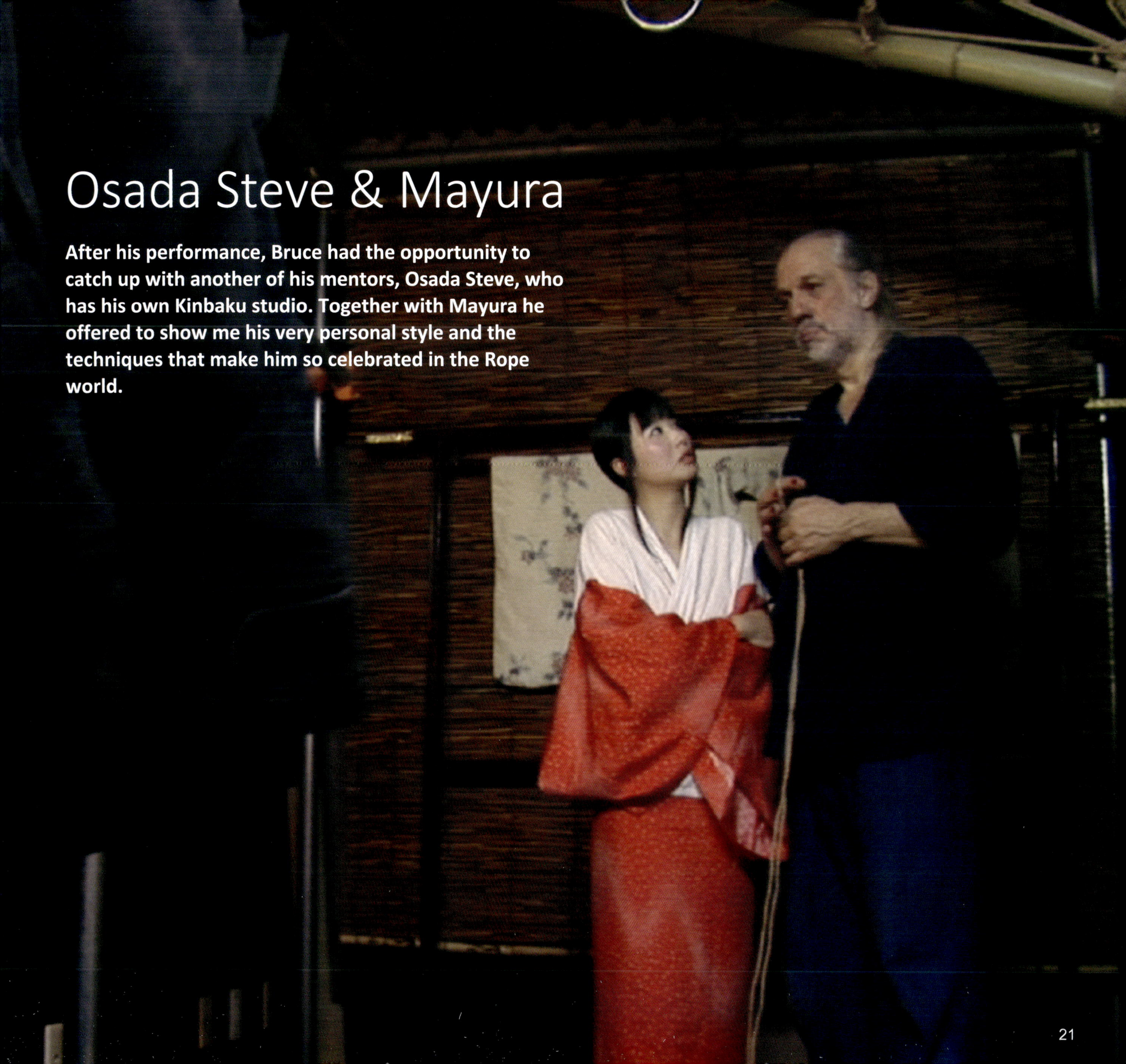

# Osada Steve & Mayura

After his performance, Bruce had the opportunity to catch up with another of his mentors, Osada Steve, who has his own Kinbaku studio. Together with Mayura he offered to show me his very personal style and the techniques that make him so celebrated in the Rope world.

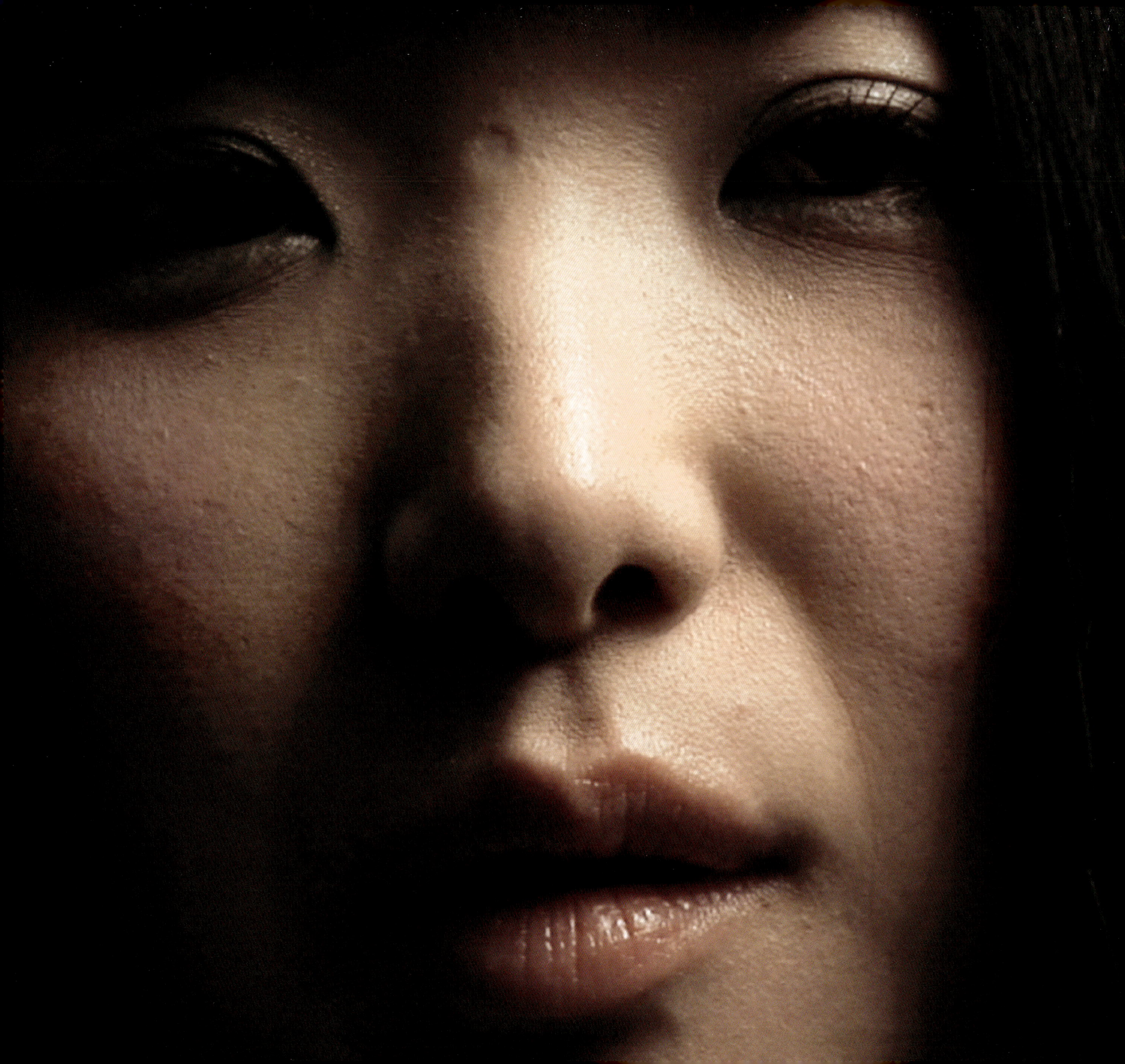

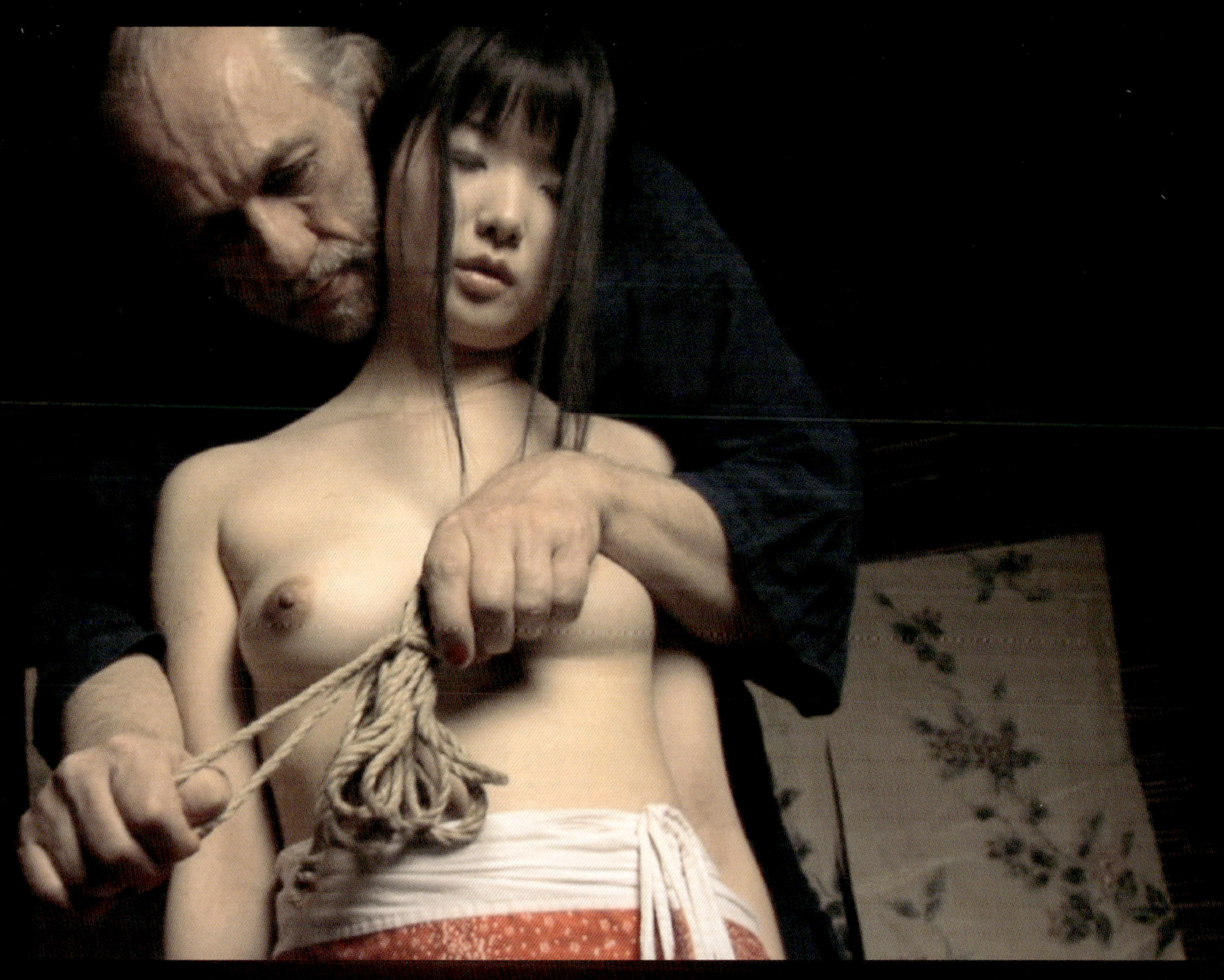

Mayura: During each show, I always close my eyes at the beginning.

And when Steve embraces me tightly with ropes, I'm feeling, you know  -  like protected, safe.

For me, doing this is not a job because I really enjoy it from the bottom of my heart.

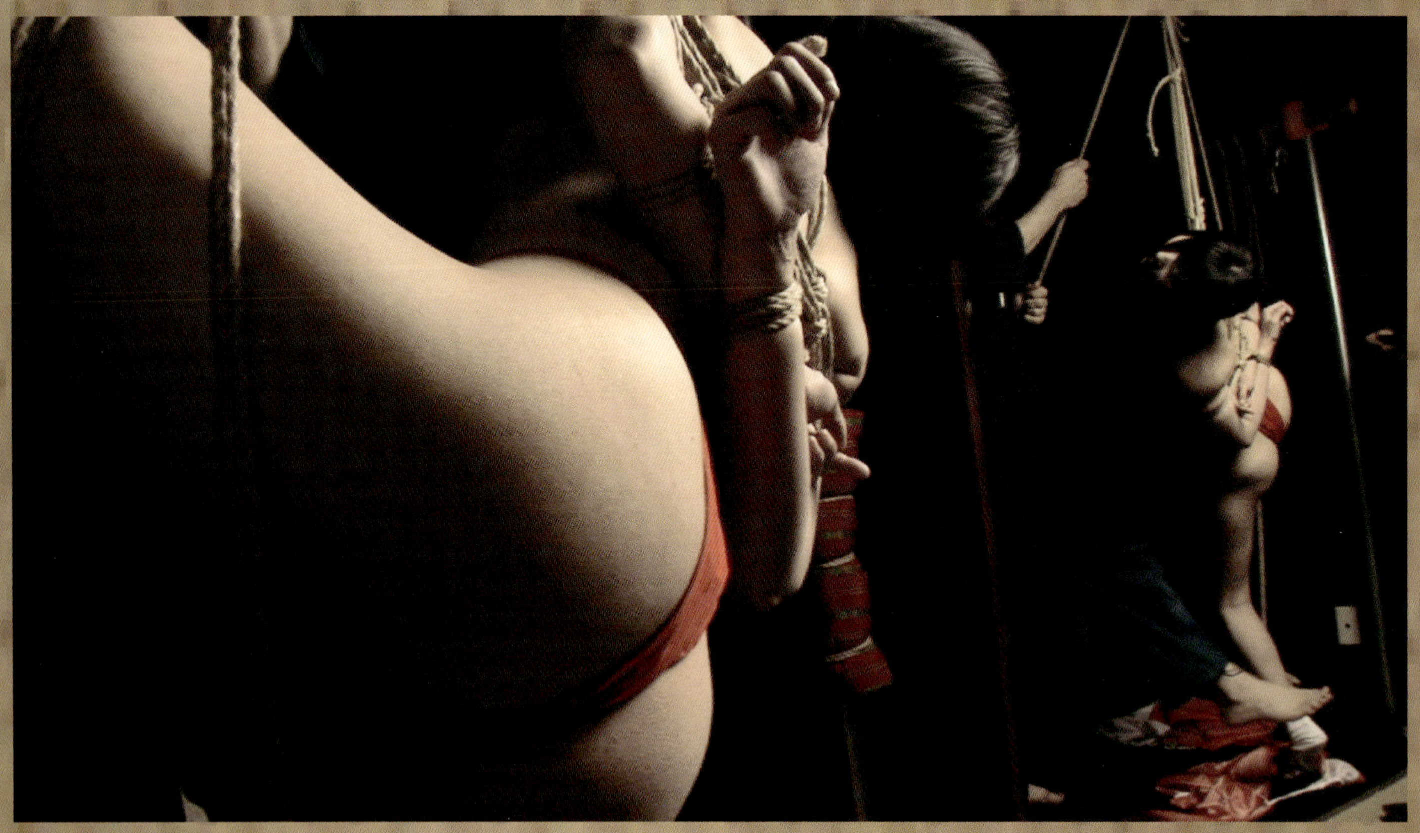

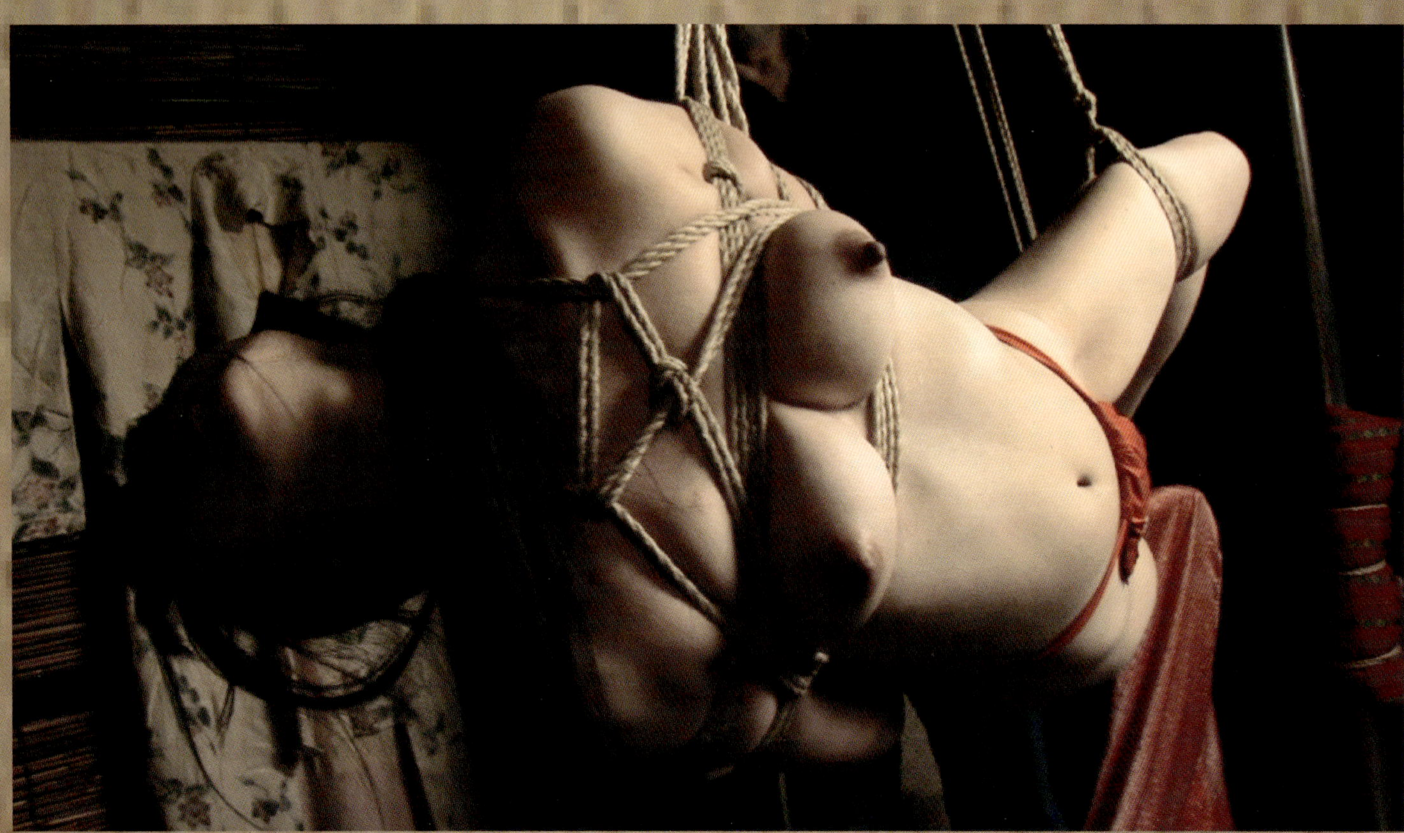

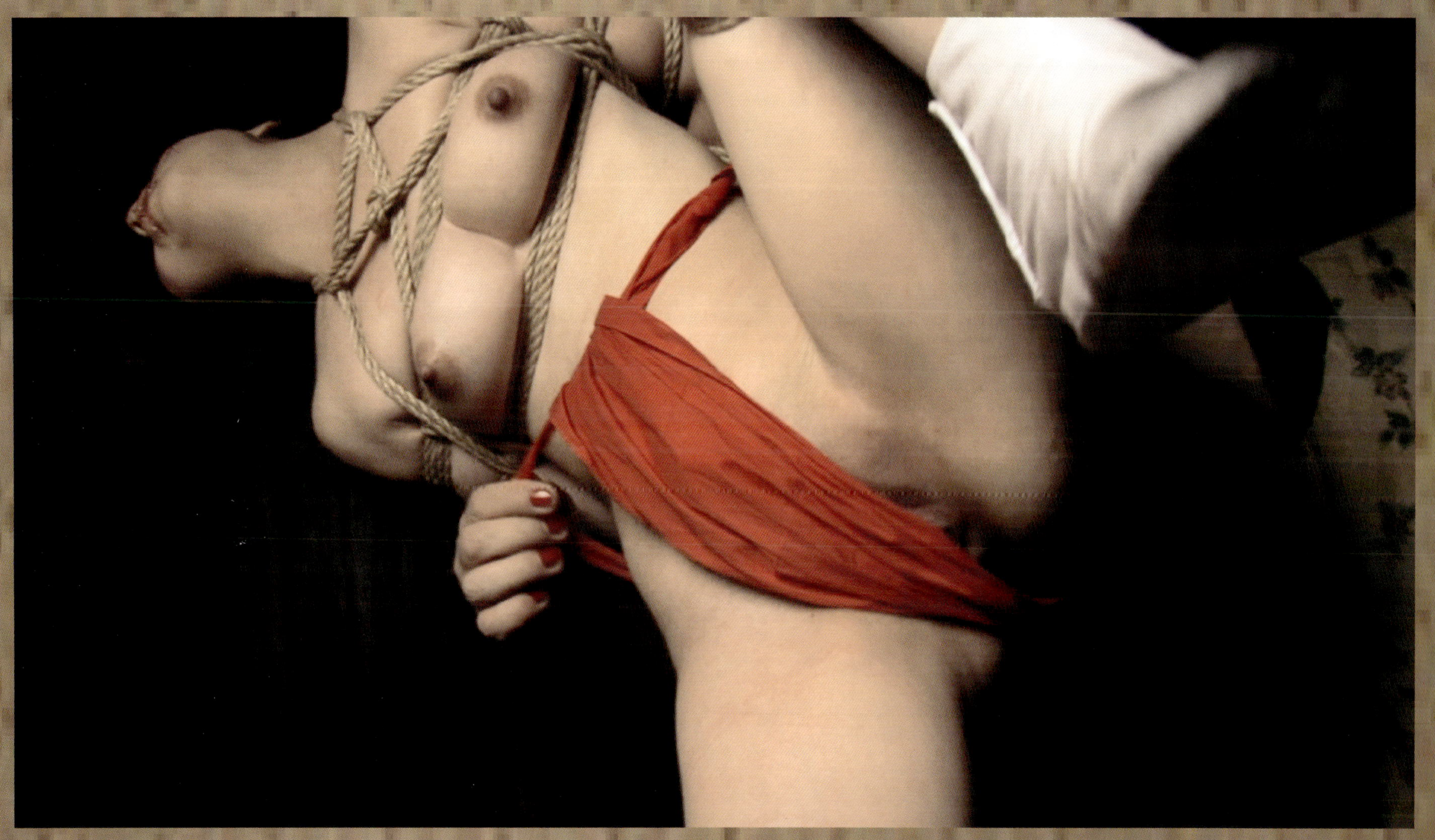

When I did Kinbaku for the first time I was 19 years old and it
was with the first man I dated.

He was 42 years old and he tied me up.  It was my first time.

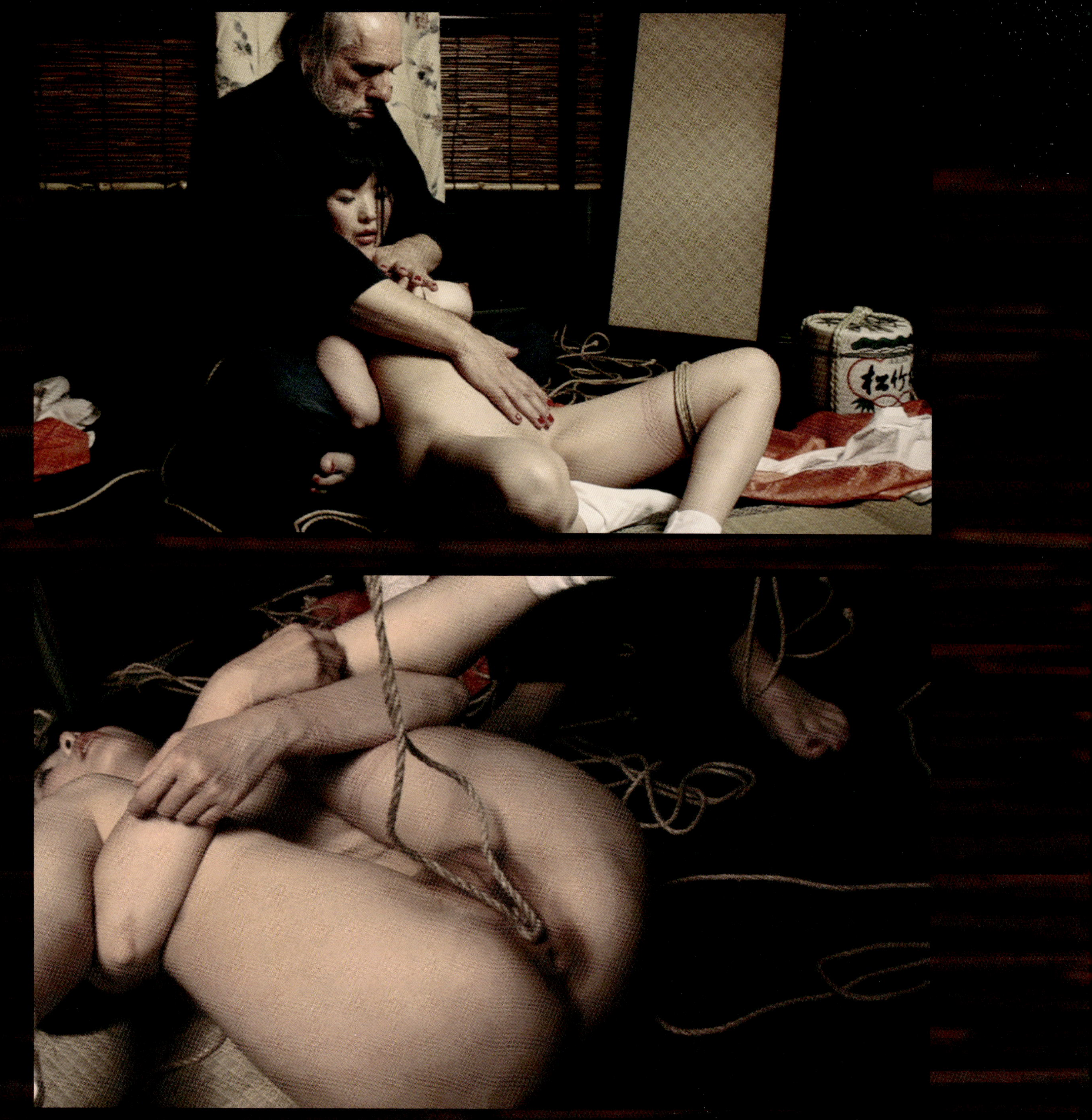

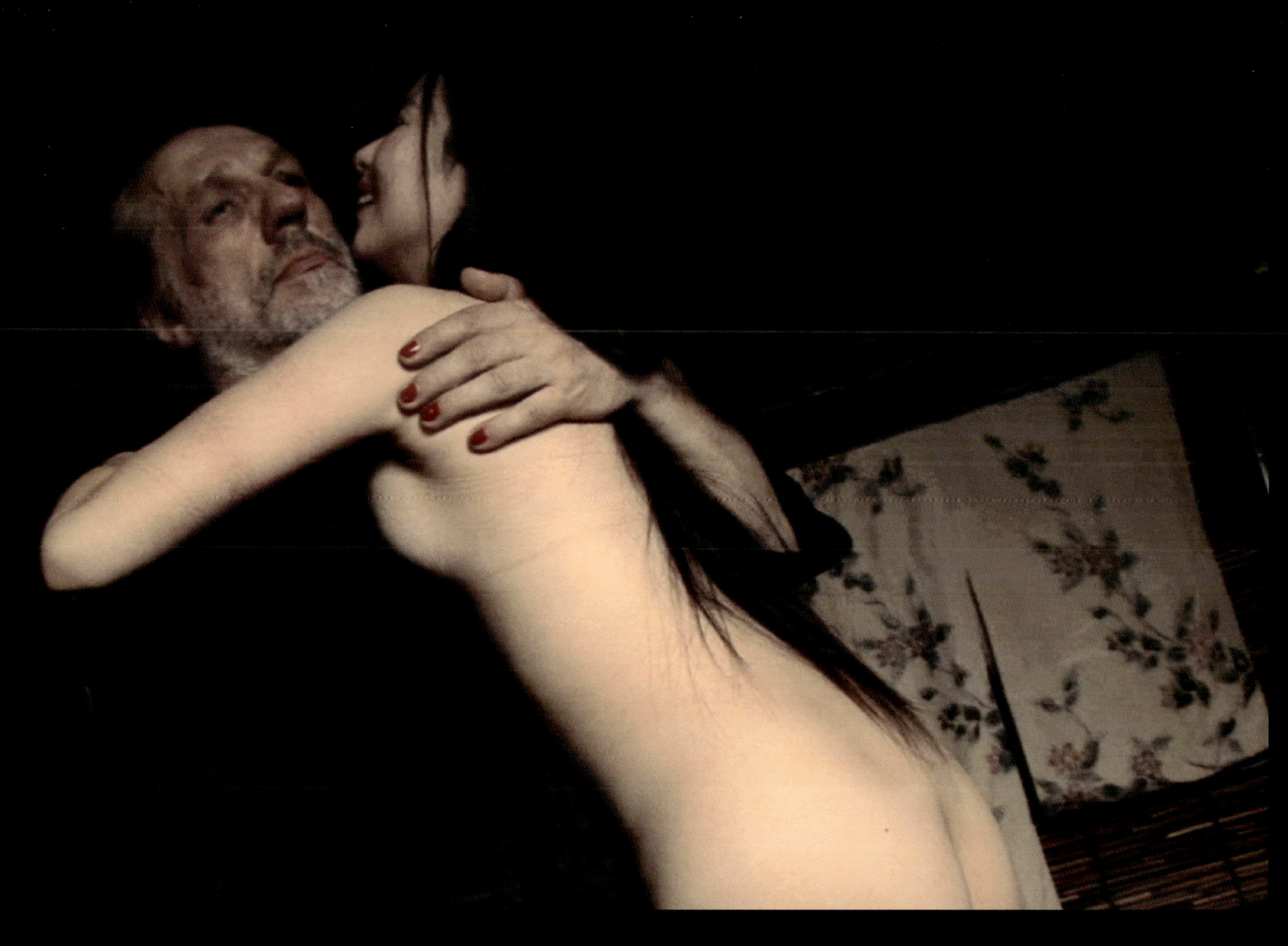

.......after the session I always feel really happy.

# Tangled Tales

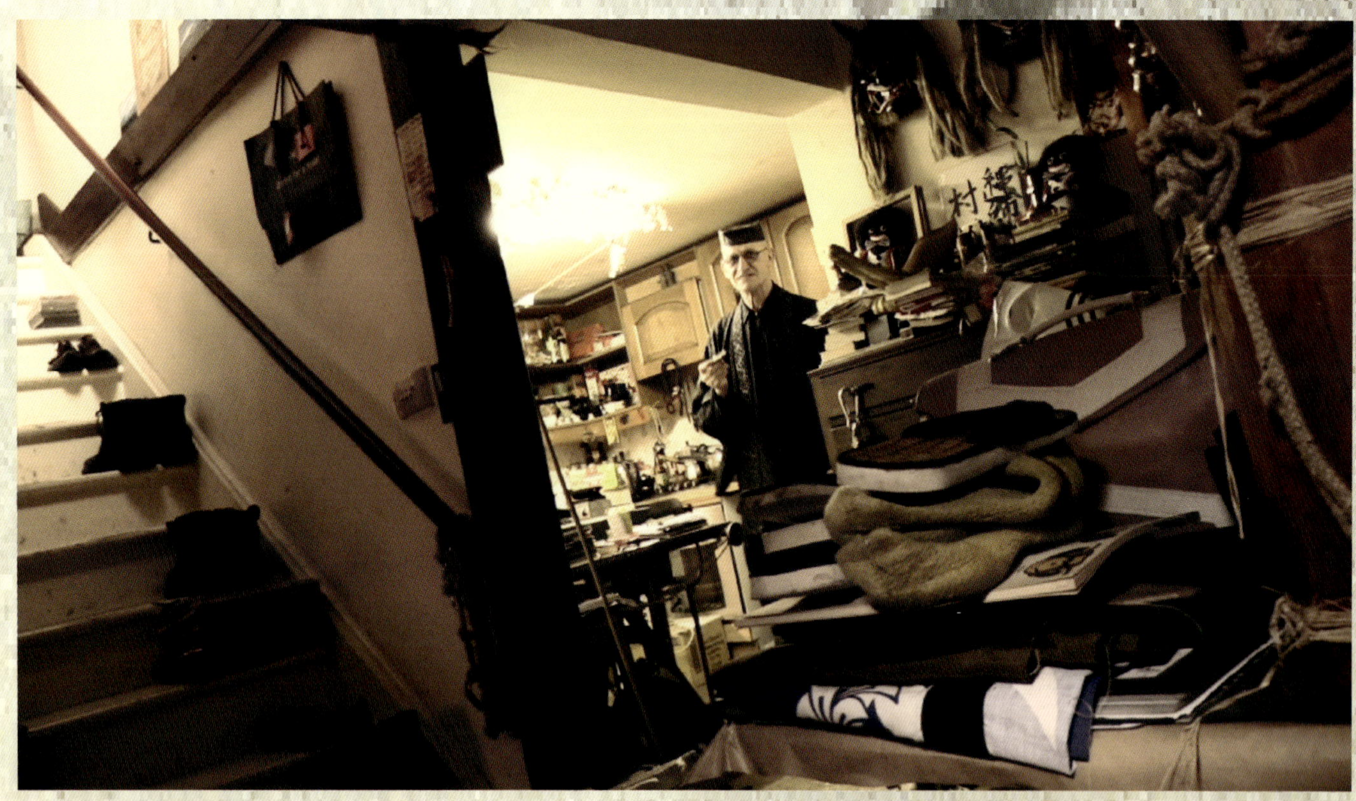

Following the visit to Tokyo, I wanted to find out more about the origins of Kinbaku.  I went to visit Jon (Nawashi Murakawa) at his house in London to learn about the Japanese origins.

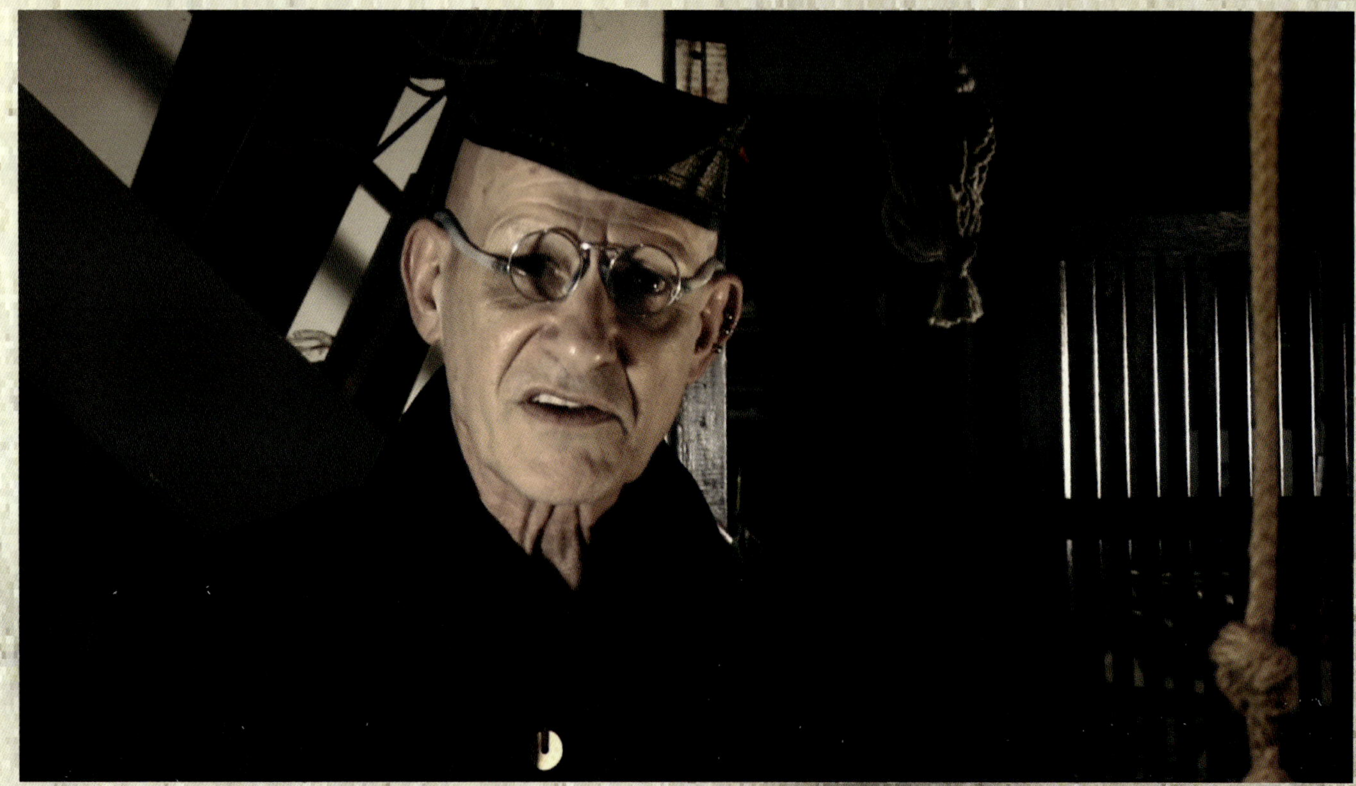

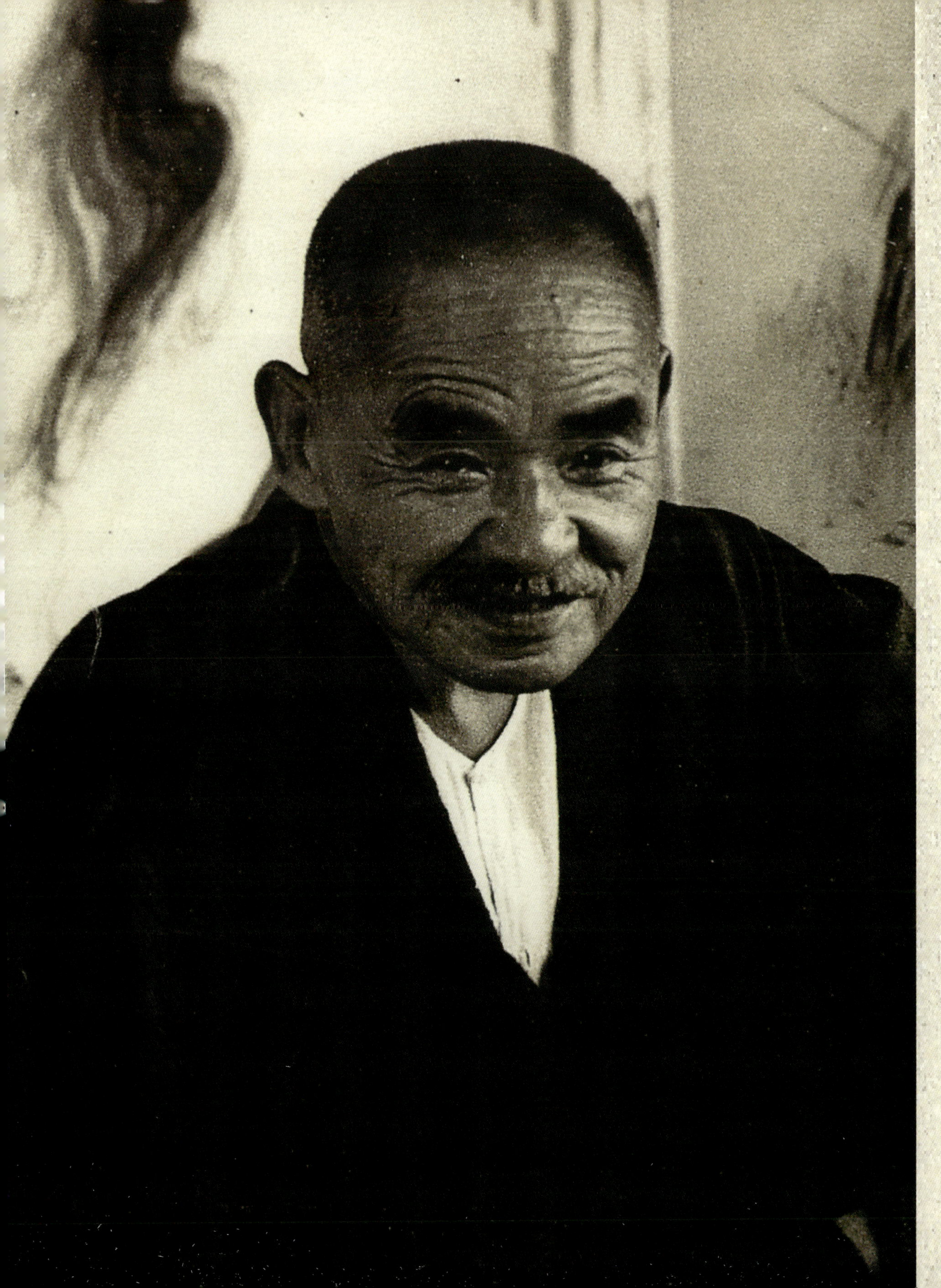

Nawashi Murakawa: The key person who has brought bondage to us and linked us to the past is Seiu Ito. He was born in 1882 and died in 1961. He was a writer, a poet, an artist and a translator. He also tied women. He's become much respected and a key person in an intellectual and aesthetic way.

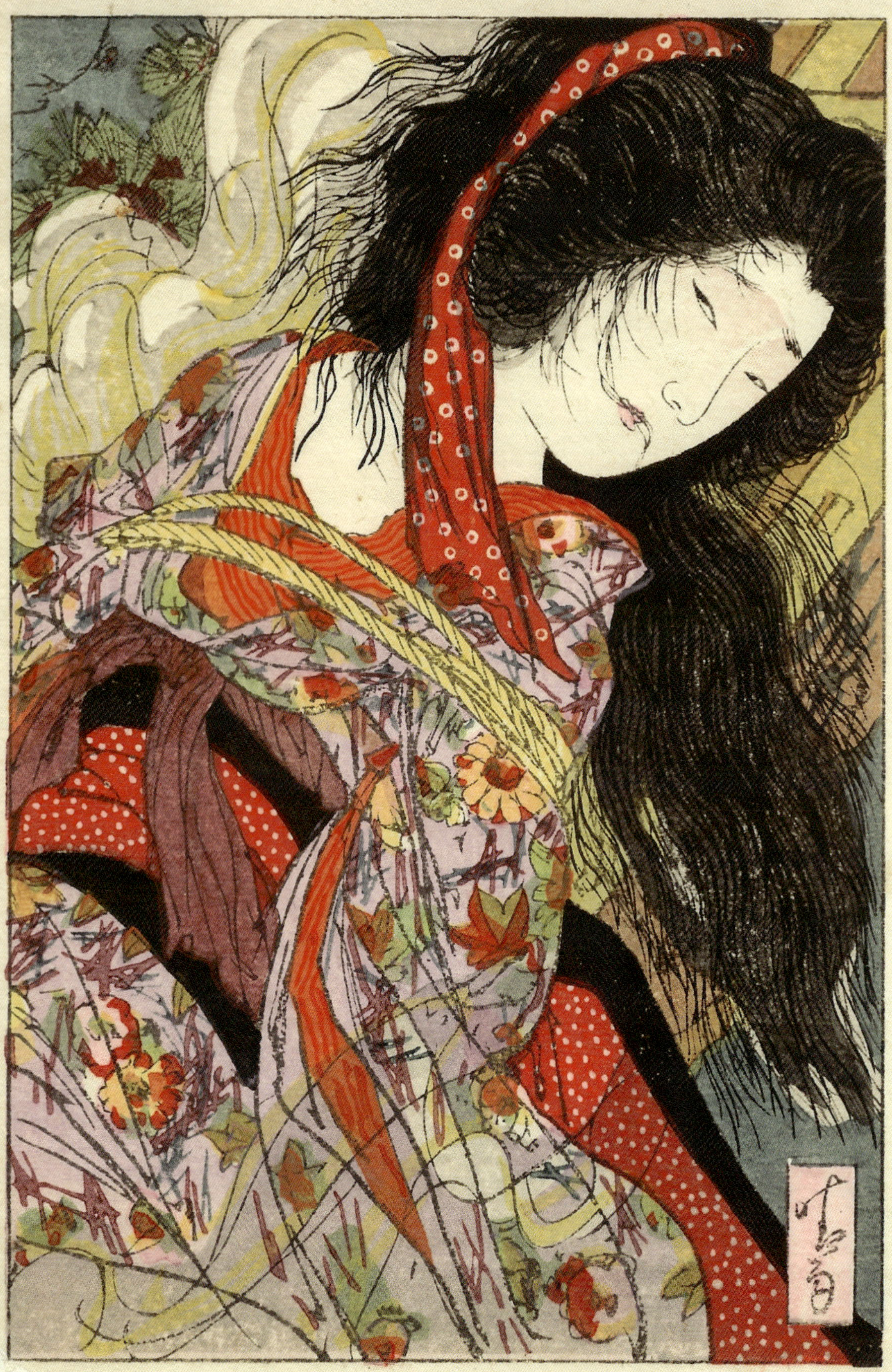

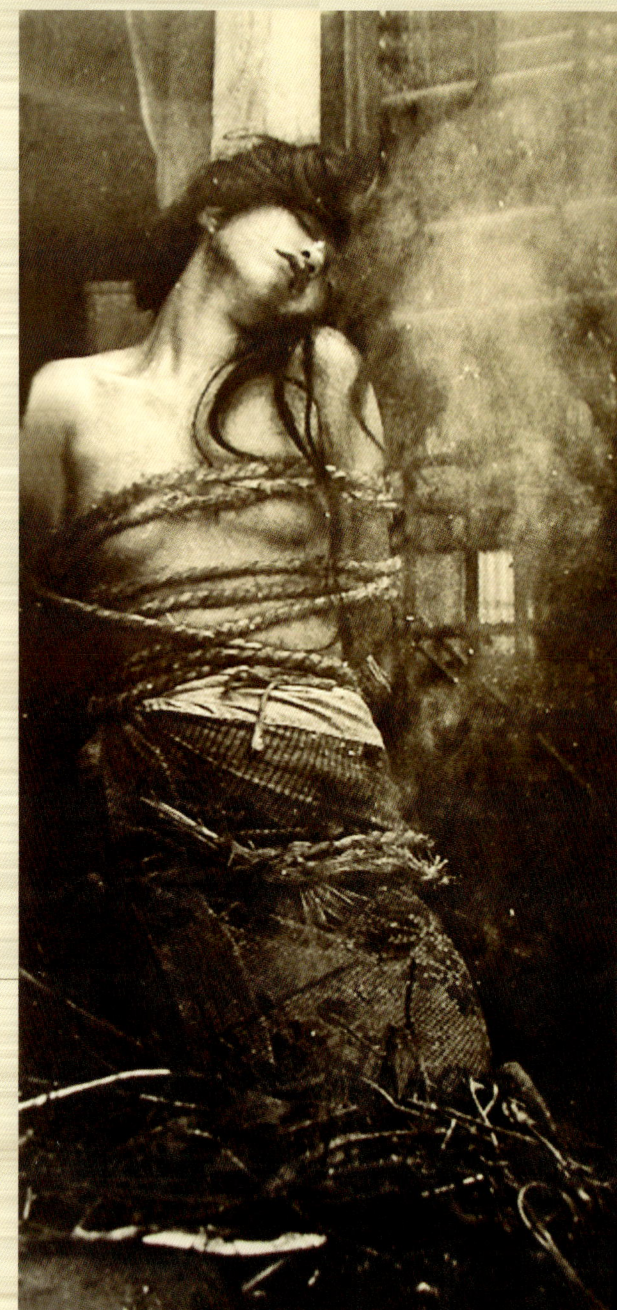

Seiu Ito's bondage is rather crude.  He often used rice straw rope, which is thin and thick: it's inconsistent in its weave. But it created a very beautiful look, especially the woman in kimono.

Seiu Ito would have been aware of the military ties seen in illustrations of medieval tales for catching and restraining prisoners.

Esinem: Tying was one of the four codified punishments. The others were whipping, pressing with stones - where basically you're put in a kneeling position with something uncomfortable underneath like a corrugated wood board. Then they'd put some large slabs of stone across your thighs.

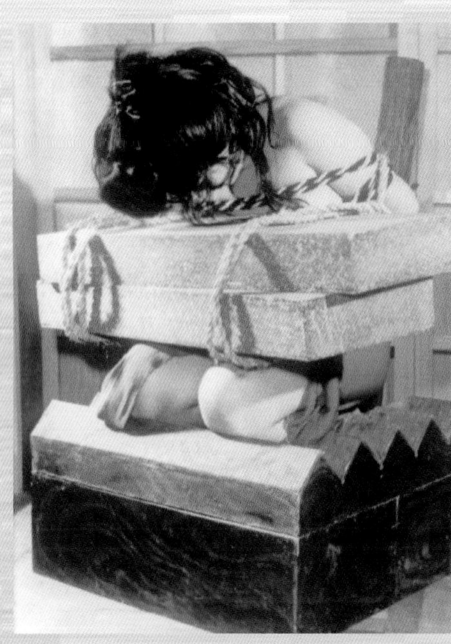

The most savage punishment was suspension. And that was normally done by just suspending someone by their arms. And if that wasn't sufficient they would also hang a rock from the prisoner.

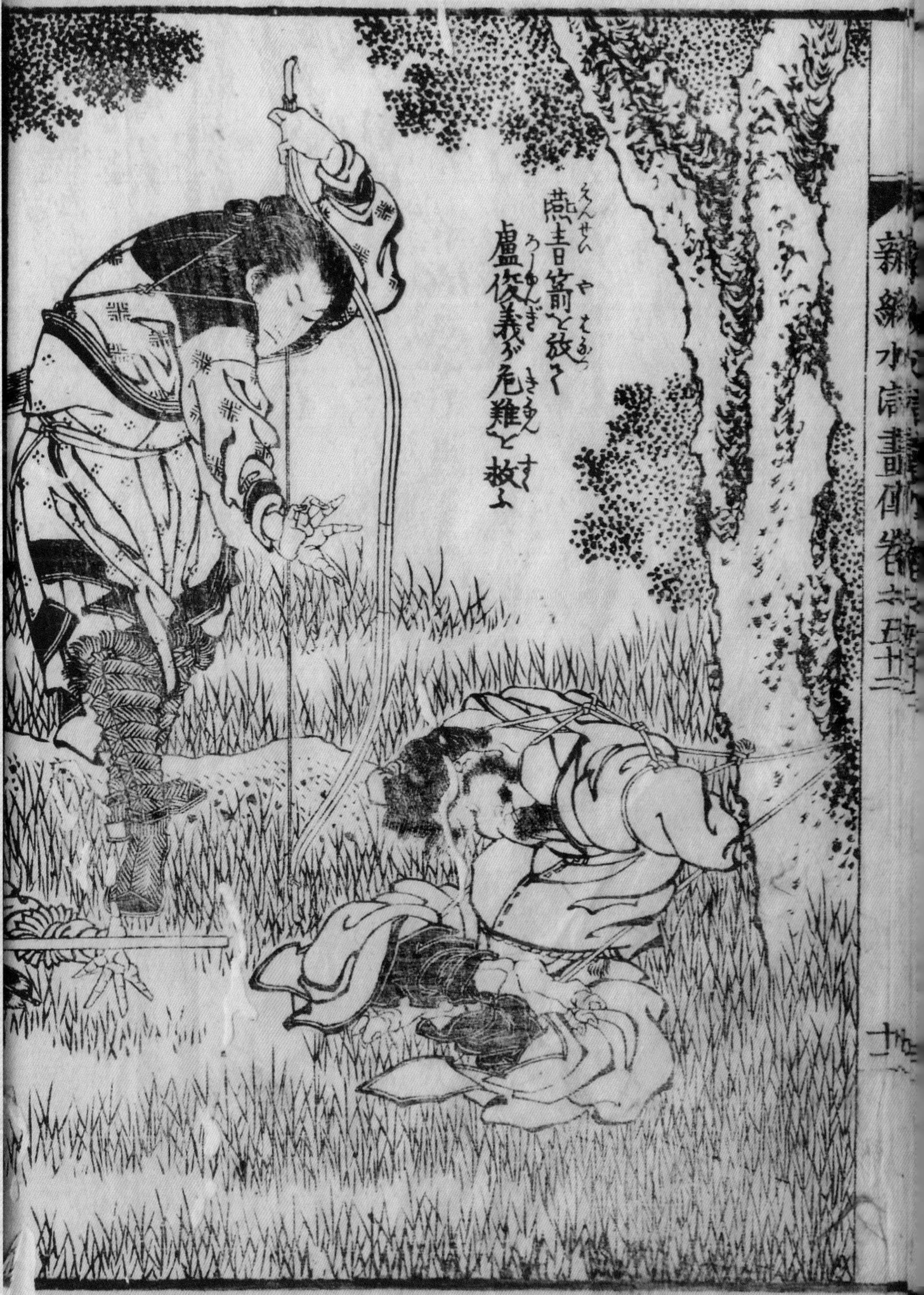

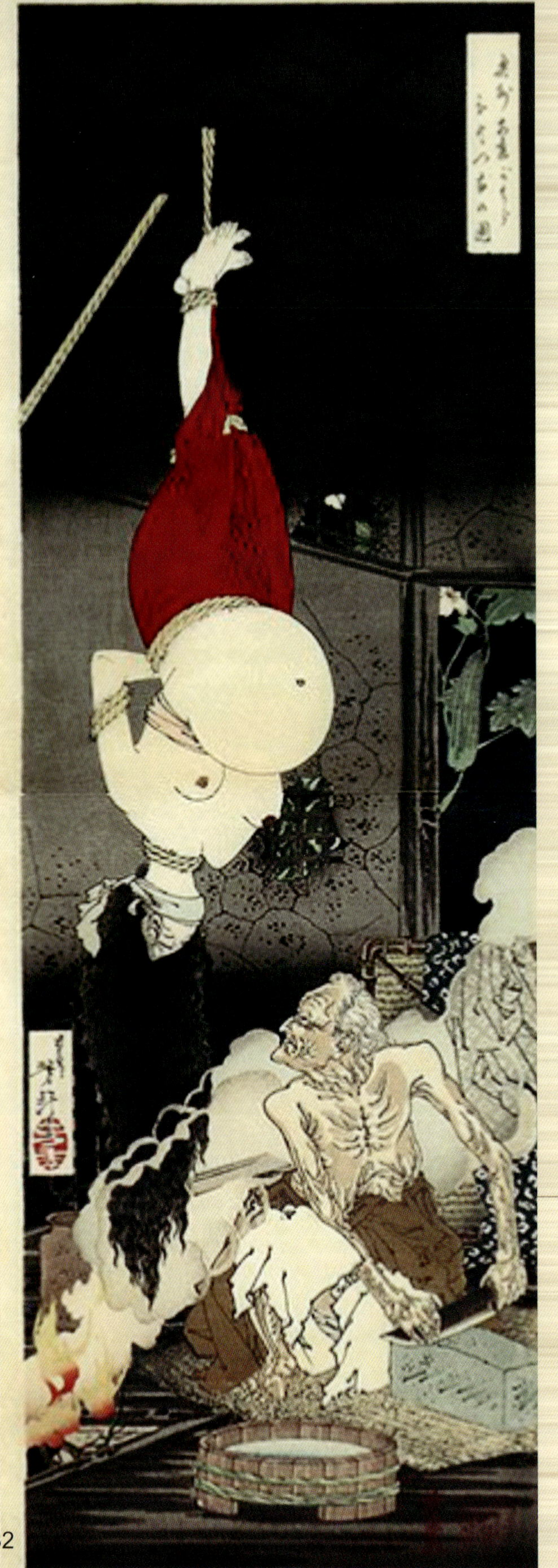

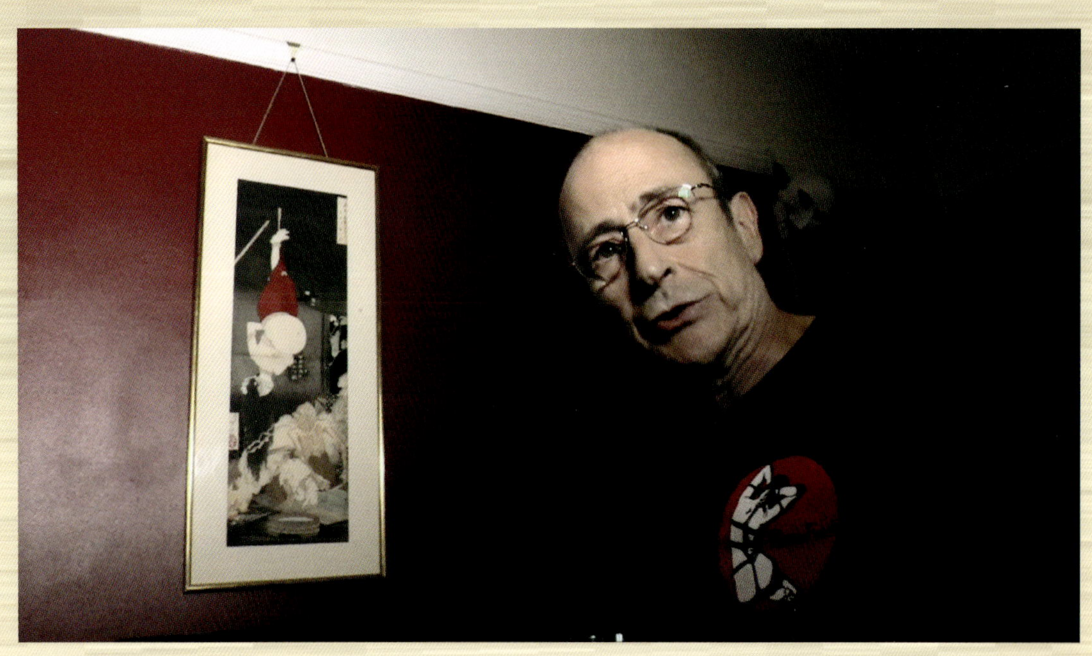

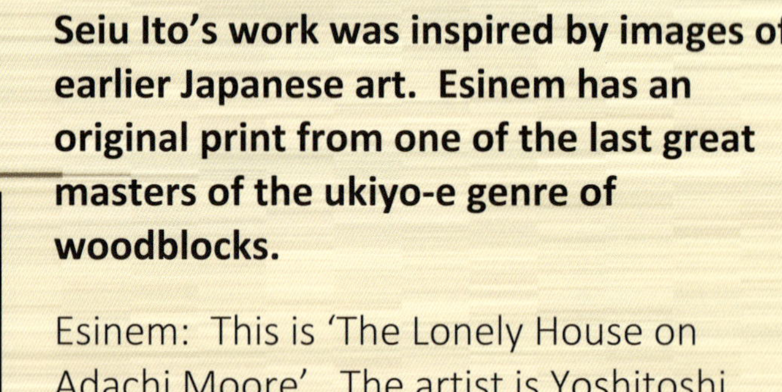

**Seiu Ito's work was inspired by images of earlier Japanese art. Esinem has an original print from one of the last great masters of the ukiyo-e genre of woodblocks.**

Esinem: This is 'The Lonely House on Adachi Moore'. The artist is Yoshitoshi.

This woodblock print was produced in 1885. Obviously it is a striking image and in fact it was actually banned by the Meiji government at the time. What you are looking at at the bottom of the picture is the Hag of Adachi Moore - a witch if you like. What she's doing there is sharpening a knife in preparation for harvesting the blood from the foetus of the pregnant woman you see hanging there. Seiu Ito actually tried to recreate this picture, as a photograph, using his own heavily pregnant wife.

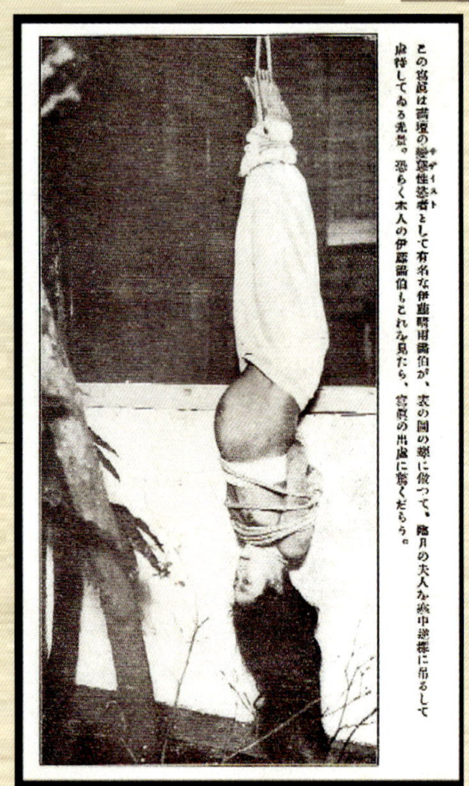

Murakawa:  Despite the good work of Seiu Ito to inspire the new bondage masters, there wasn't that much interest.  Then World War Two occurred and that actually regenerated interest, especially when Americans came to Japan, because they brought their publications including girls tied on the front of cheap detective magazines.  These magazines, such as those of Eric Stanton, inspired the Japanese to reinvestigate the subject.

Obviously they couldn't read the text, but the pictures could tell them everything.  The darker side of sexuality that Eric Stanton expressed appealed to the Japanese because it also contained humiliation, and degradation and shame culture of its own kind.  Shame culture is a key thing to understand about Japanese bondage and its developments in the more modern world.

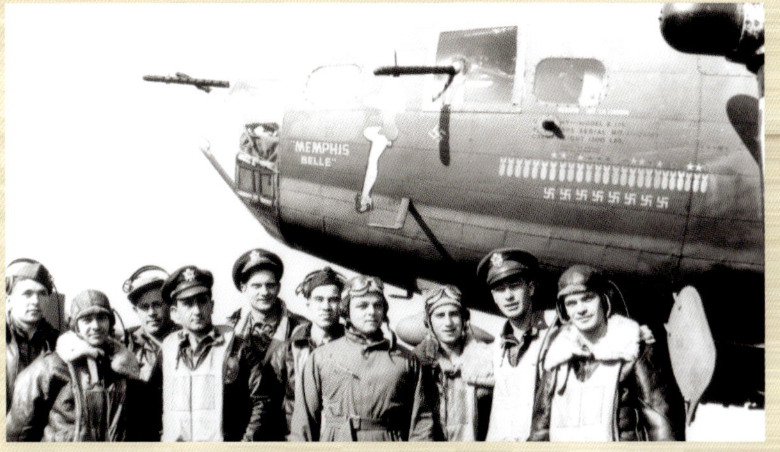

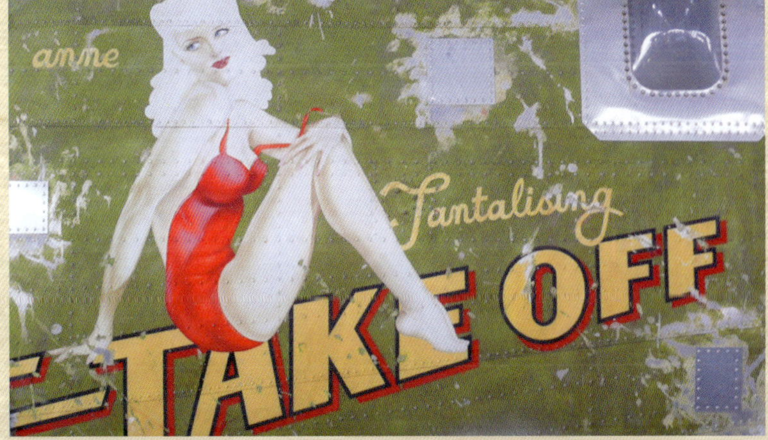


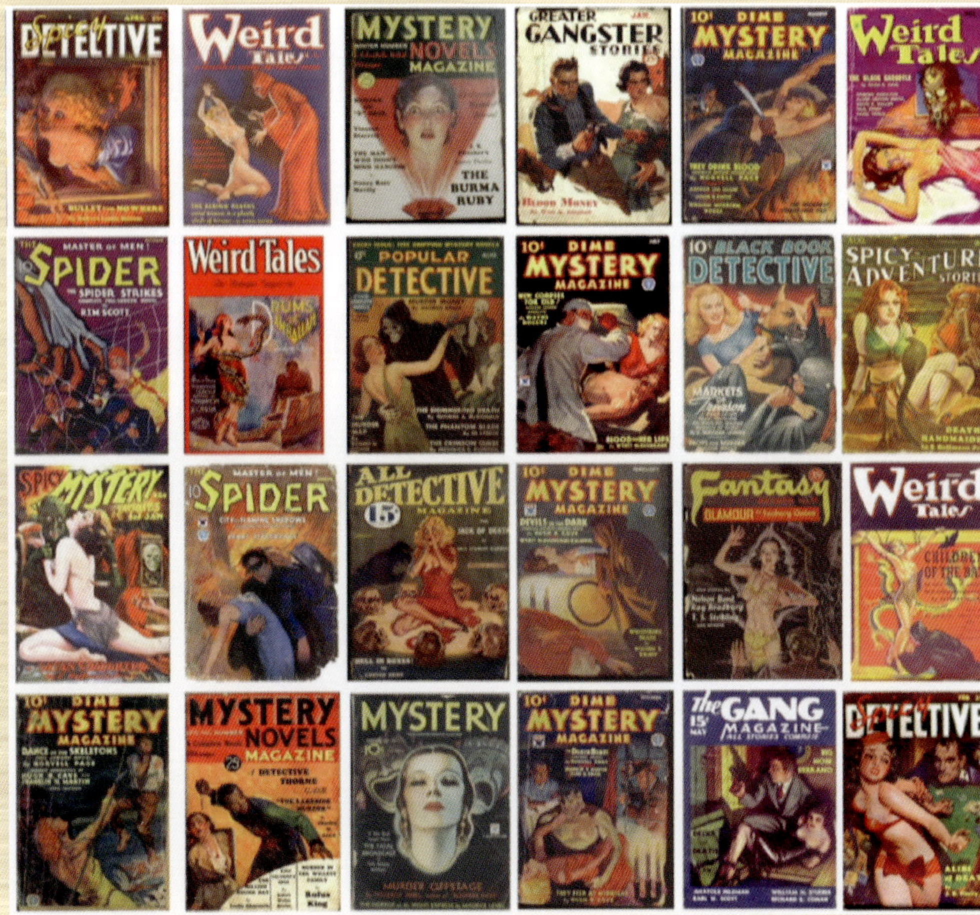

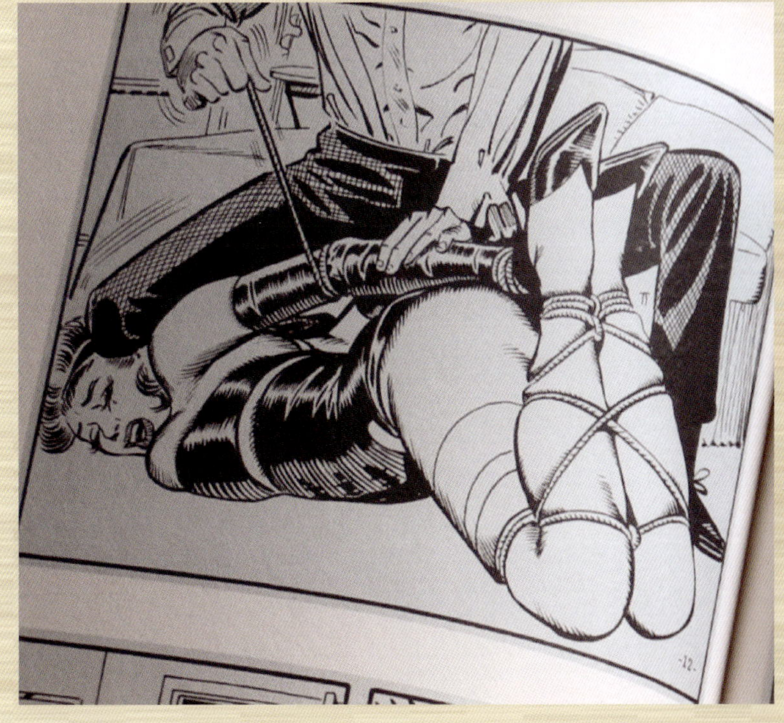

# Tokyo London Ties

Following Esinem and Nawashi Murakawa success in Tokyo, a return visit to London was arranged in late 2011.  Kinoko Hajime brought with him a teaching team called Ichinawa-Kai, the bondage master Kazami Ranki and other Japanese performers. They attended 'The London Festival of the Art of Japanese Rope Bondage'.  This was held at the Resistance Gallery hosted by Garry Vanderhorne.

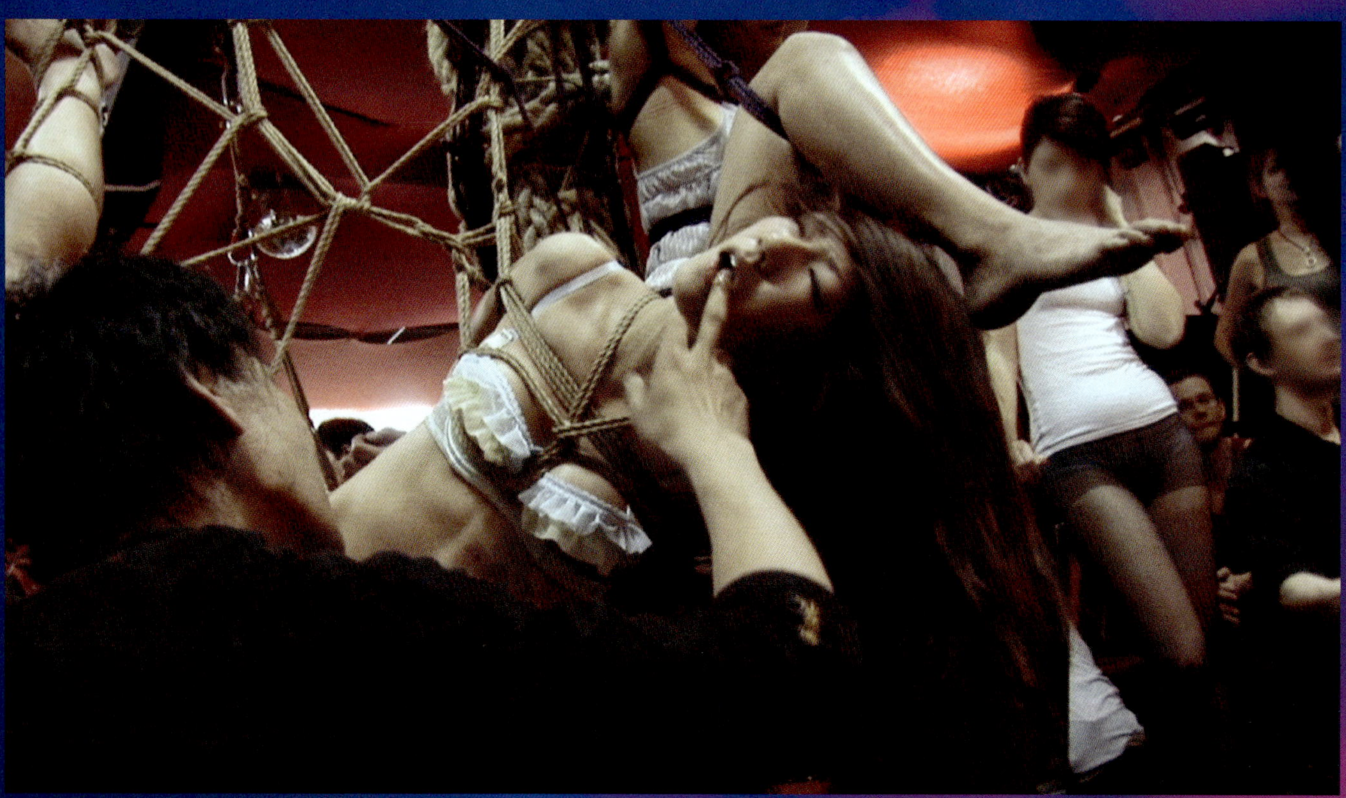

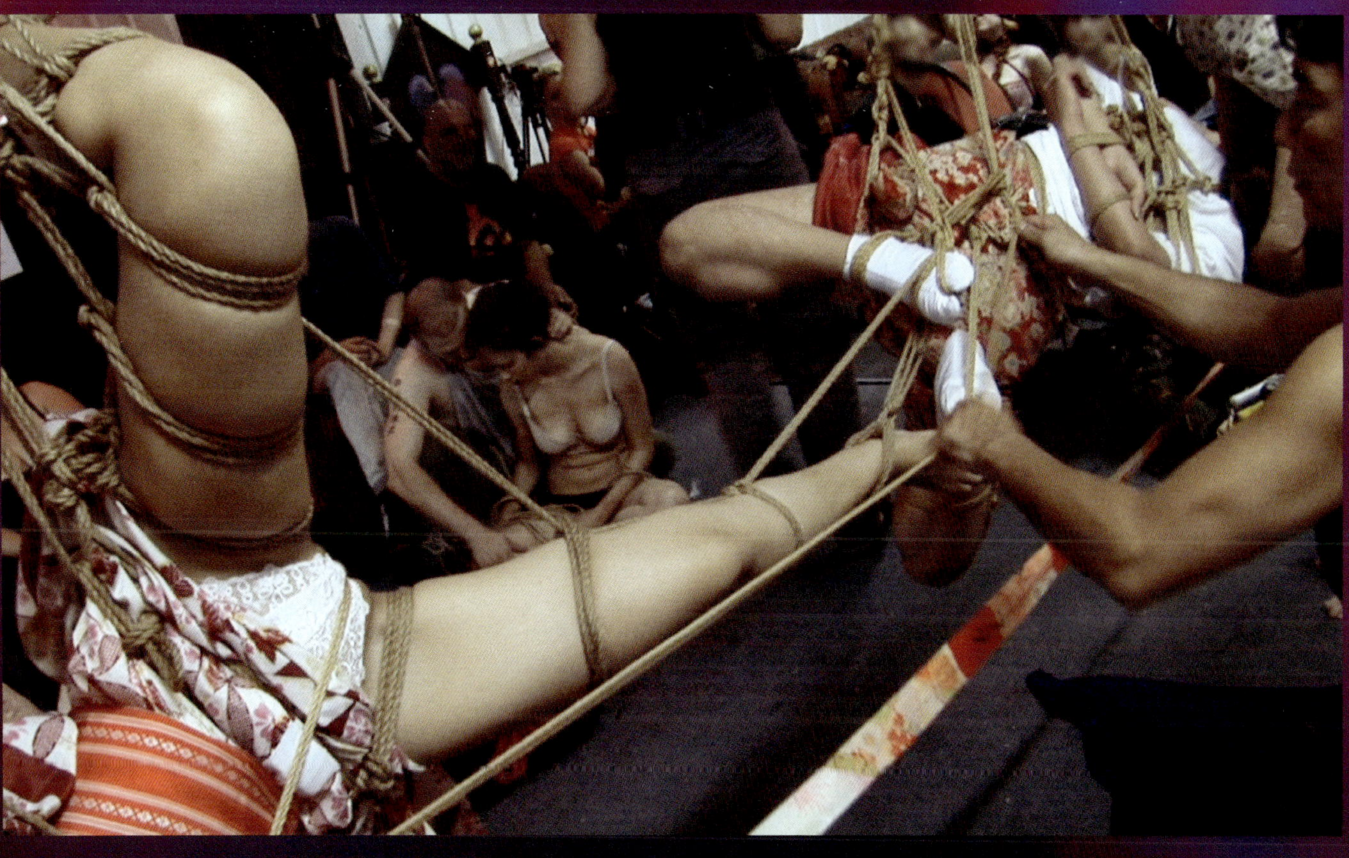

The Ichinawa-Kai team ran workshops to teach the intricate rope tying techniques used in Japan.

It was mainly young women being tied, but it was not only men doing the tying.

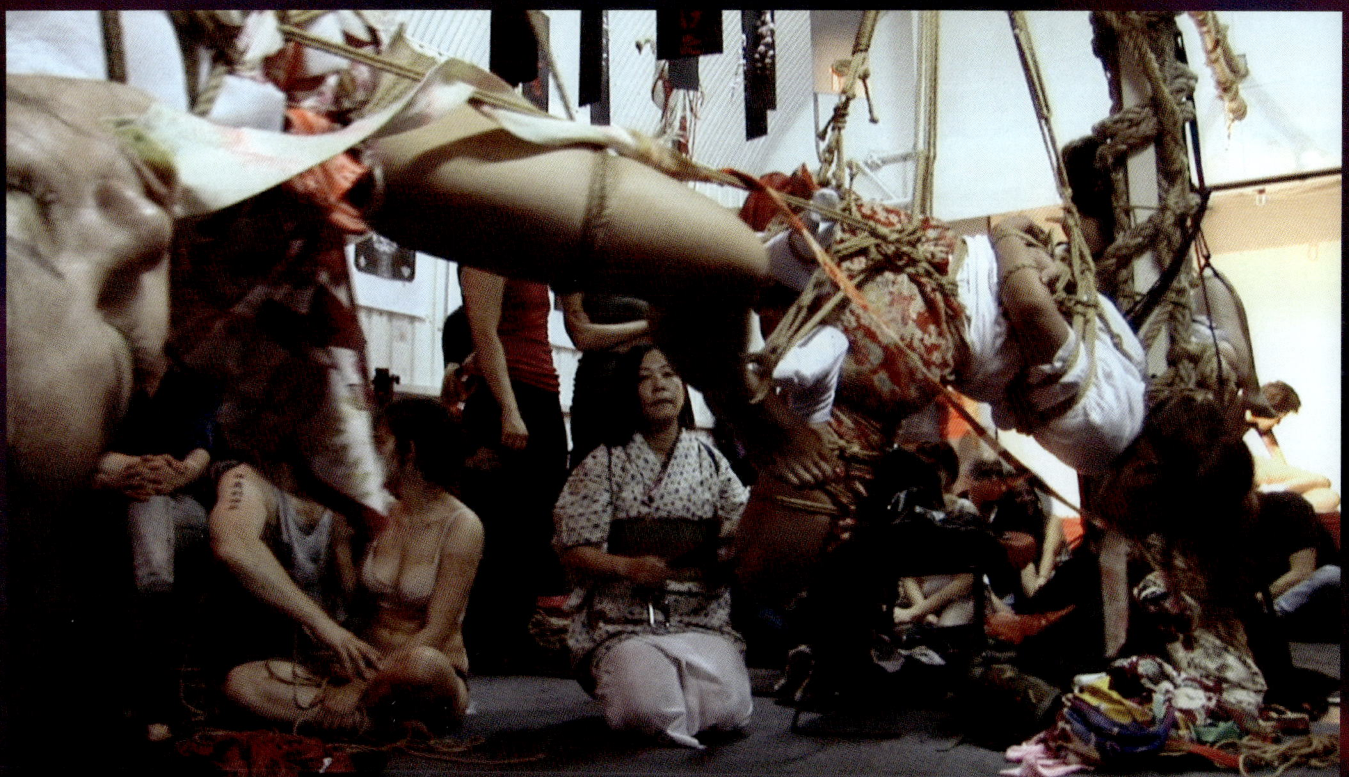

This was certainly an exhibition of erotic skills making me wonder if the Japanese were simply putting on a show.

So I wanted to find out how it was, particularly for the women who had signed up for the weekend.

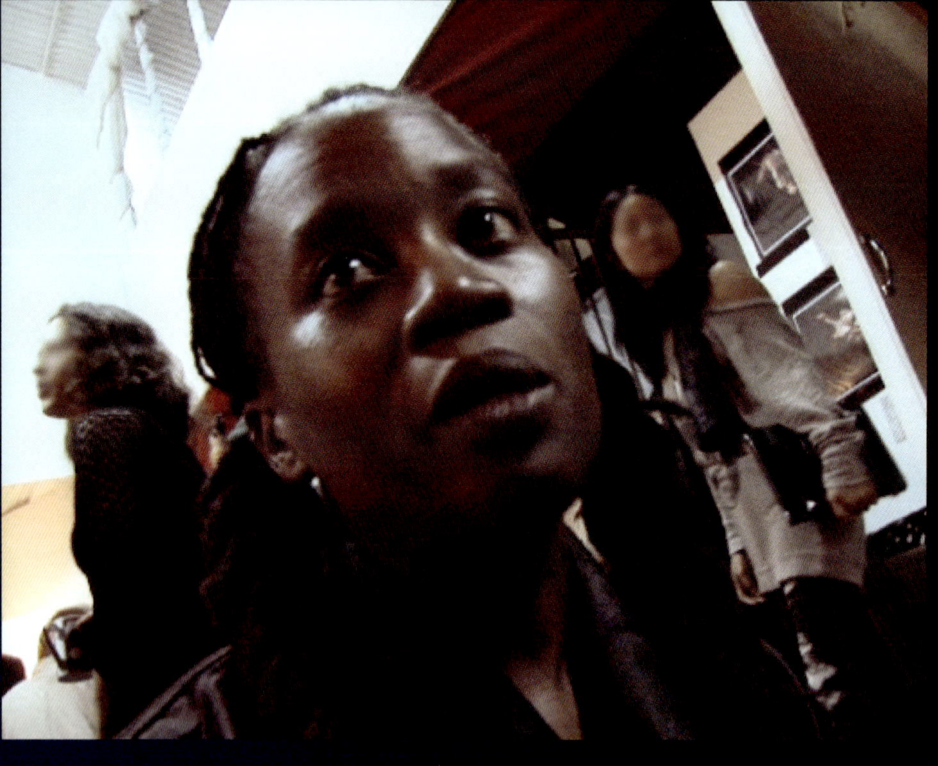

Kitty Mooschief:  I love Japanese rope bondage, I love the art form, and I am completely fascinated with it.  I have been into the fetish scene for 15 years and since discovering rope, I have been suspended by five people: I feel very fortunate.

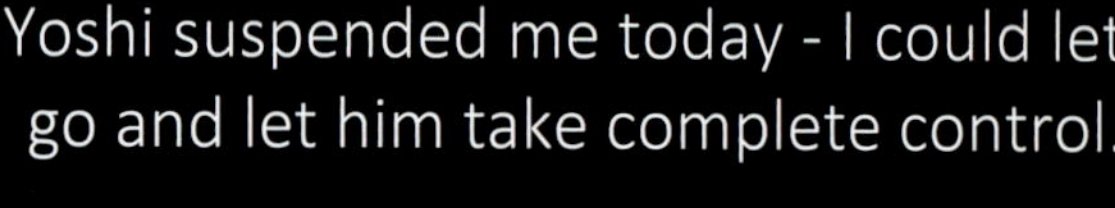

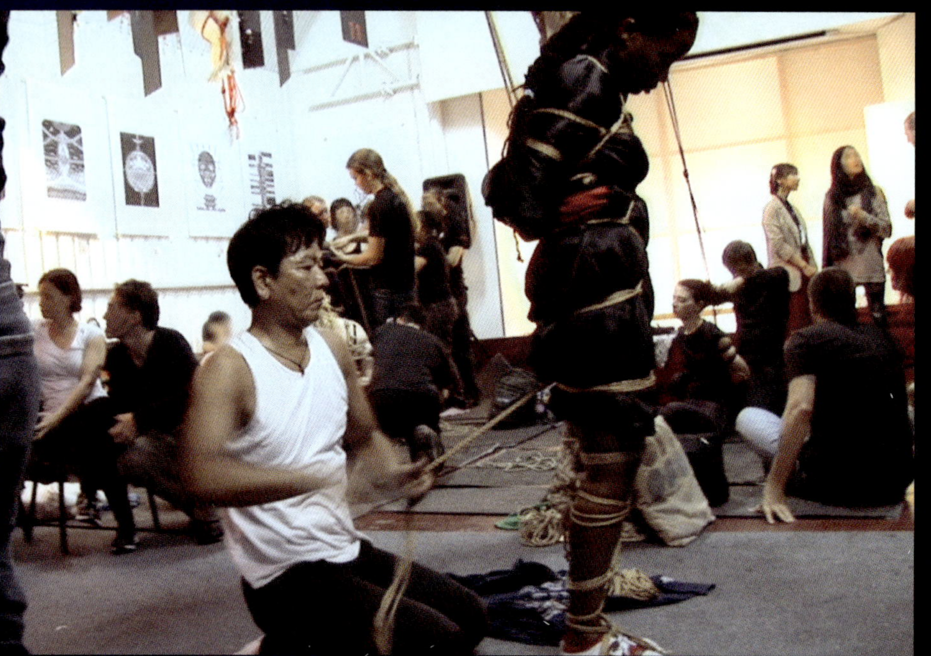

Yoshi suspended me today - I could let go and let him take complete control.

I see this as art such as dance, painting, music.

As for comments that this is not good for women.  Well I am a woman; I like to be tied up and I like to tie up.

I see it as a very positive experience.

# Kazami Ranki & Gestalta

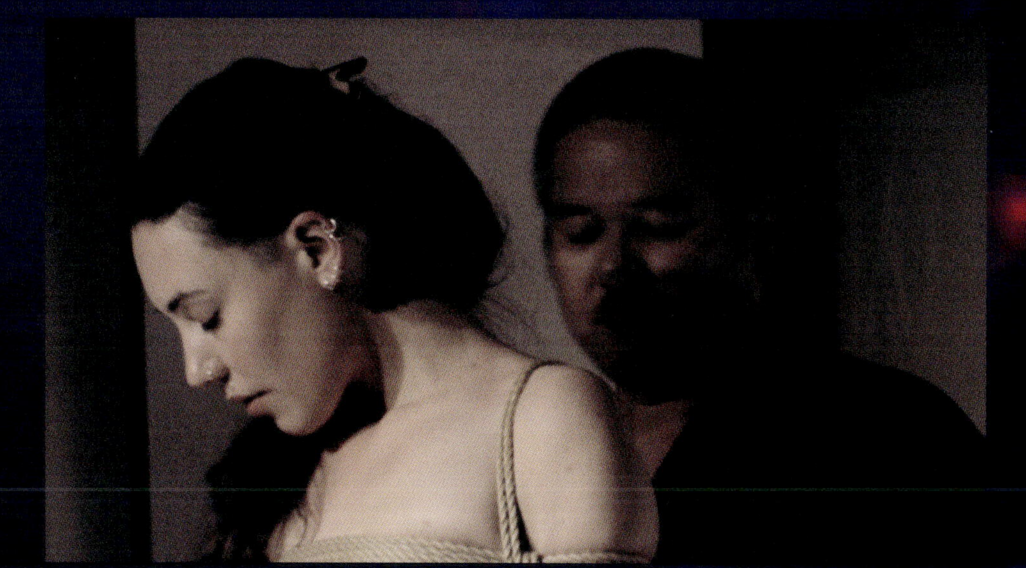

**Following the daily workshops the evenings were devoted to performance. Gestalta had the opportunity to put on a show with Kazami Ranki.**

Gestalta: Well I met Kazami I think finally on the Friday afternoon before the performance we were to do in the evening. He has quite a reputation for being quite sadistic. He has the nickname 'The Atrocious Nawashi'. But a few people have told me that in real life he is a very, very nice person. And he really is. He is a very sort of smiley, jolly kind of person.

So we did this very traditional show. It was very much sort of rope based with none of the extra elements - the wax and the needles that you quite often get. It was very nice actually and sort of focused just on the tying.

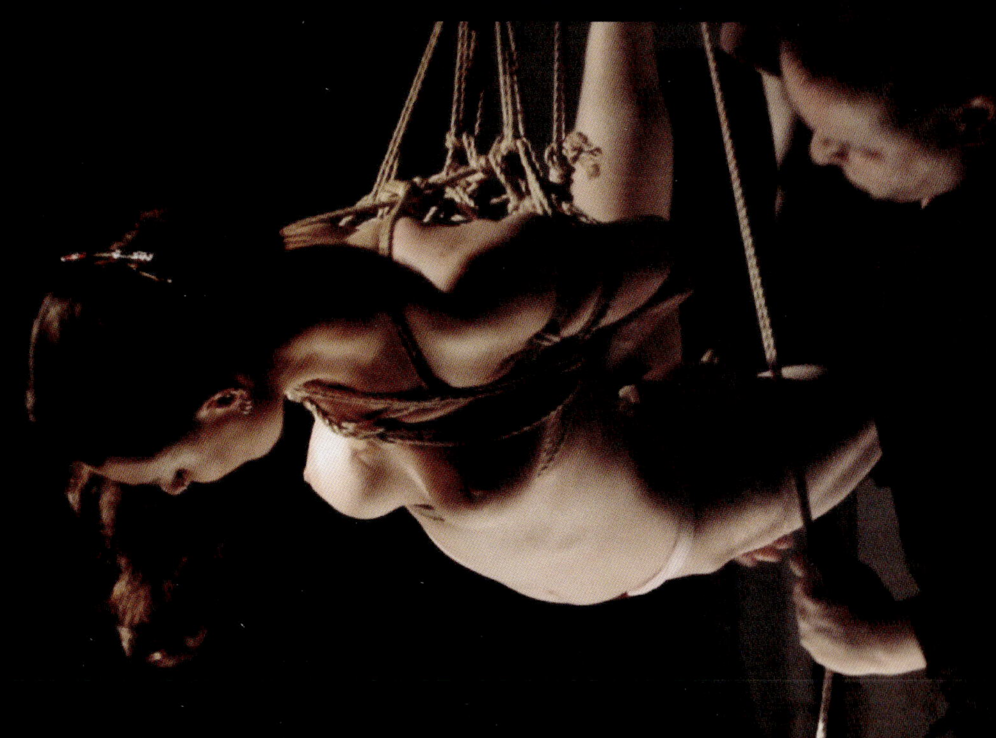

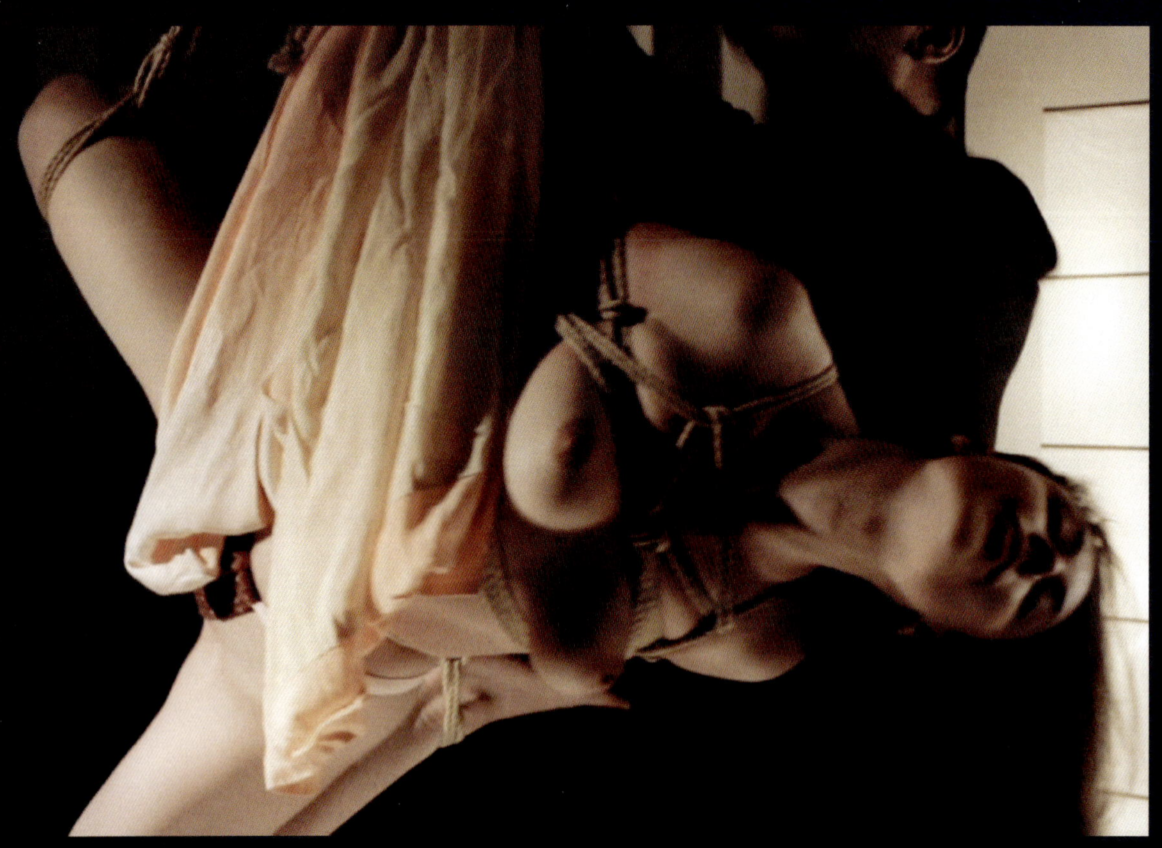
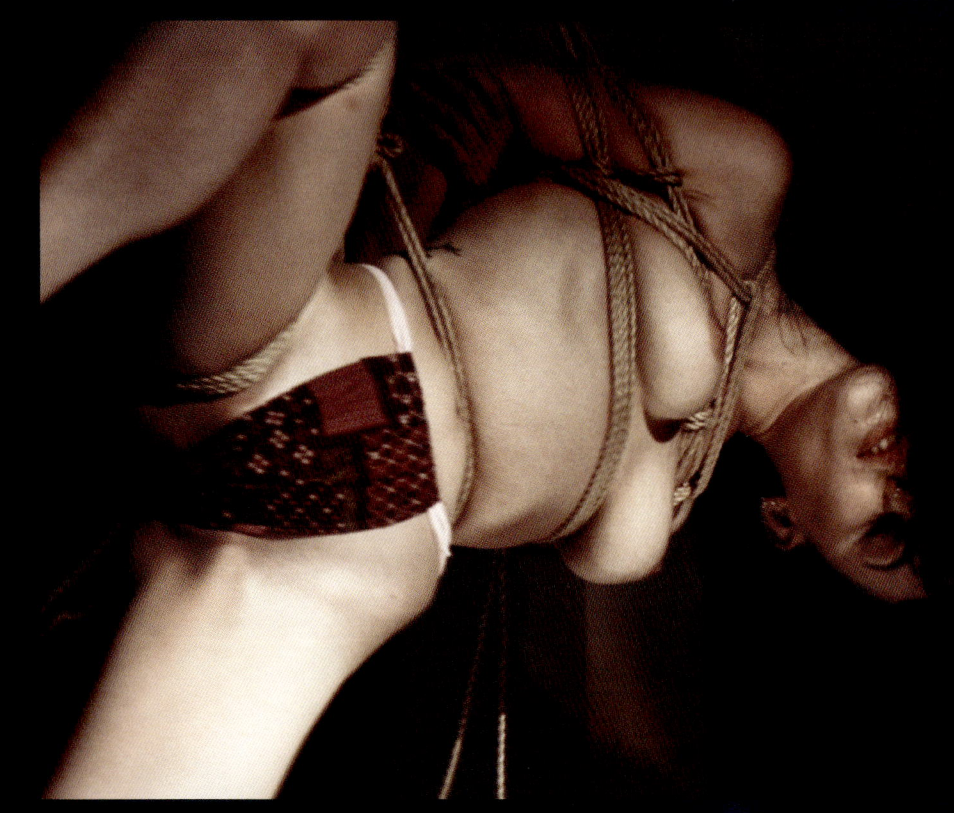

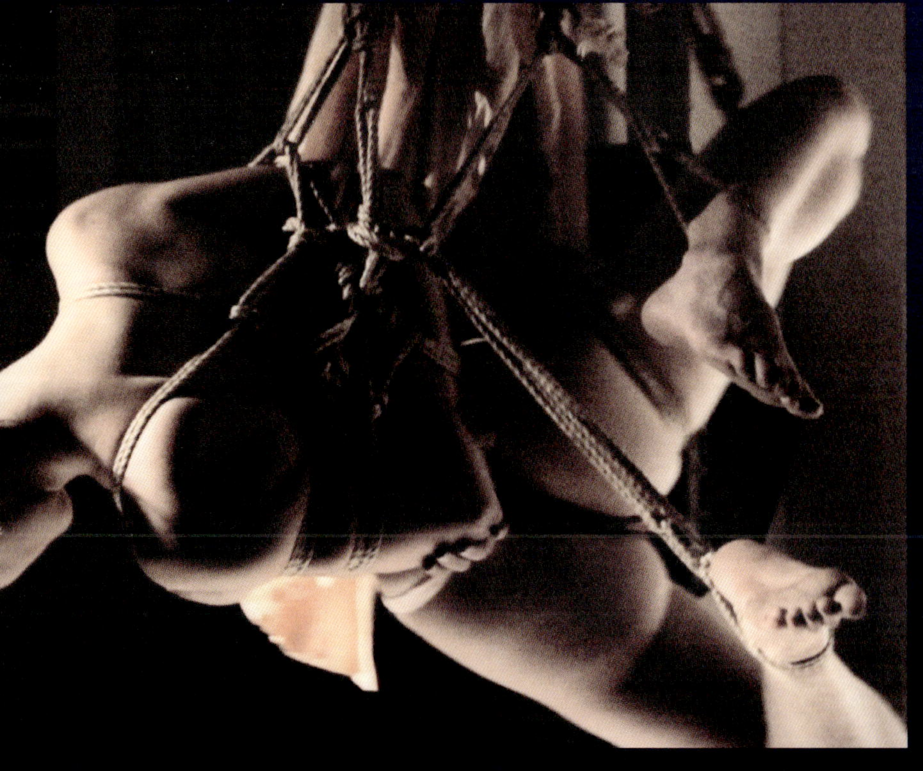

It was my first ever single ankle inverted suspension.  Just a lift right from the floor with one ankle which I was expecting would be quite a scary experience.  But actually it really wasn't at all.  It was very, very relaxing.  I think I was vaguely aware during the show I think that my ankle started twitching a bit and then I realized I was upside down and I was like, oh, that's a very nice feeling.

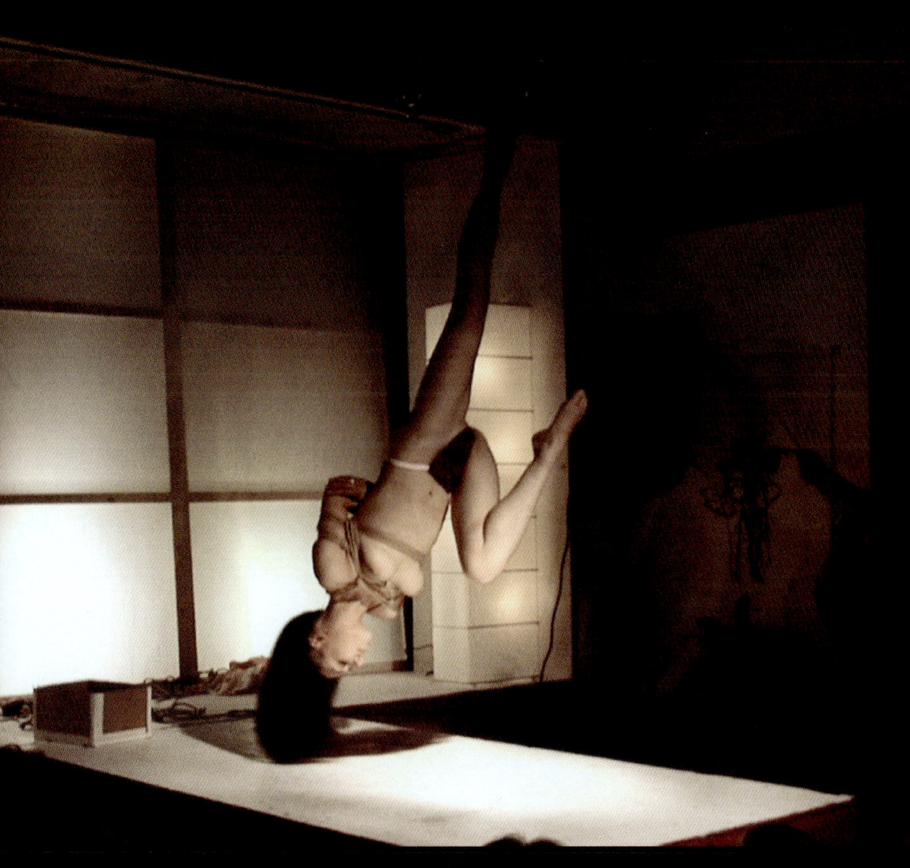

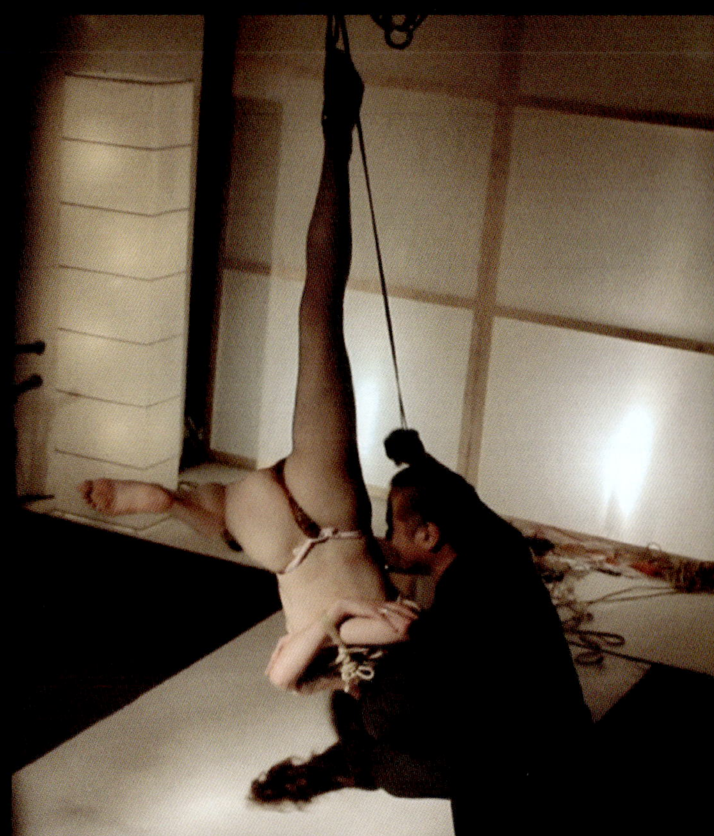

# Nawashi Murakawa
# &
# Susie-Wong

**Somewhat ironically it was our own Nawashi Murakawa  who put on the most Japanese of performances.**

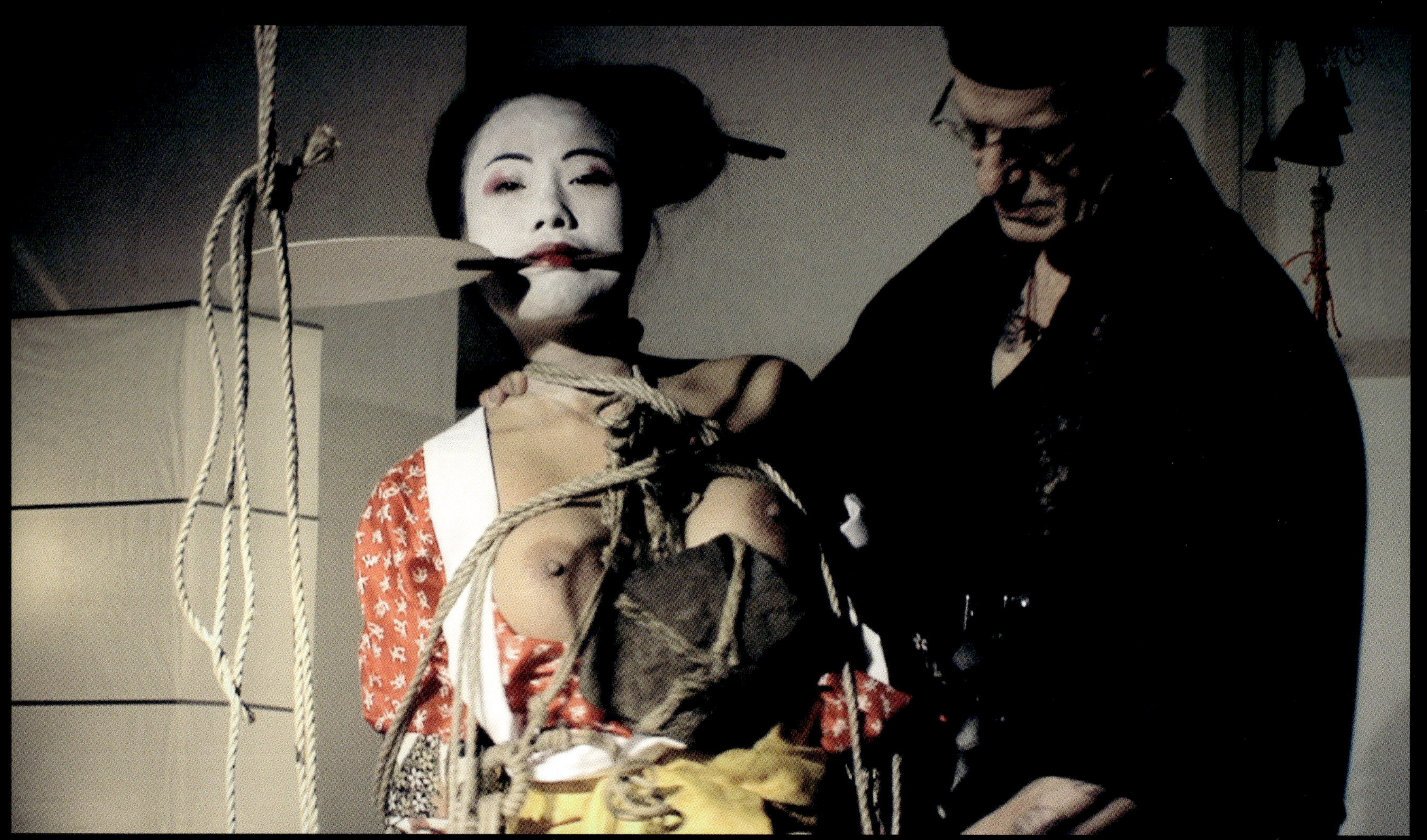

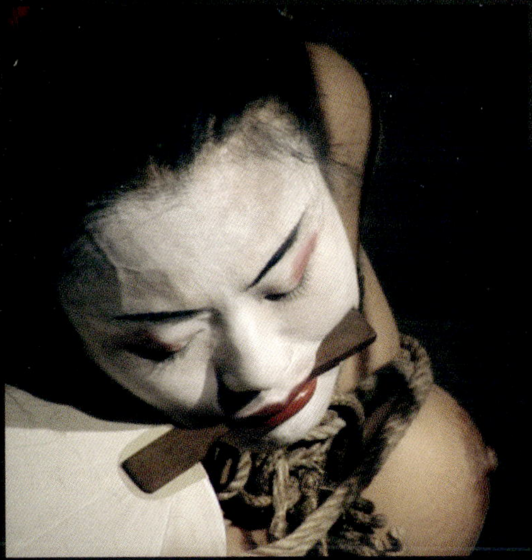

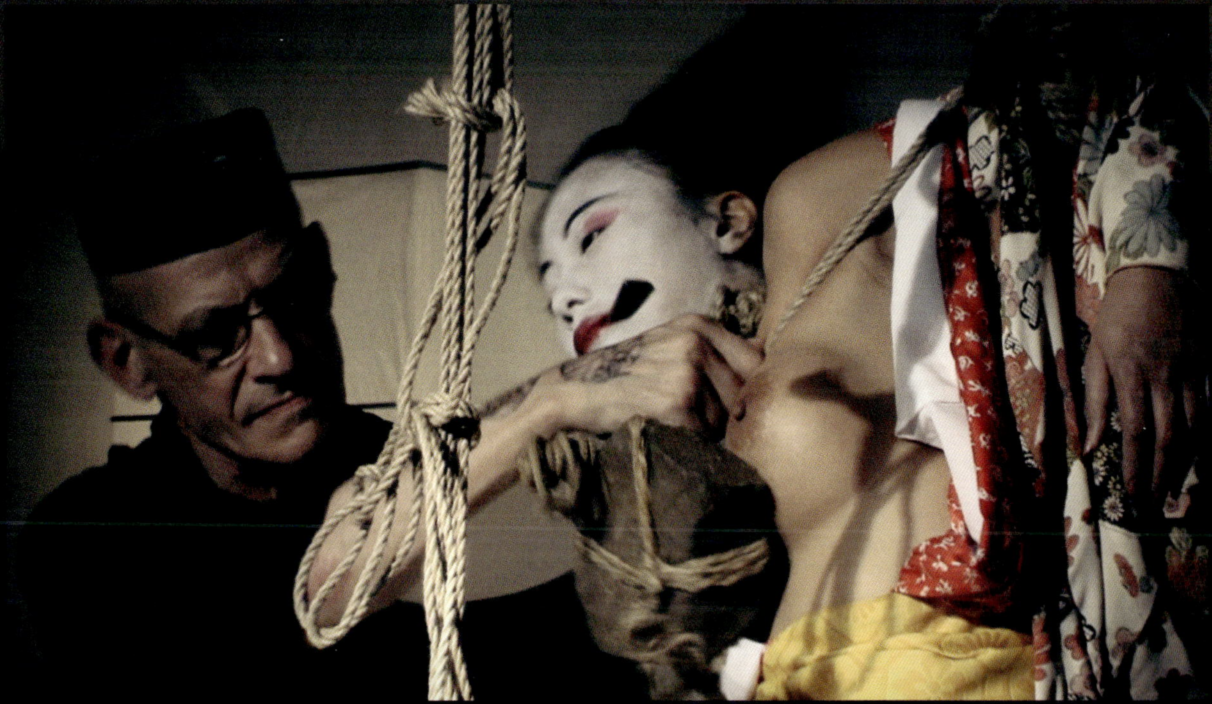

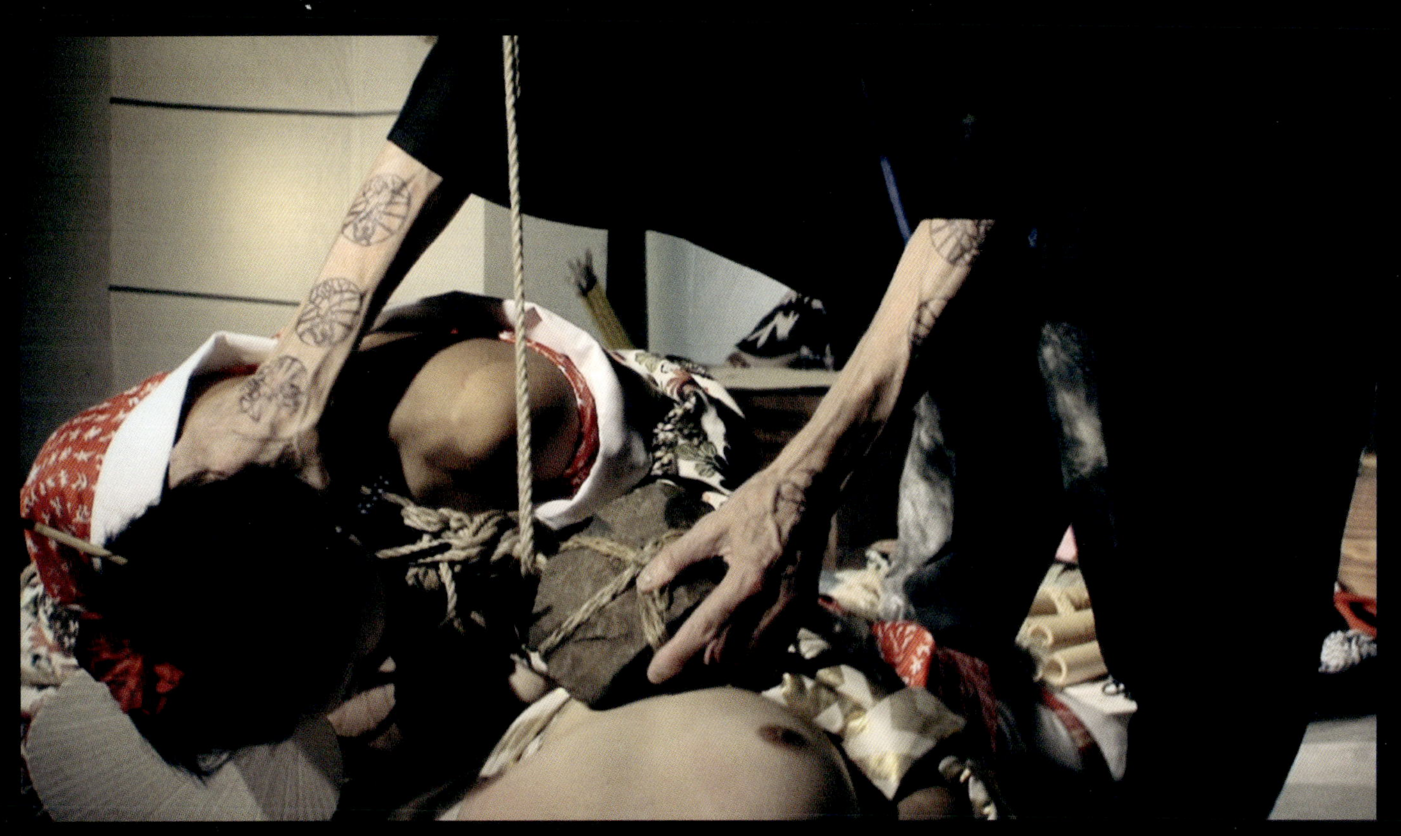

Murakawa:  The shows I do are not particularly technical because I'm interested in telling a story and a narrative. My performance told the story of a lost and lonely country girl who comes to work in the Yoshiwara district of Tokyo, in the Edo period.

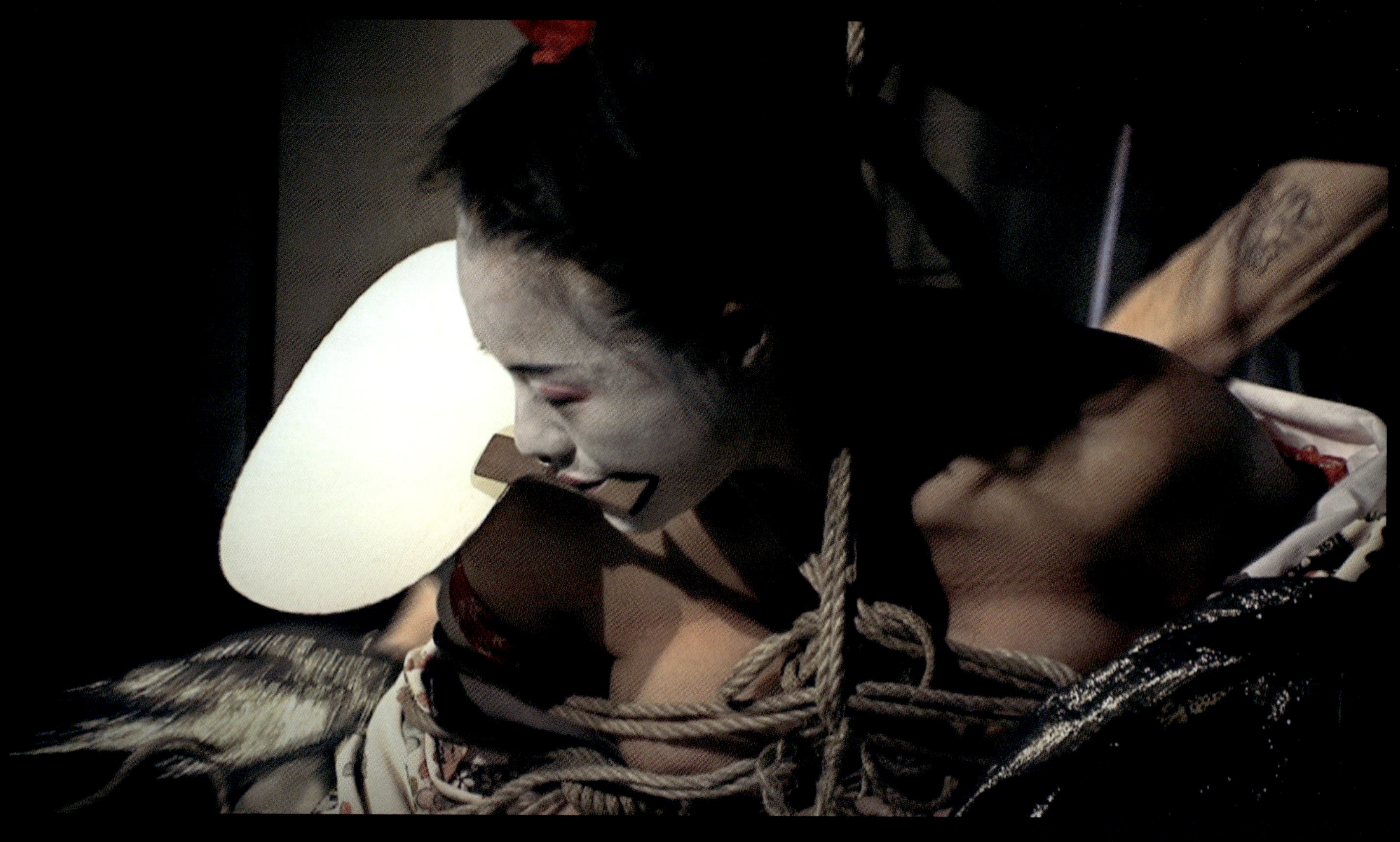

I'm trying to express how this girl is lost in this new glittery world.  She's a girl in a gilded cage but has a hollow life with no meaning and feeling she wants to go back home really.

It's not just a show of technical rope bondage.  I am trying to create an atmospheric world of Japanese tradition and drama and beauty using rope to tell part of that story.

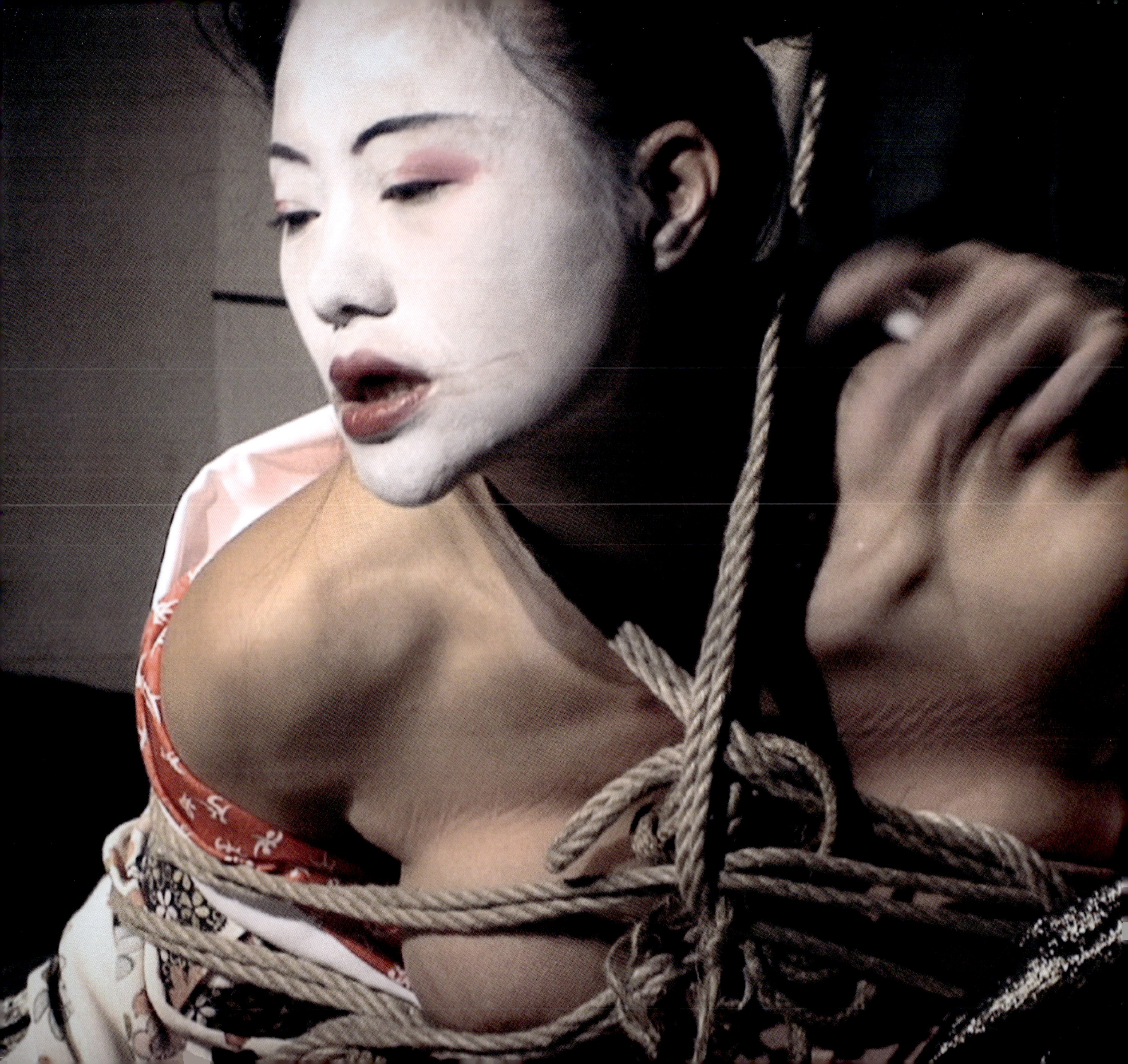

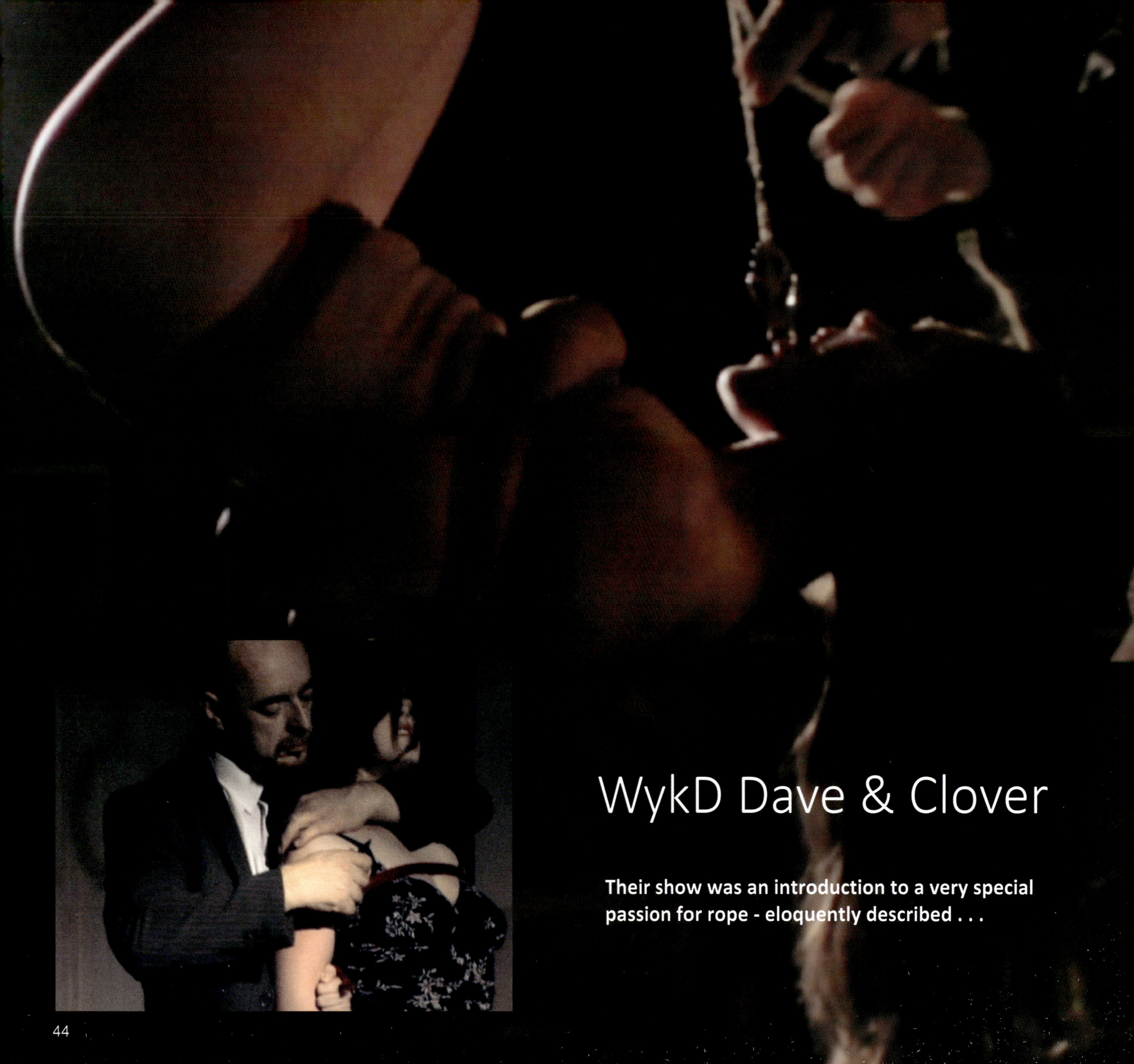

# WykD Dave & Clover

**Their show was an introduction to a very special passion for rope - eloquently described . . .**

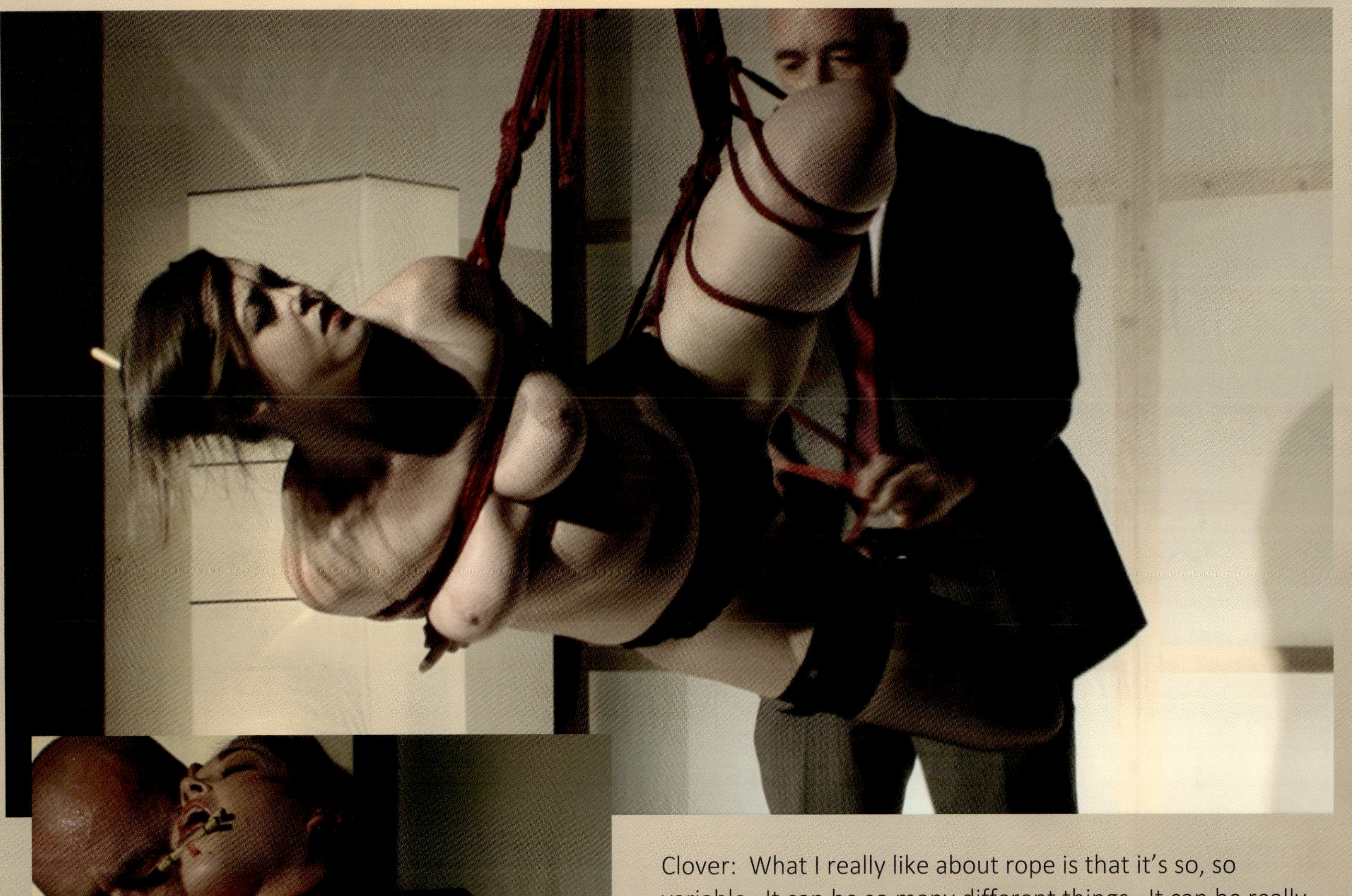

Clover:  What I really like about rope is that it's so, so variable.  It can be so many different things.  It can be really painful and it can be really pleasurable.

WykD Dave:  I feel loving. I feel protective. I can feel elated. It's a very concentrated emotional intenseness.

Clover:  I think it can be difficult to get people to understand the contradiction.

WykD Dave:  There isn't really a conflict once you understand that the person is enjoying that.

Clover: And I think if you experience it and you're not that way inclined, again, you're not going to understand it because it's going to be a massive ordeal.

If I'm in very sensual rope, it's quite a nice floaty feeling, where it's very calm and peaceful. And then when you're enduring some torture or stress, it's a different kind of mindset. You're still floaty but it's still painful. But it's nice.

For us, rope and everyday life have kind of merged a bit. When we come home from work we'll do all our domestic chores and stuff we need to do and then we'll make time to do rope together. For us it's like making love or having sex. It's just about the biggest stress reliever and afterwards you just feel renewed.

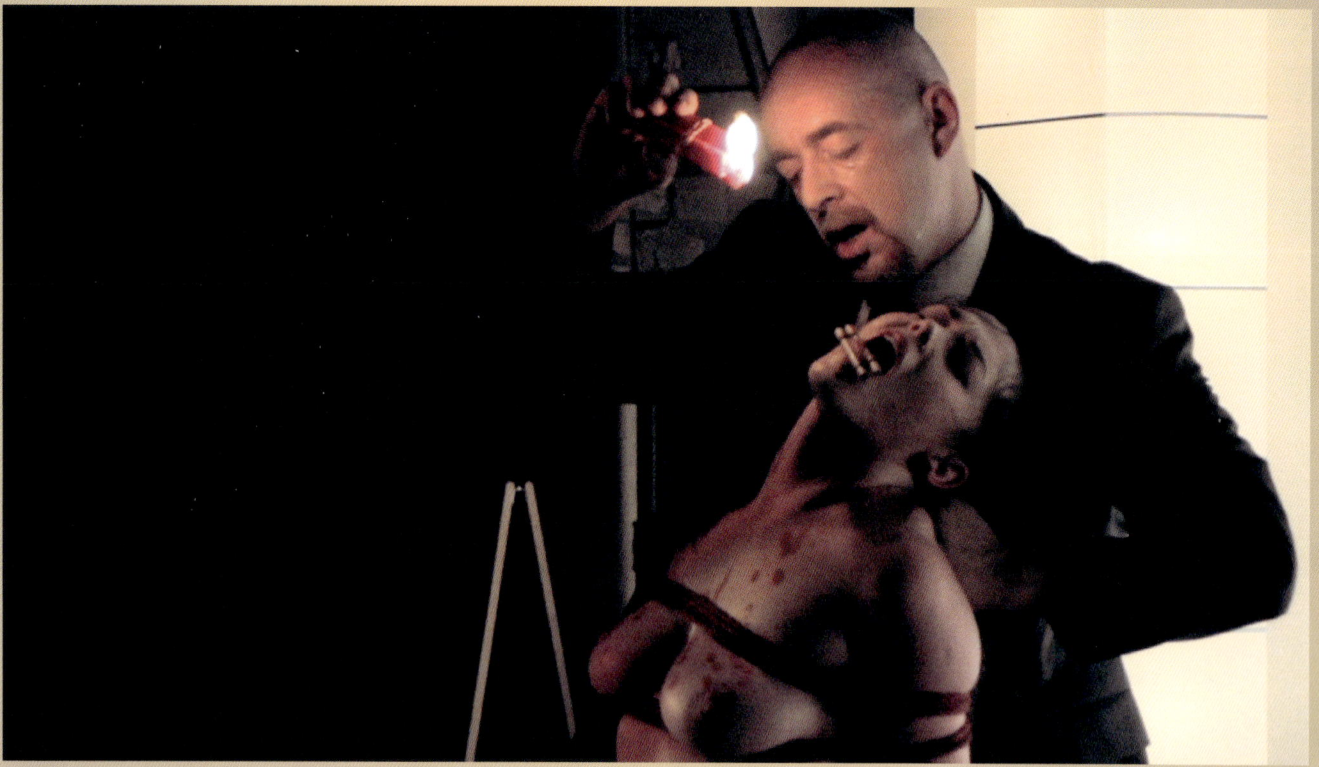

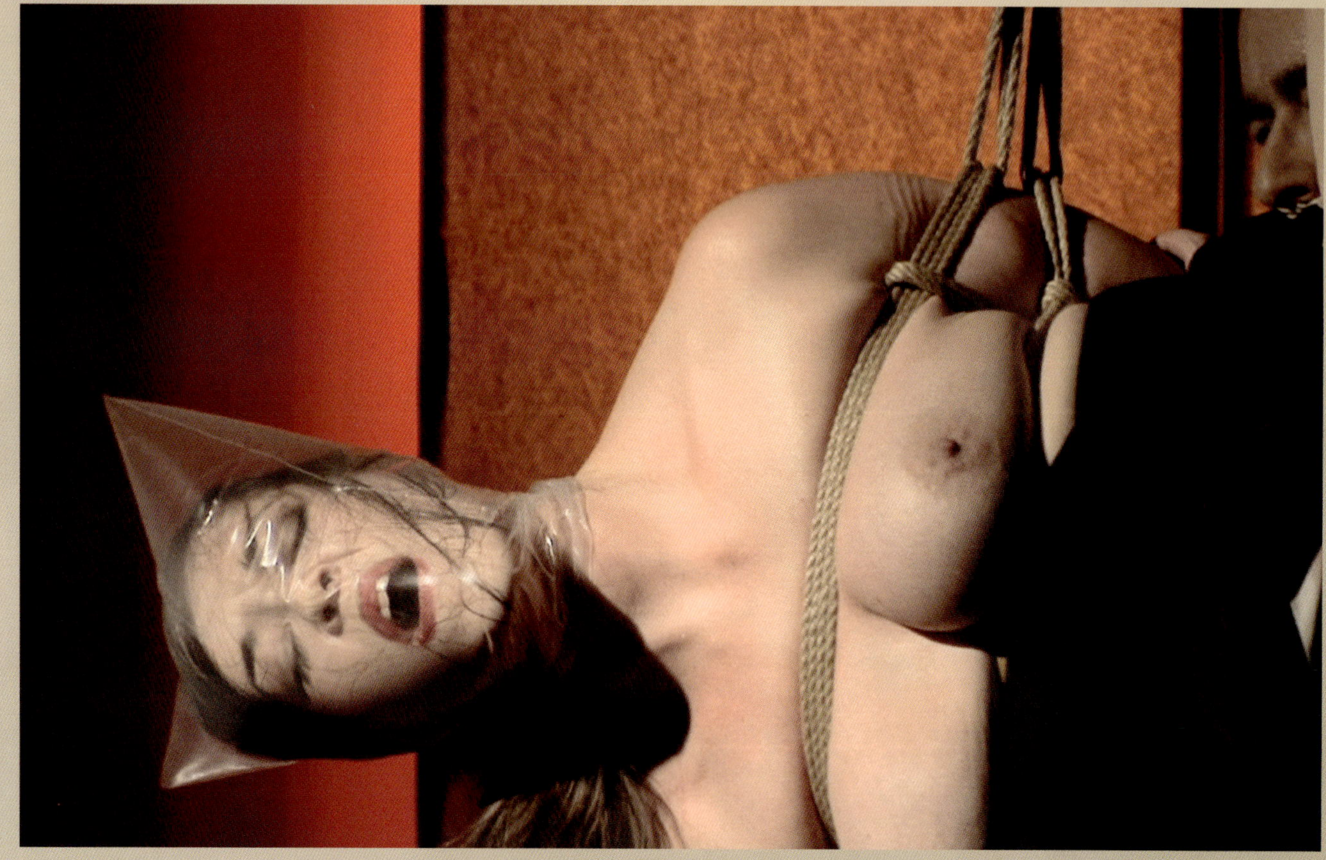

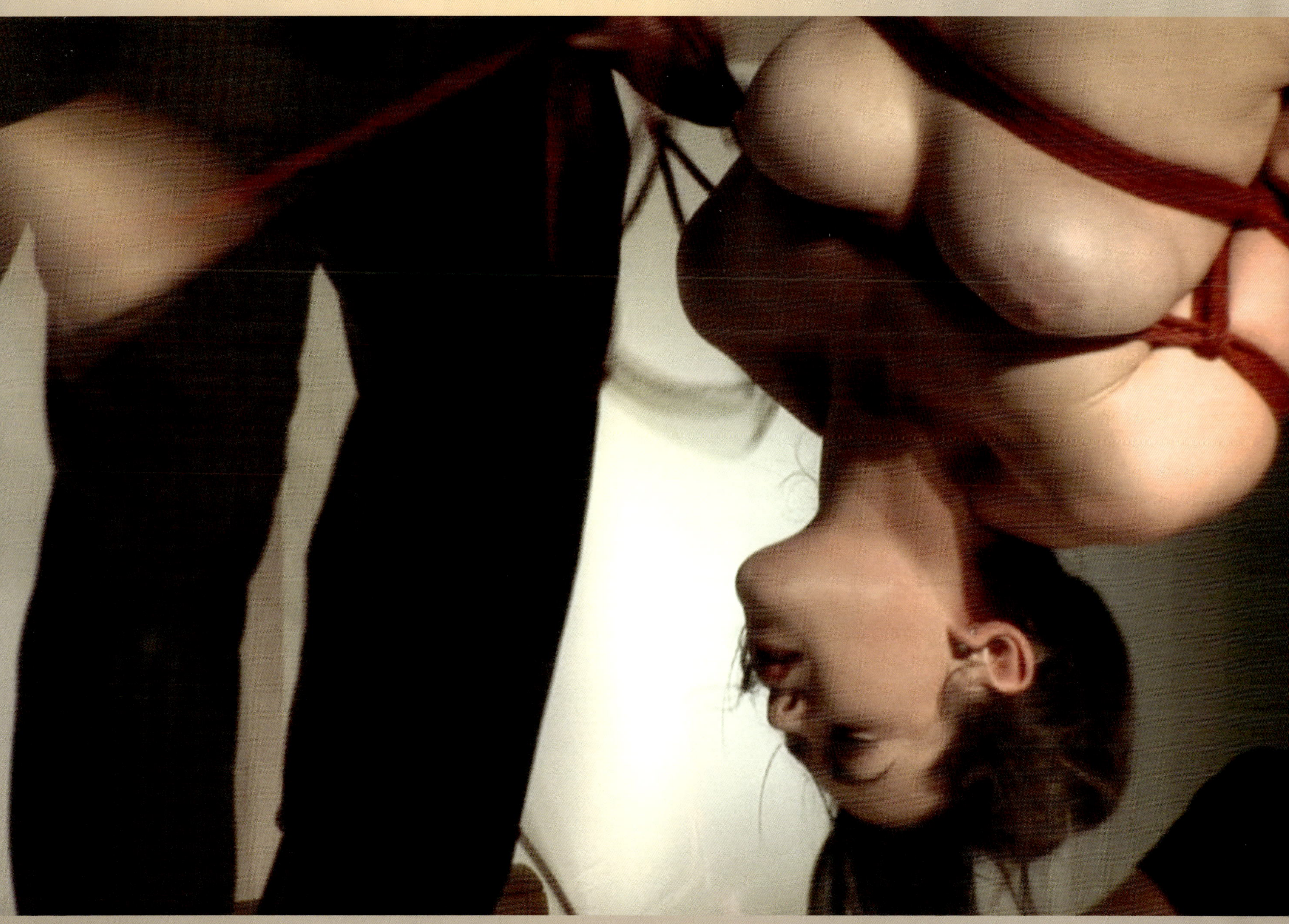

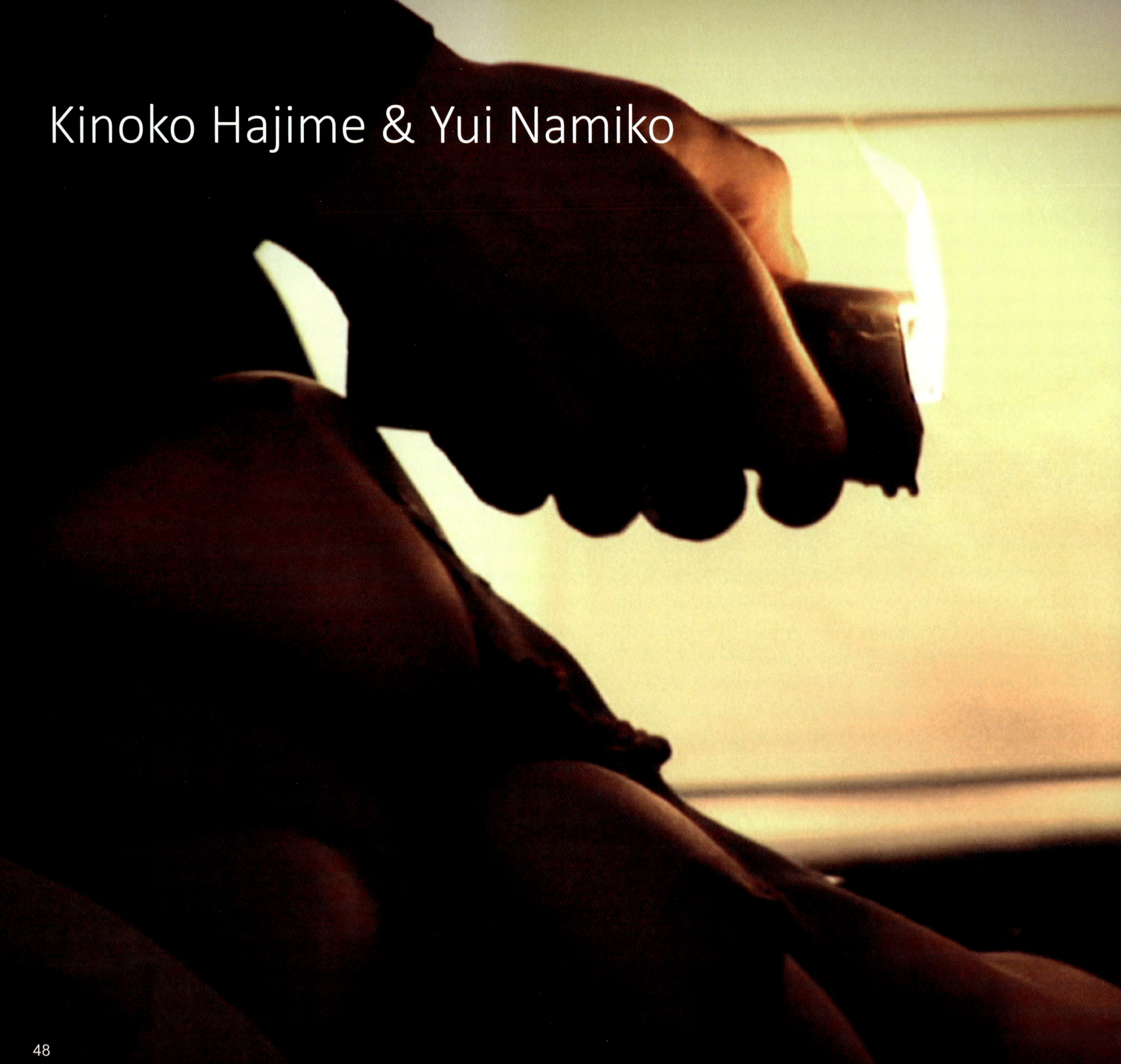
Kinoko Hajime & Yui Namiko

**It was the performance of Kinoko Hajime in 2011 that was the most keenly anticipated.  It was his show at the previous London festival that had so perturbed me.**

Clover:  The show in London that Kinoko performed in complete silence completely gripped everybody.  You could have heard a penny drop in the room.  He just captured everyone's attention.

Every time I see him perform it blows me away again and again.  Looking at the models he uses for his performances, I find them very inspiring; just watching them and seeing how they are in rope and how they approach things.

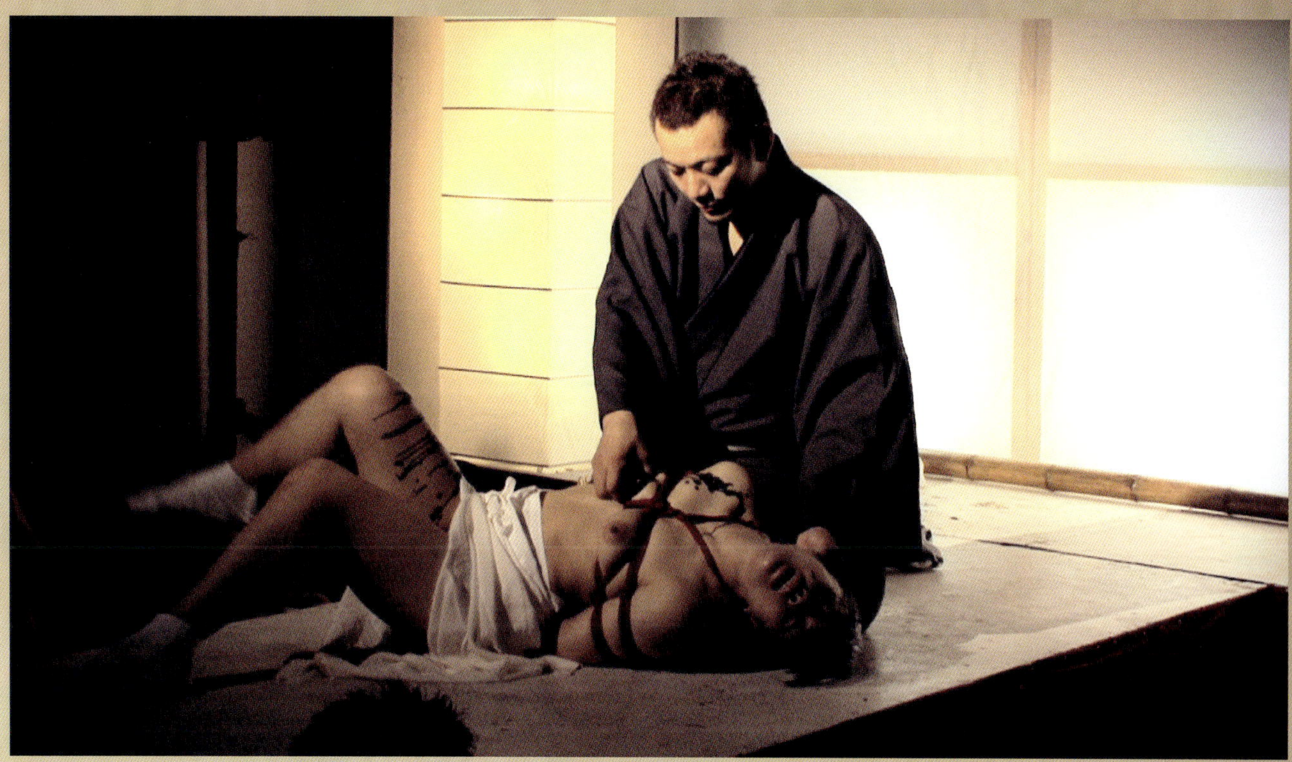

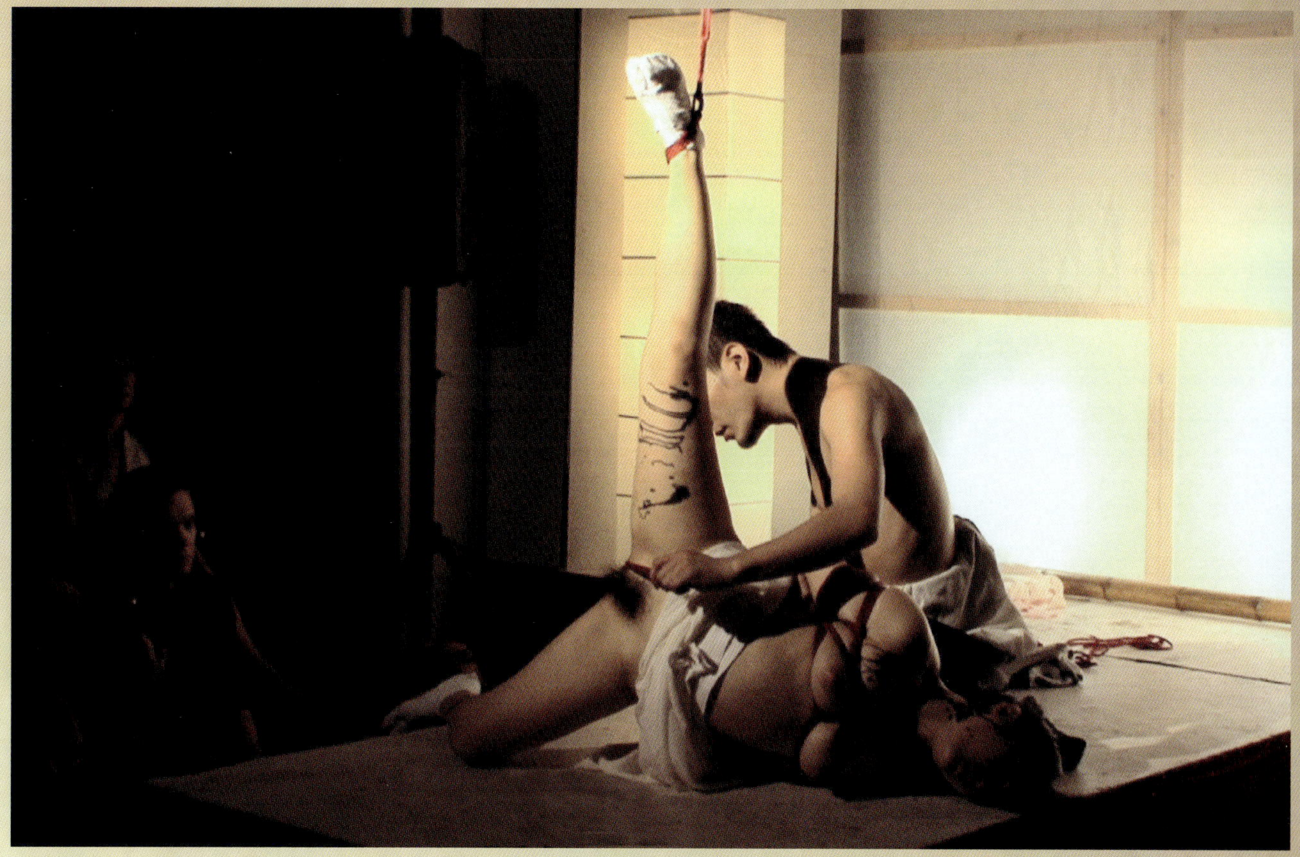

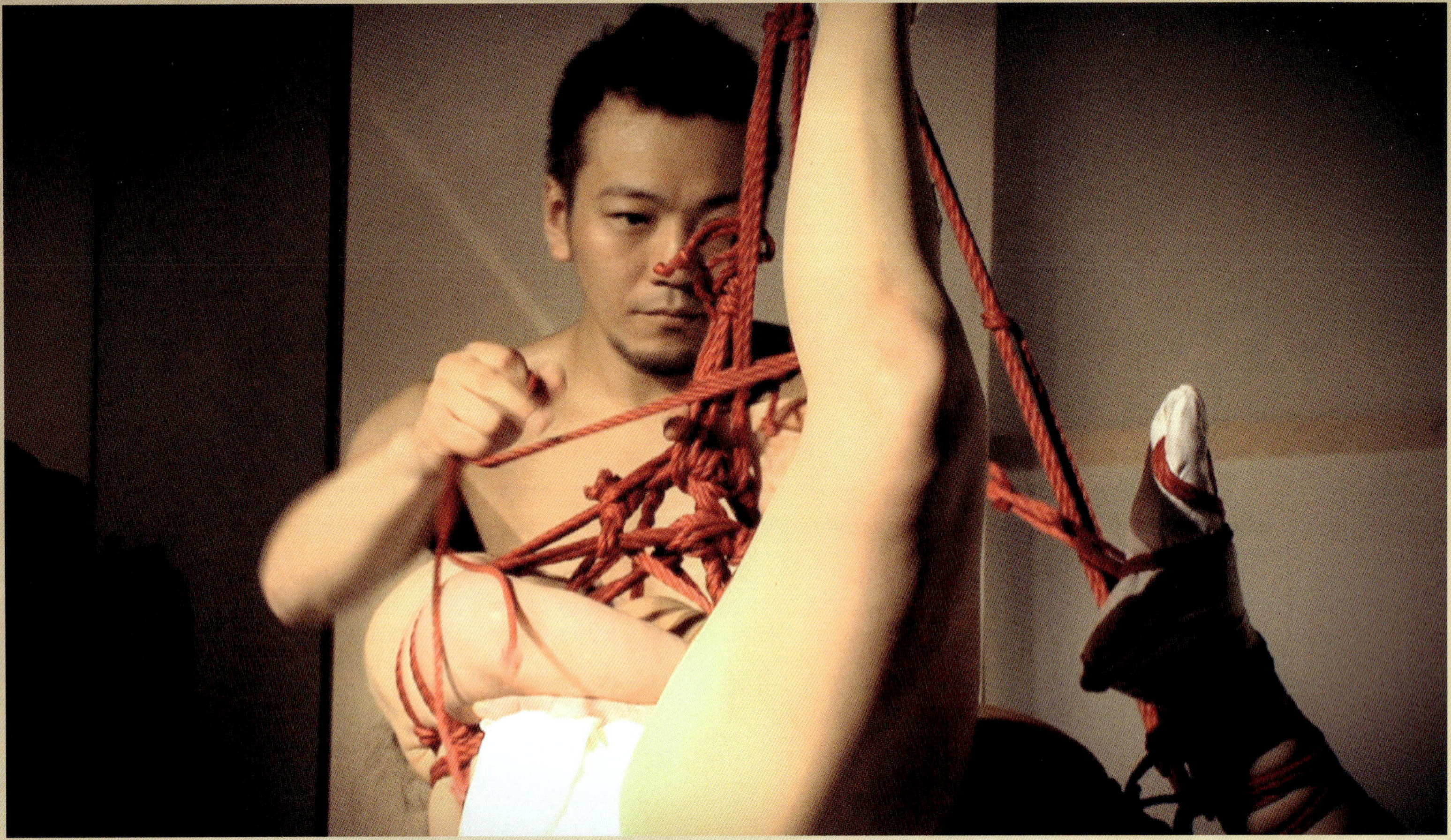

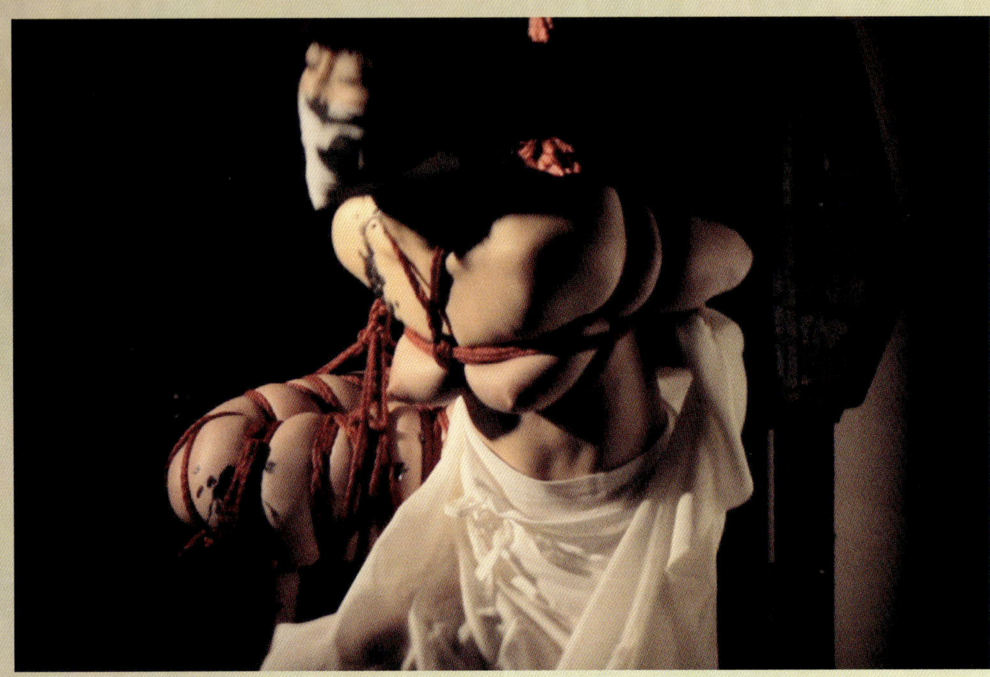
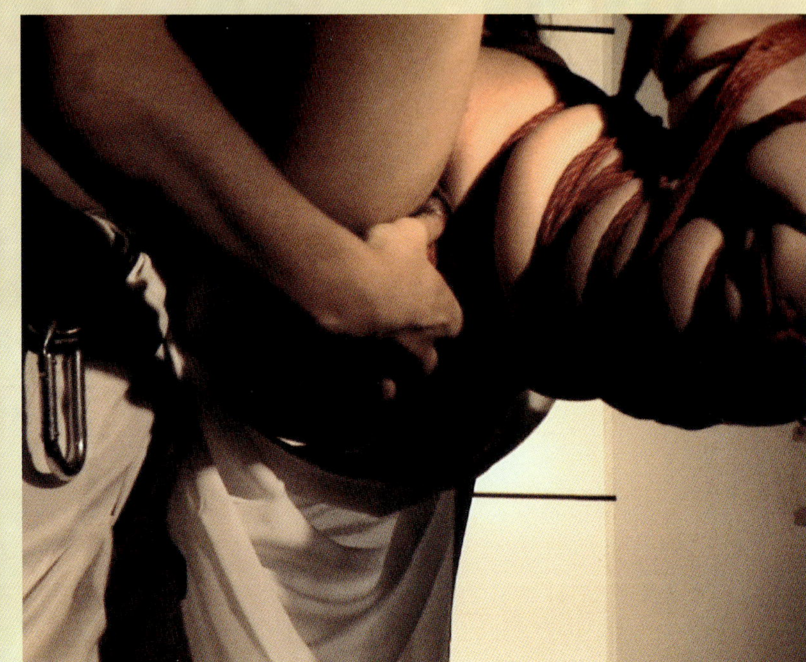

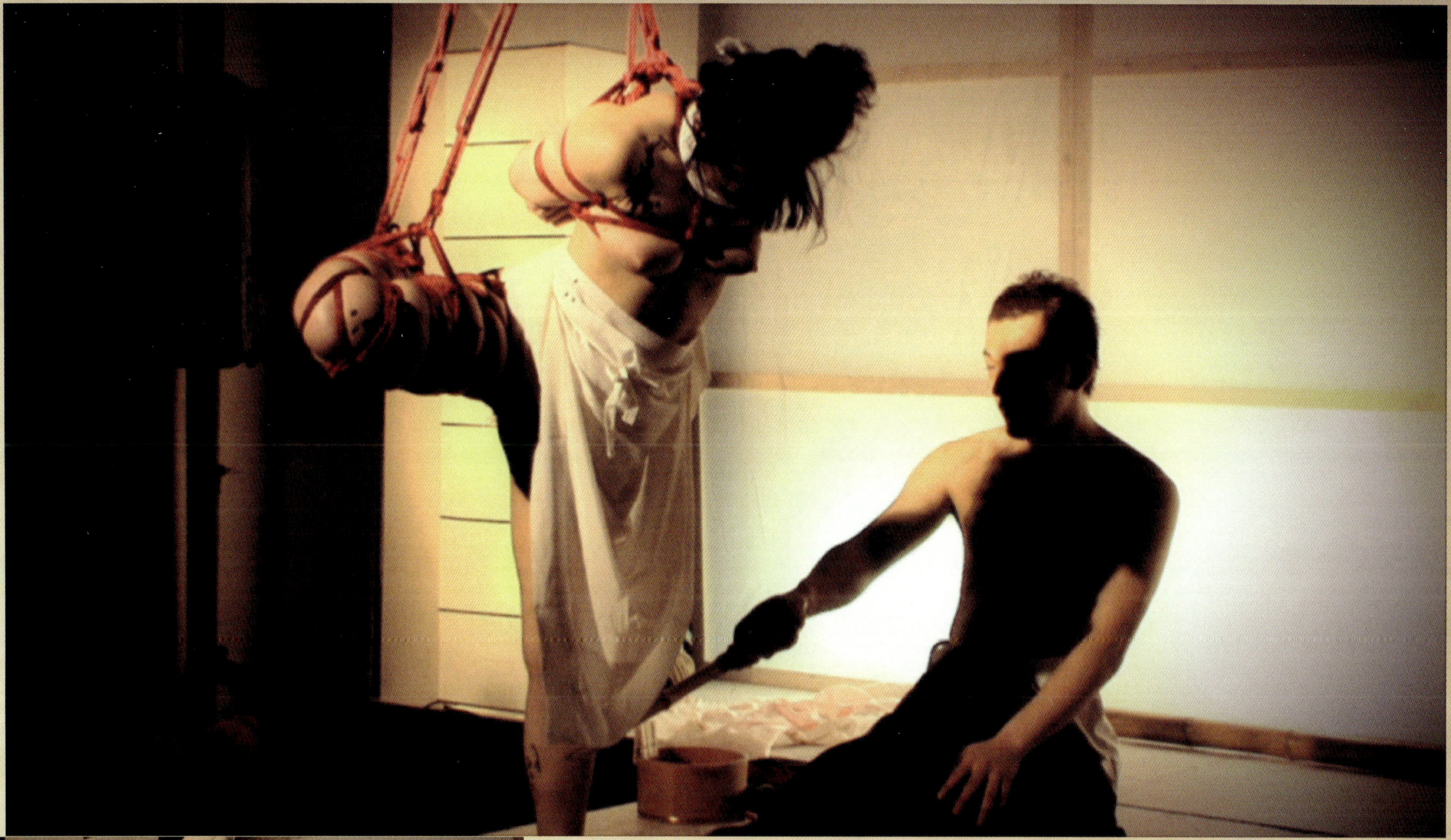

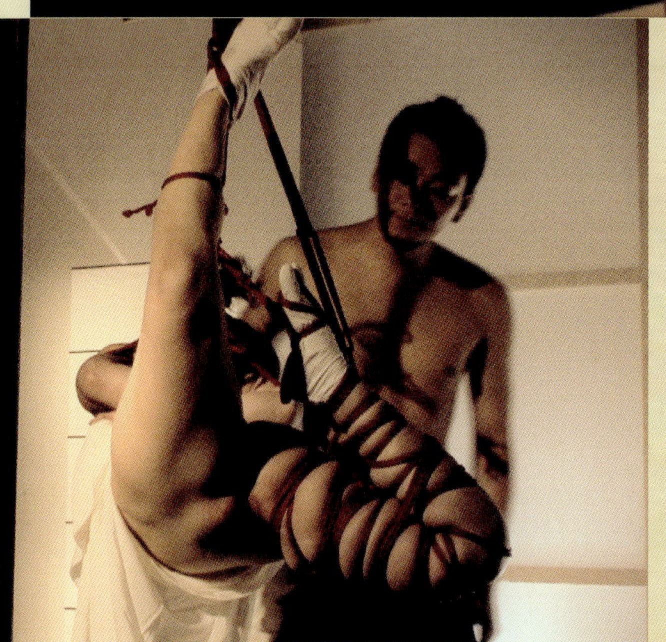

Clover:  I've never seen rope like that before on stage. I found it completely overwhelming.

I think he has completely revolutionised rope in Europe.

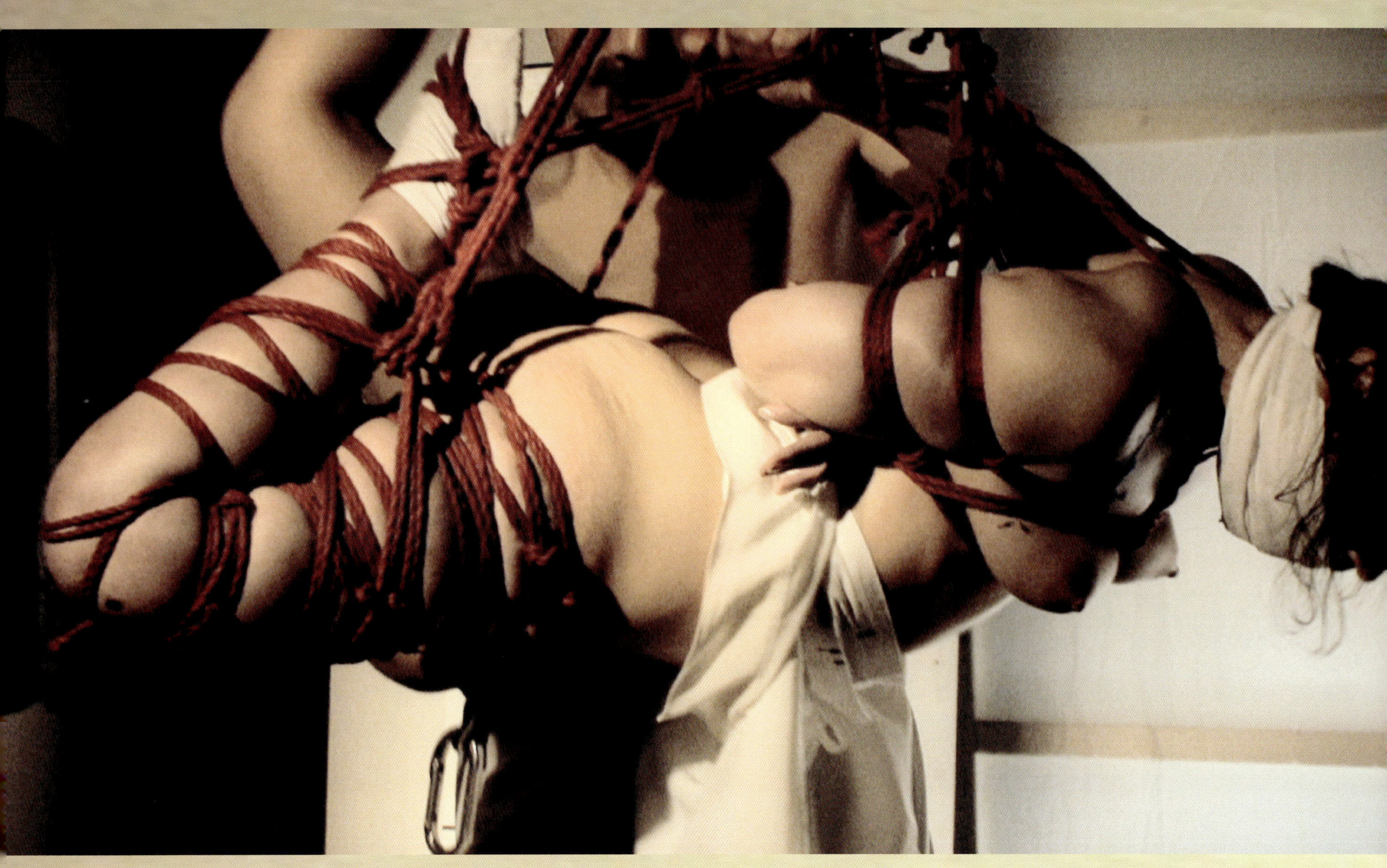

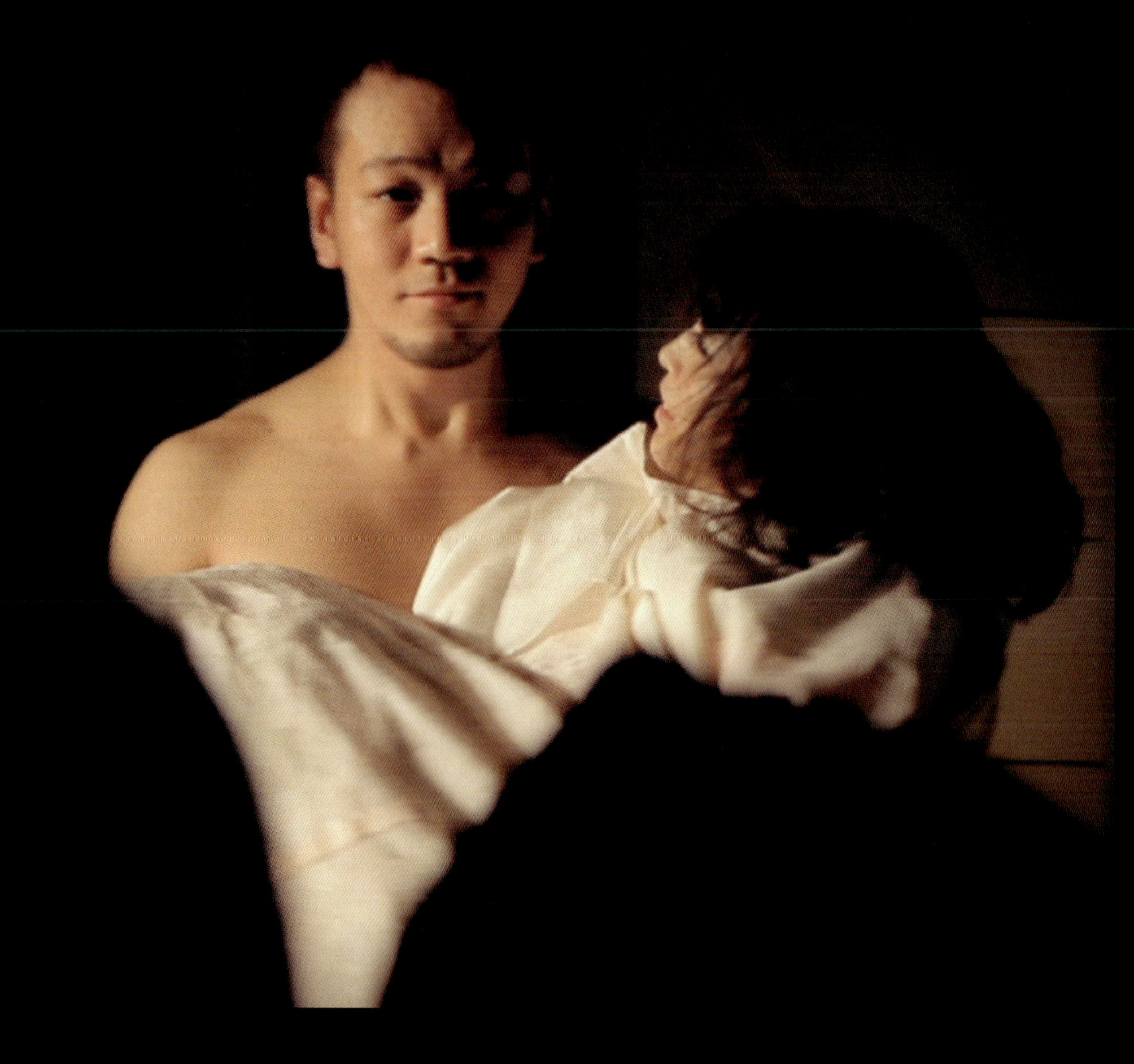

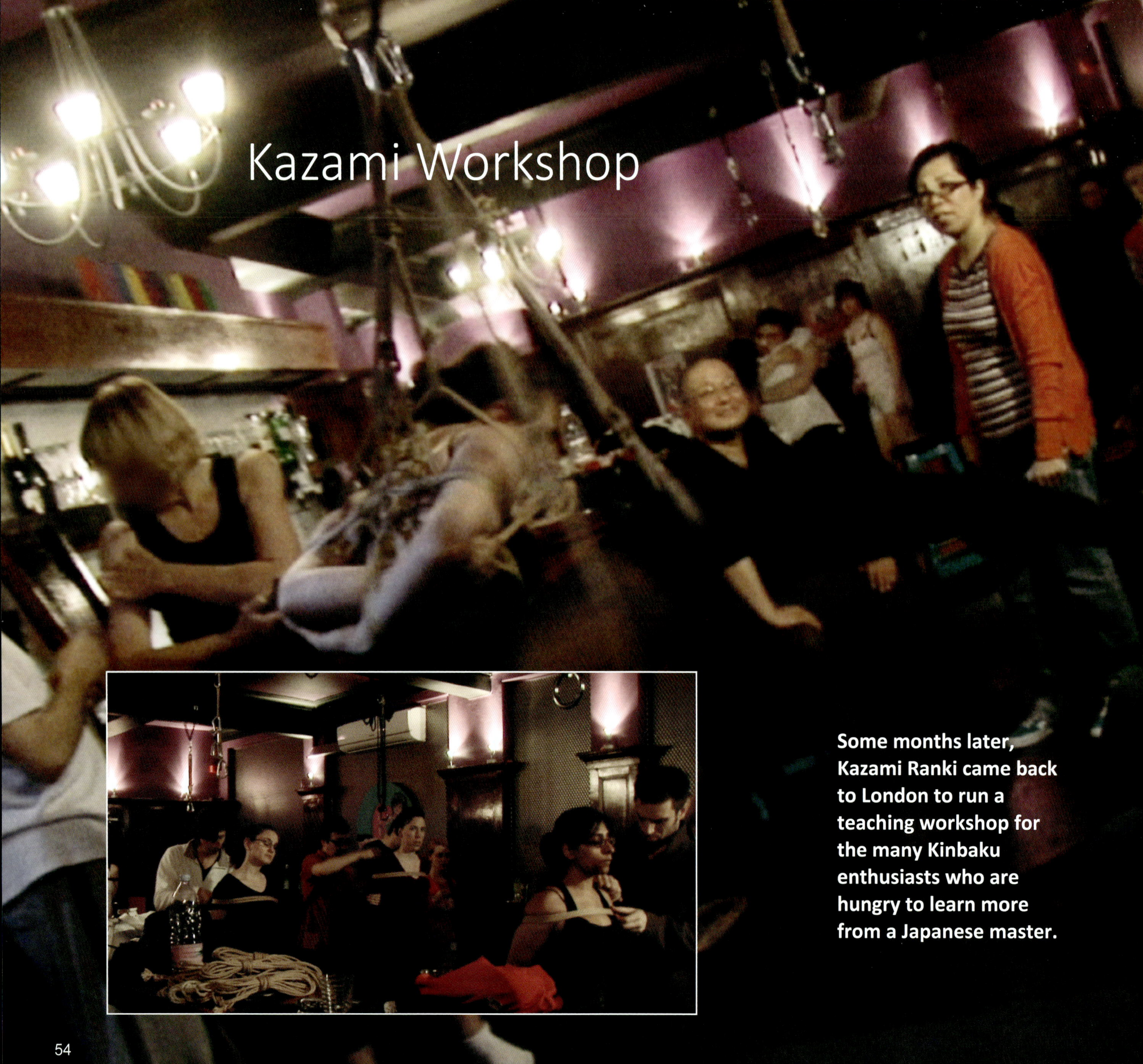
Kazami Workshop

Some months later,
Kazami Ranki came back
to London to run a
teaching workshop for
the many Kinbaku
enthusiasts who are
hungry to learn more
from a Japanese master.

**Ichigo did a performance with Hedwig after one of the workshops.**

Ichigo:  I think you've got to have a lot of respect for Kazami because when you know someone is that experienced, you tend to fall into that trust so much easier.

He knew what he was doing and he was good at communicating and he was also asking if I was OK.  He's just lovely.

I like restraint.  I like the feeling under a kind of control and the play fighting factor of it.  And then there is the more sensual side.  I think there's so many things that you can explore about rope.

I have a partner already.  He's my long term boyfriend.  Obviously we have an open relationship and I'm allowed to play with women.  I do prefer women topping me more than men. It's just a lot more sensual.  I only crave the male side of things from my boyfriend.  So it's kind of balanced.  It's nice, I get to be a big raving lesbian!!!

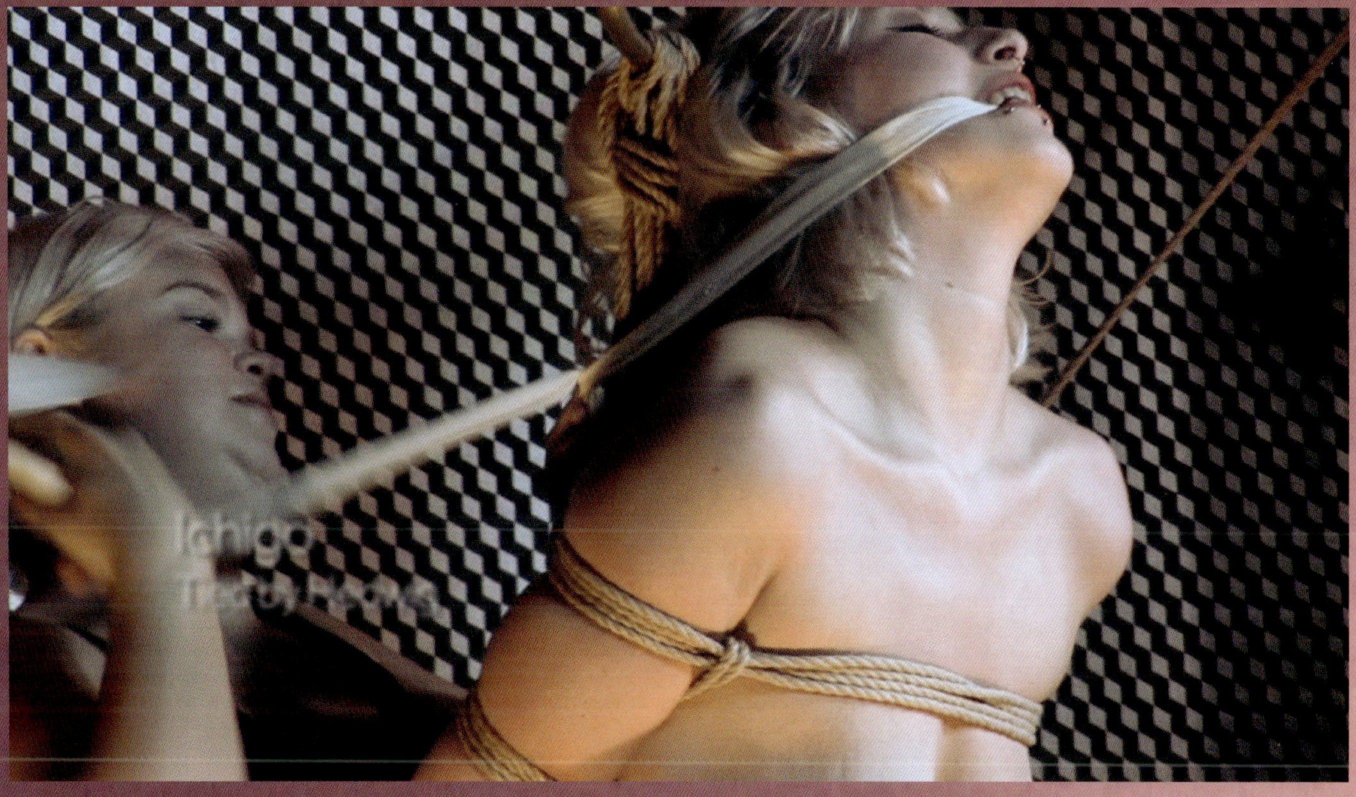


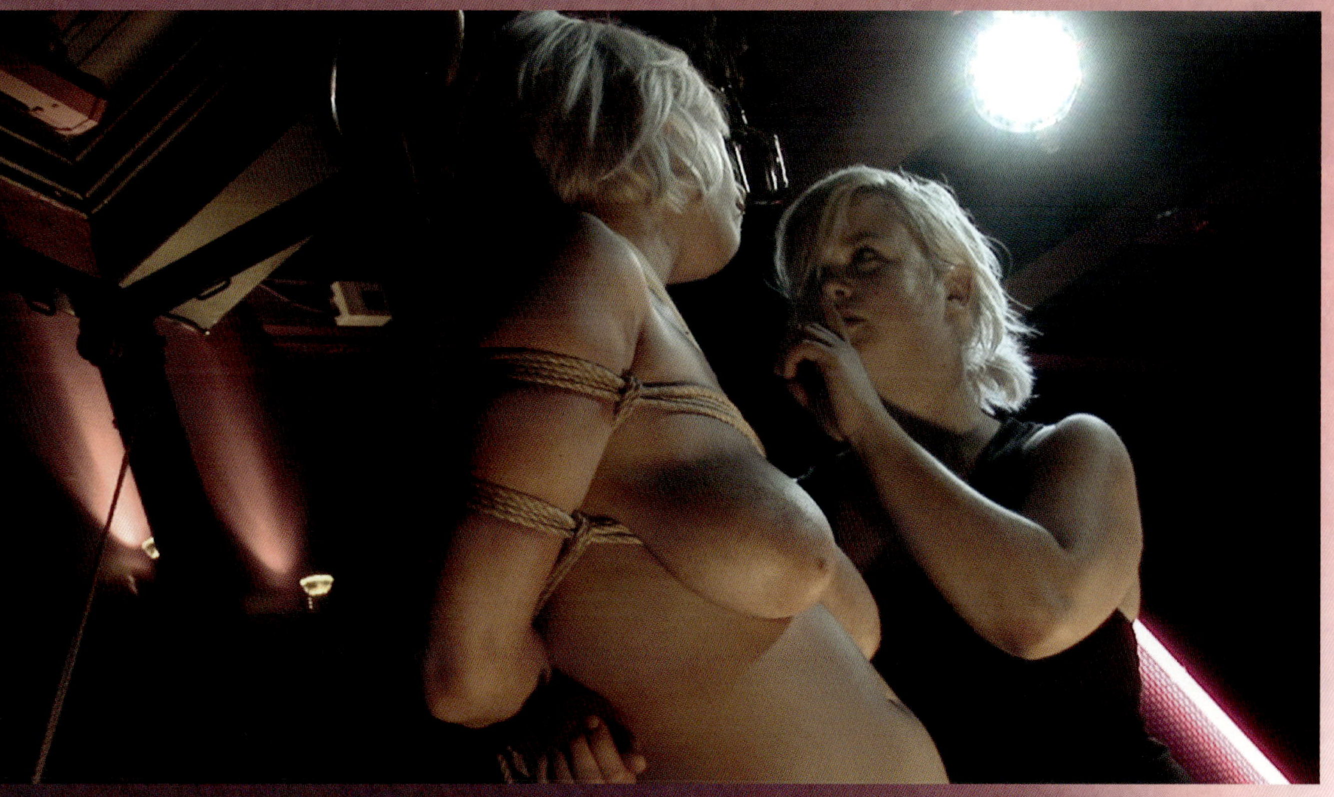

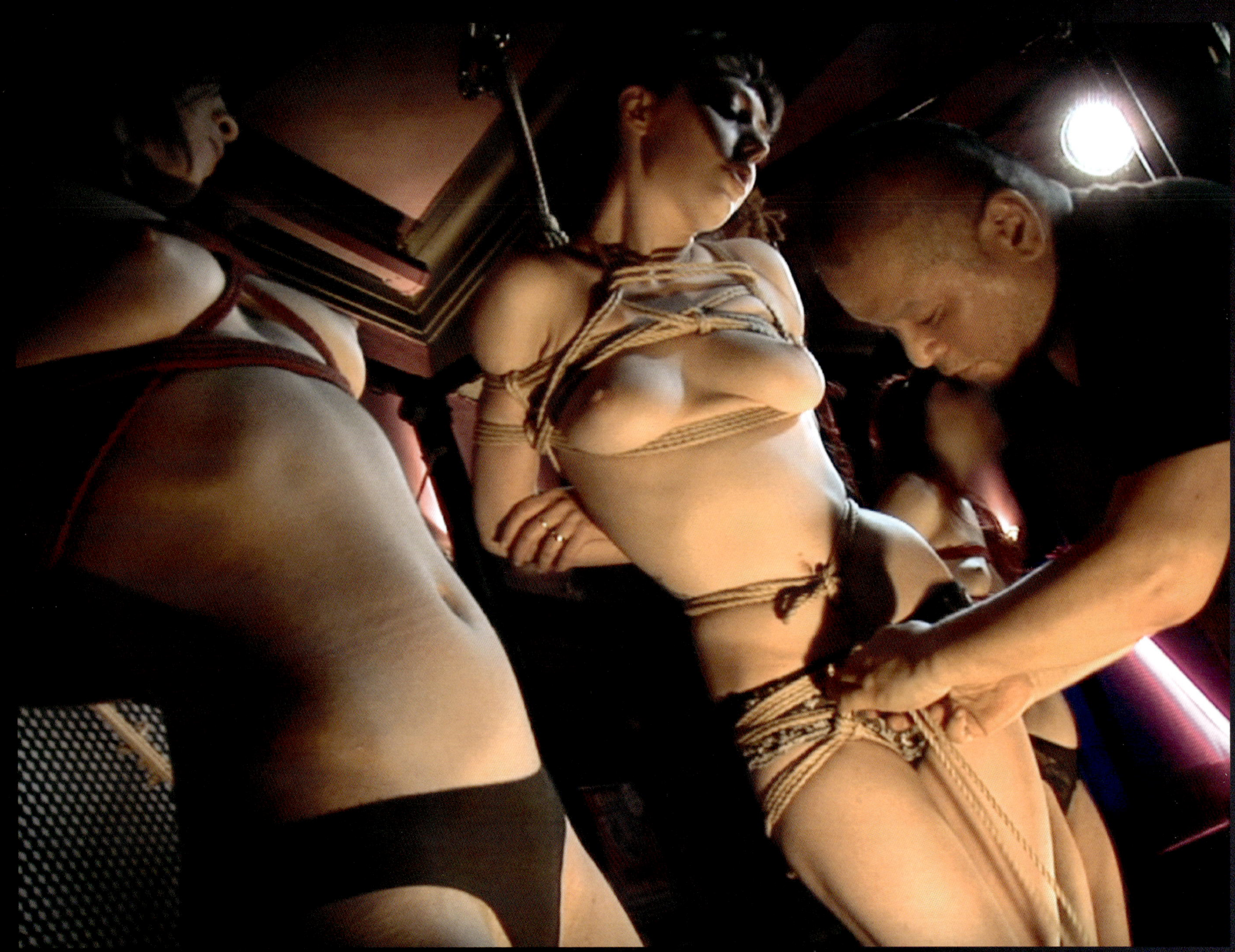

Towards the end of the workshop, Kazami gave a demonstration of advanced suspension with Gestalta and two other volunteers.

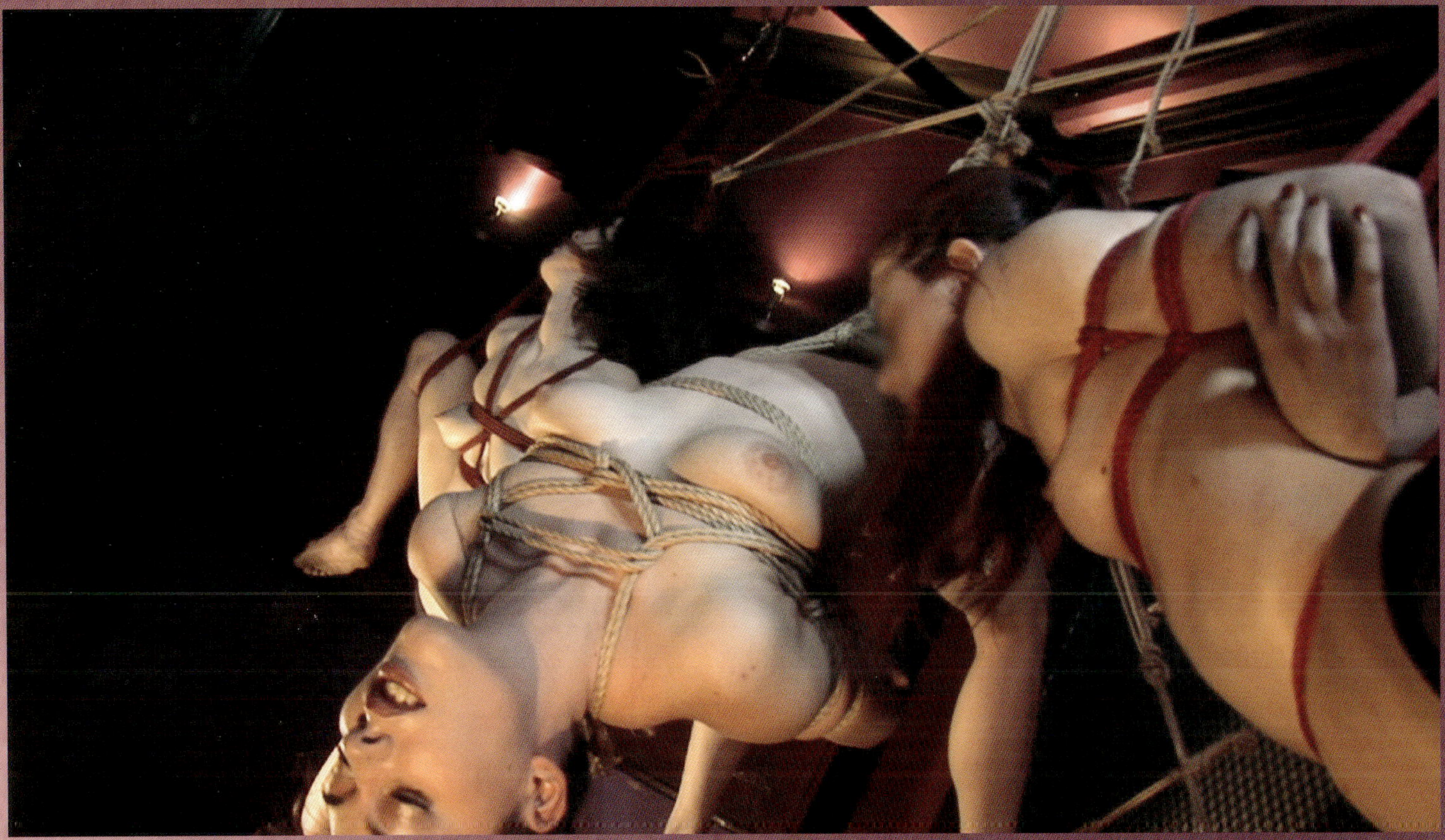

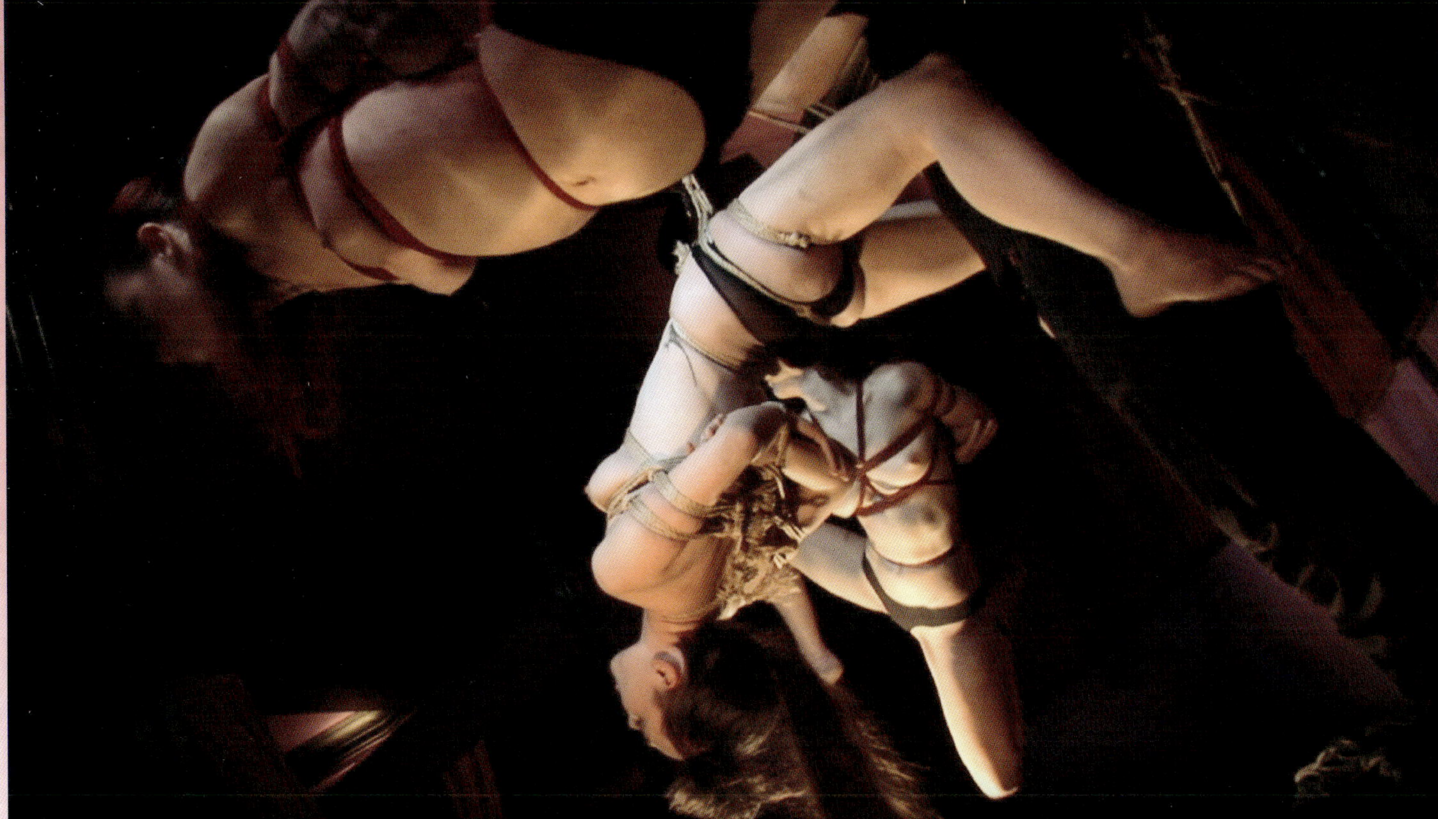

Midori:  It's certainly exciting for a lot of fellows to be technically proficient at something.  So there's a tendency for an individual man, woman, any gender to enjoy an engineering or artistic aspect of it.  This certainly is a way of sex and pleasure that would allow for that sort of exploration.

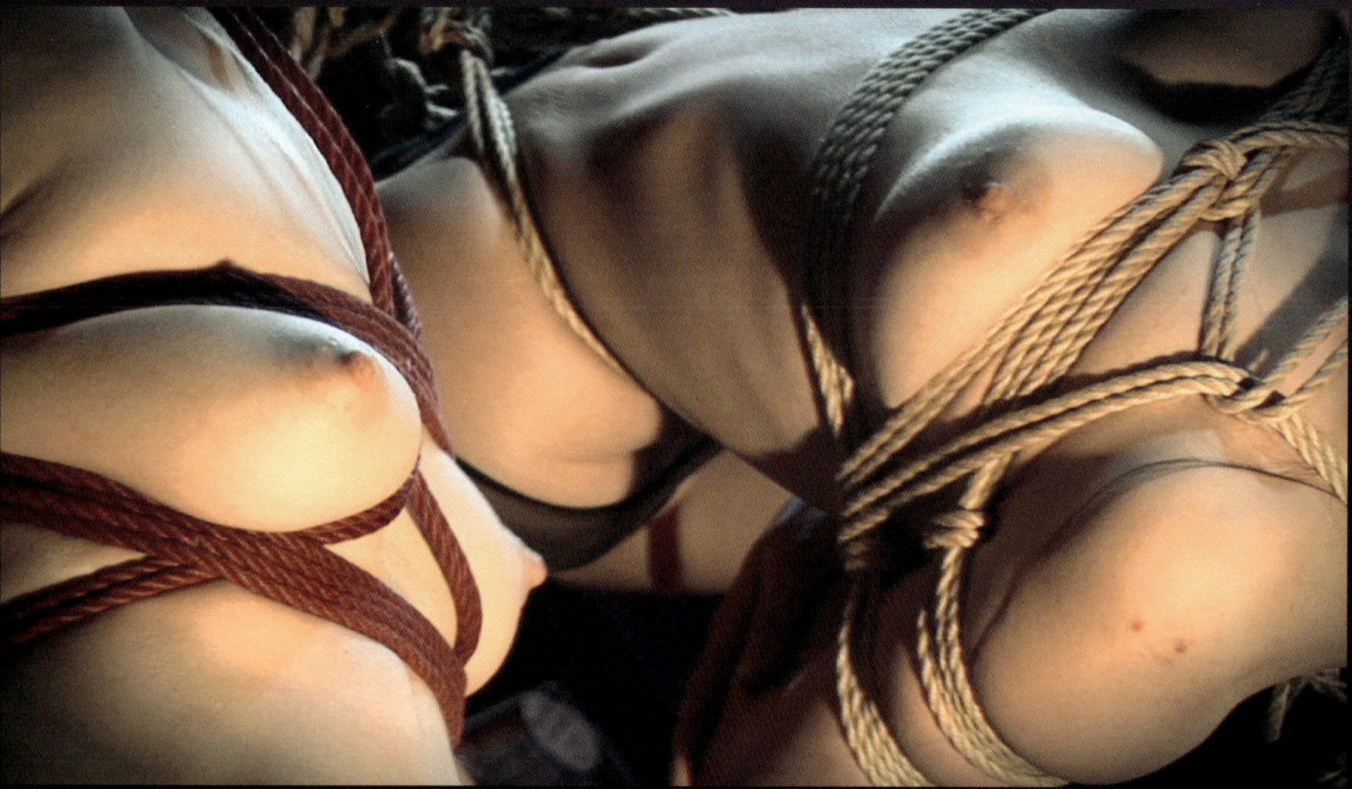

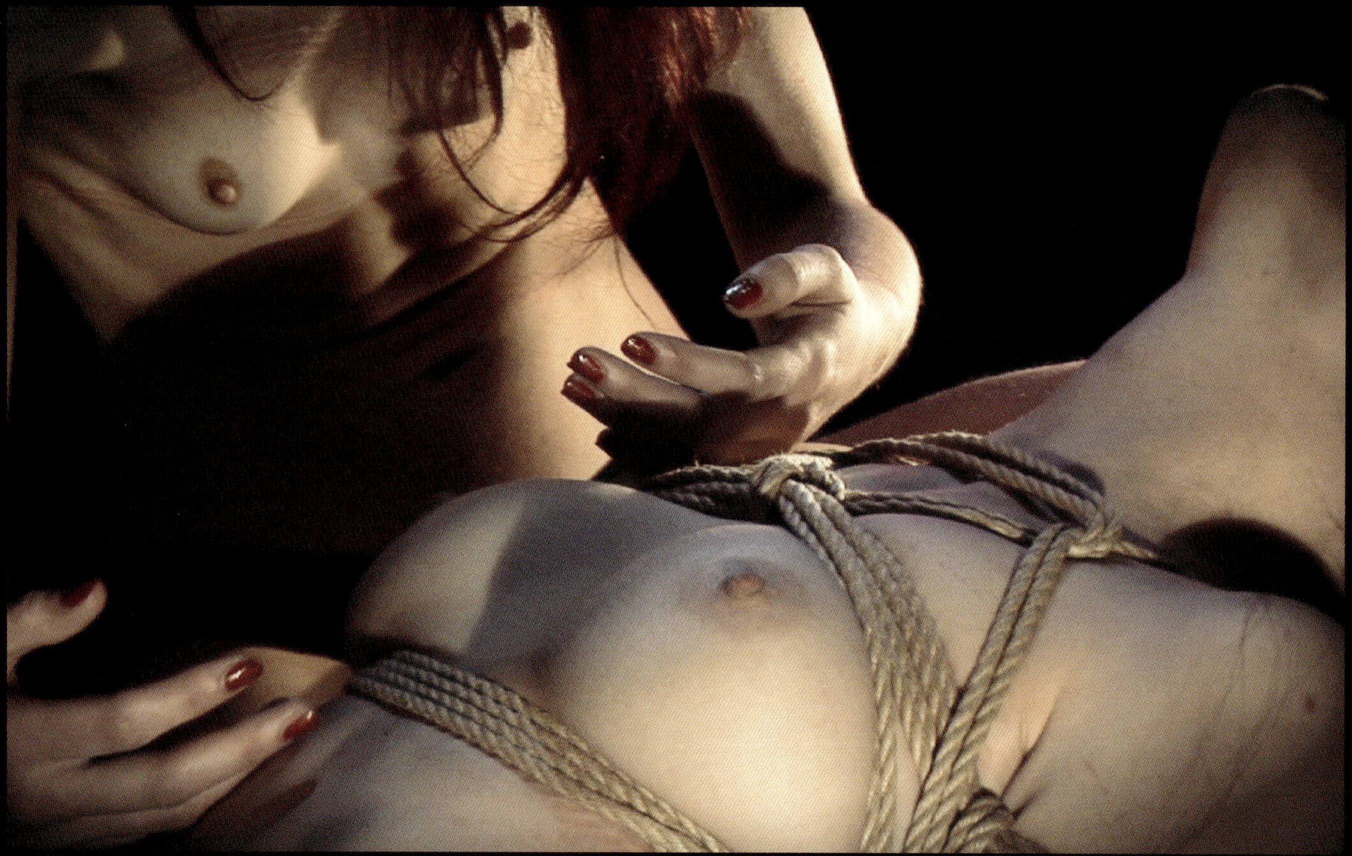

Midori: Many women say that guys will talk about the technique but rarely seem to talk about the person they're tying, or the emotional connection and nuances.

And a lot of women that I've talked to find the endless argument about the technique of a tie to be rather tedious and they just want to get on with having sexy fun.

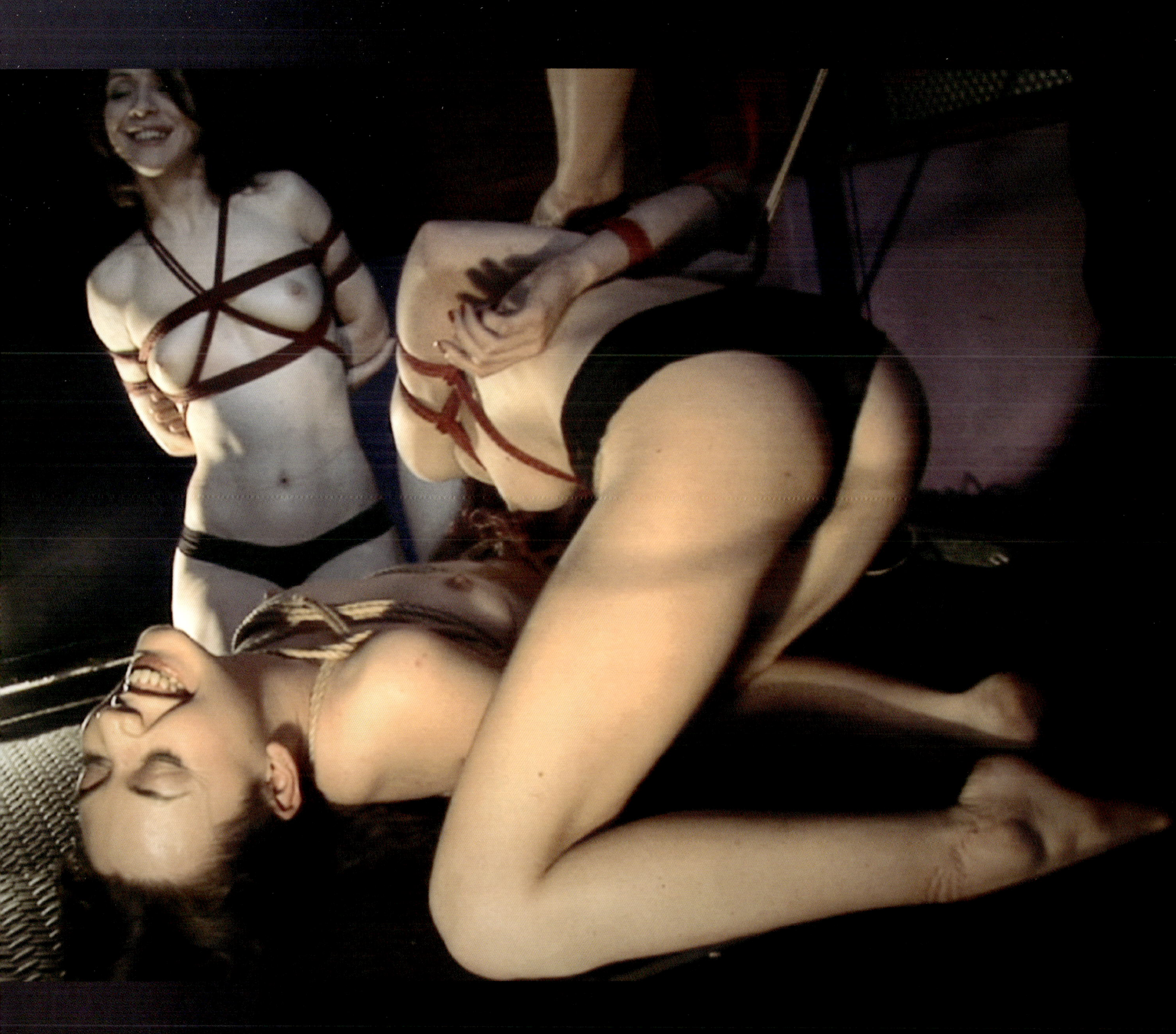

# Chapter 2

## CREATIVE TIES

In this chapter we explore how Kinbaku is used in various art forms.  It provides unexpected benefits, helping people in surprising ways, revealing the pleasure of rope.

## Midori

In London's fashionable Covent Garden an event took place in a window of a well known emporium for women.

Coco De Mer invited Midori to create a sculptural installation  . . .

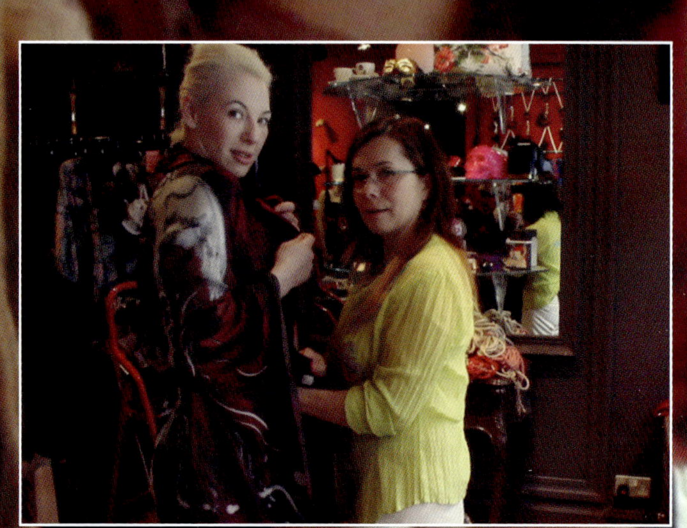

Midori:  Coco De Mer is a lovely sexy shop in Covent Garden, London, for lovers and the lovers of beautiful sexy things.  I am thrilled because here's a window in a store, weekday afternoon in Covent Garden and people are walking by when they suddenly realise that what seems like a window full of flowers holds a woman.

So I create seasonal representations: so it's my expression of flower   beauty   decay.

The window is full of the delicate and viciousness of nature.

My human subject, along with the flower subject, is Dolly Dangerous, a fantastic burlesque performer in town, and we've been long time friends.

It is the interaction with the people that show up there that's really precious.  Some are people who receive my newsletter and come to watch, others are passers by on their way to get coffee.

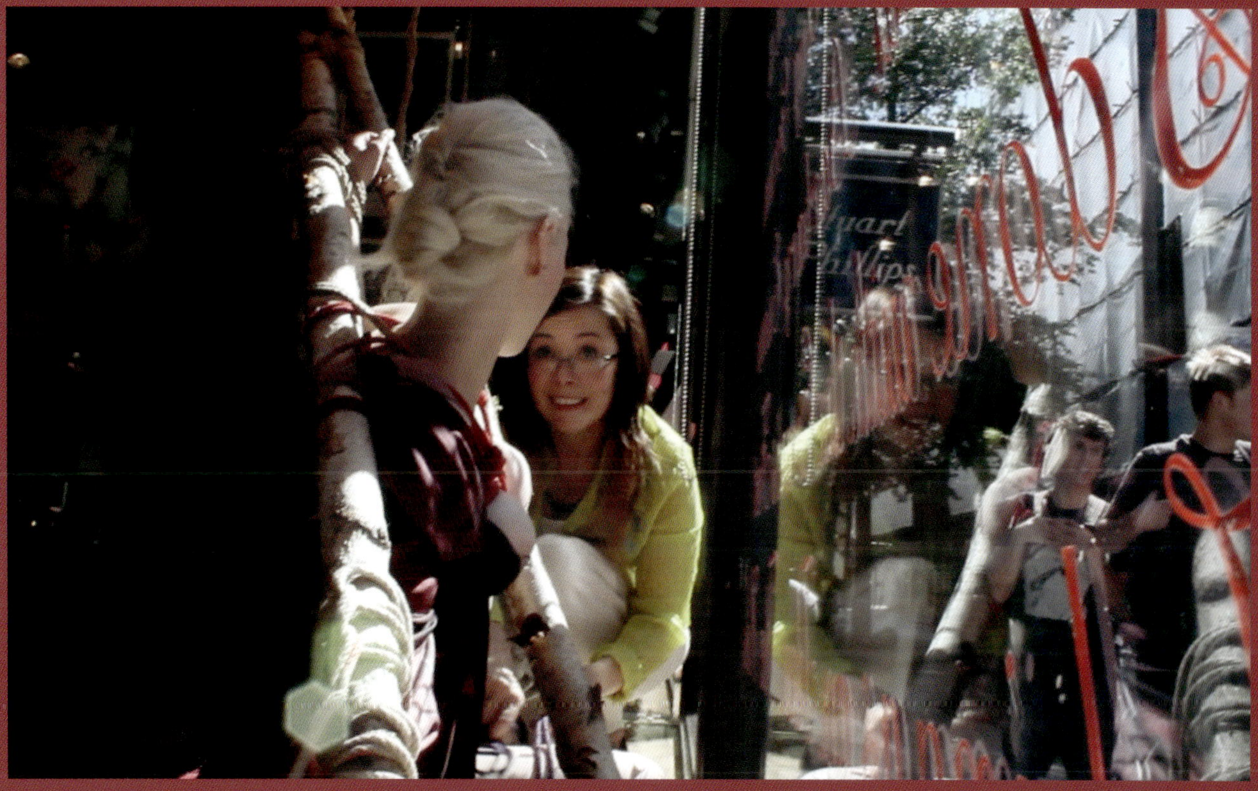

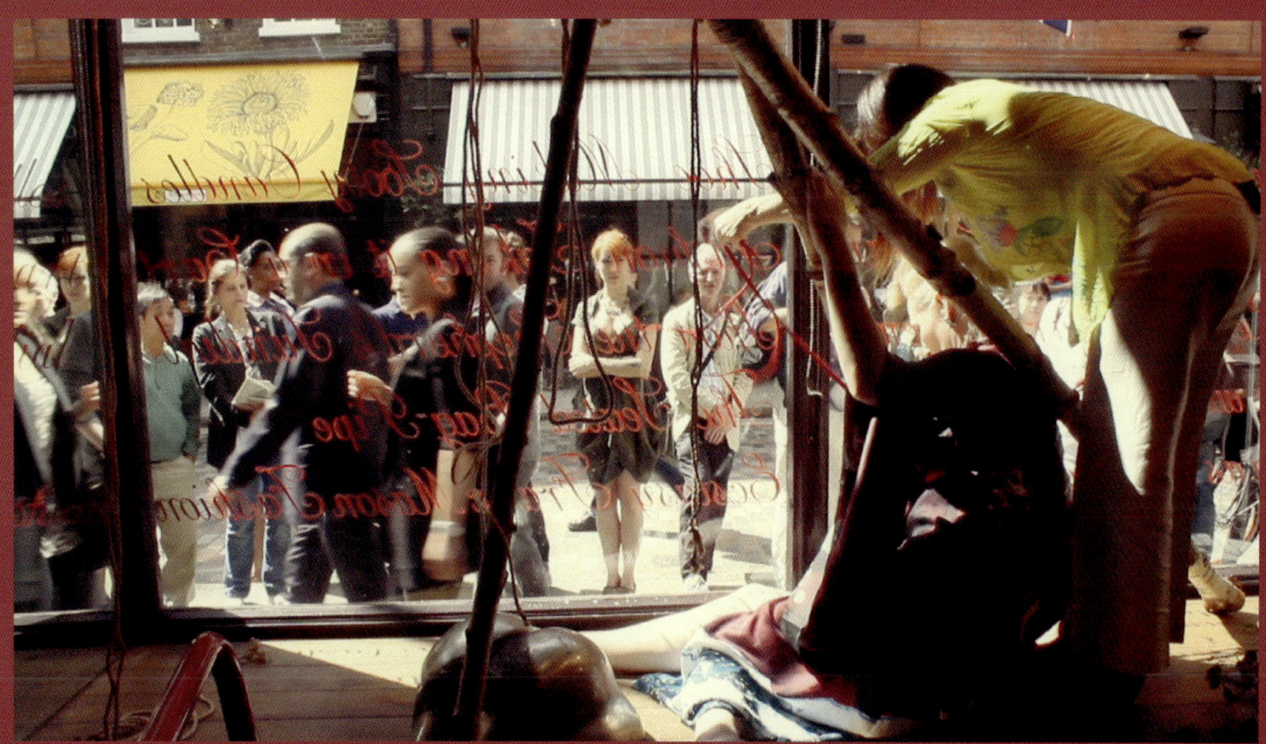

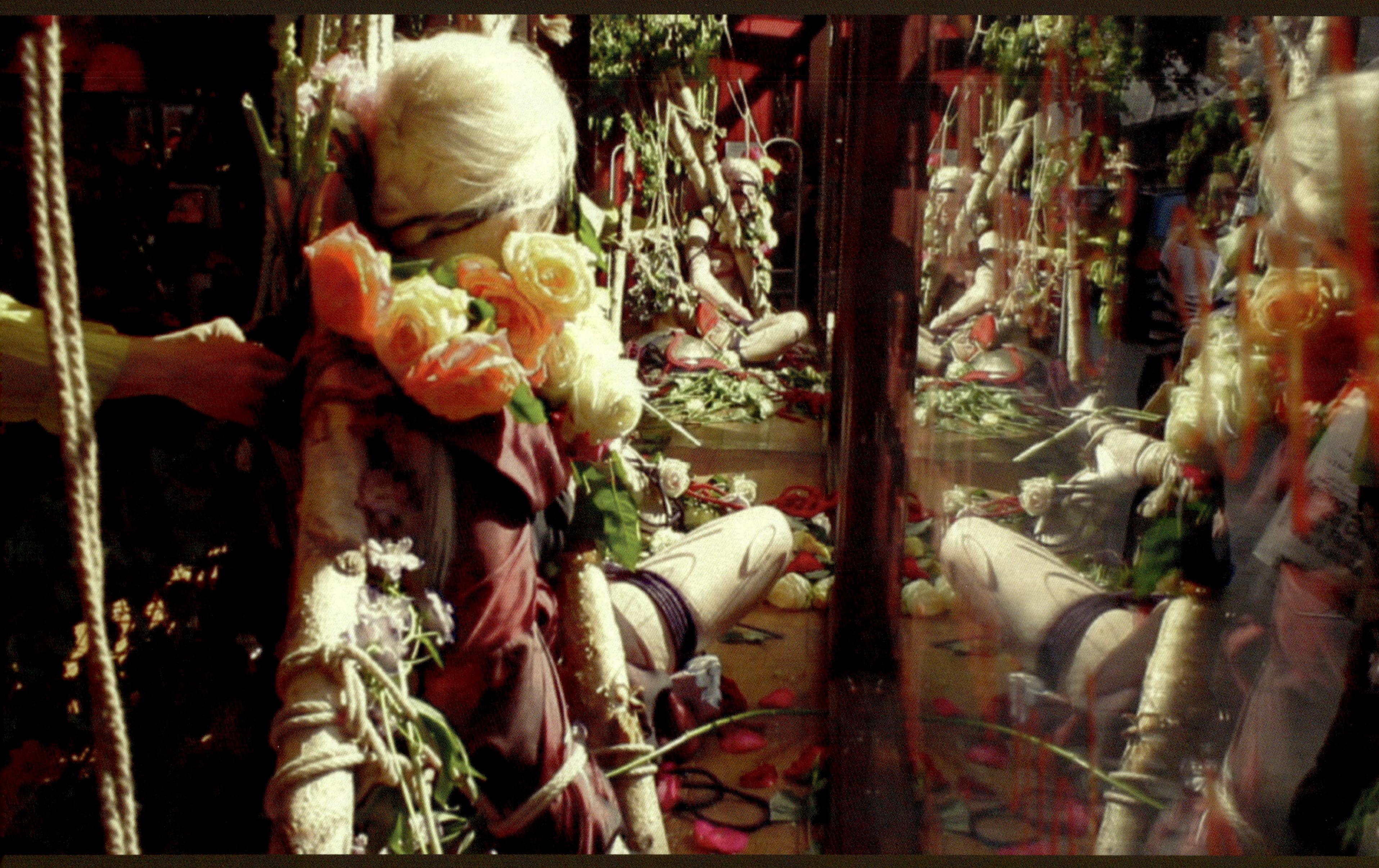

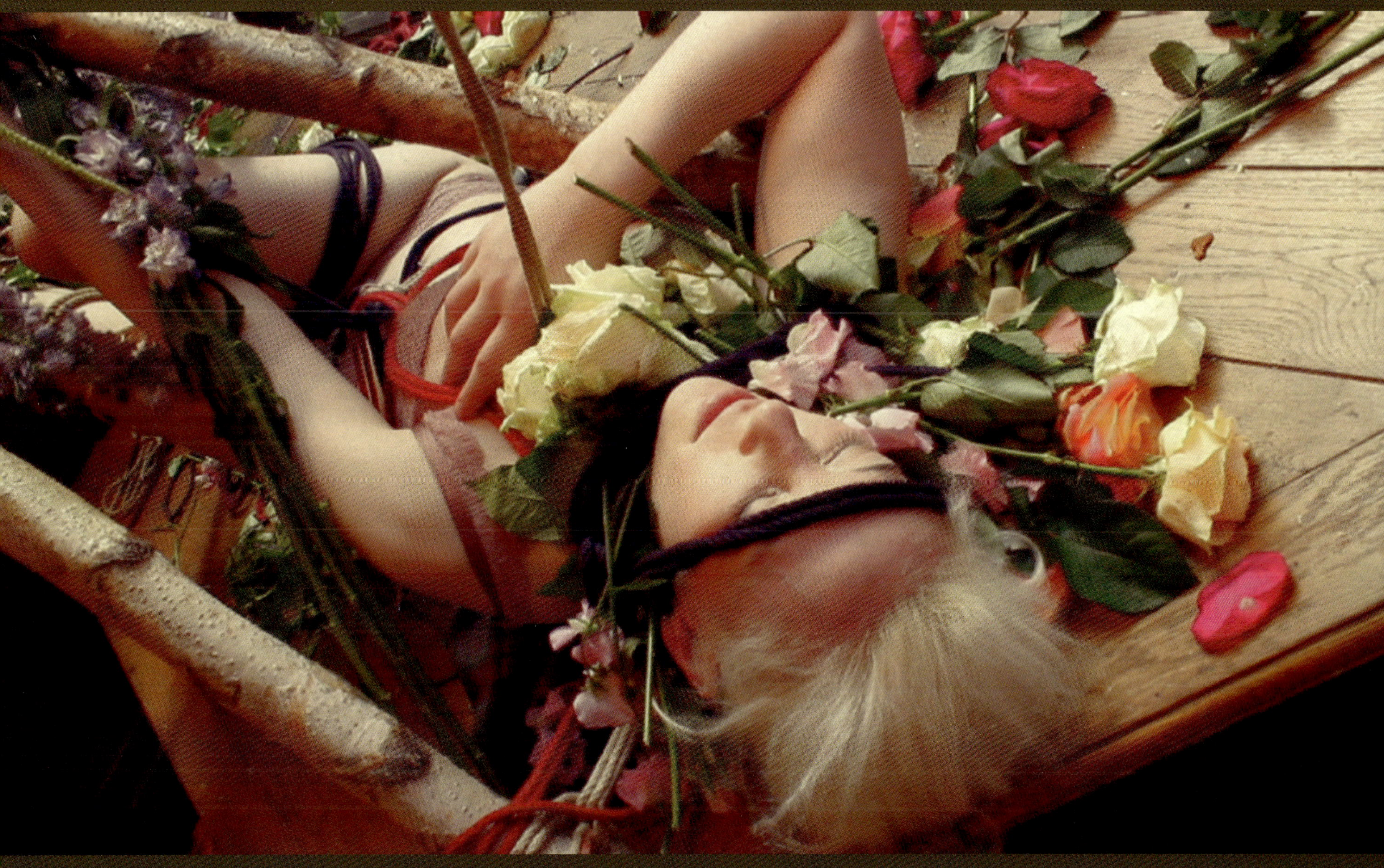

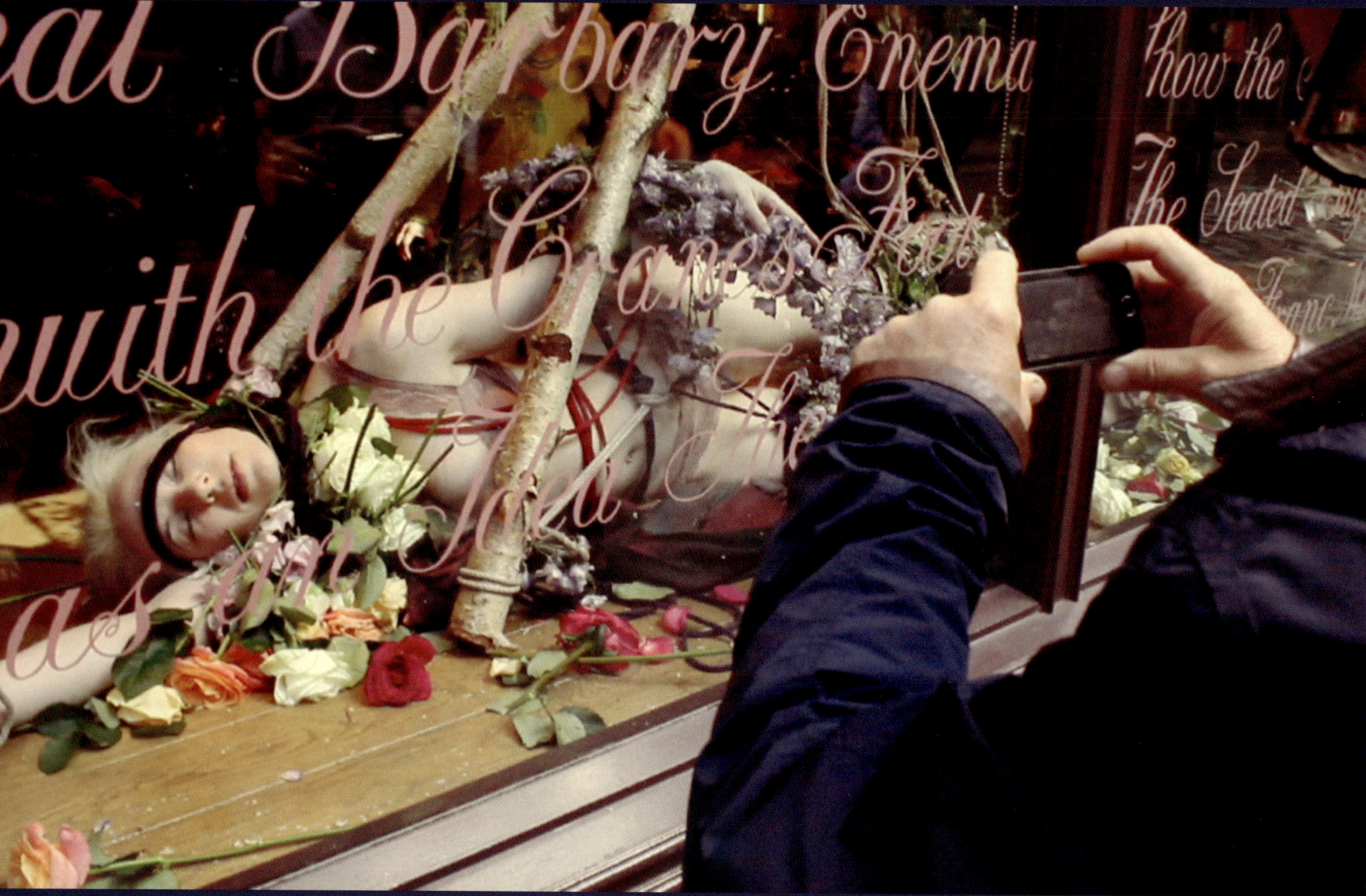


Midori:  Dolly had fun.  We always have fun.  But I think she's also a bit of a trickster as well with that beautiful alabaster skin, she can look like a mannequin.  So I think she likes to play little tricks on people walking by because she'll look at them and - wink - cheeky.

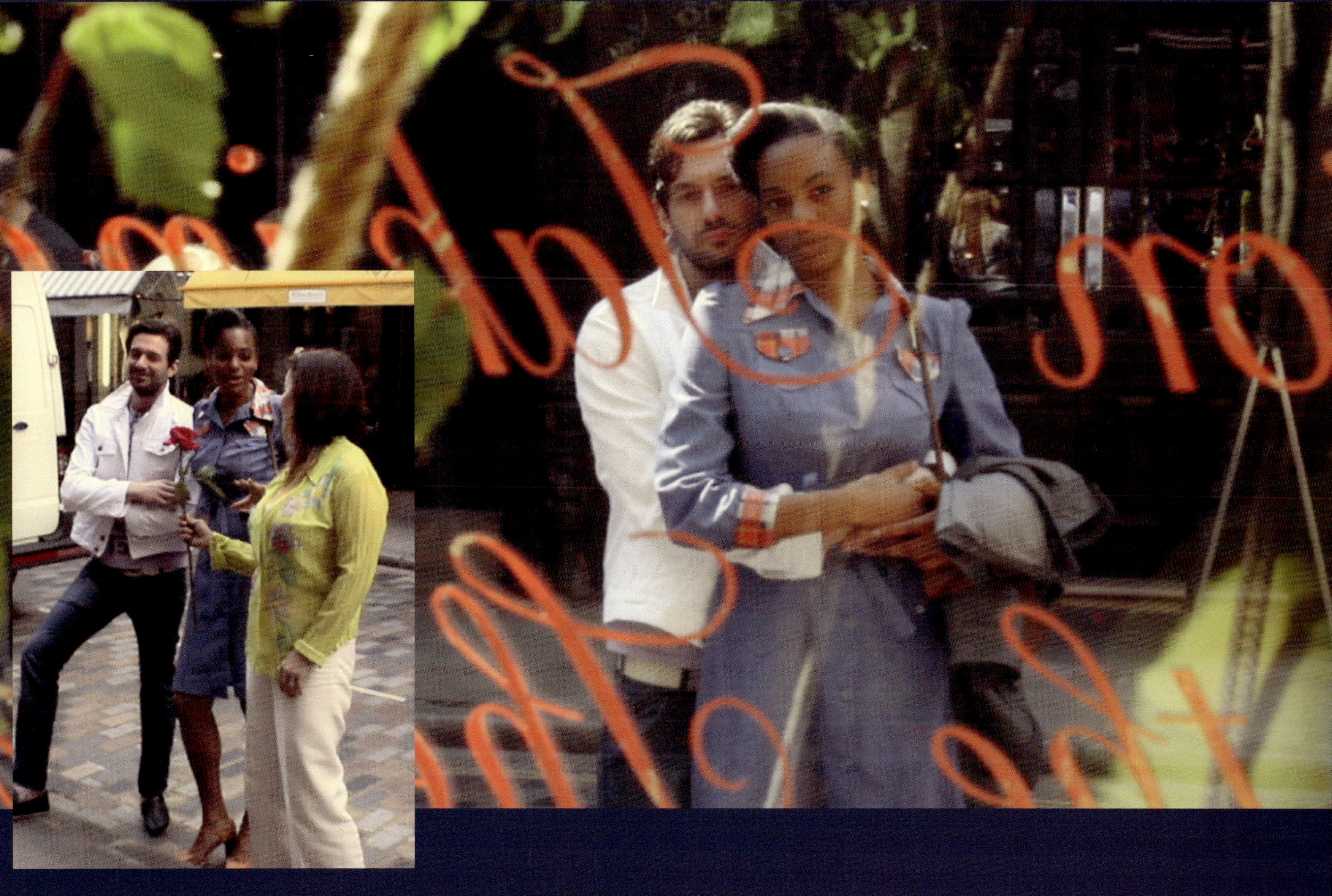

And what I like doing at the end of the performance, I'll find somebody to give one of the red roses to; a little connection with the others.

# Dances with Rope

## Simona Martini

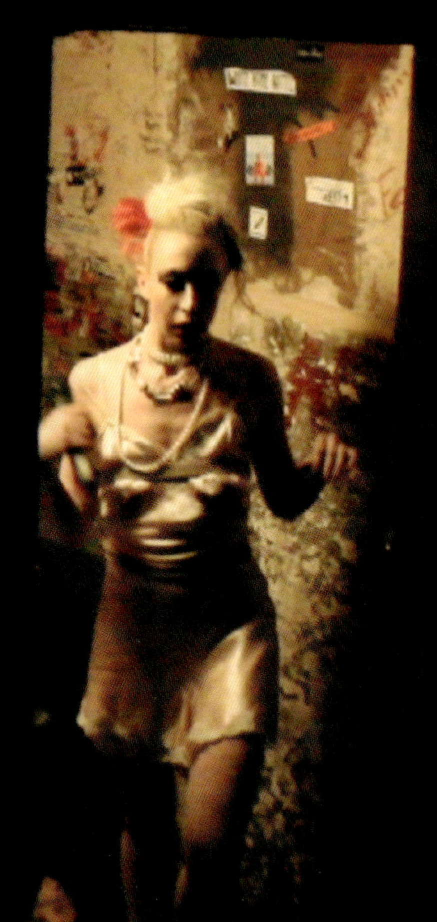

There are other kinds of rope performance art as Simona Martini demonstrates with her band Maleficent.  She also adds another component - dance.  Being trained at the Royal Ballet School, she brings a lifetime of performance skills to the rope scene.

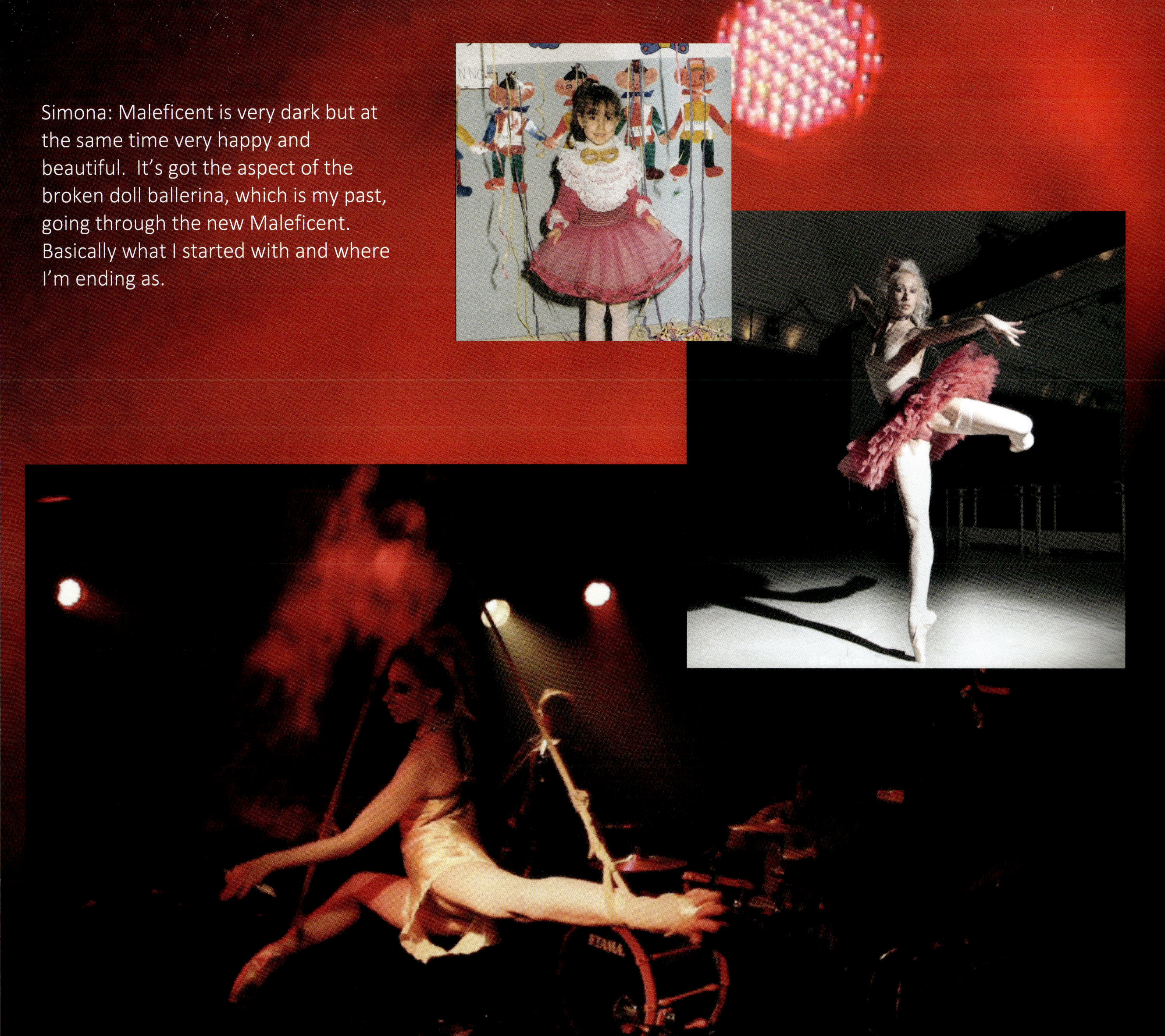

Simona: Maleficent is very dark but at the same time very happy and beautiful.  It's got the aspect of the broken doll ballerina, which is my past, going through the new Maleficent. Basically what I started with and where I'm ending as.

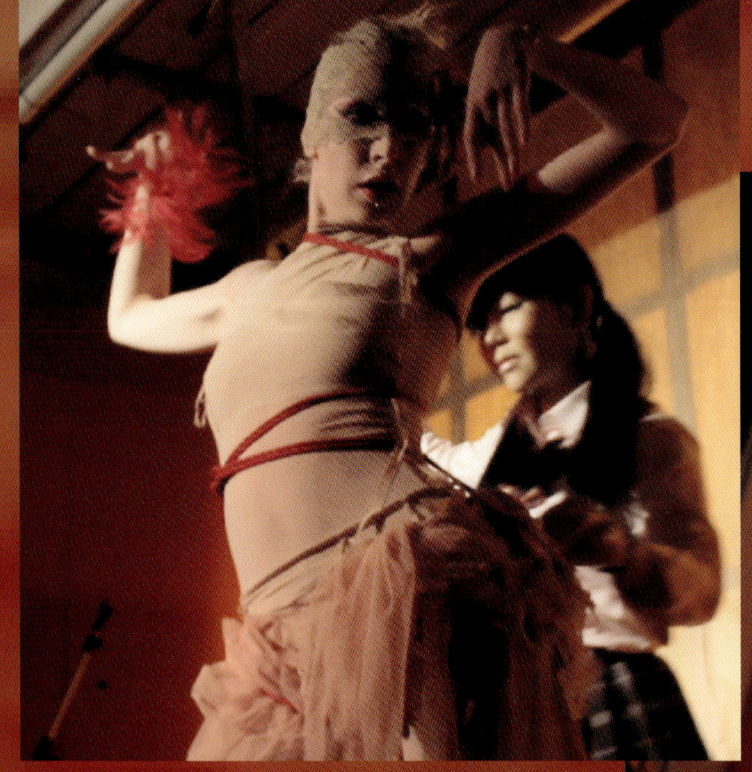

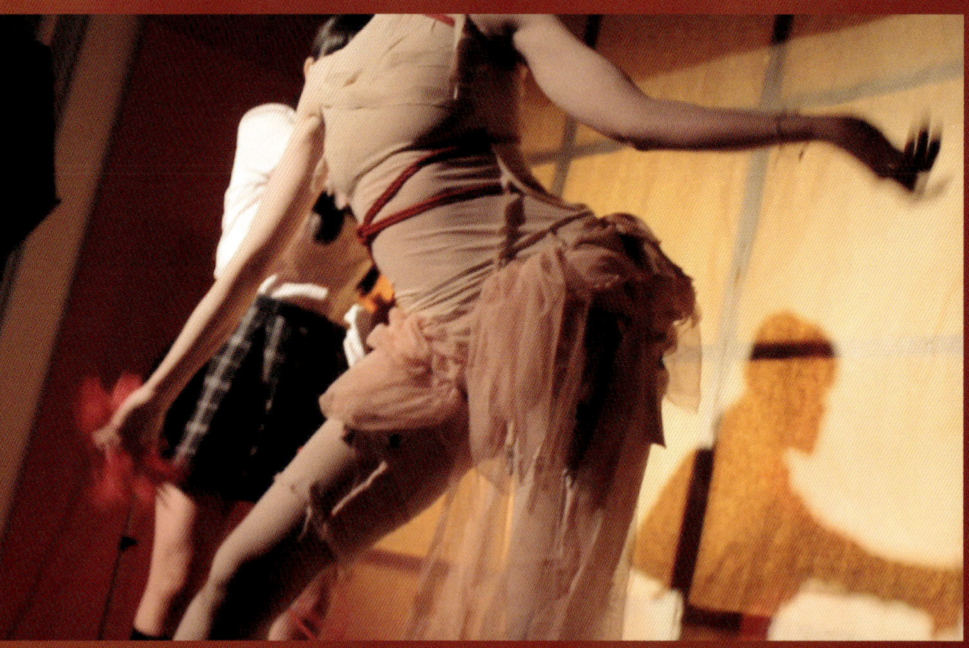

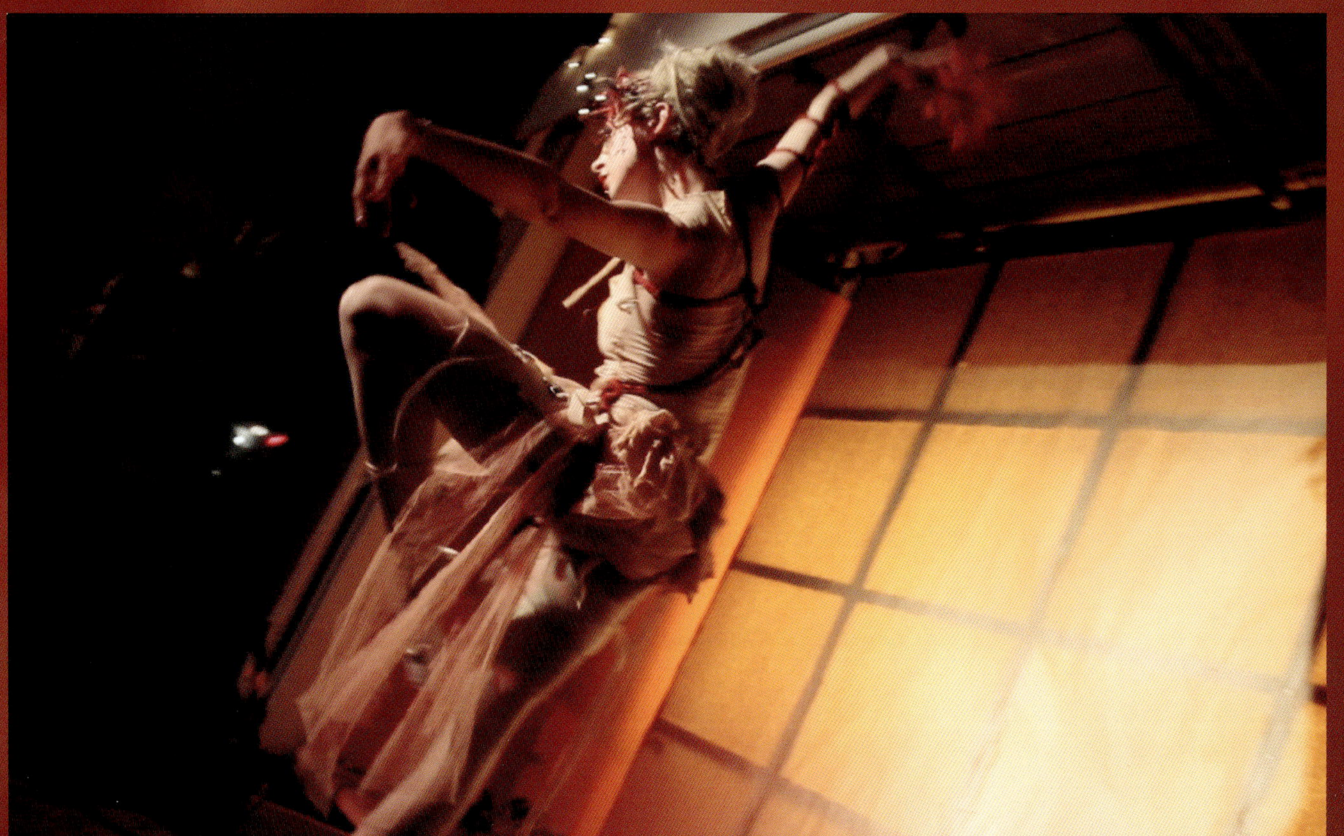

Simona: I've been doing suspension for a while now and what we've been creating is like this beauty of the ballet, but at the same time, with the bondage rope suspension.

It doesn't look like a normal Japanese bondage suspension, but it's more kind of artistic.

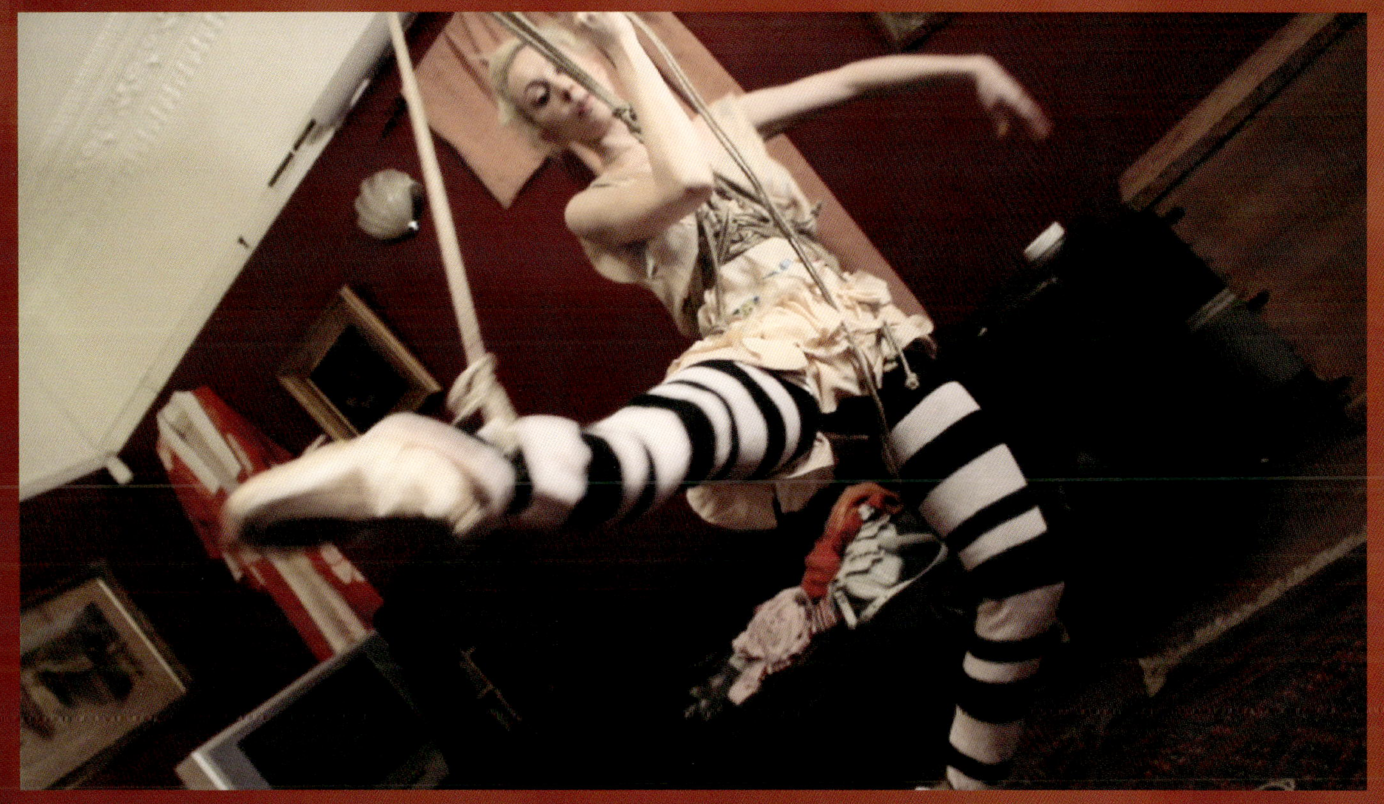

I would love to create a ballet, contemporary choreography, together with help from  Esinem and choreographer Siân Williams.  I can personally relate it with the ballet because it's got this beautiful aspect to it but at the same time it shows the pain you're going through during the time you're practicing.

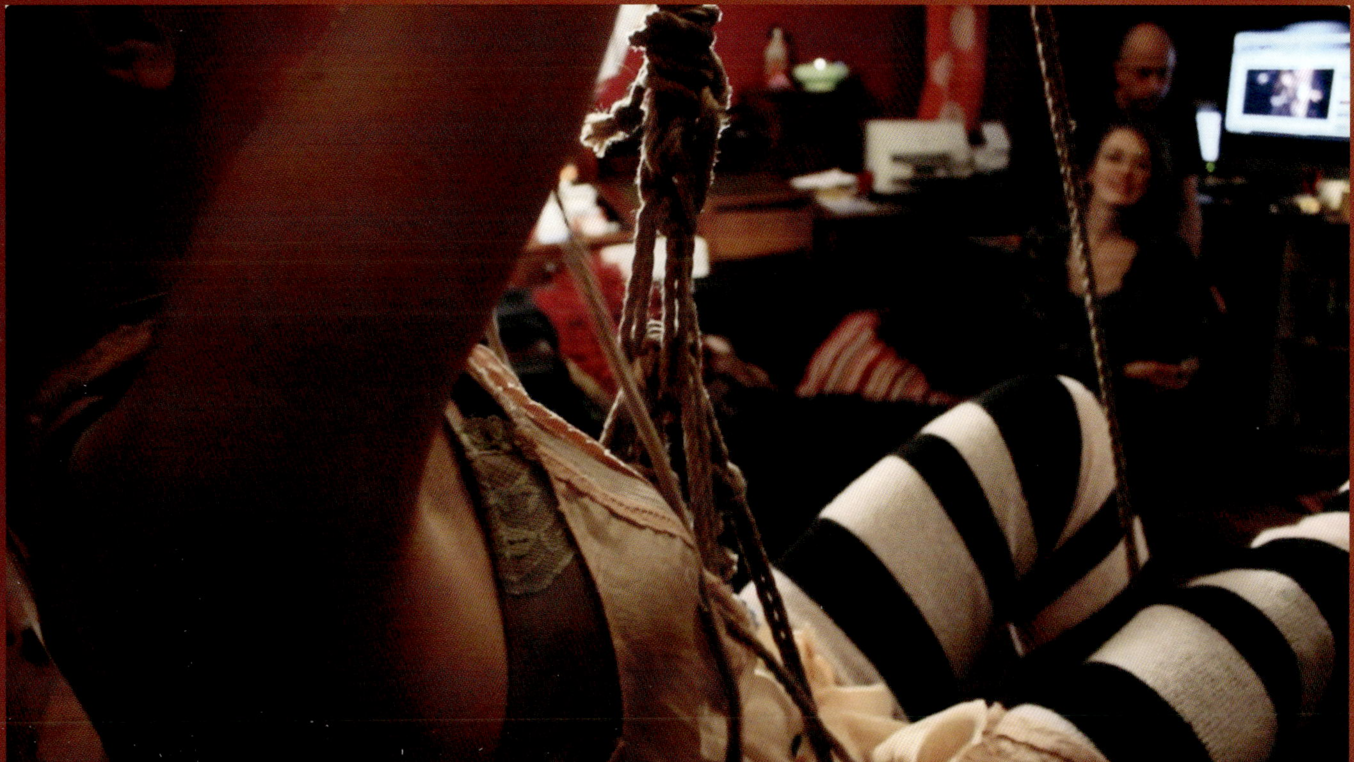

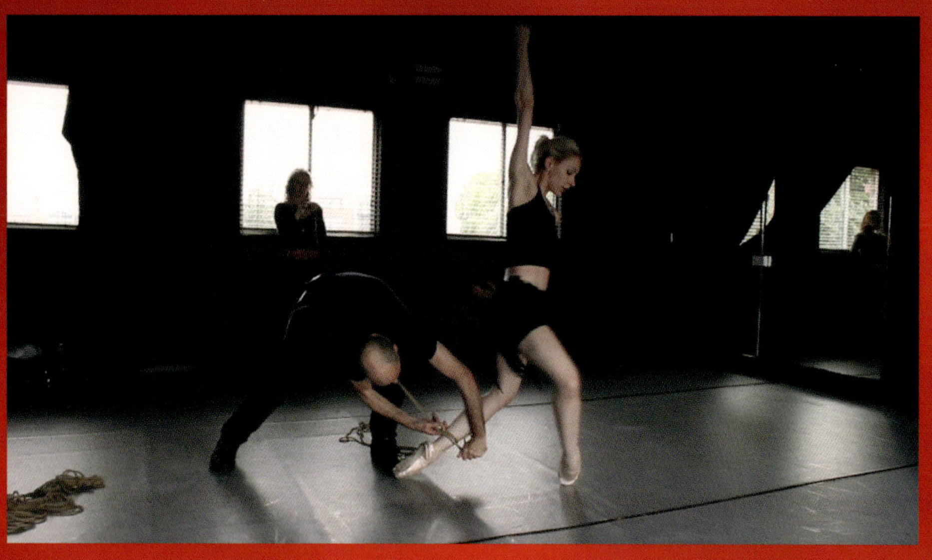
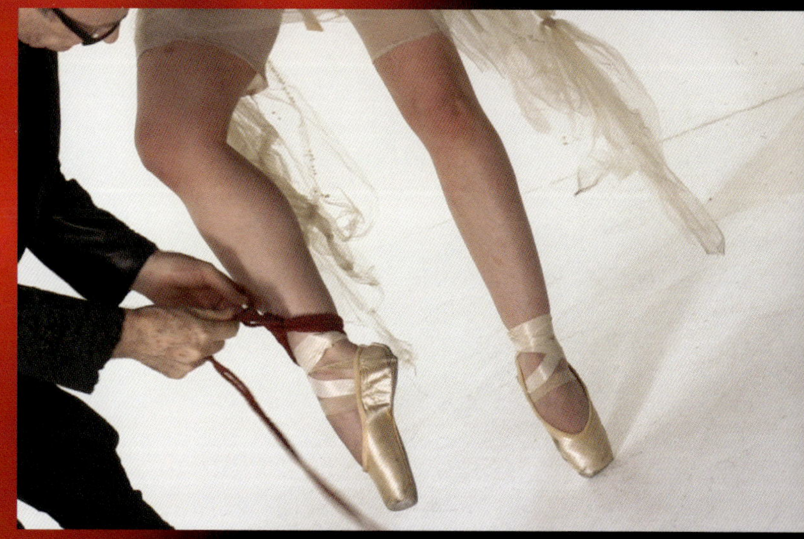
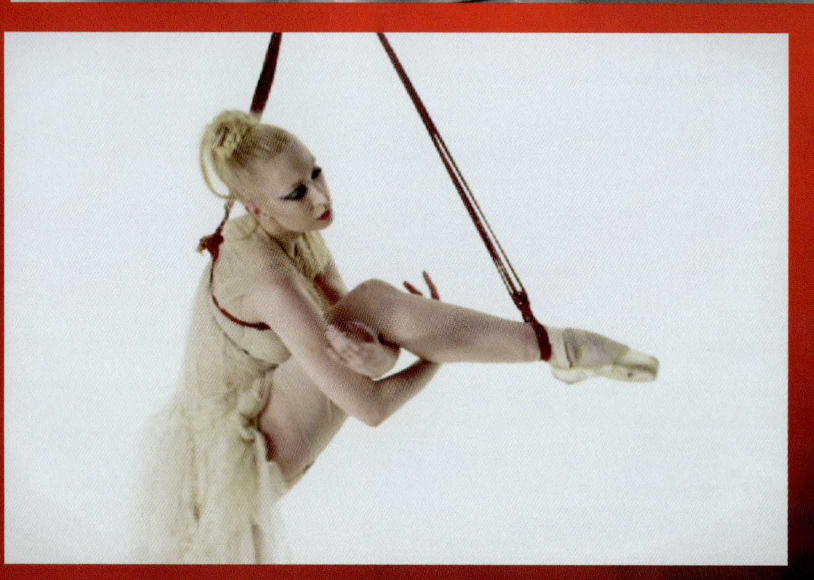
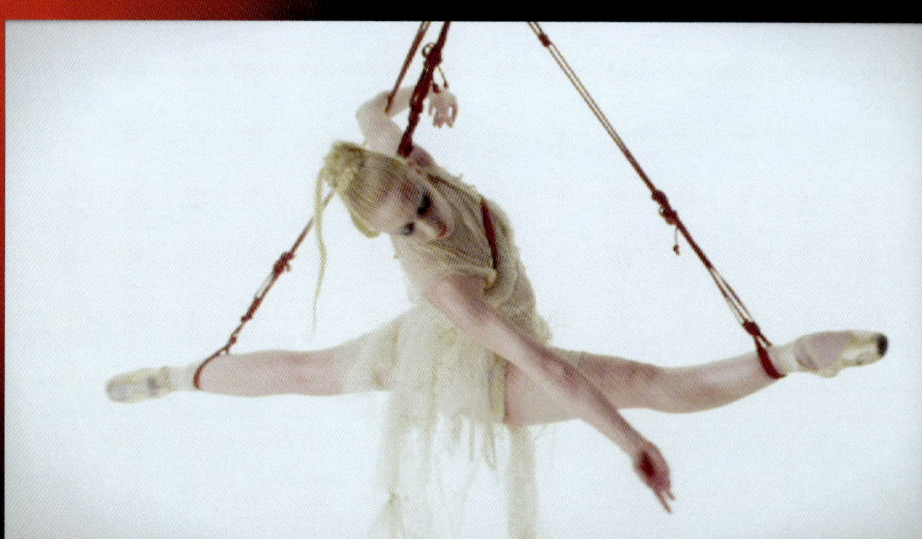
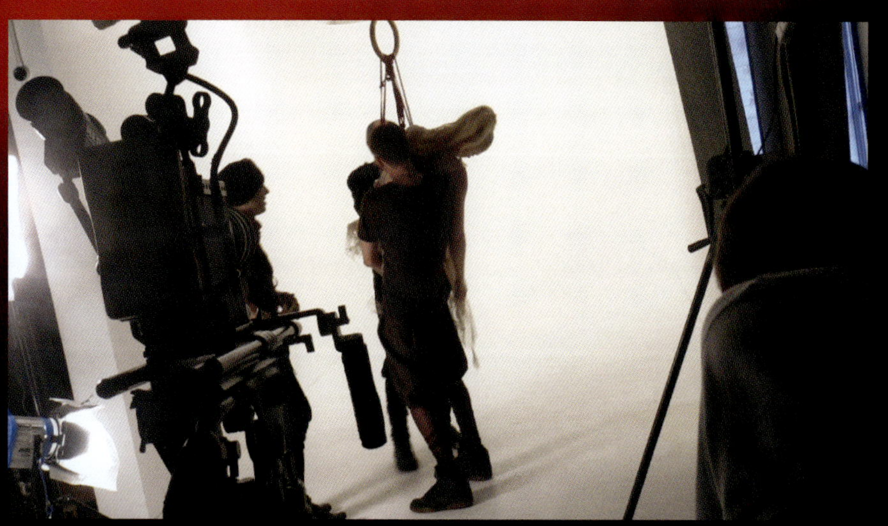
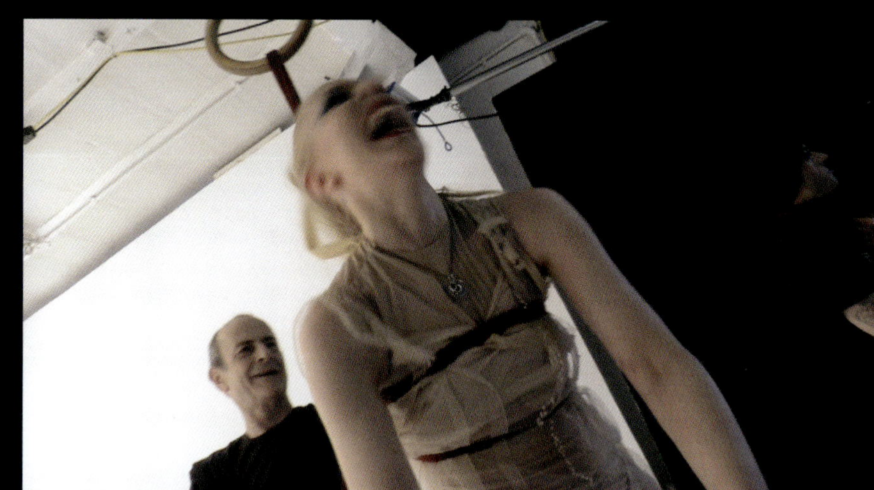

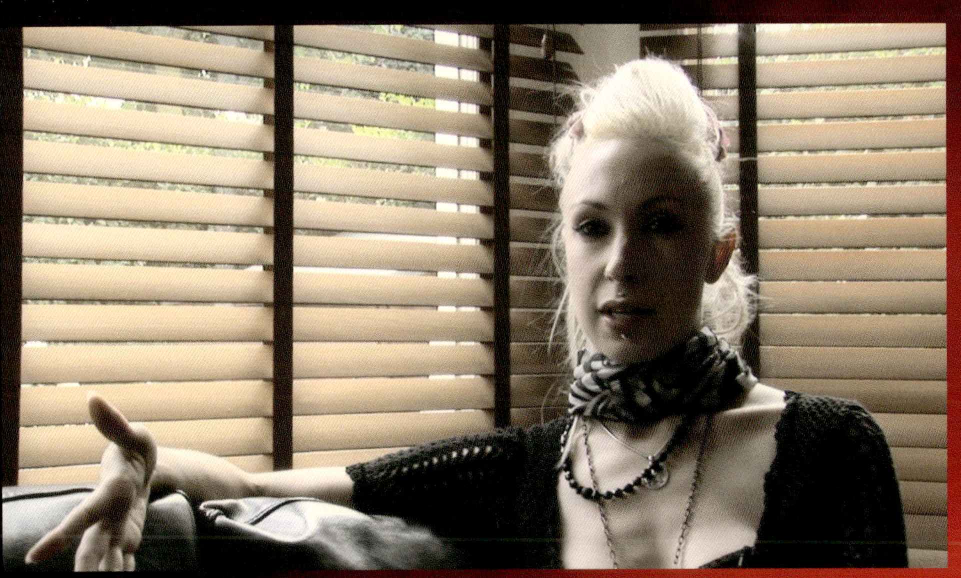

Simona:  These two aspects of beauty and pain create a balance, the black and white in my life.  You know, either really dark or really beautiful.  And that's kind of my personality as well.  It is what our band is about.

**Simona and her band Maleficent filmed a music video of one of her songs.**

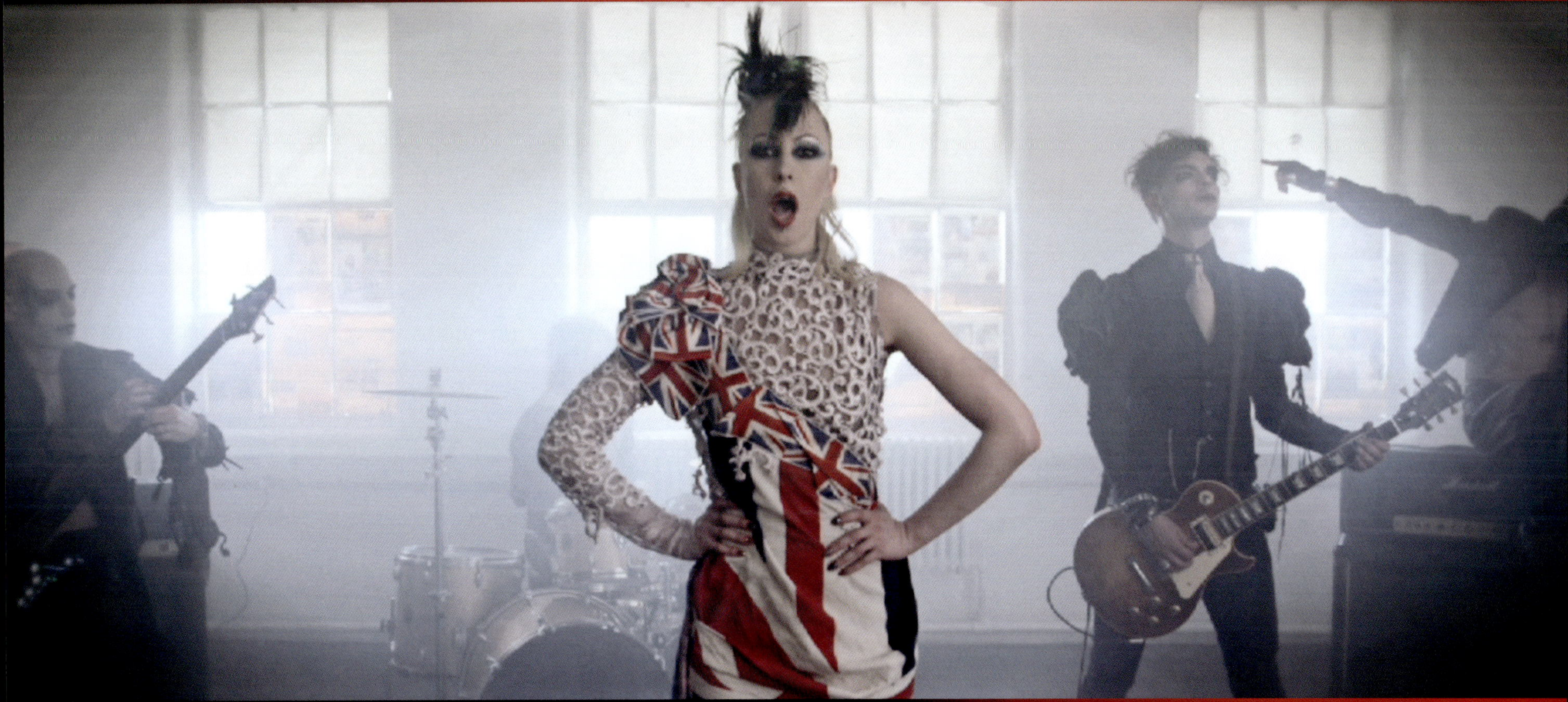

Simona:  All our songs are really emotional and they're telling a story.  And with the bondage and the ballet, what I would like to do is, like, create this kind of feeling of beauty, but at the same time you know pain and suffering which are kind of associated with bondage to the ballet.

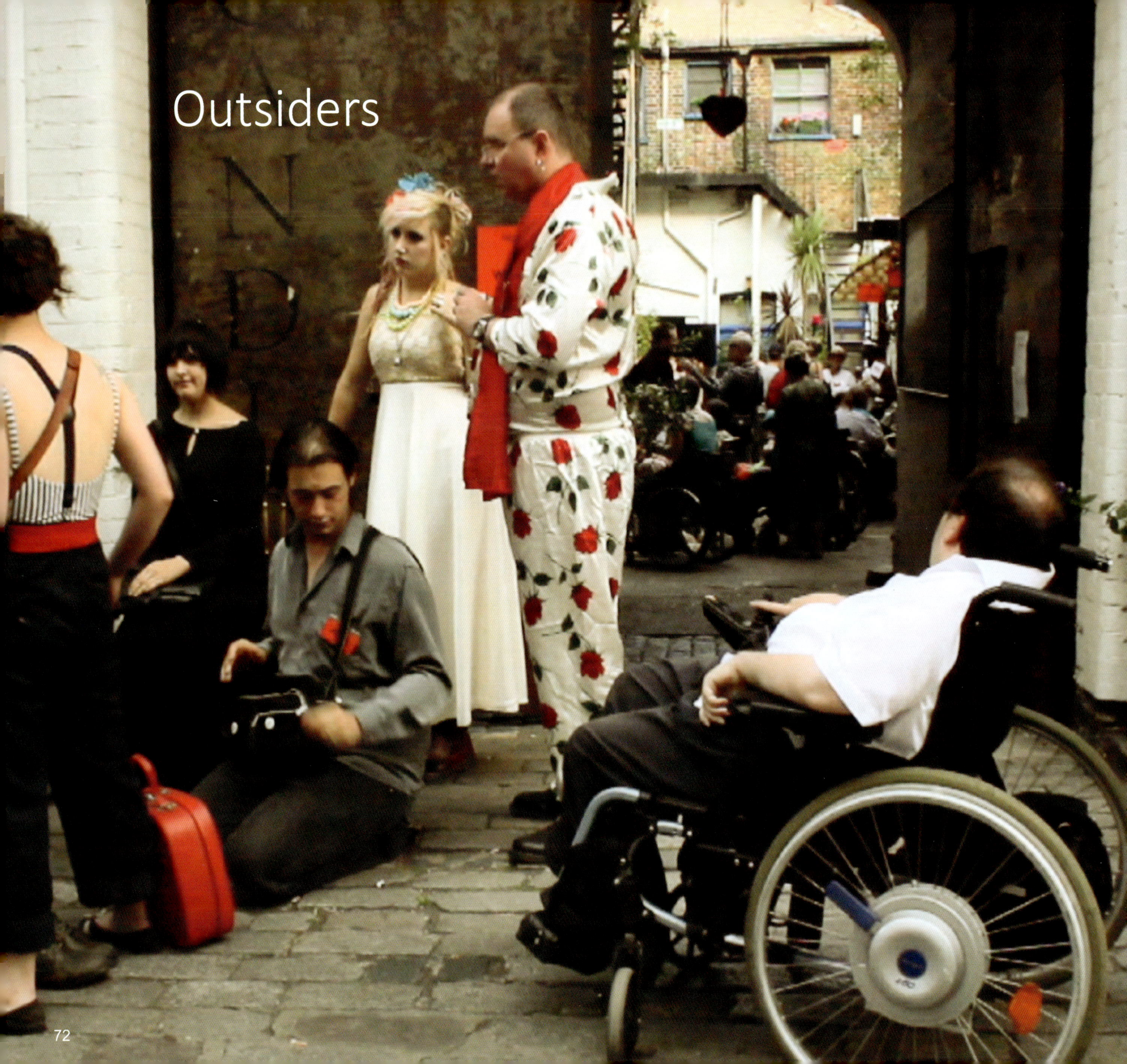
Outsiders

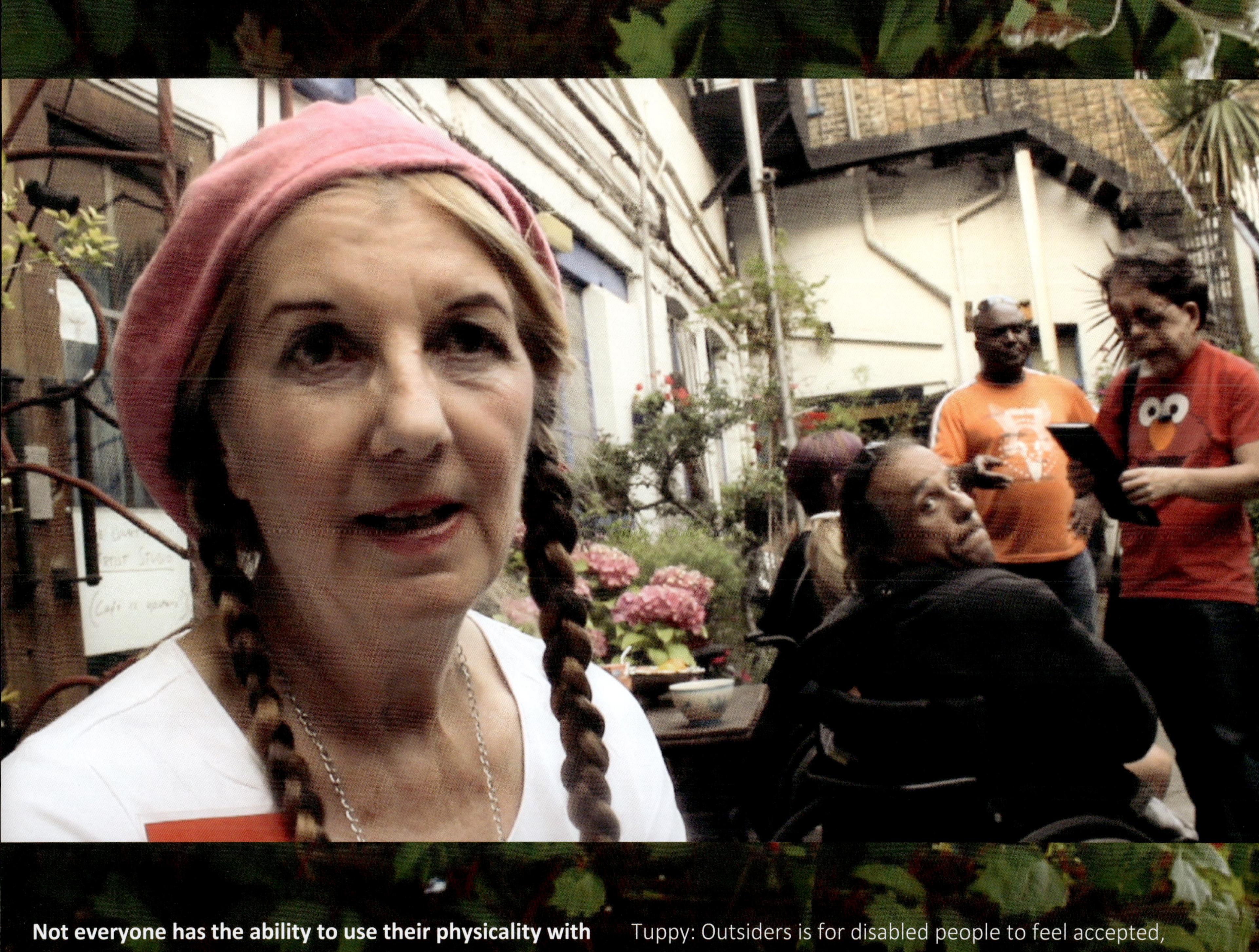

**Not everyone has the ability to use their physicality with abandon.  At an event in North London we see other ways to discover sexual freedom. The event called 'Outsiders' was organised by Tuppy Owens.**

Tuppy: Outsiders is for disabled people to feel accepted, feel that we acknowledge their sexuality, and give them confidence and encourage them to find whatever it is they want in life.  Usually it's a partner.

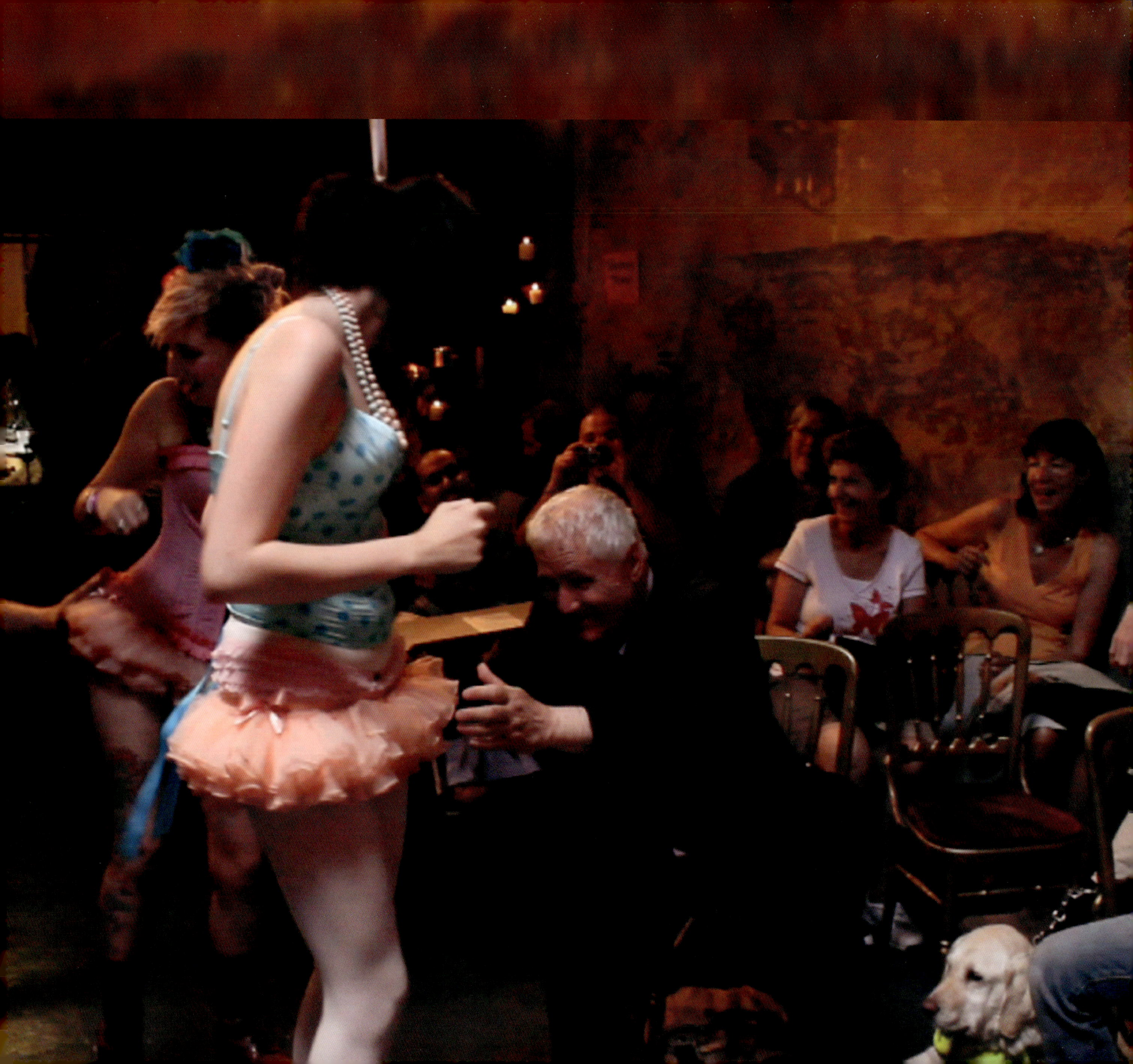

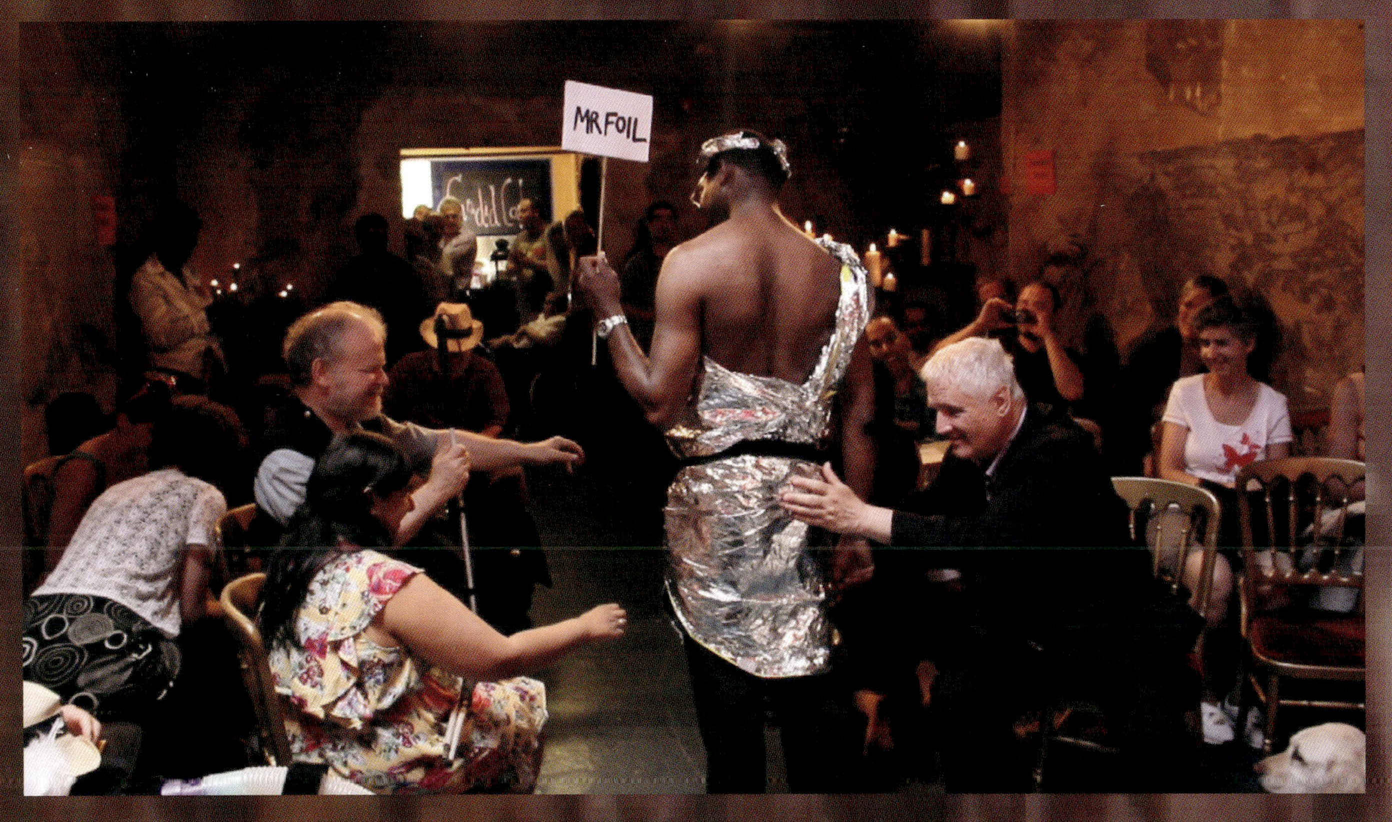


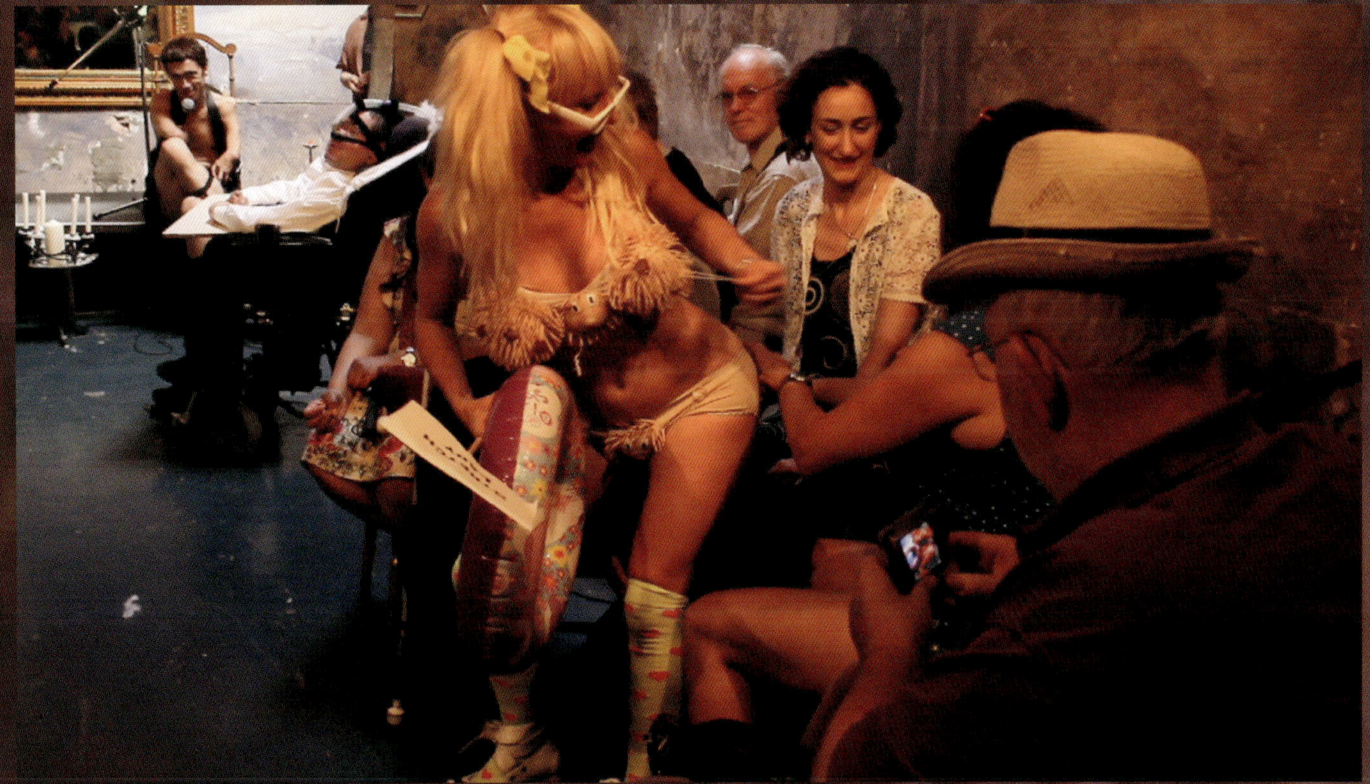

Tuppy:  This event was an experiment because we've been running Outsiders for a long time: 32 years.

We are treating disabled people like anybody else who may be gay, straight, fetishistic.  They may be into the same range of things as anybody else.  We call ourselves a little microcosm of acceptance.

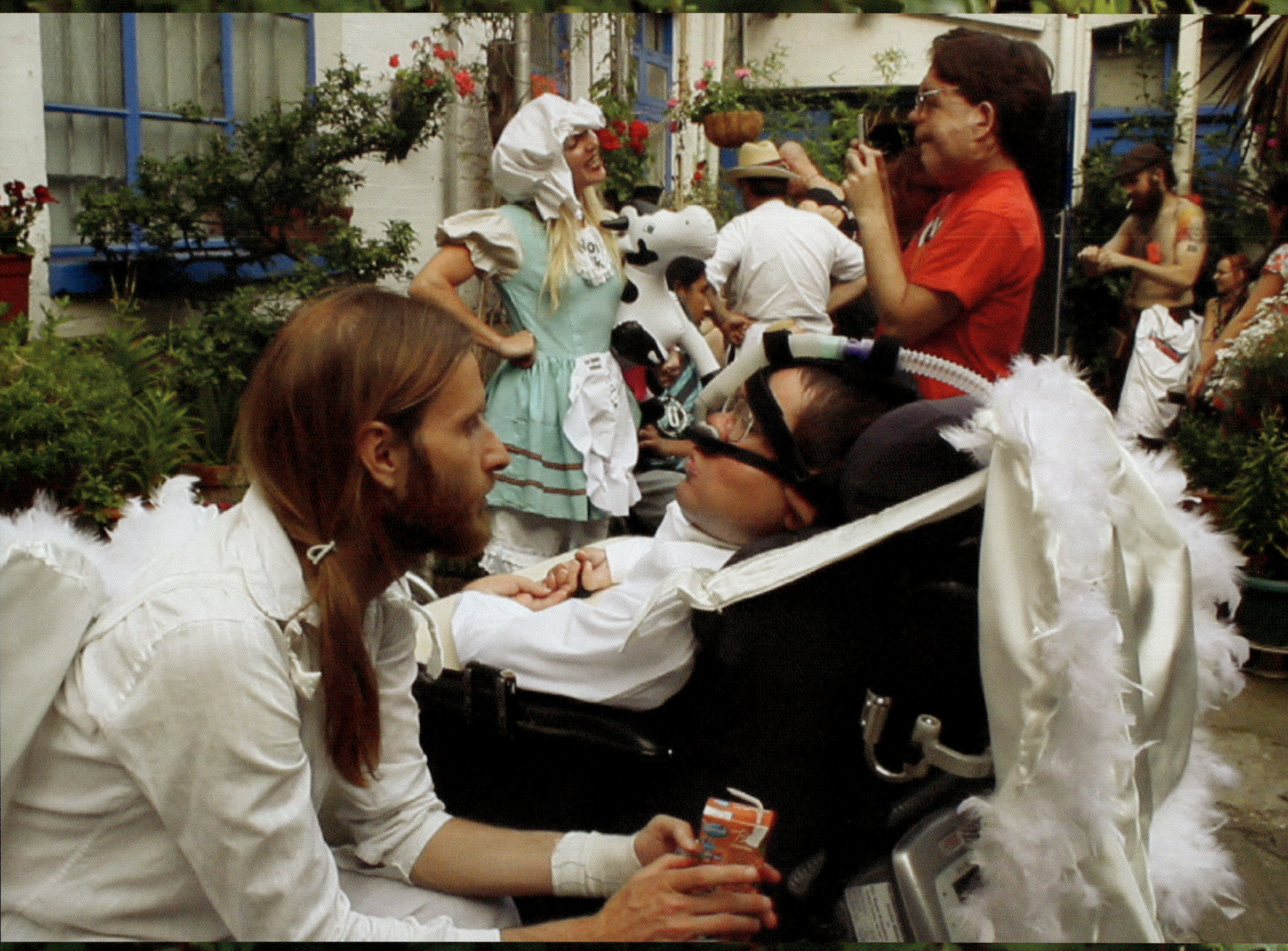

Tuppy:  I wanted to put on an event where the Outsiders had an opportunity of being tied up but I didn't want to do it with just any ordinary bondage person.  I wanted to do something that was very artistic and beautiful and fun and didn't look harsh, but looked like a magical thing happening.

I asked Jon ( Nawashi Murakawa ) because only he really manages to do that.  So I was very keen that it would be him that was doing the bondage and he's obviously made three people very happy today.

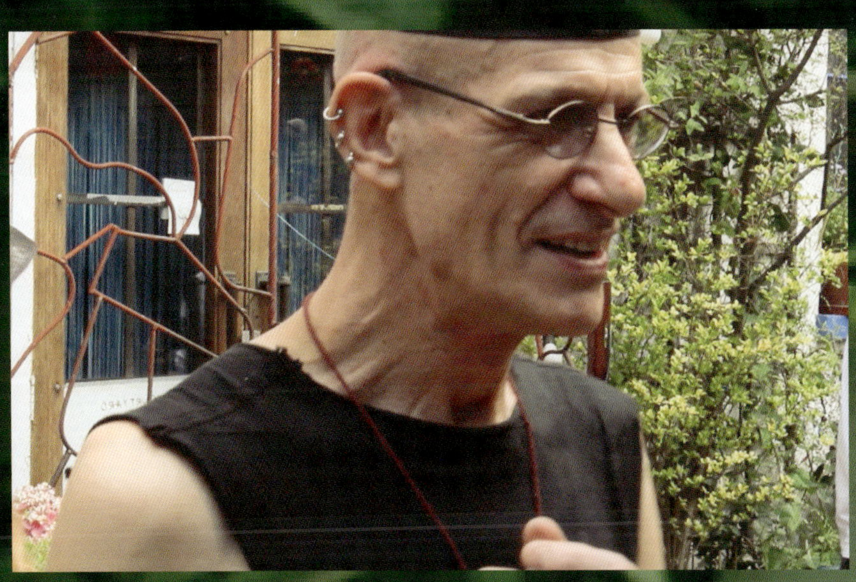
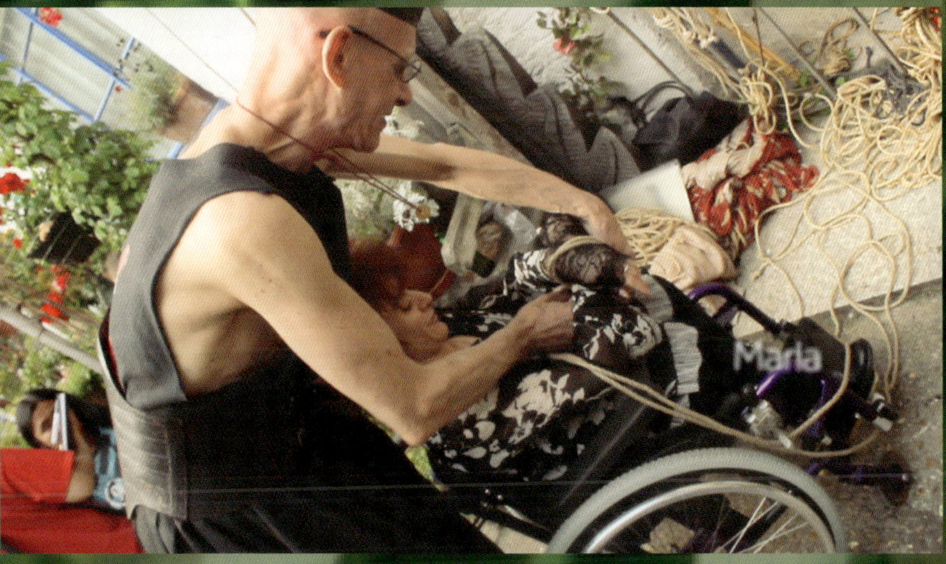

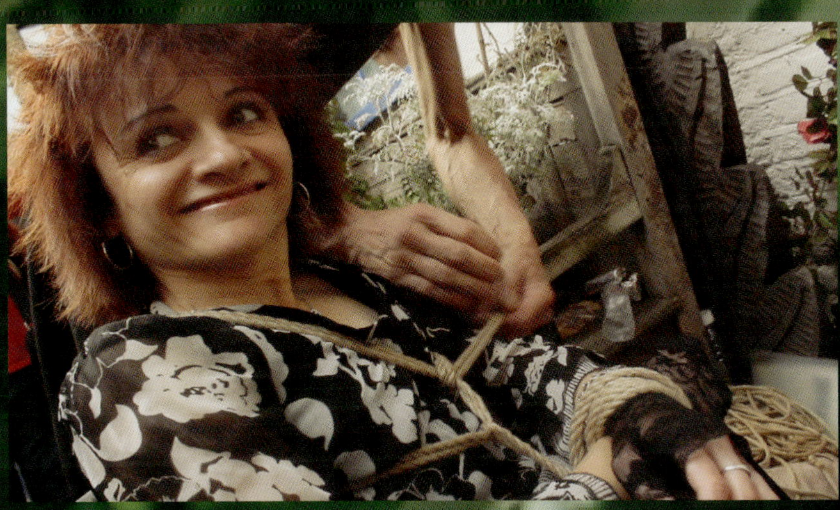
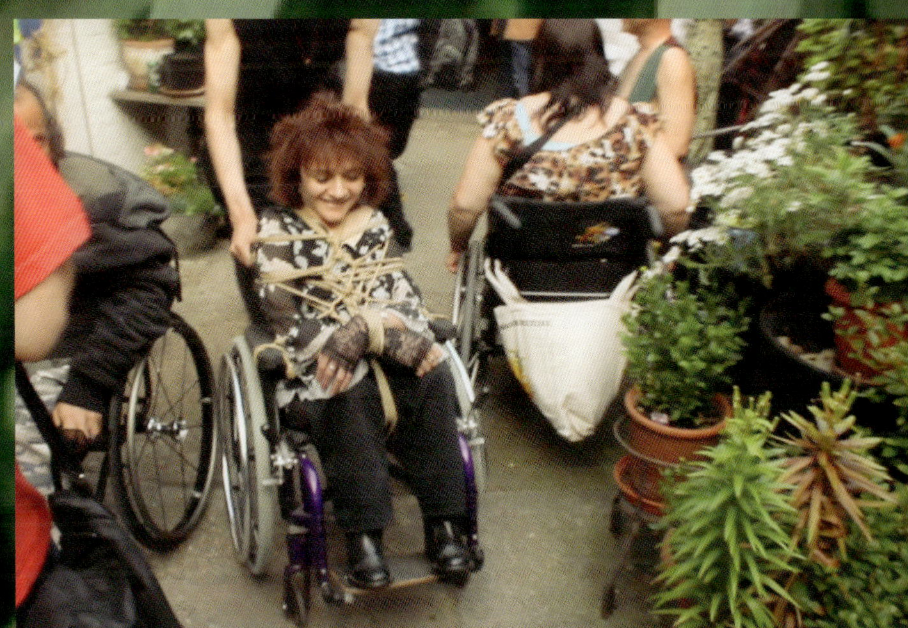

Maria :  I was put on this earth for people to have challenges!  That was quite an amazing experience.  And it felt so good when they came off as well.

Bob Bentley:  Have the ropes left any marks?  Did it hurt?

Maria:  Marks a little bit, that's fine.  And no, no, it didn't hurt.  It felt good being secure and then equally good being released.

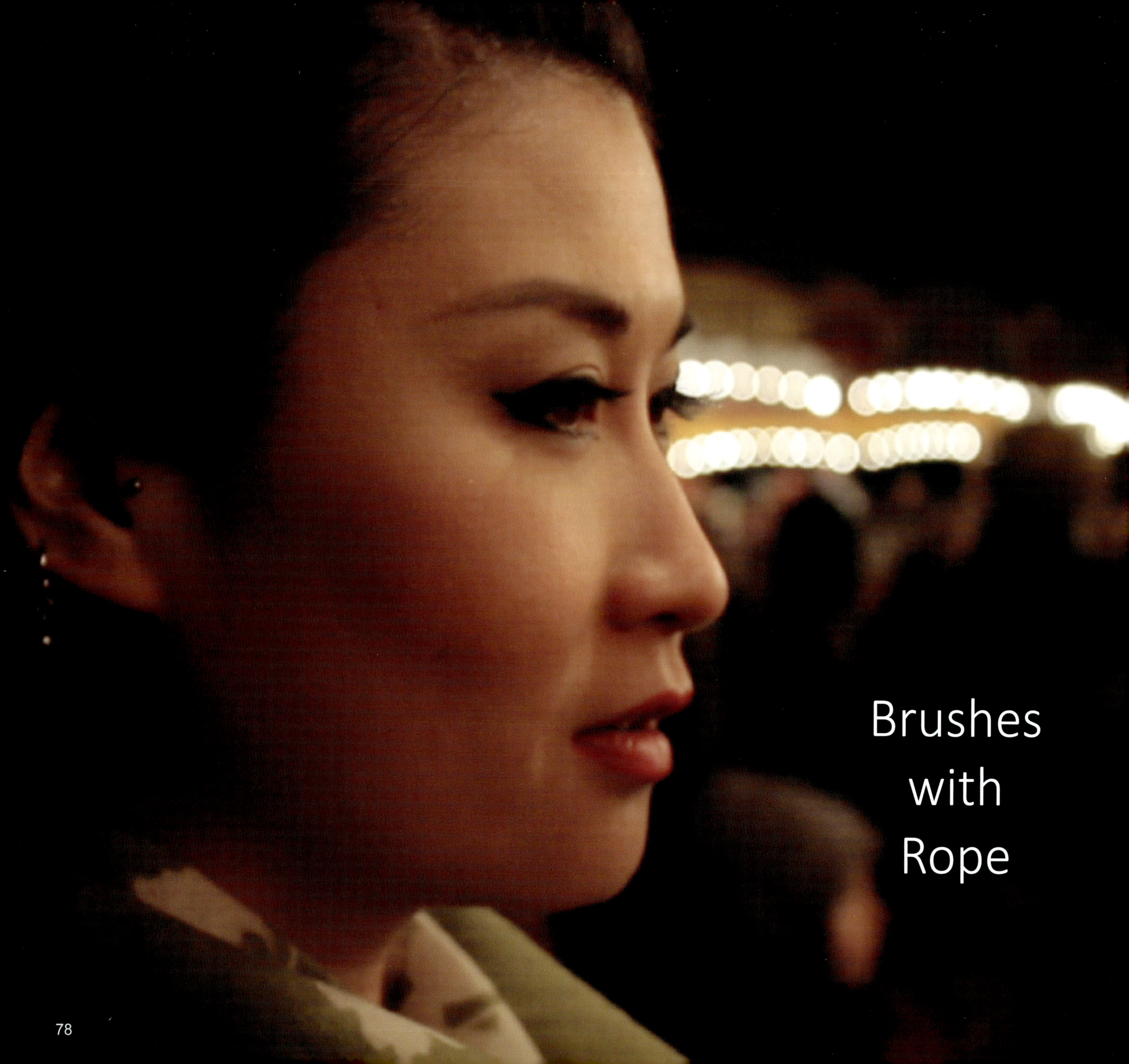
Brushes
with
Rope

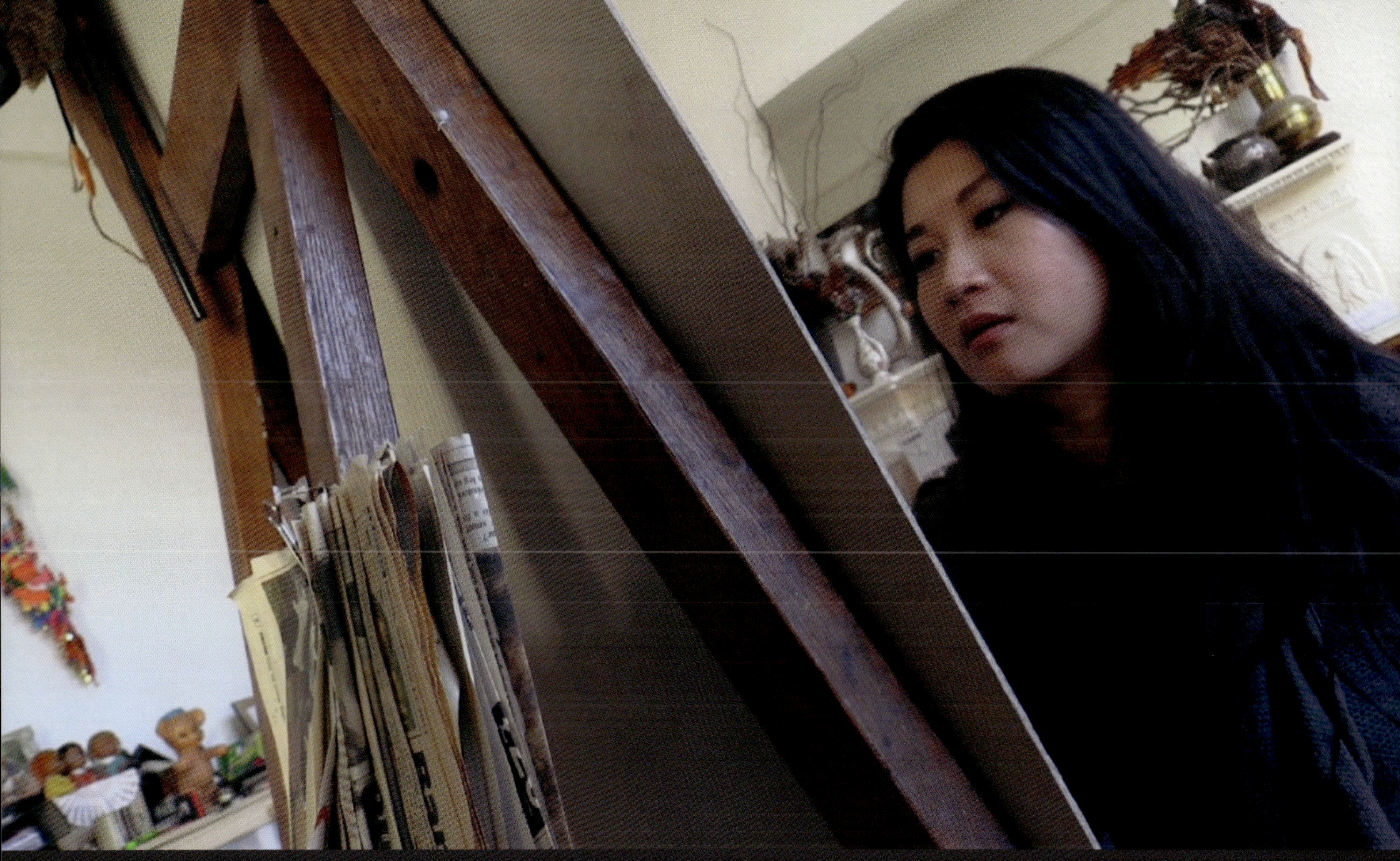

**Chinese artist Xue Wang  went to the Outsiders event specifically to meet Jon and to find out about rope bondage for one of her art projects.**

Xue Wang:  I wanted to do a bondage theme but I didn't know where to start or how to get this until I met Jon.  I want to have a bit of extreme in my picture.  So kind of imagining me in the picture and having all these things happening, I might want to just experience a bit of pain to make this whole thing work.

My subject - a girl.  You can always see me painting a girl with big eyes and big head and a small body, it is my motif.  She always appears in this weird concept and surroundings.  I think, in a sense, it is myself, but she's always blonde with big blue eyes.

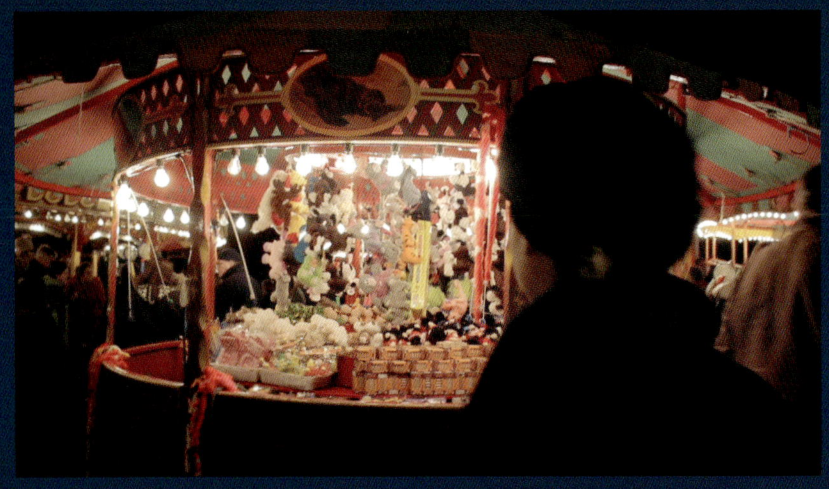

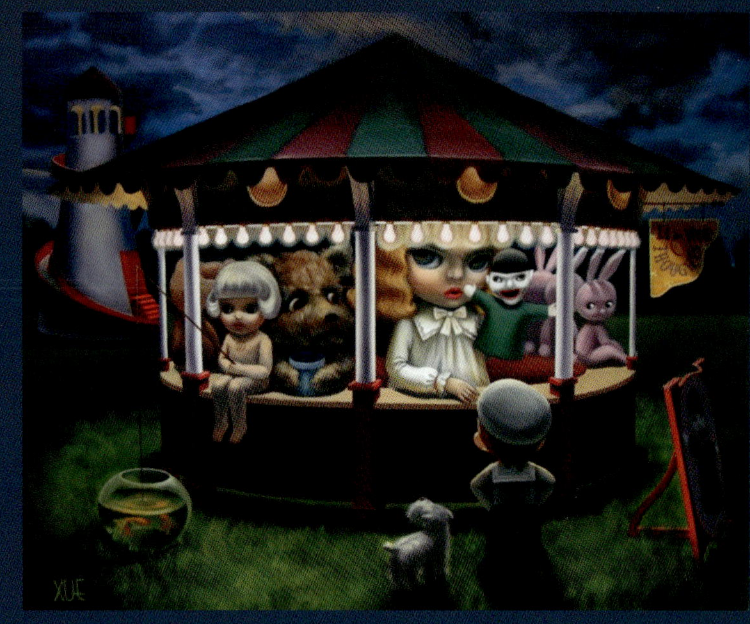

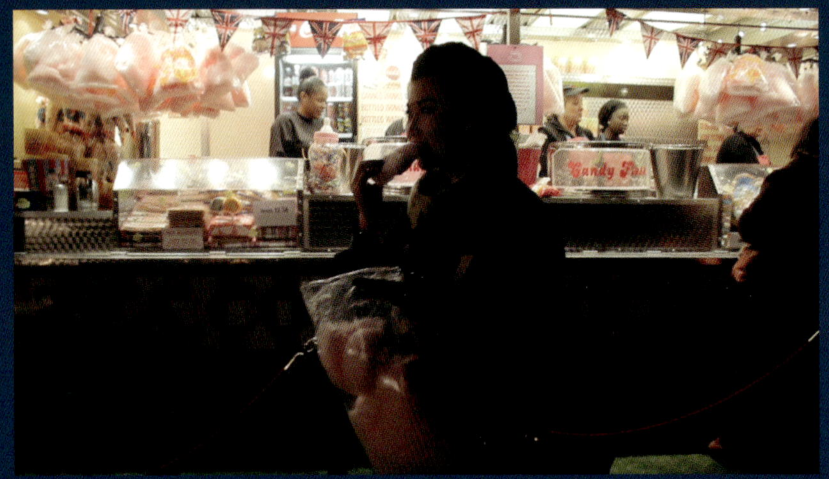

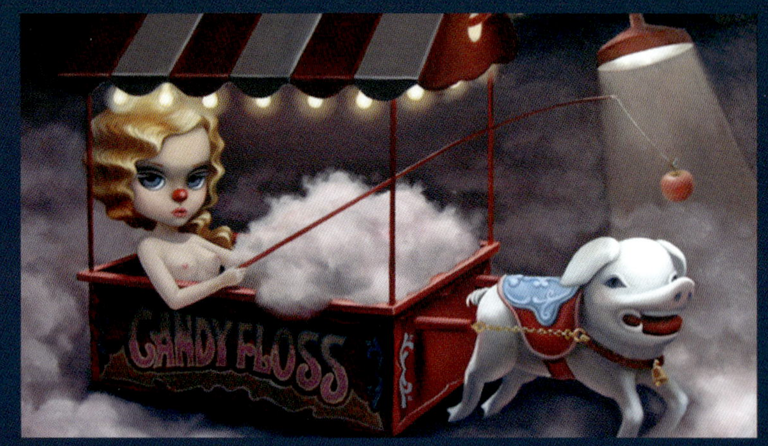

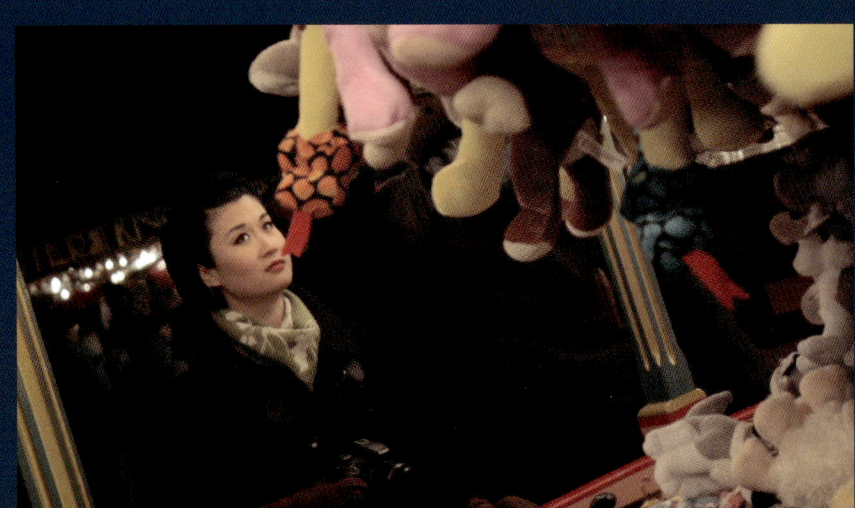

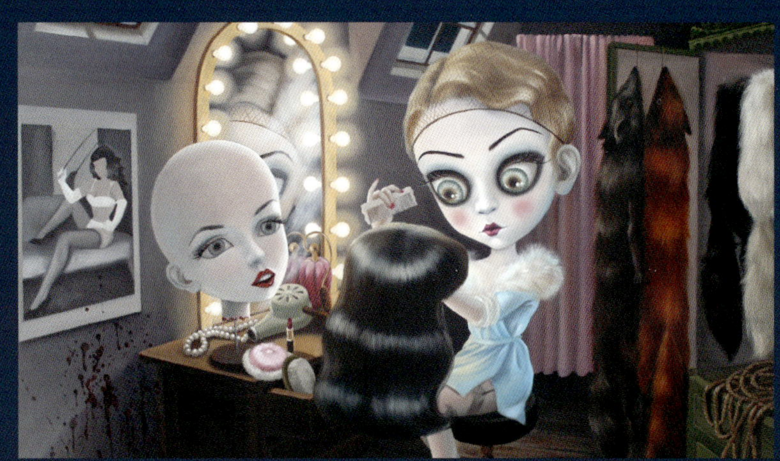

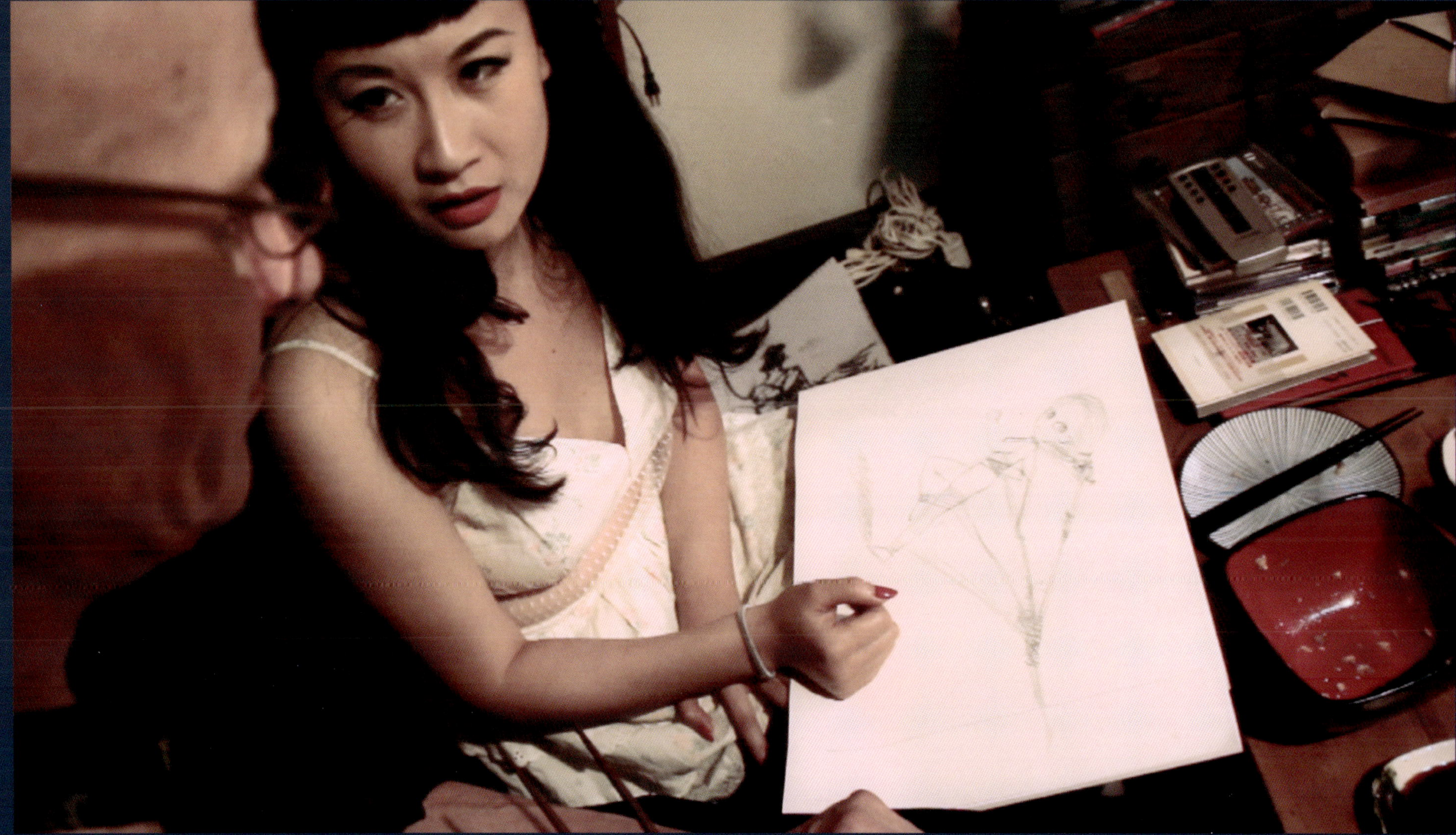

Xue:  I want to really feel it.  So that's another thing of why I want to do it with Jon.  I don't want to just look at the model appearing in front of you and have bondage on her.  I want to experience how the whole thing feels, so you get a deeper understanding I guess.

Jon: When I do Kinbaku I like to tie people to something, maybe not all to the same point.

Xue:  You've just given me another idea. I want to do it on a tree.  And when I do the painting afterwards, I'll have different characters around her doing weird stuff.

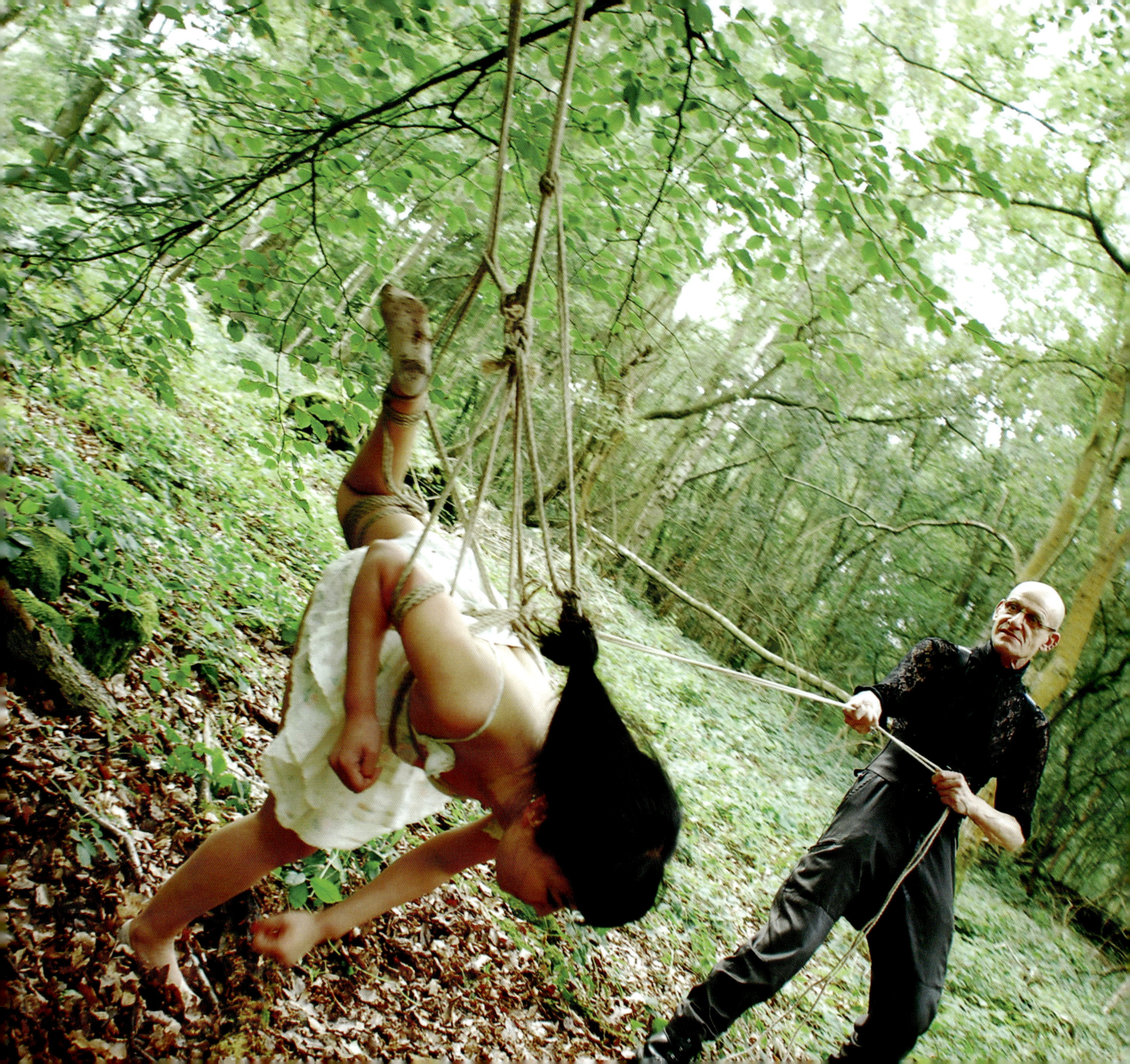

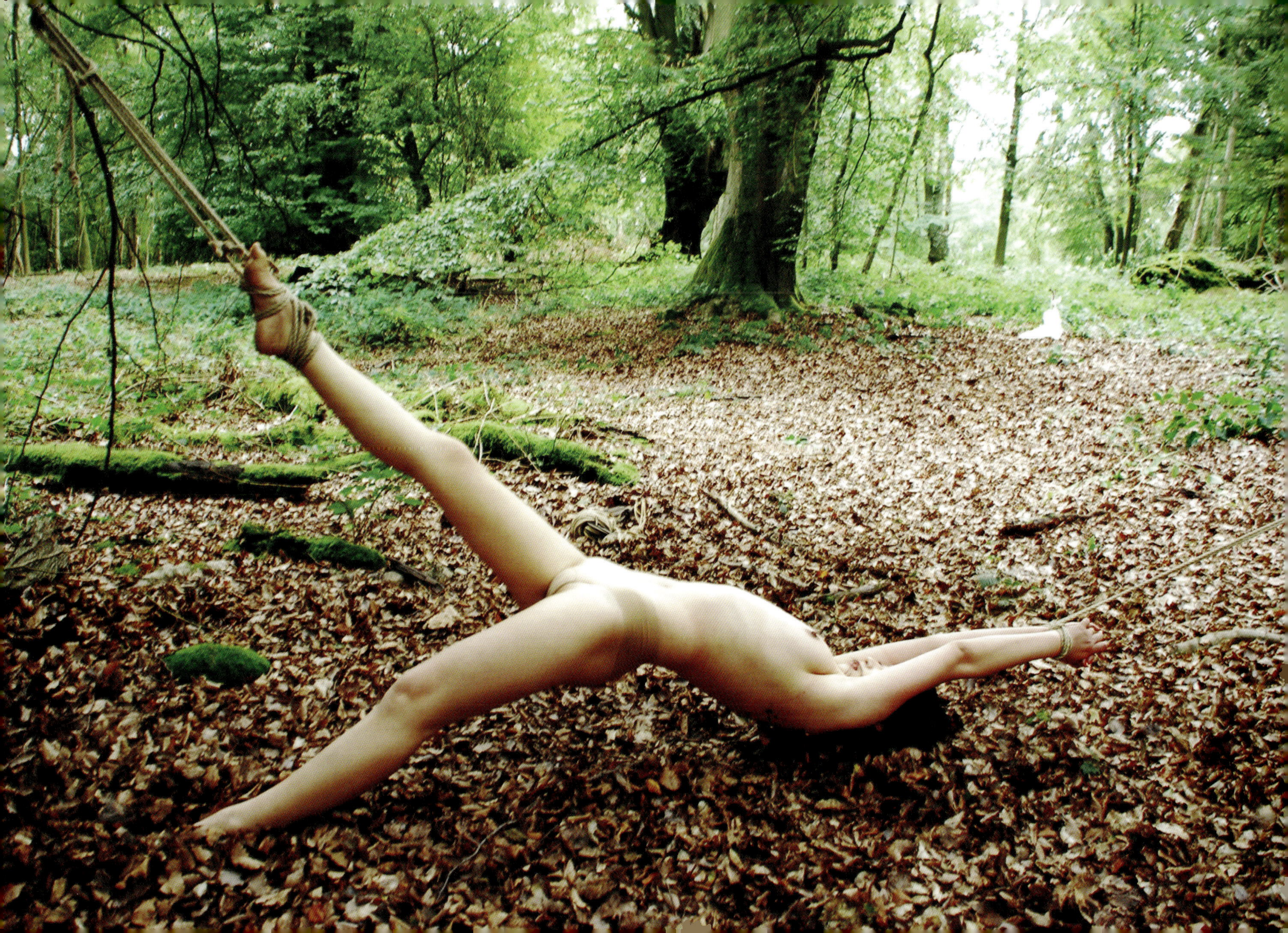

Xue: In this one - she's kind of falling, but in my painting I would have a toy or a figure trying to pull her to stand up.  Here she is quite relaxed.  She have her eyes closed and two arms are crossed in front of her.

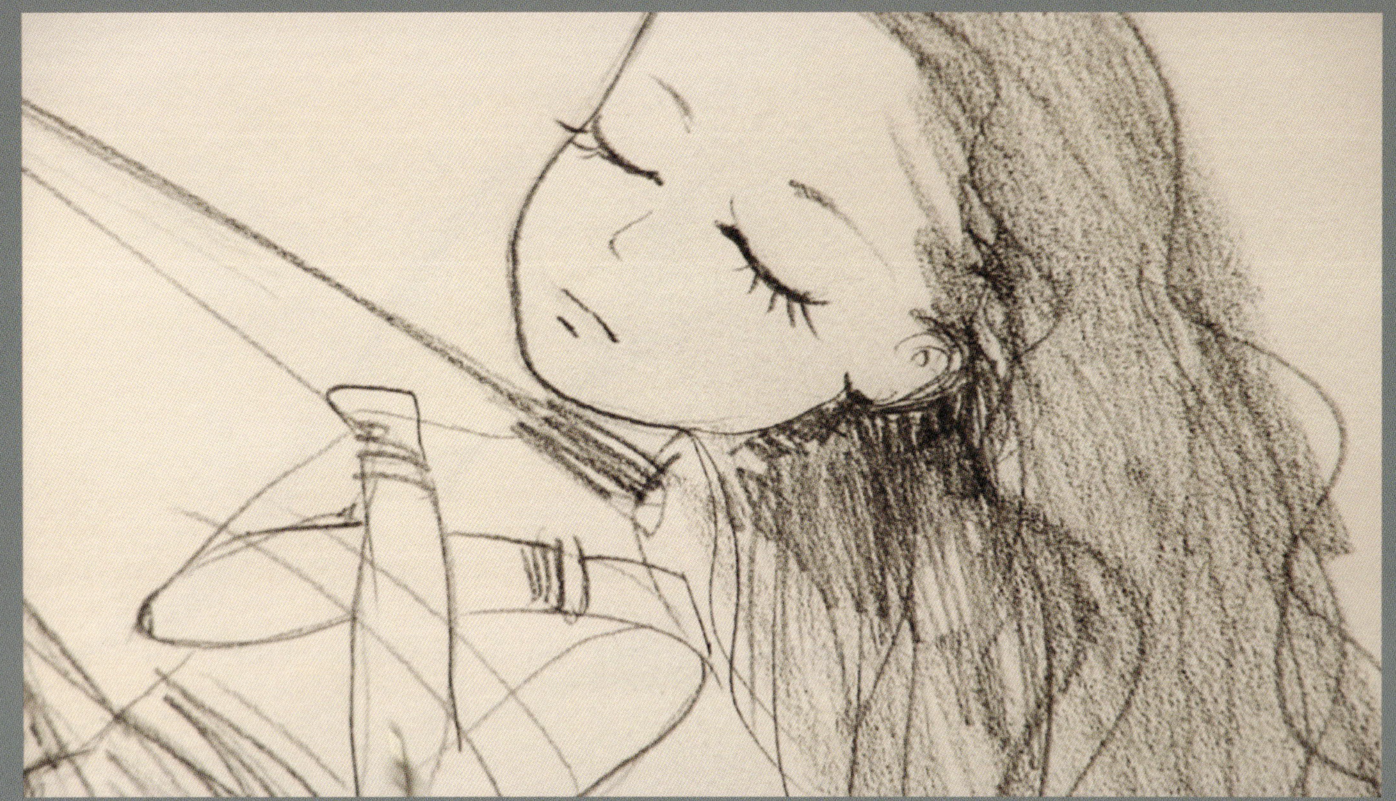

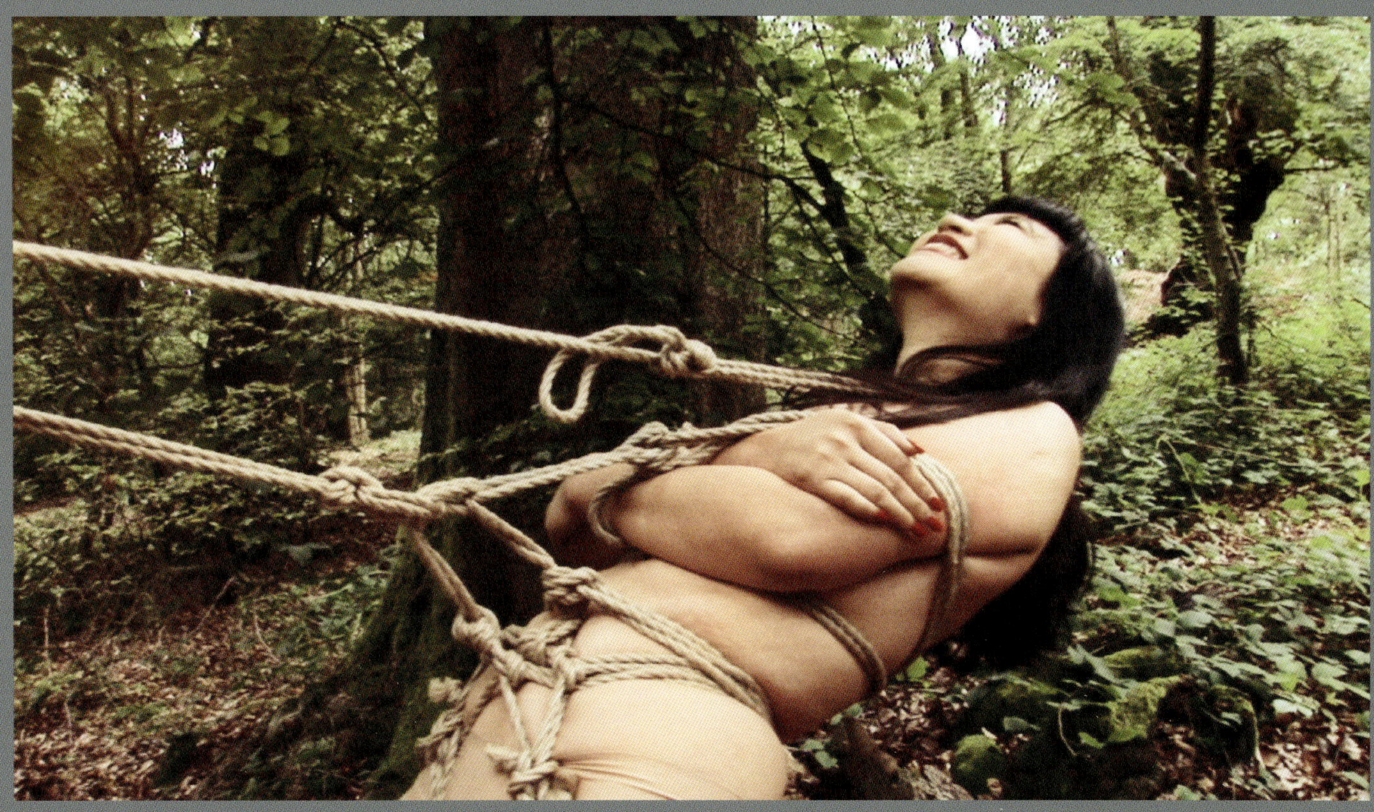

We've practiced it and that's in real life how bondage will work.  I think the ideas got developed.  In this picture, the second girl is kneeling.  She's pulling her hair and squeezing milk into her mouth.

Before I started to paint on the canvas, I do, like a colour study, to see what the colours will look like and the actual little piece fits into that frame.  So I just put them together and it looks really nice.

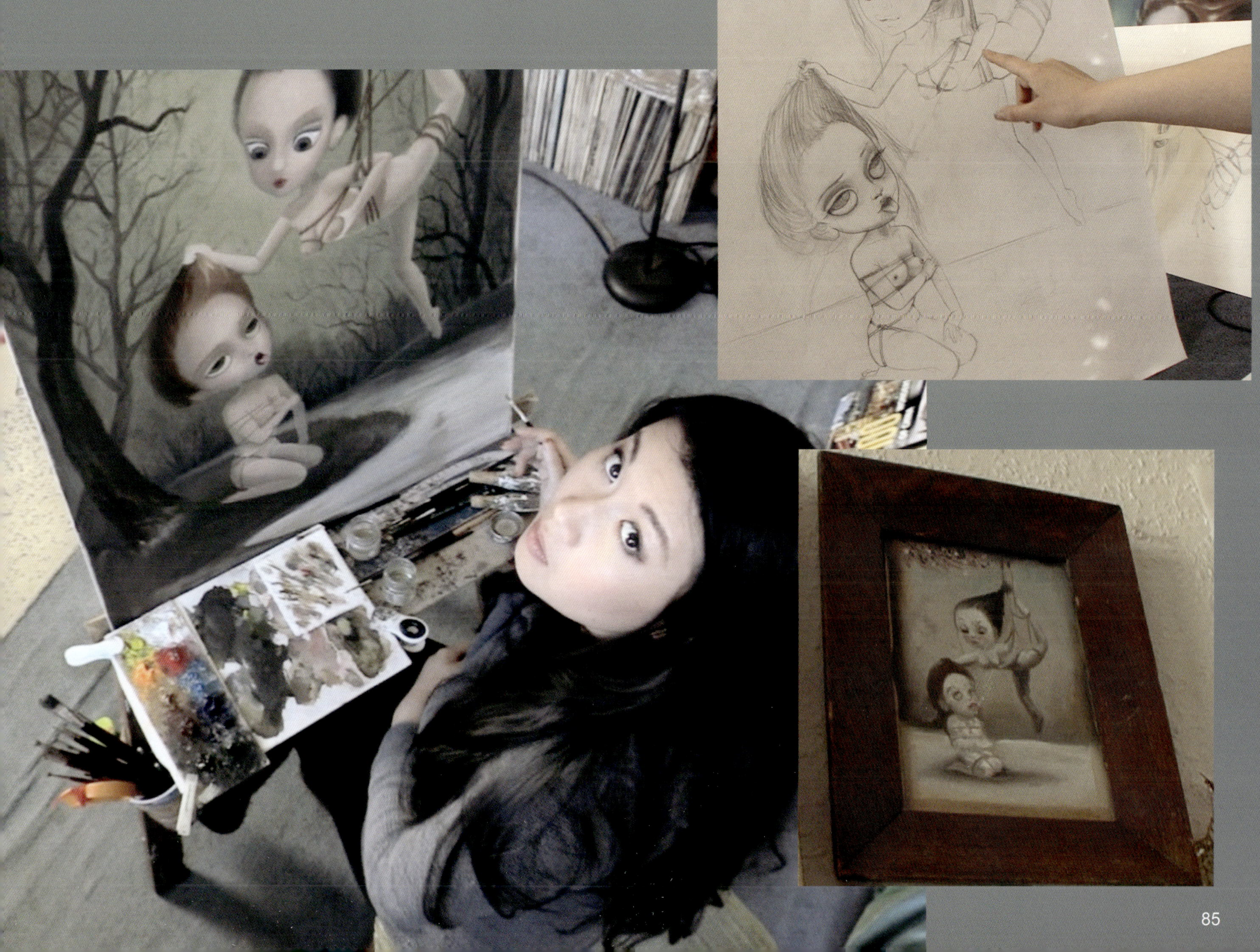

It's looking so much different from my original thoughts.  I think this painting is more personal than any of my other works because I haven't modelled in any of my paintings before.

The newest theme is not just the physical experience, it's the spiritual experience as well and is about paranormal activity.  The girl is breastfeeding a ghost in the night.  And the ghosts have got little milk tokens so they come, in the night only, for milk.  They're ghost babies.

I used to have nightmares when I was little.  I'd cry and wake up with tears in my eyes and can't breathe.  I've got sketches where I collect all my thoughts, dreams, inspirations.  I write them down for my work.

I think in the night it's just - mysterious.



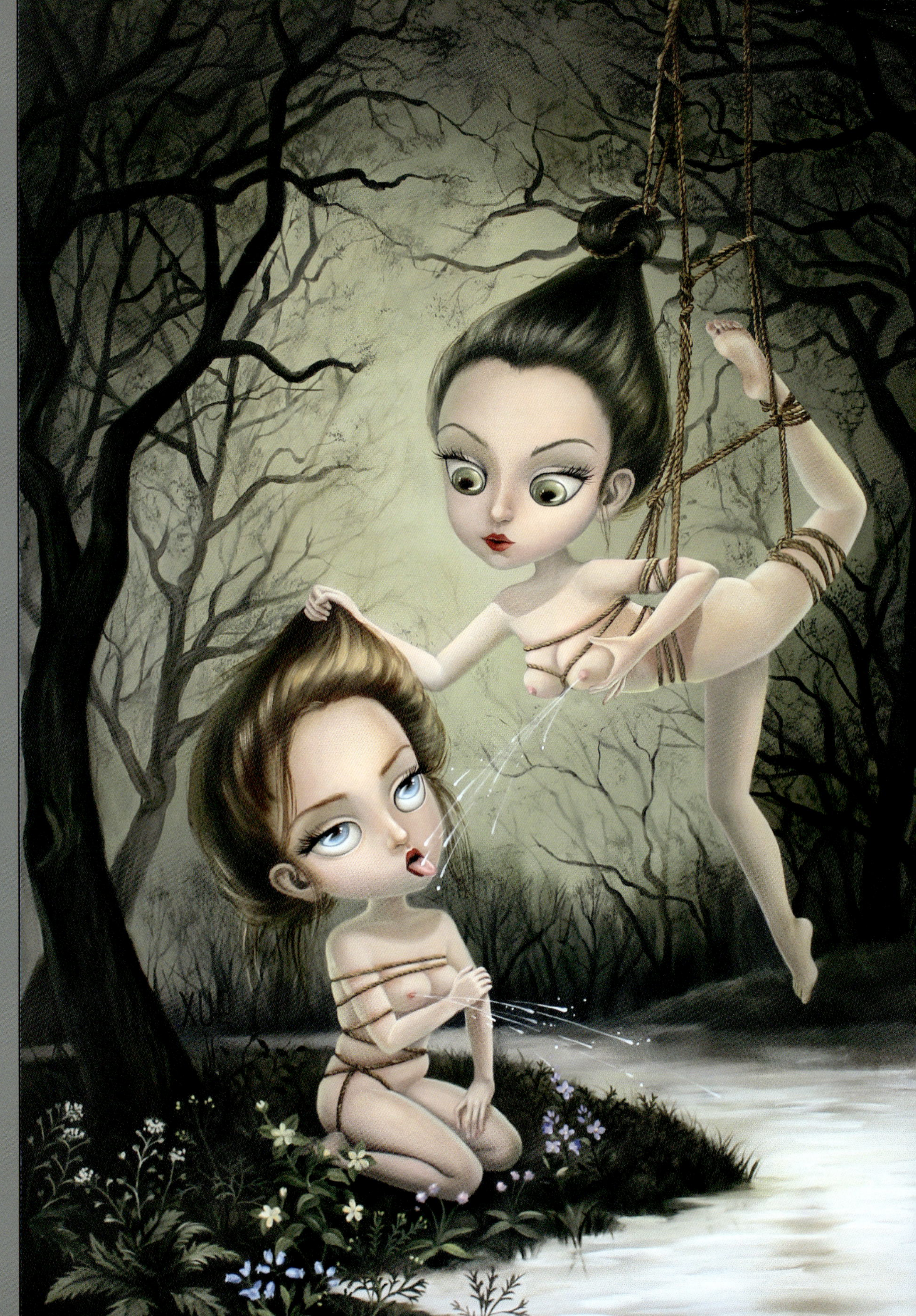

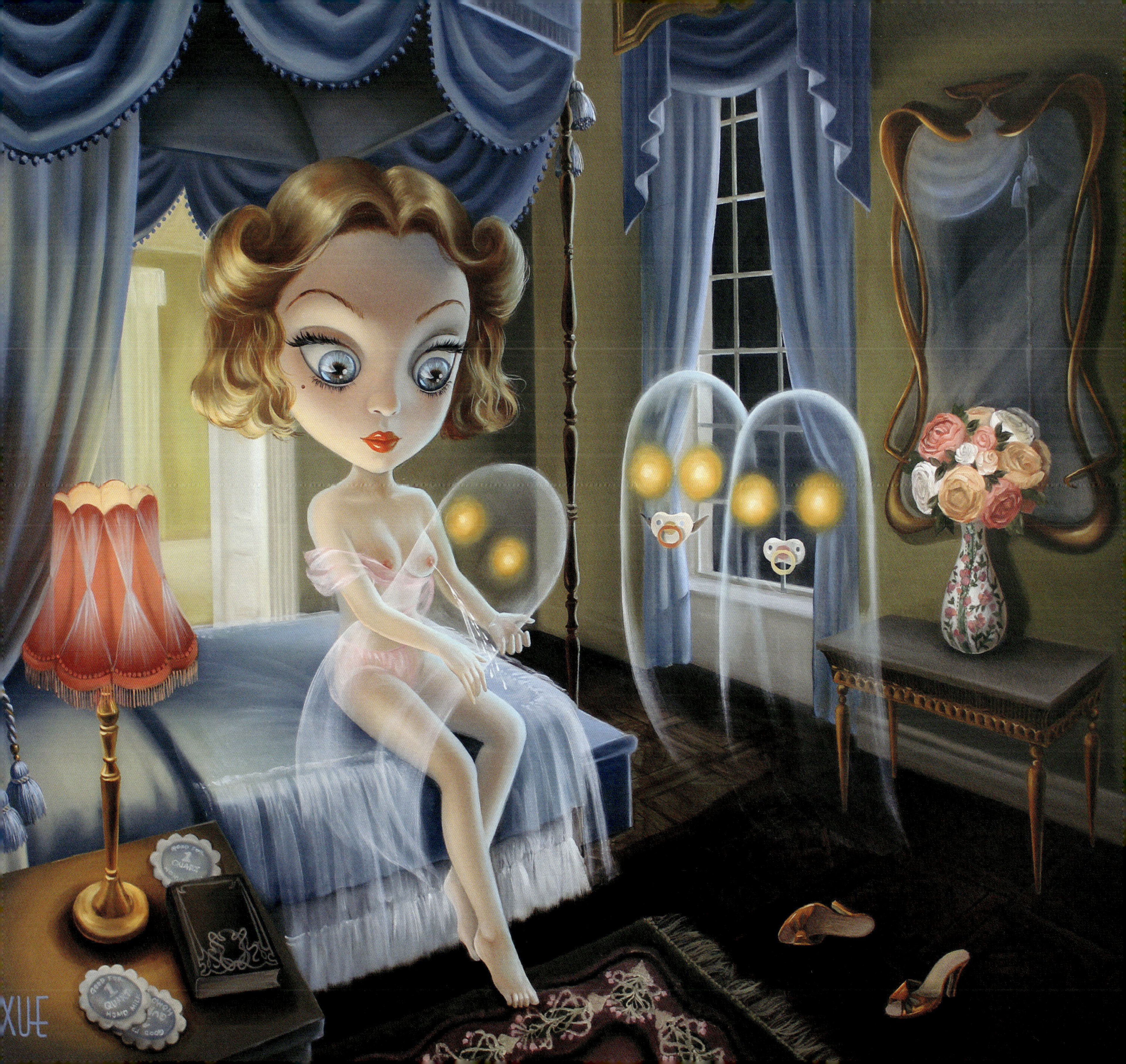

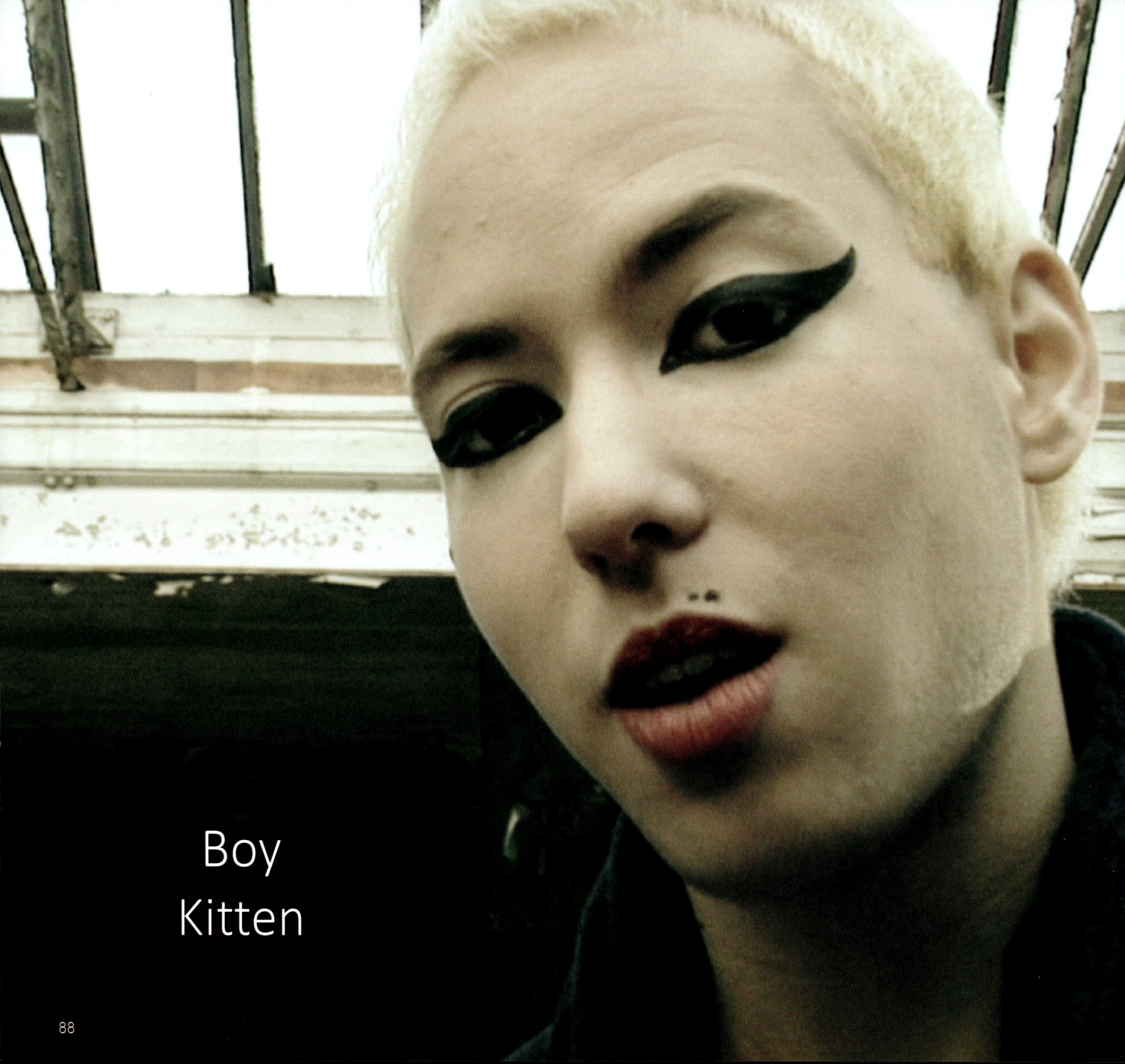
Boy
Kitten

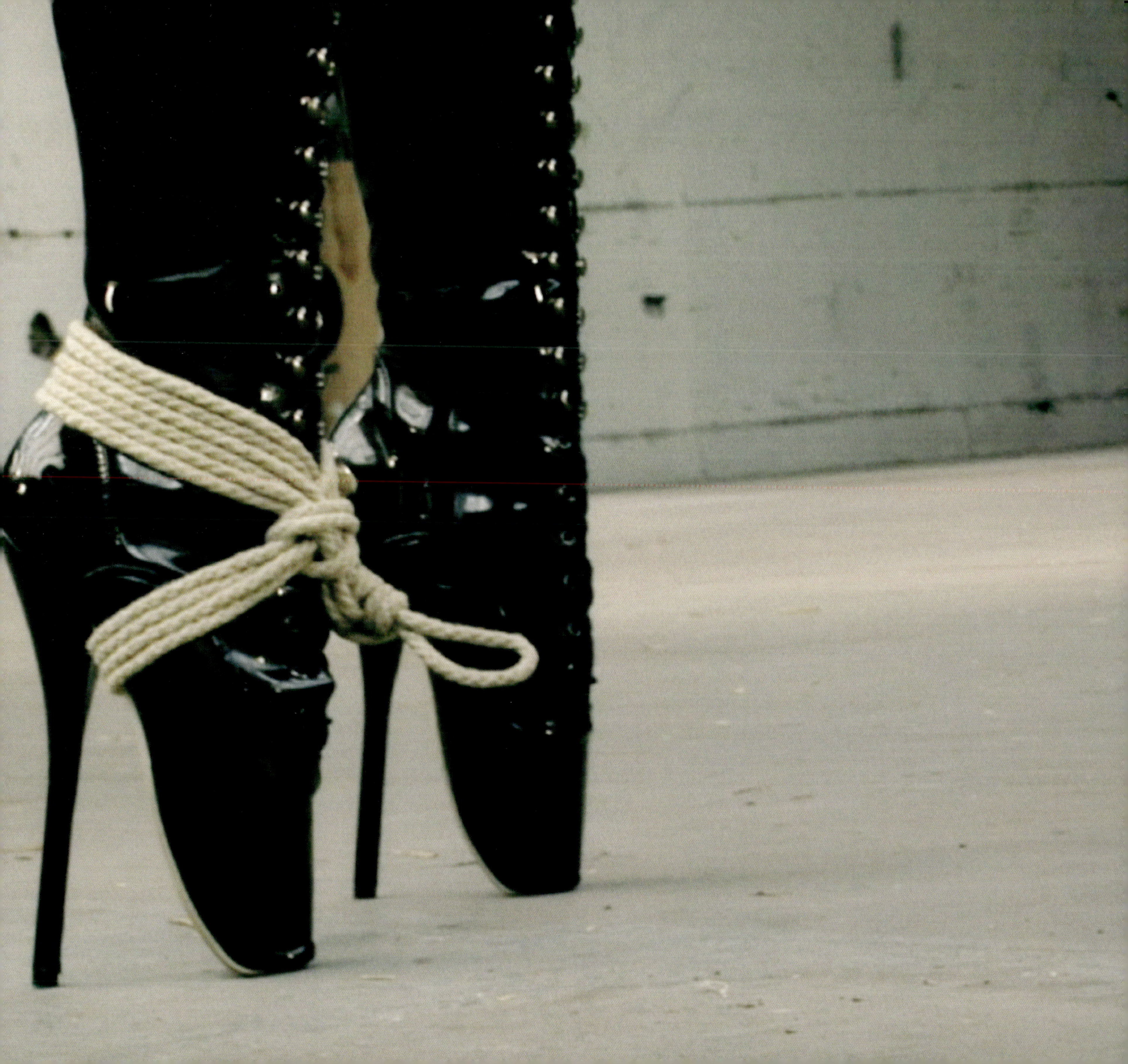

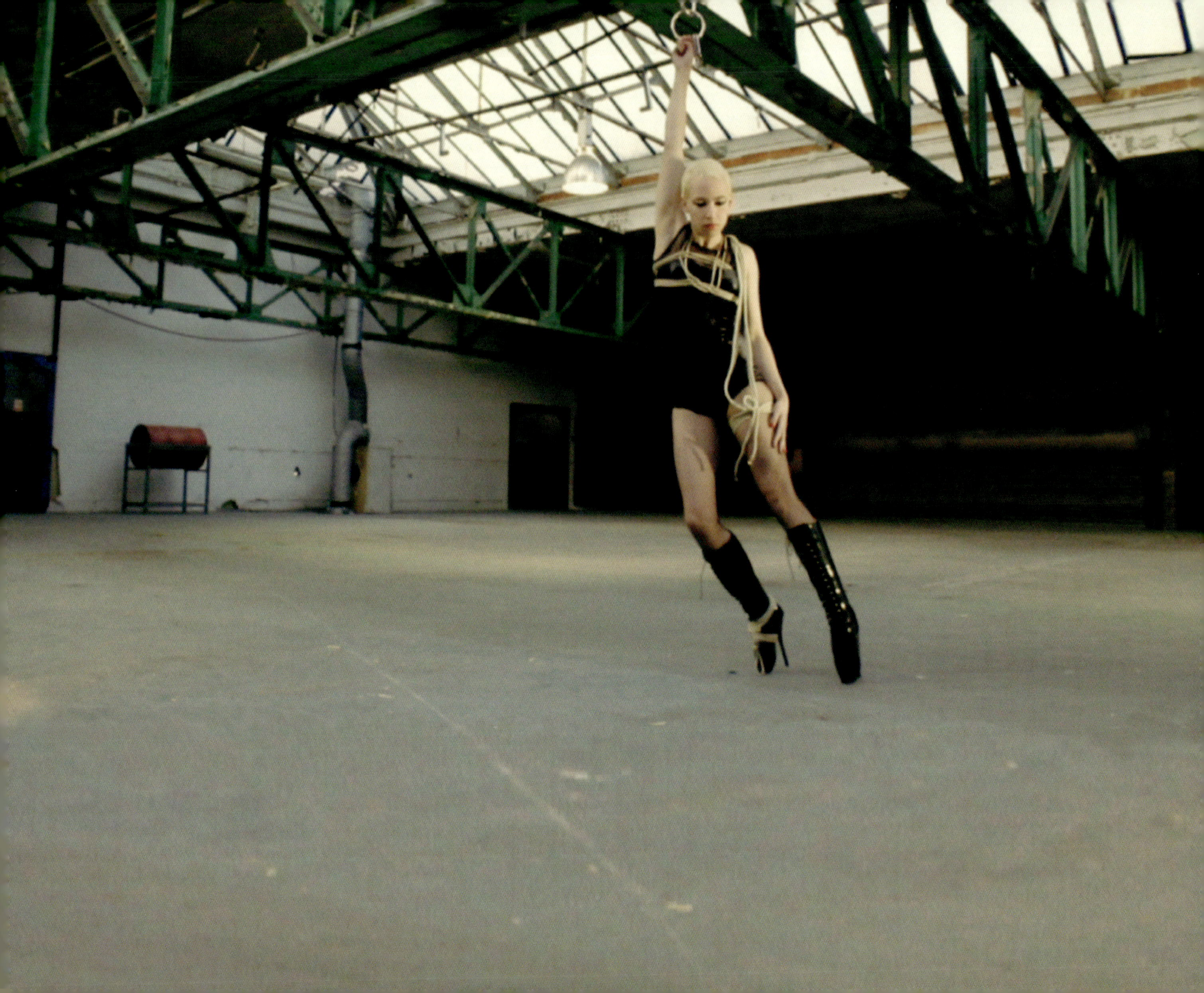

**Boy Kitten has devised ways to use ropes by himself, without a performance partner.**

Boy Kitten: This self suspension is a lot more difficult than it would have been even six months ago when I was doing this at the Erotic Awards.  I've got a chronic pain condition, just in my thumbs, but it's in both thumbs so it means doing something like this takes a lot of strength and a lot of pain.  It's something I've only had for the last few years and it has got steadily worse.

I'm a masochist.  I can put up with more pain than the vast majority of people, but the pain in my thumbs is more than I can cope with.  I just hope that I can carry on doing this for as long as possible.

Because I really do, you know, love doing it and it's such an exhilarating experience.

My rope work is a lot more precious than it was before.  I guess I give every performance as if it could be my last.

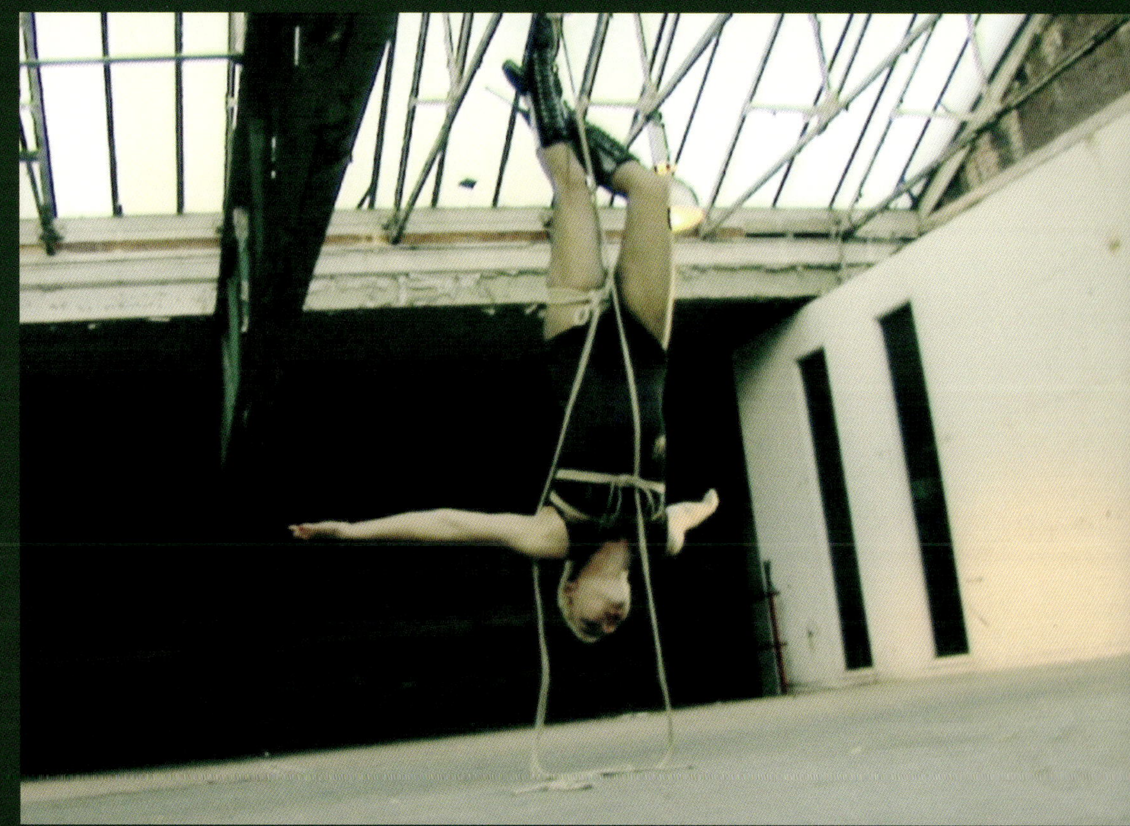

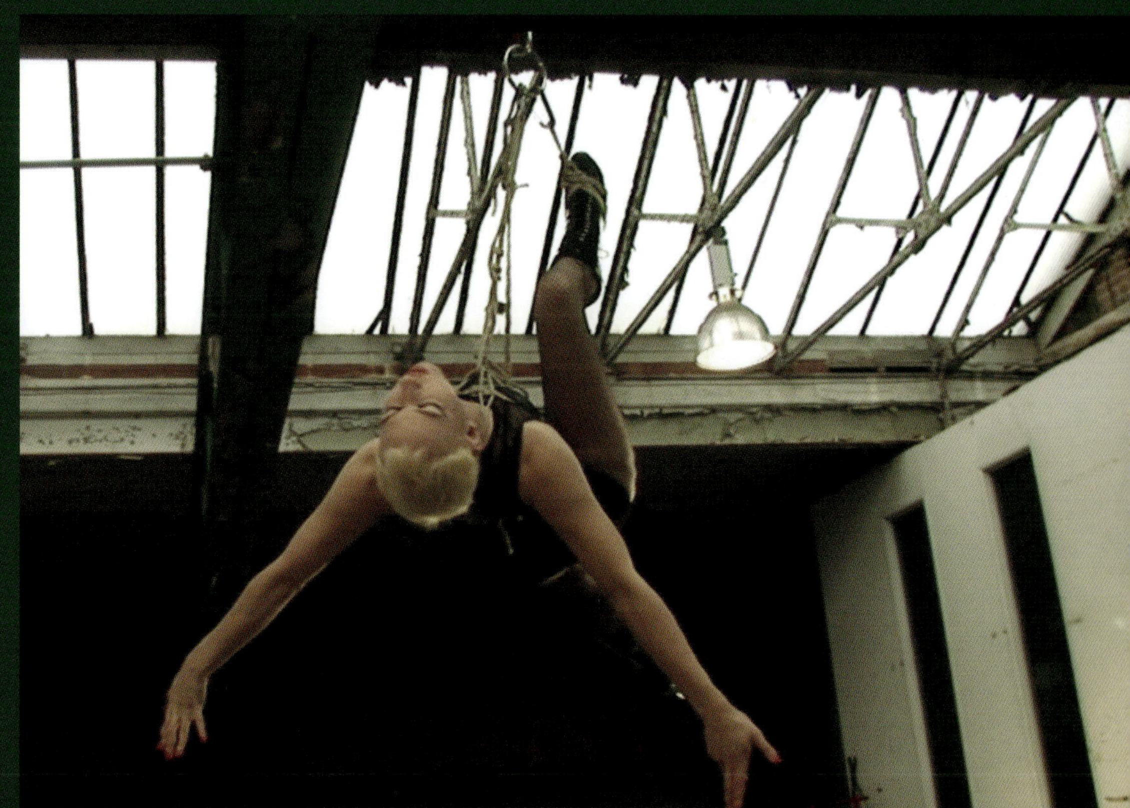

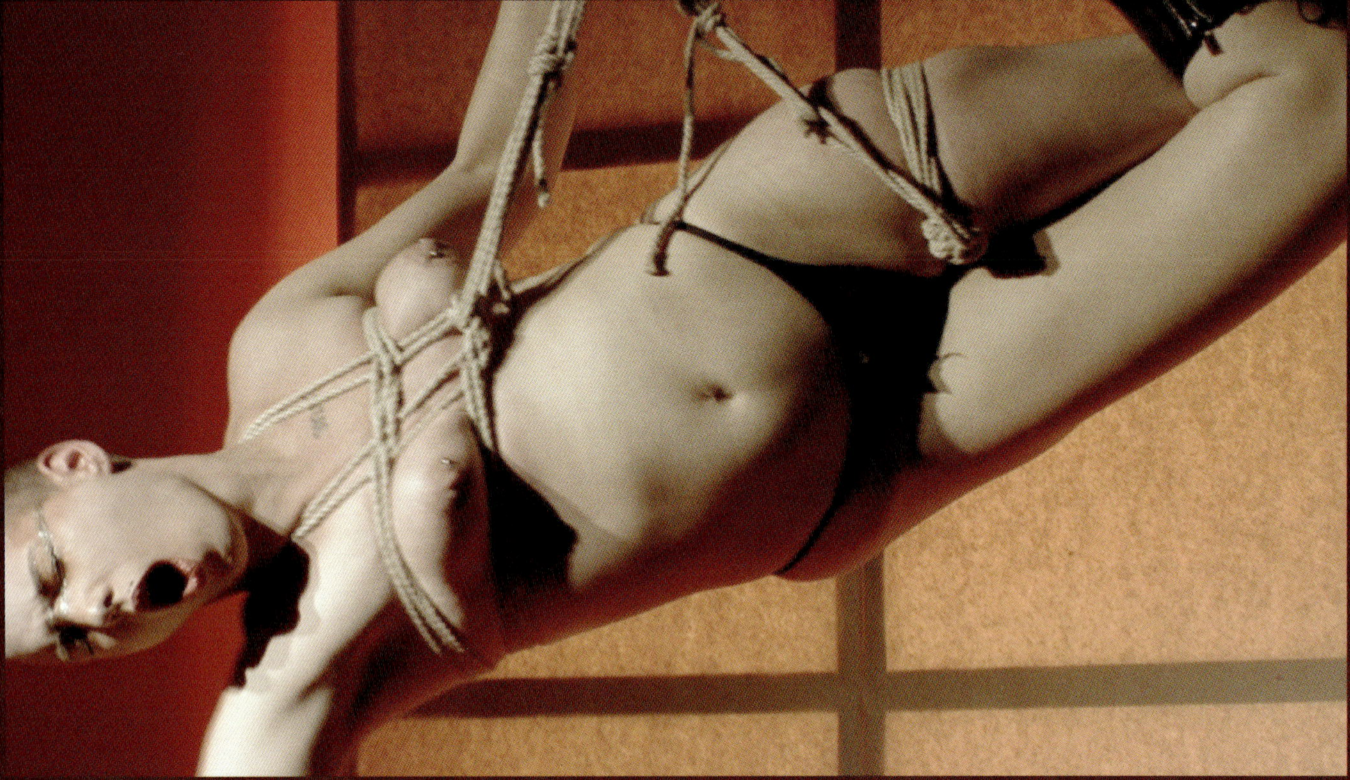

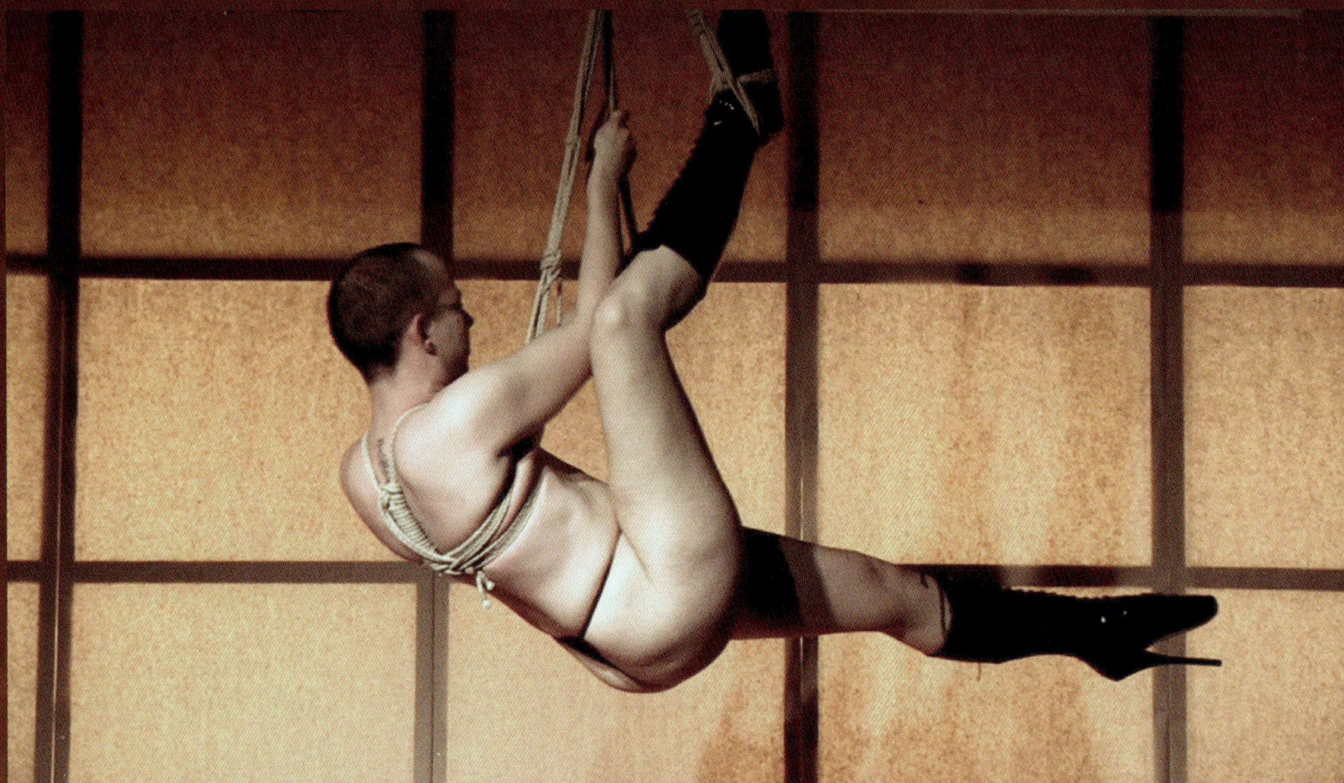

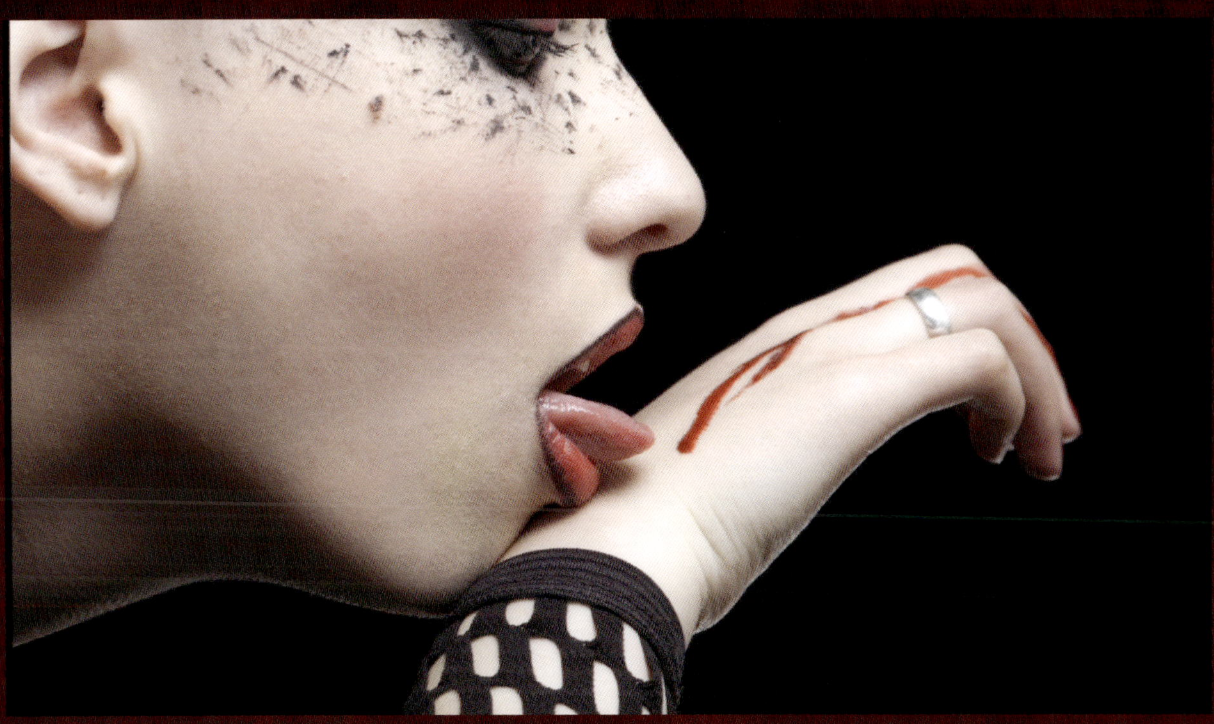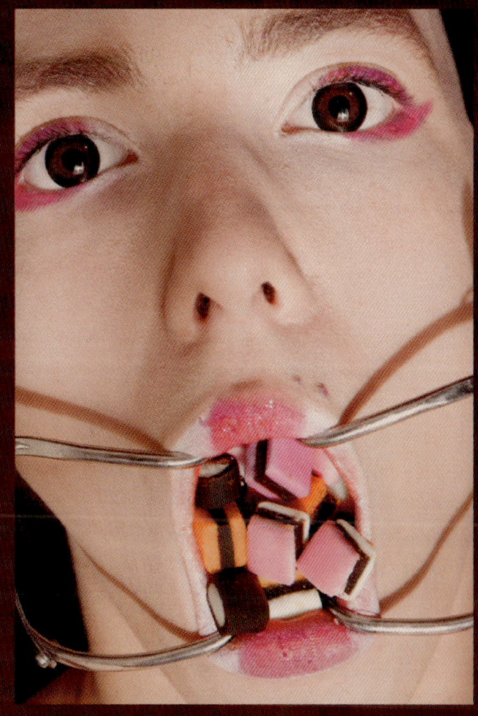

Boy Kitten is muse and model for photographer Rod MacDonald. They have been partners for many years and together they express his particular sexuality and are proud to display it - in a London exhibition at Sh! Women's Erotic Emporium.

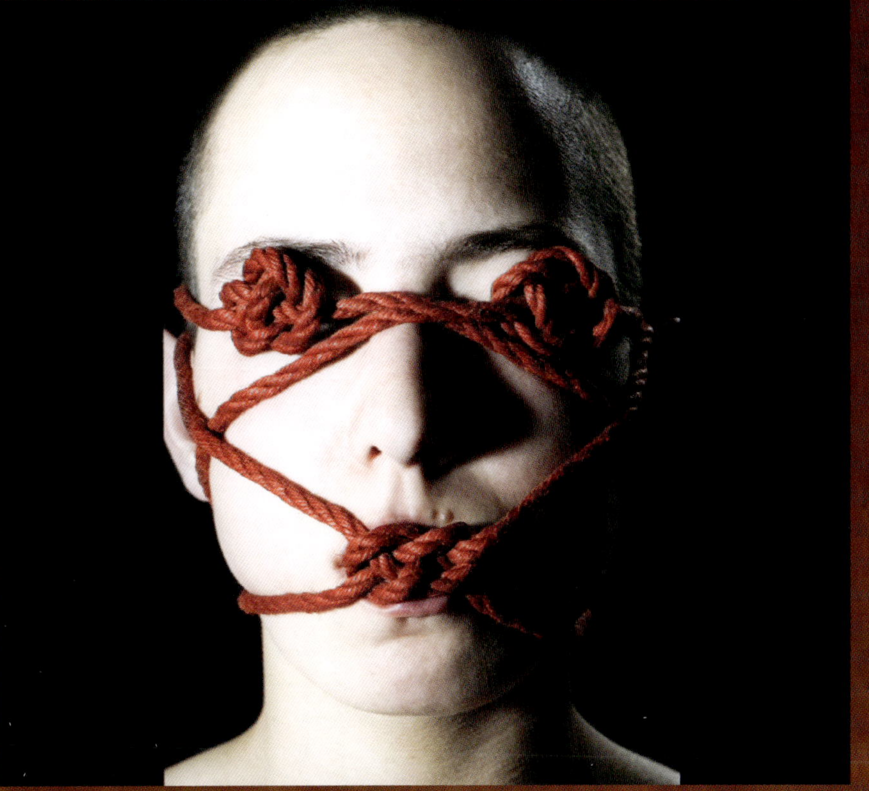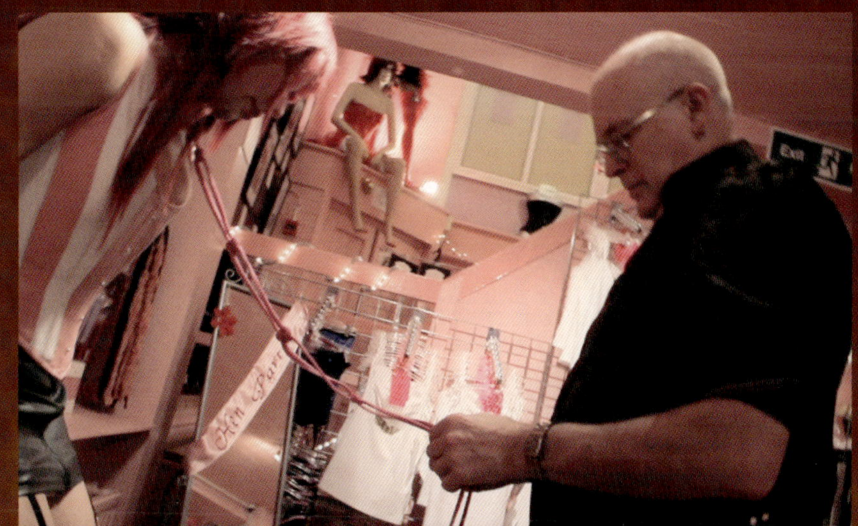

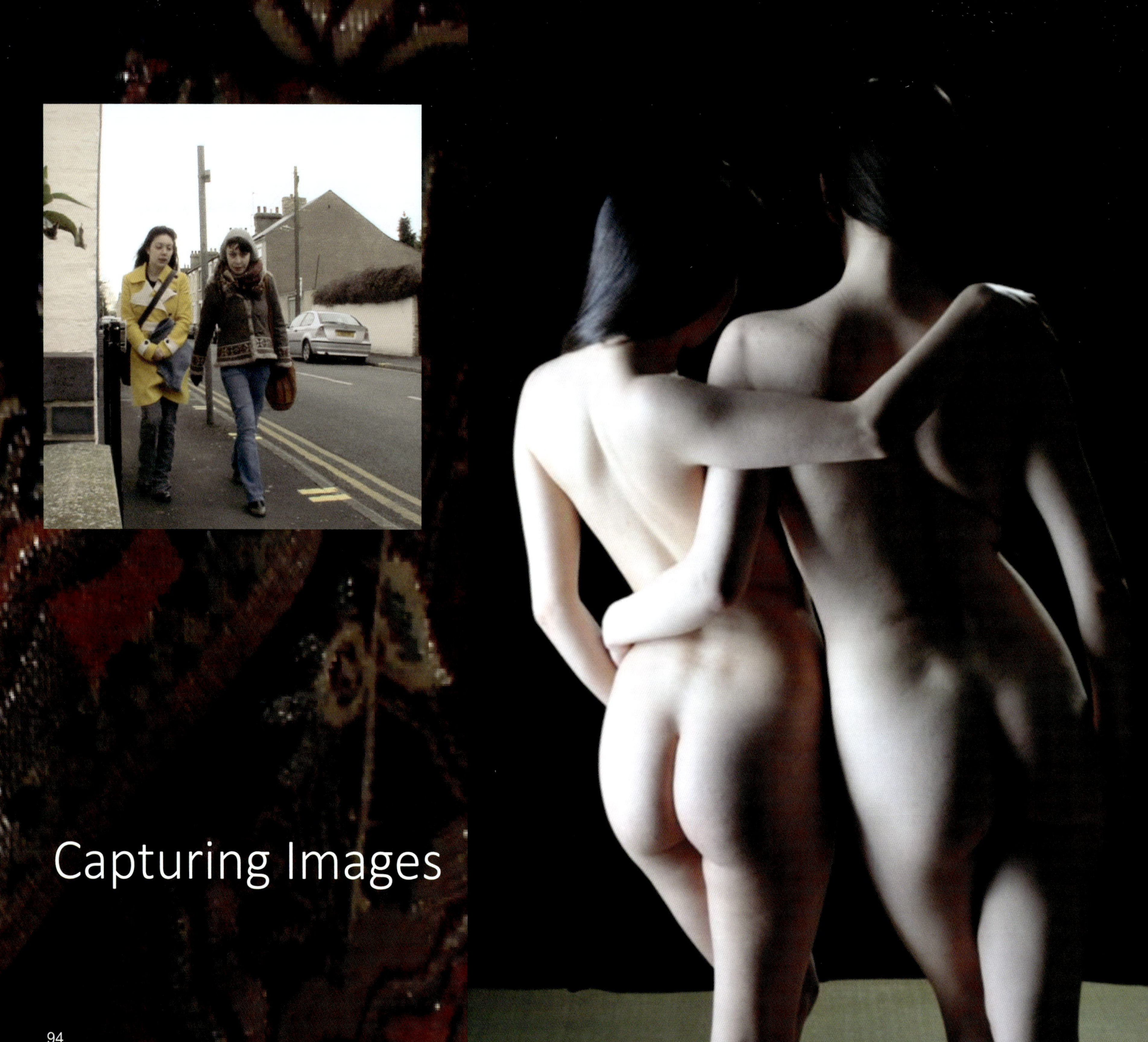

# Capturing Images

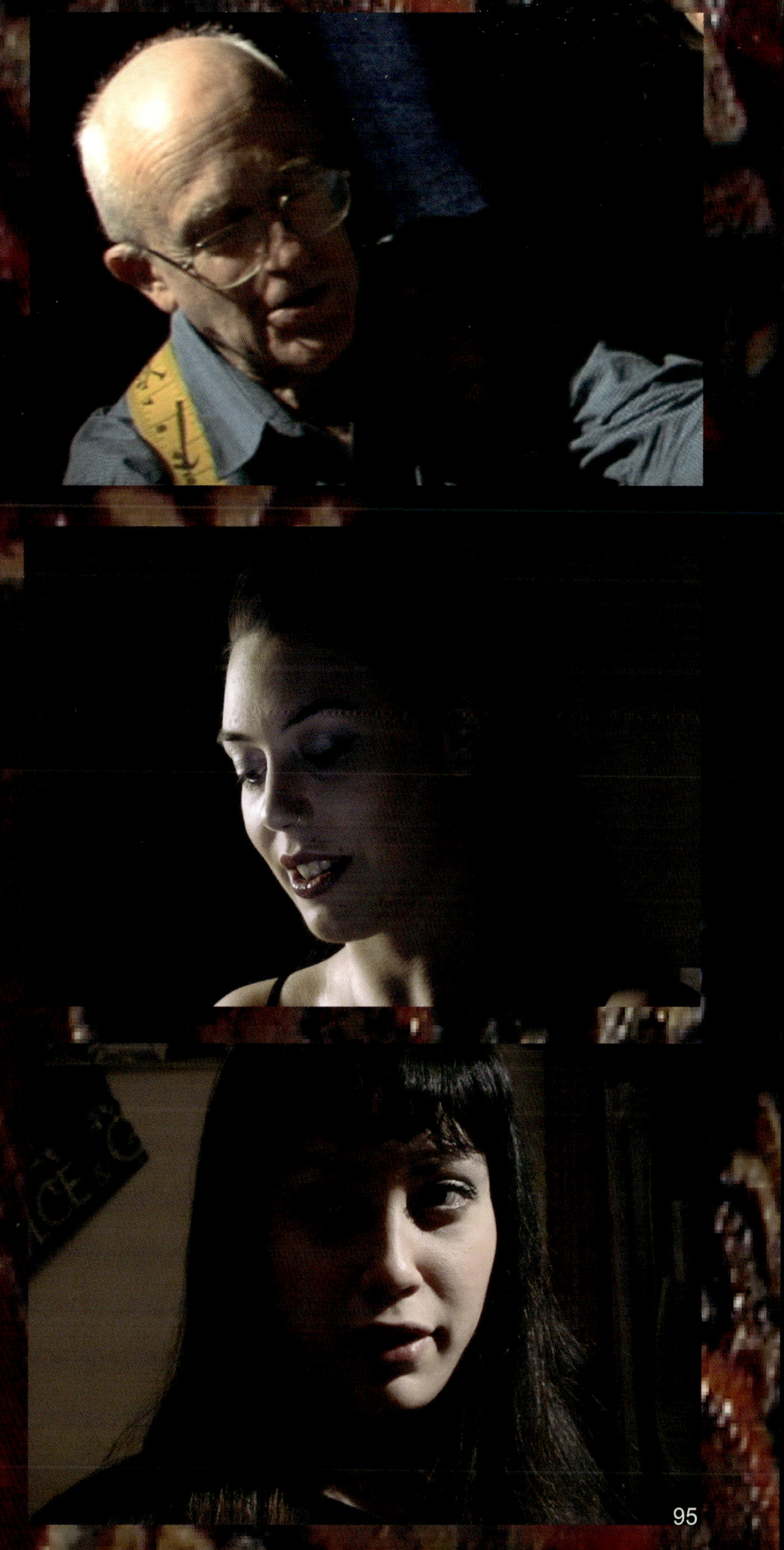

**Rod MacDonald has photographed Gestalta for many years.  On this occasion he has been enlisted by her for his rope skills - to assist in an art video she is making with her house mate, Rebecca.**

Gestalta:  Well basically the film is sort of divided into three main parts.  Normally when I'm trying to come up with an idea of something, I have about a million notebooks lying around and I start scribbling until something makes sense.  So yeah, I did this in the case of this film.

When I decided to make this movie with Rebecca and Rod, part of it was down to the fact that we all live very close to each other.  Well Becky lives in the same house as me and Rod lives 10 seconds around the corner.  That made it quite convenient.  And also, just the fact that I know them very well.  Rod and I have been working together for four or five years now.

Rebecca:  Well Gestalta had this idea for a movie that she wanted to make and I suppose she decided to cast me in the lead role given that I was available and willing and an able bodied human being in the vicinity.

This was pretty much one of my first introductions to the rope bondage scene.  I hadn't really done any modelling in that style before.

Gestalta:  Certainly the last year or so I've actually really begun to enjoy being on the other side of the camera: a lot more fun.  Well, to some extent, a lot more than I enjoy being in front of the camera.  I feel like I'm having more creative input.

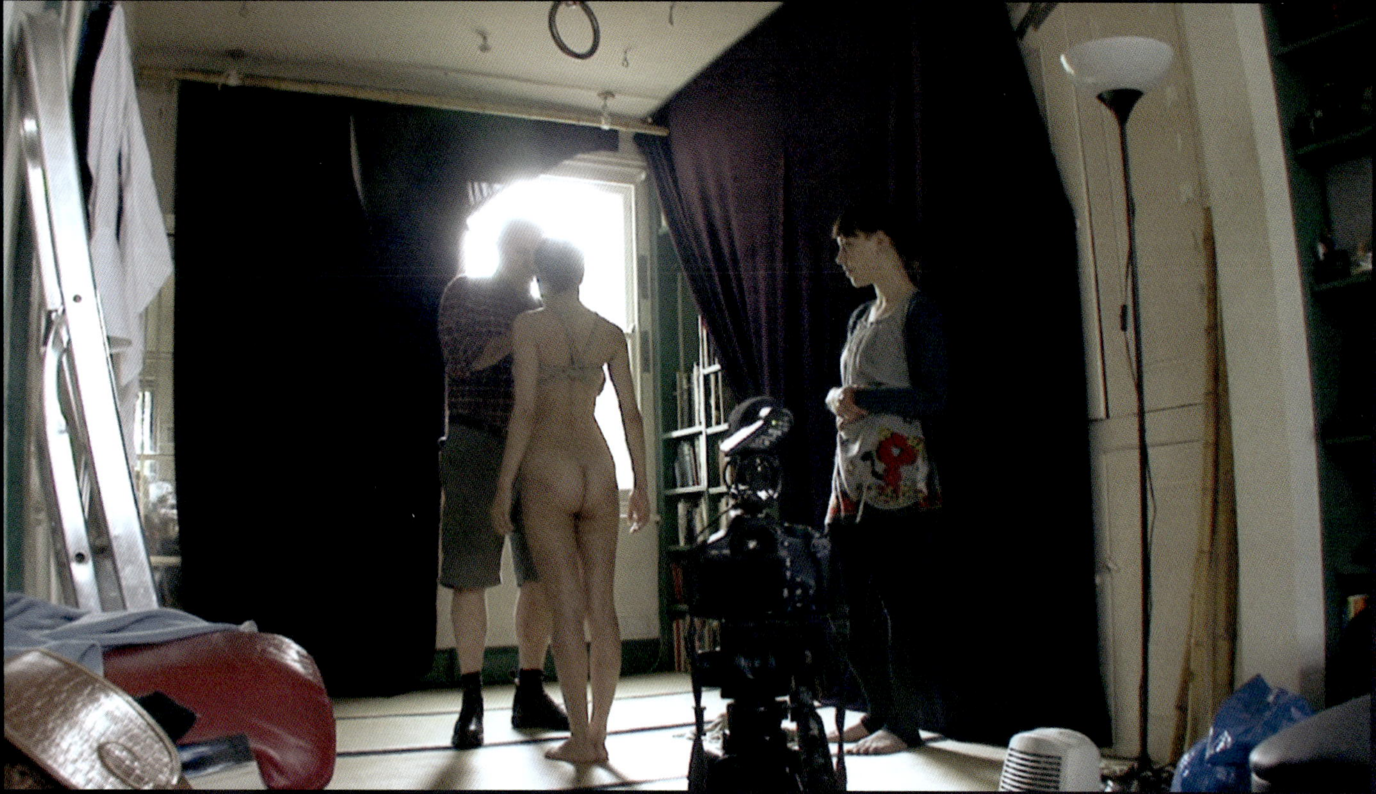

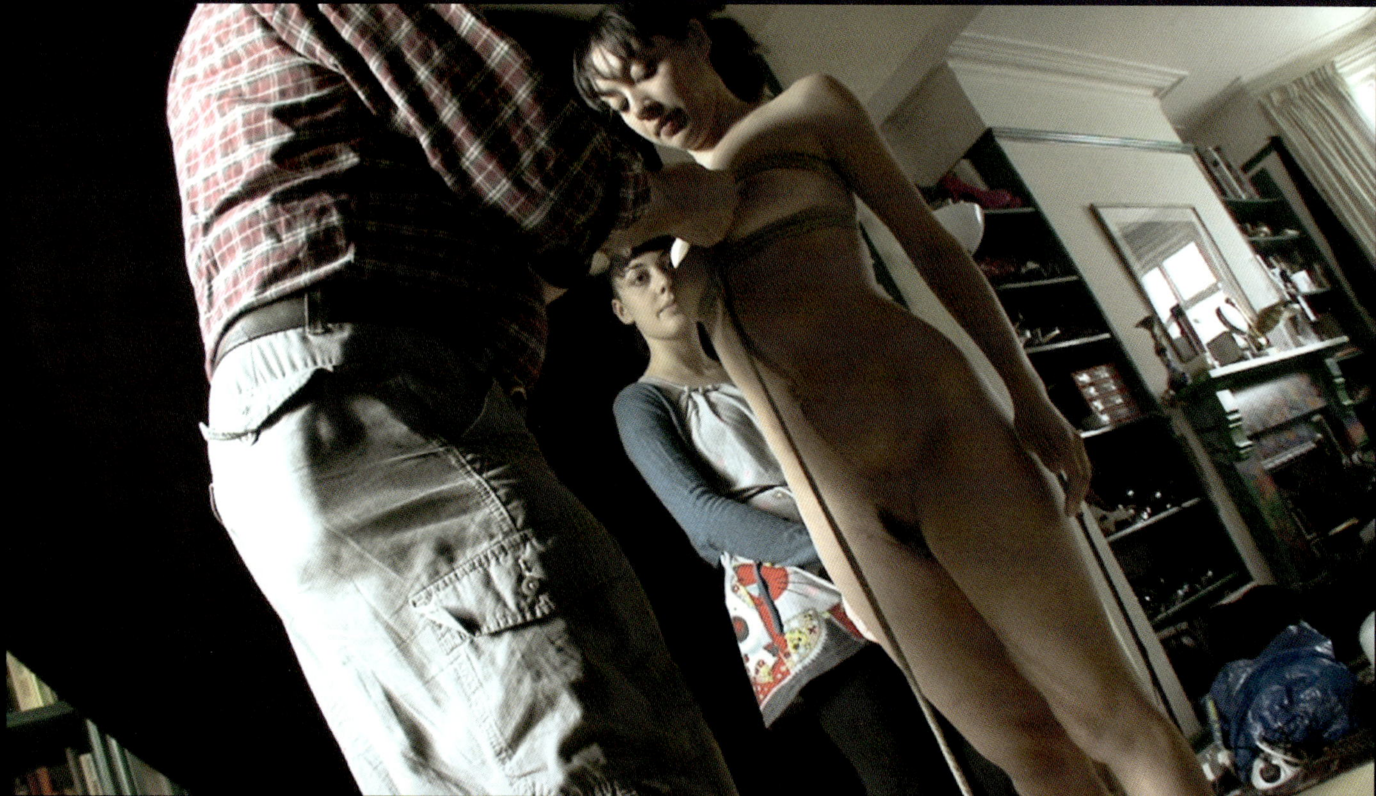

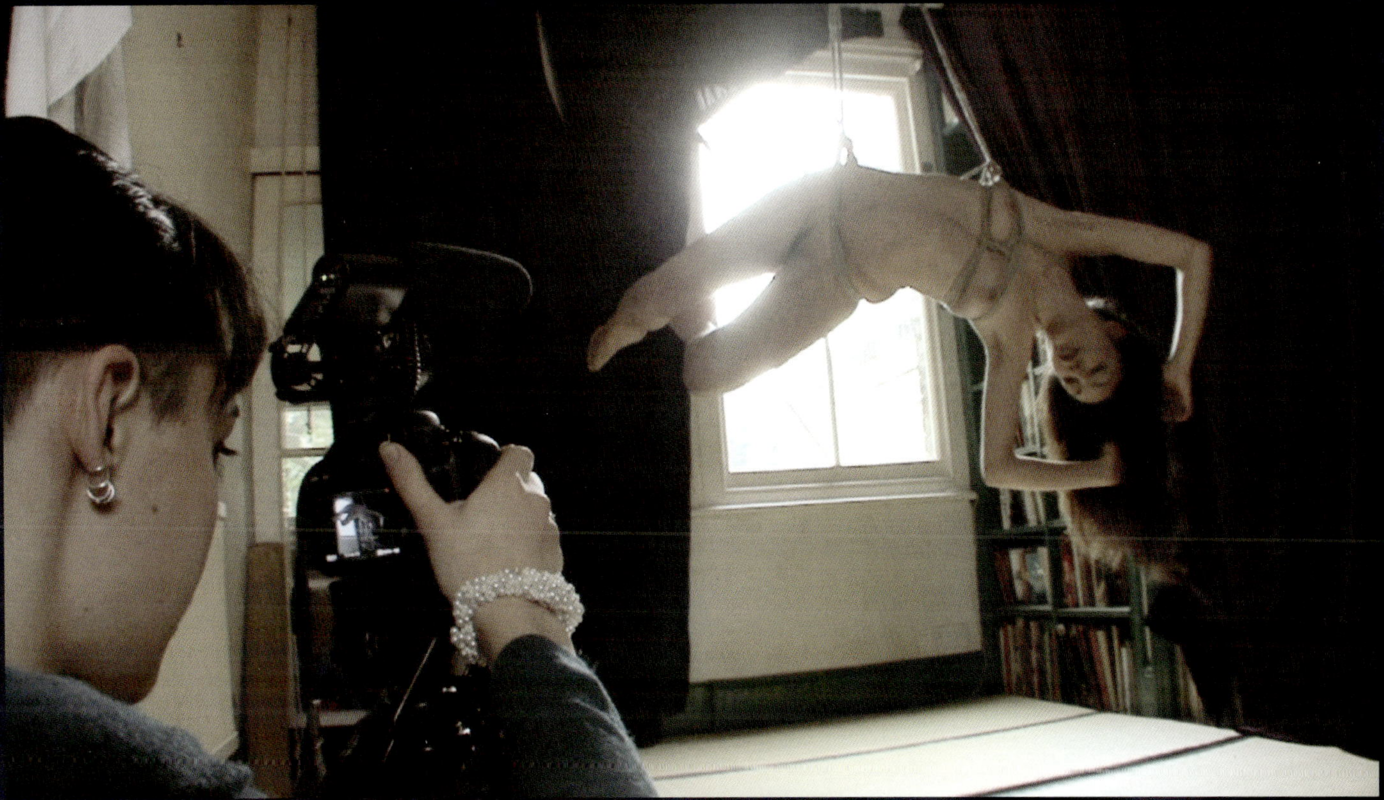

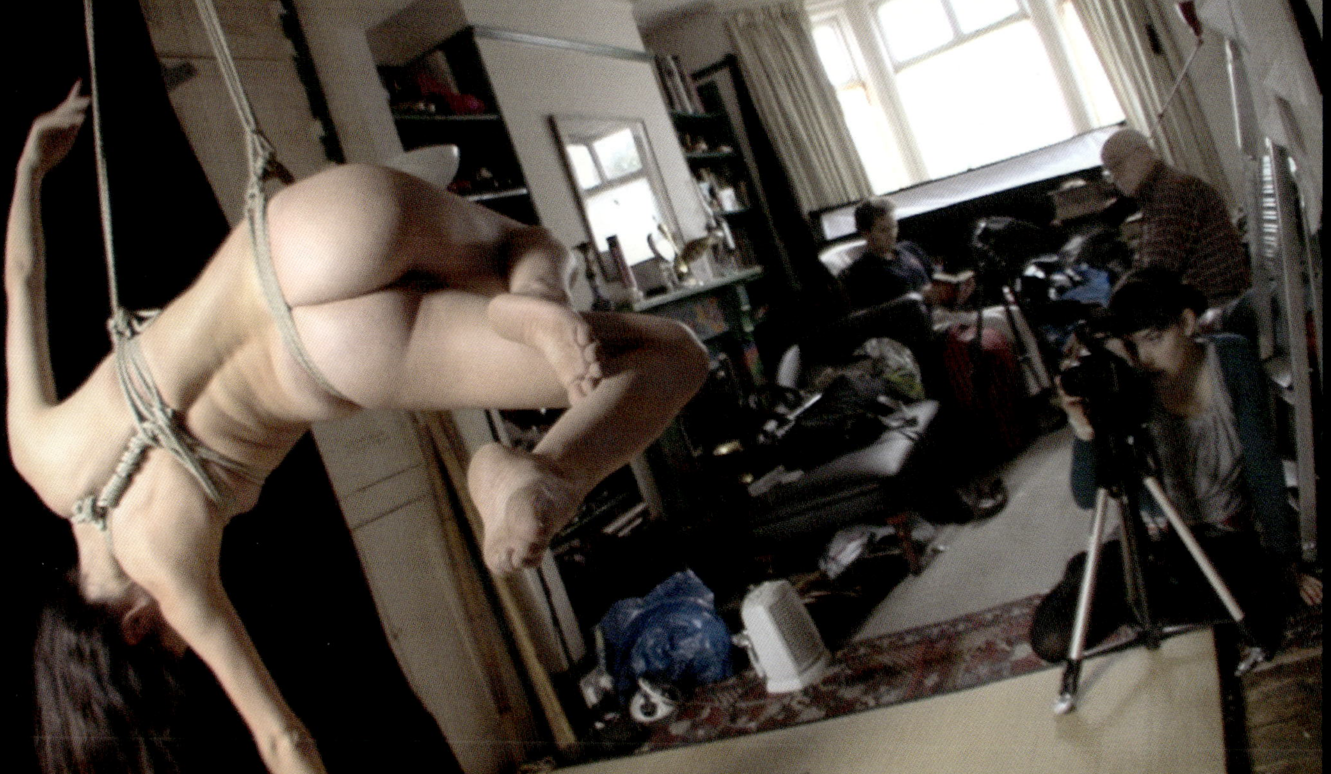

Rebecca:  I got the distinct impression during the planning stages of the concept development that I was playing the part of Gestalta.

Gestalta:  No, she's not representative of me. The film I suppose was more of a kind of emotional film.  Becky is somebody who is portraying emotional responses, but I think they are quite generic. They're not really specific to any one particular person.

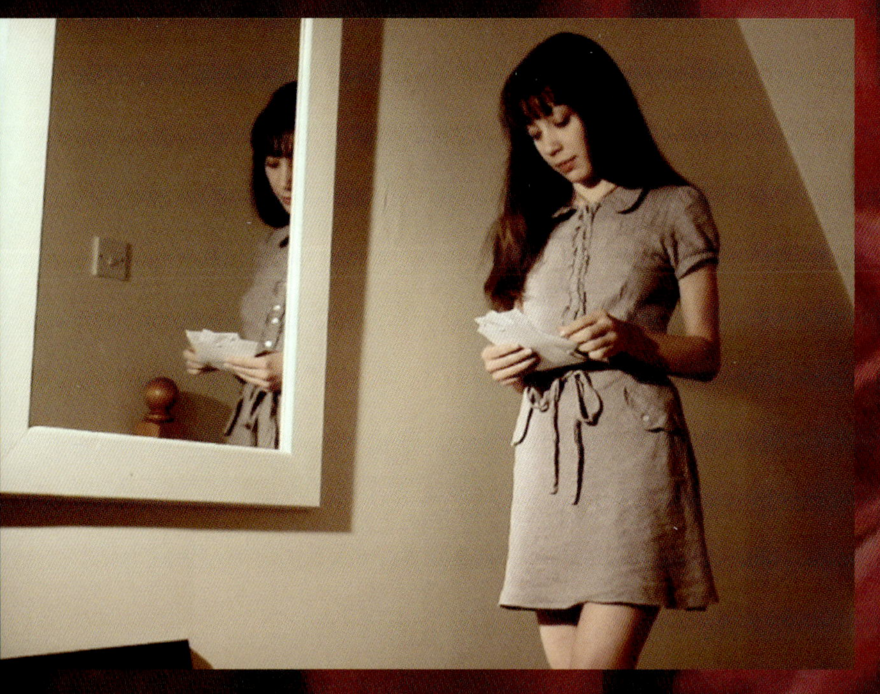
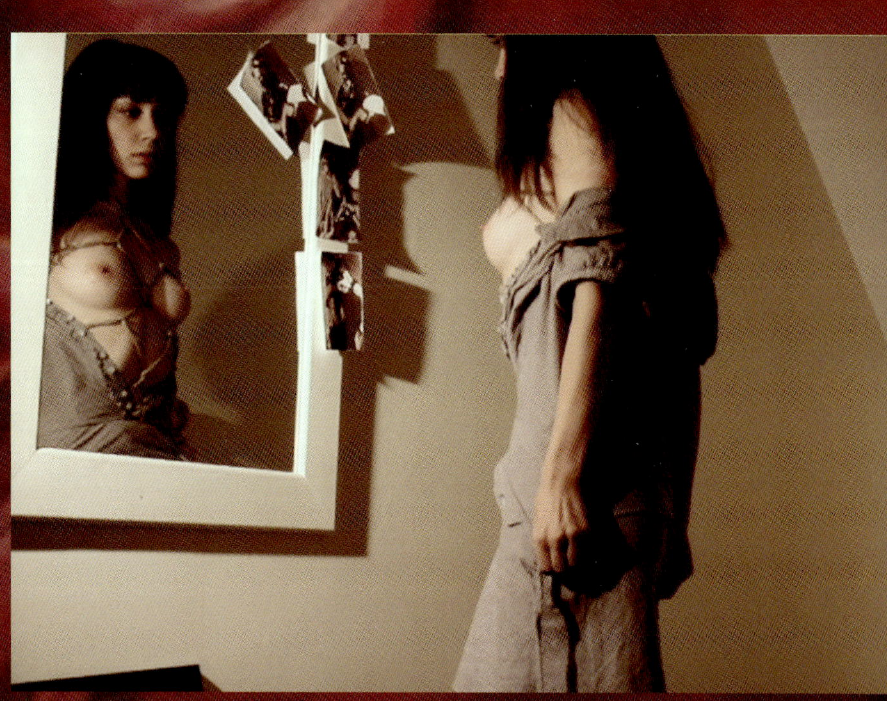

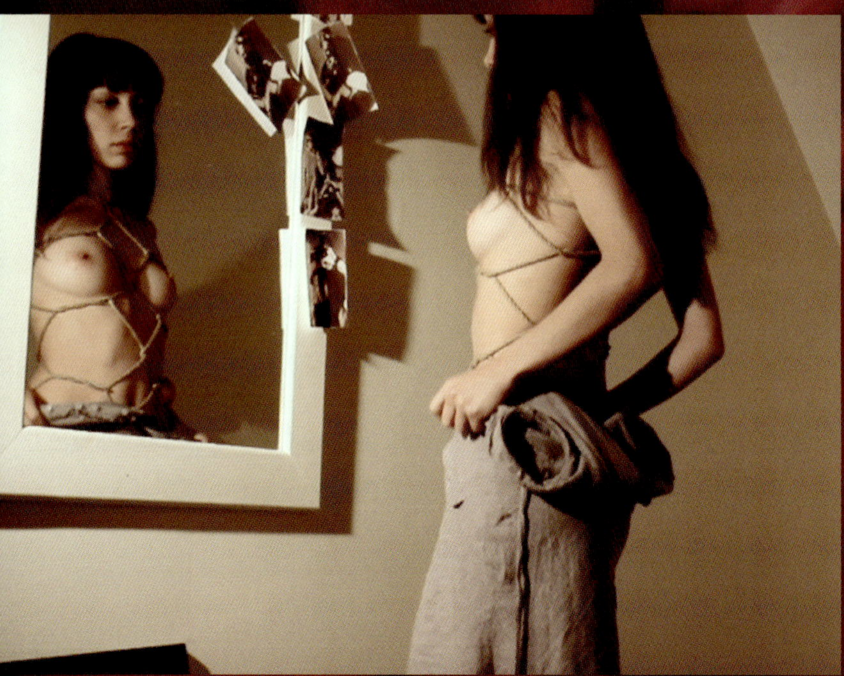
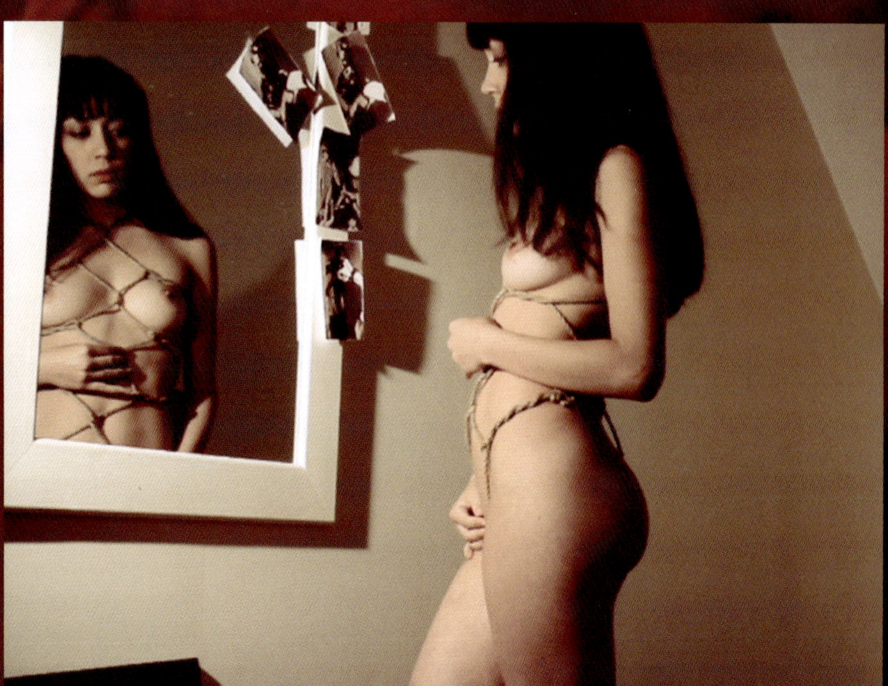

Gestalta: Possibly the only parallel that there is between Becky's character and mine within the film is the rope that she's wearing under her clothes, which is something that I did go through a bit of a phase of doing.

Rebecca:  There was a rope tie which was called a Karada which is a sort of tortoise shell shape of tie that just goes around the torso, and I had that on for some of the scenes. So we used a tortoise in the shoot.

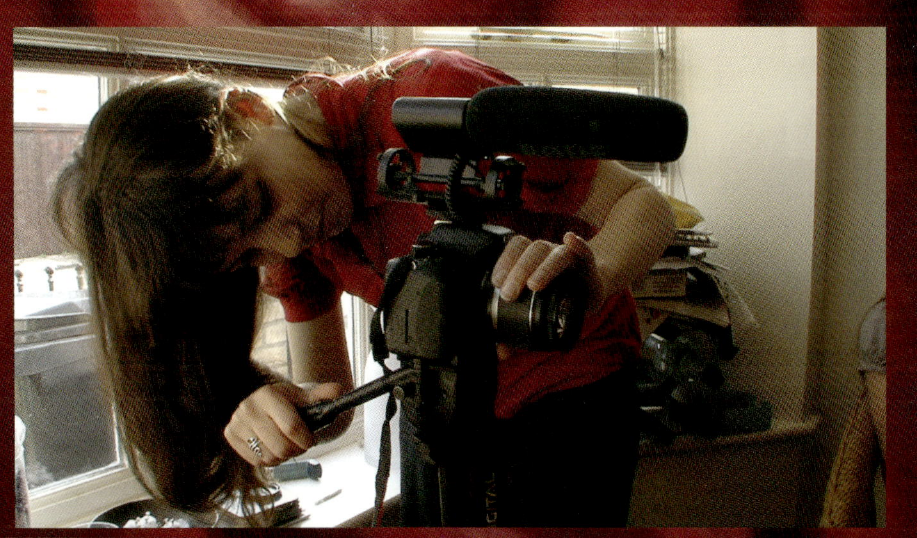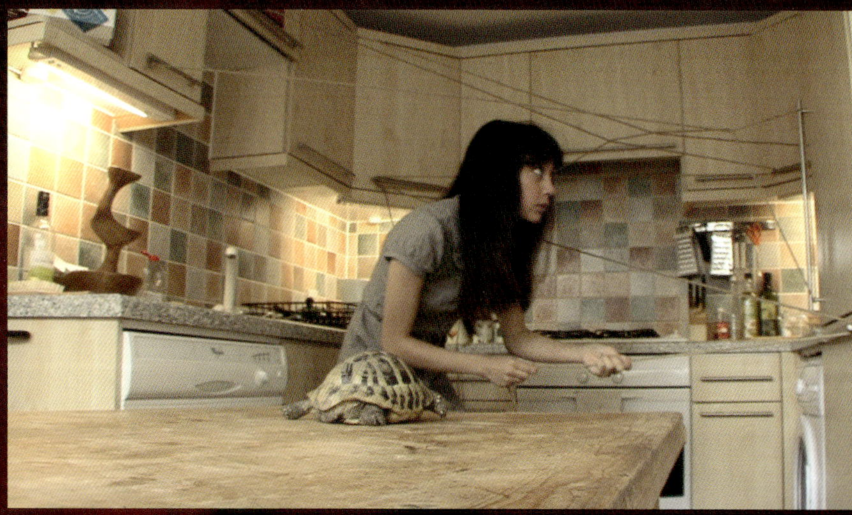

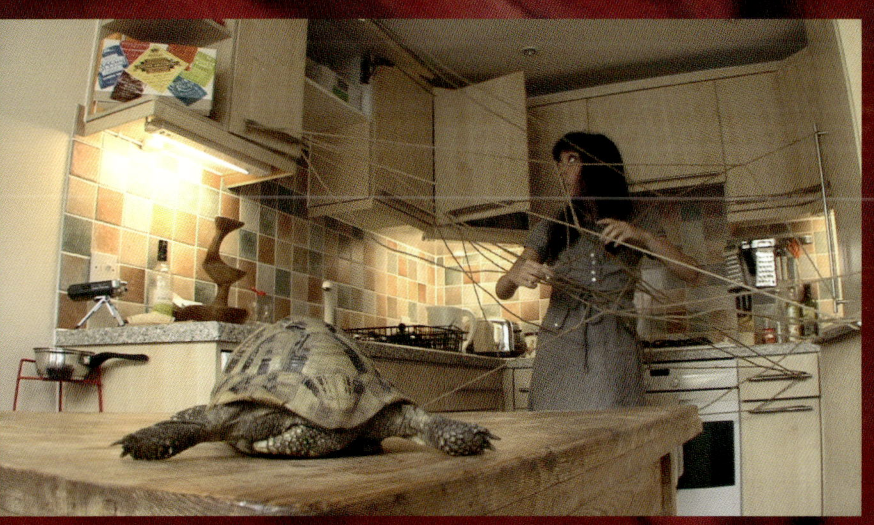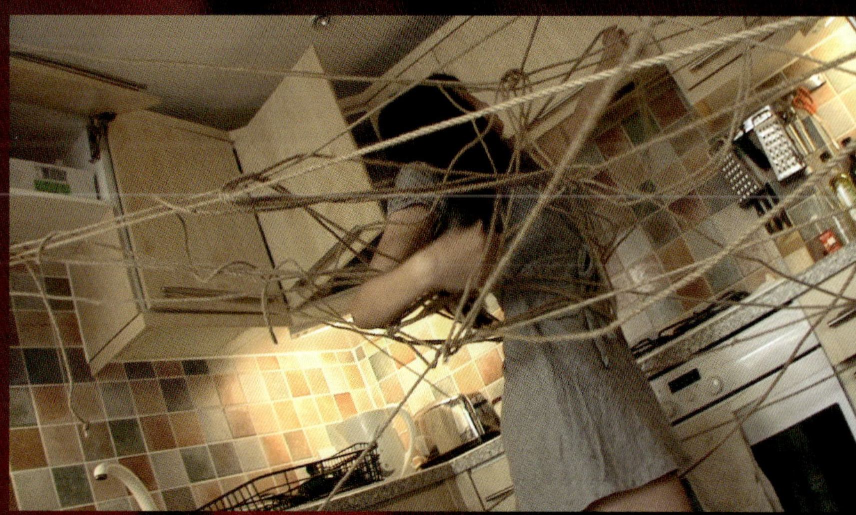

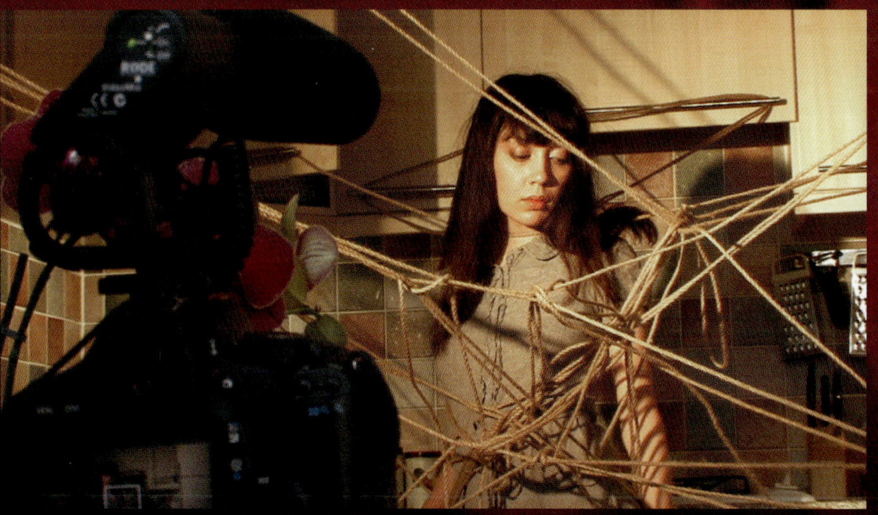

The whole movie was inspired by a Japanese film called 'Undo'.  Within this film there is a character who develops what her doctor strangely terms as 'obsessive knot tying syndrome'.  And as a result of this, she ties up just about everything.  This scene in the kitchen was inspired by that film.

Gestalta:  We used Beck's bedroom as our makeshift office so here is Becky on her computer and I've spent the last few months editing the film.

Rebecca:  The film was Gestalta's vision and I'm interested to see how it turns out. From what I've seen, it looks pretty neat.

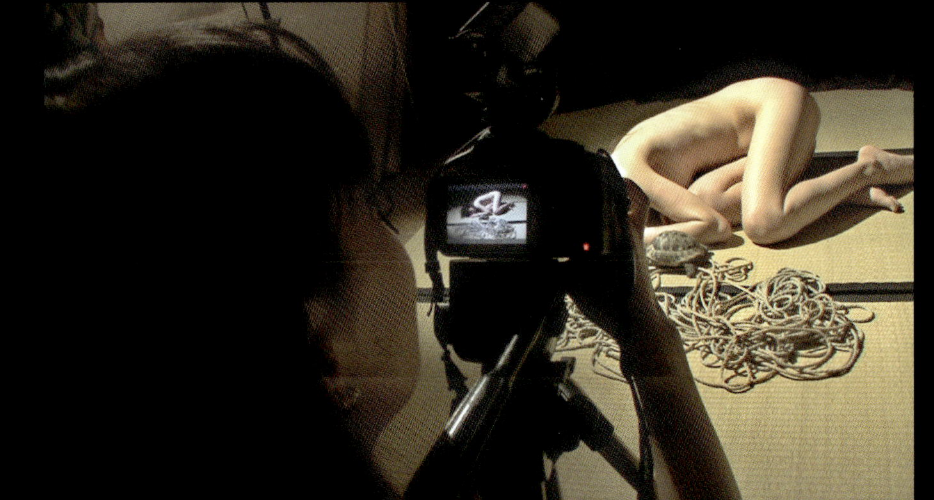

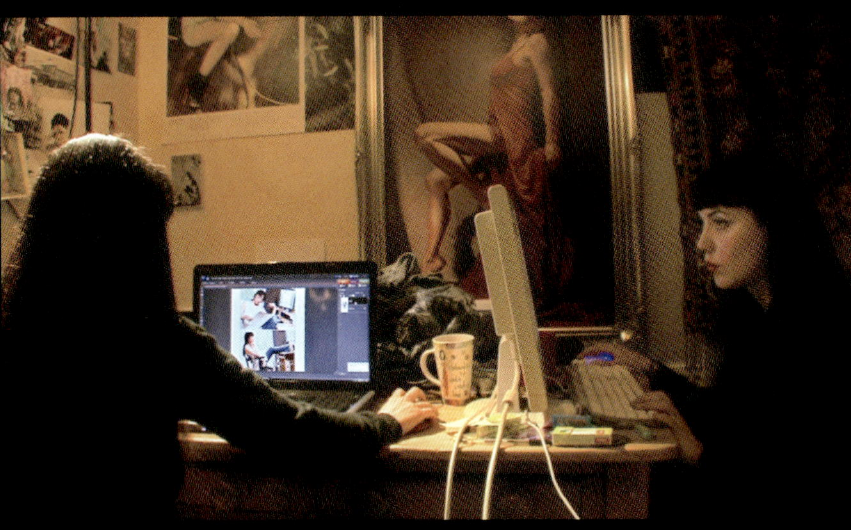

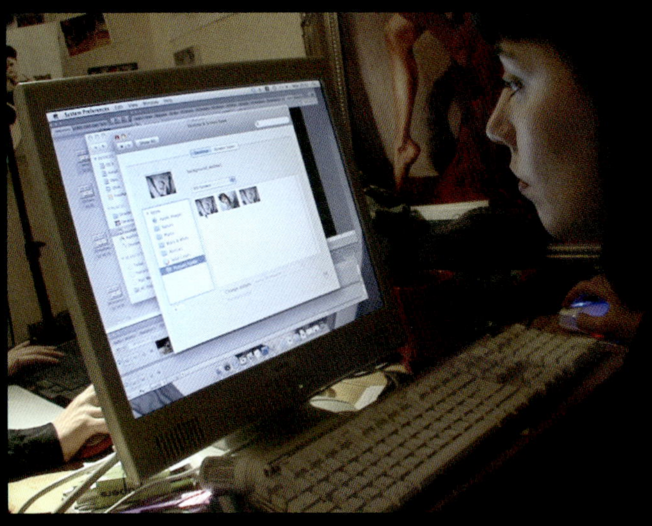

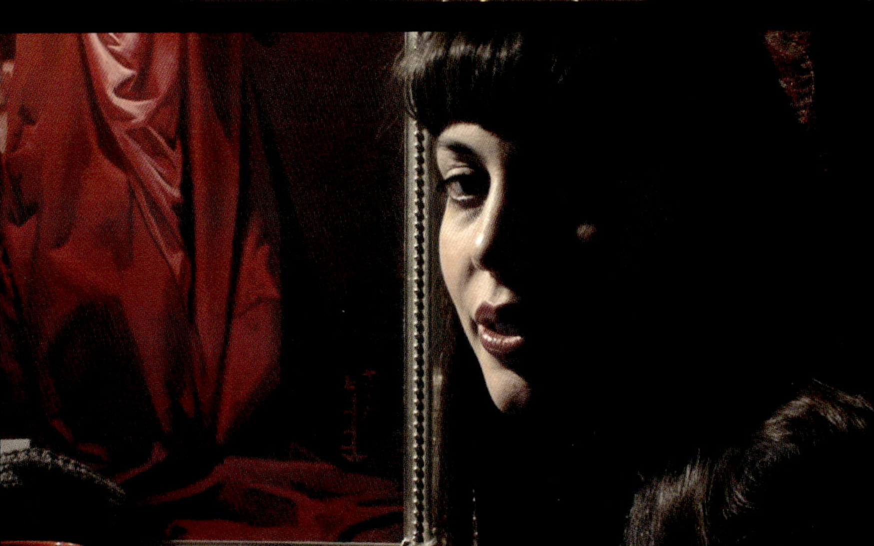

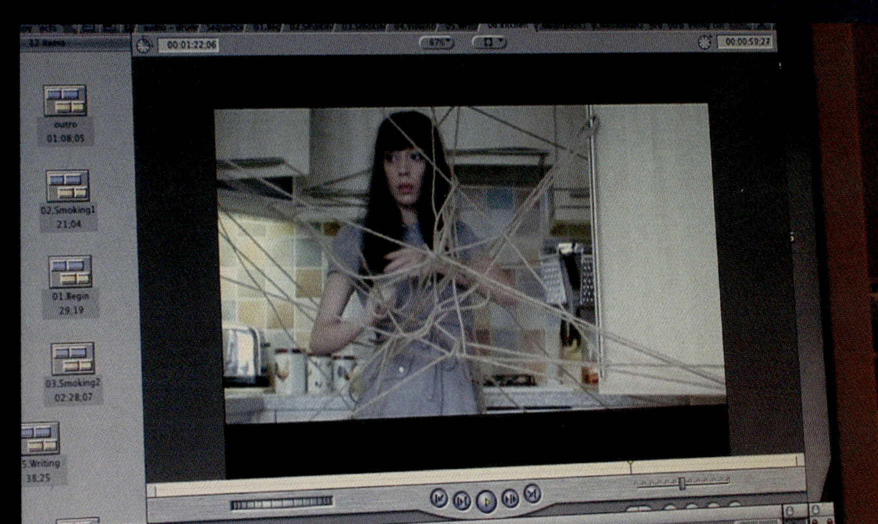

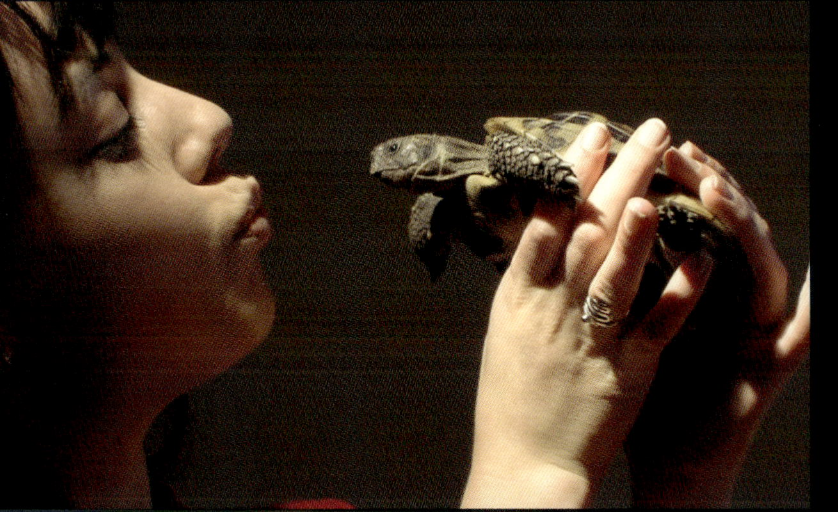

Rebecca:  I'd definitely be happy to do more wor[k]
involving rope and bondage and suspensions.  As
this was my first introduction to it, I didn't really
know whether I would find that I had any sort of,
like, rope bondage fetish.  And it turns out that I
don't really.  I'm pretty neutral about it.  But
artistically it's a very interesting medium.

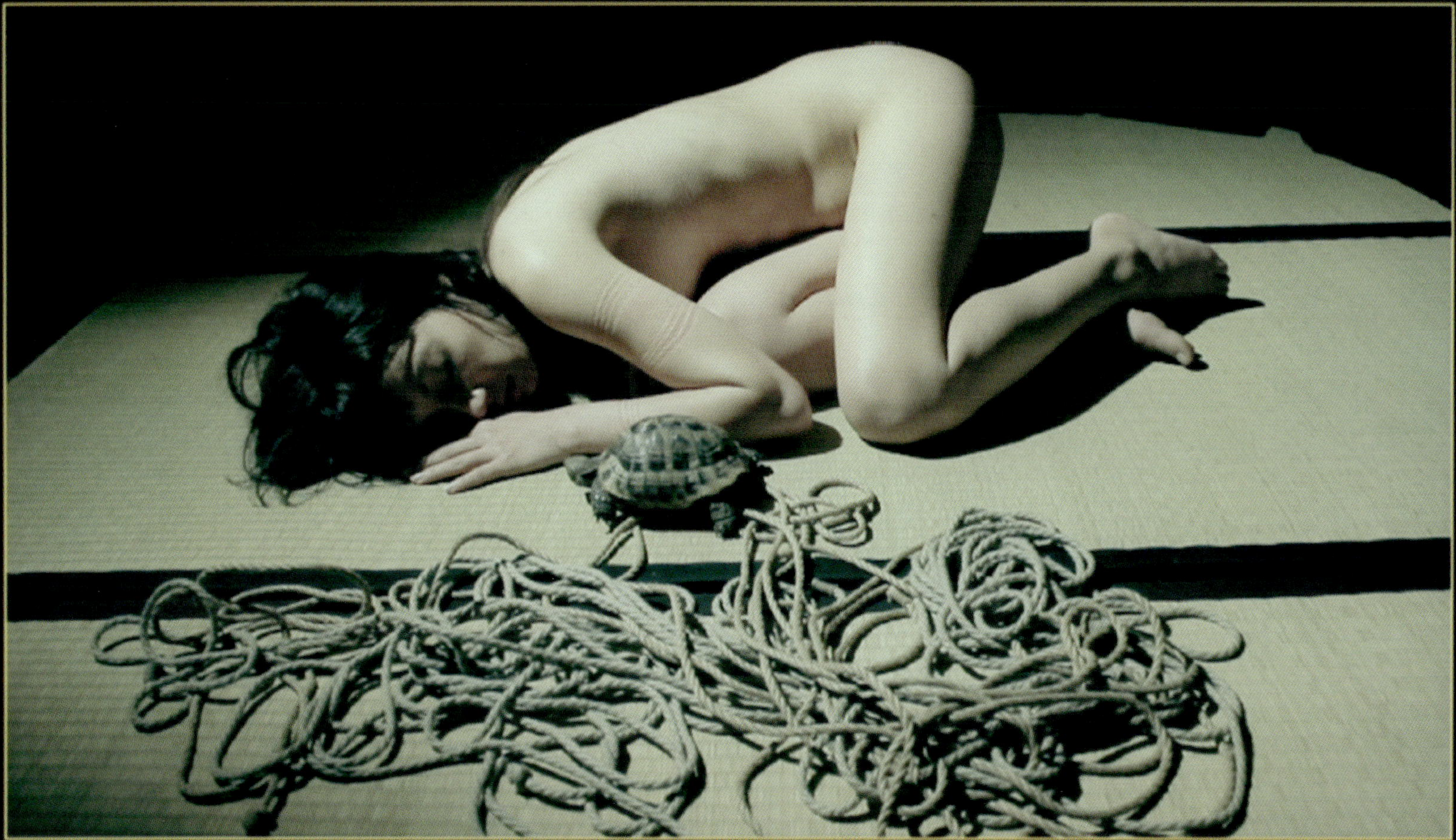

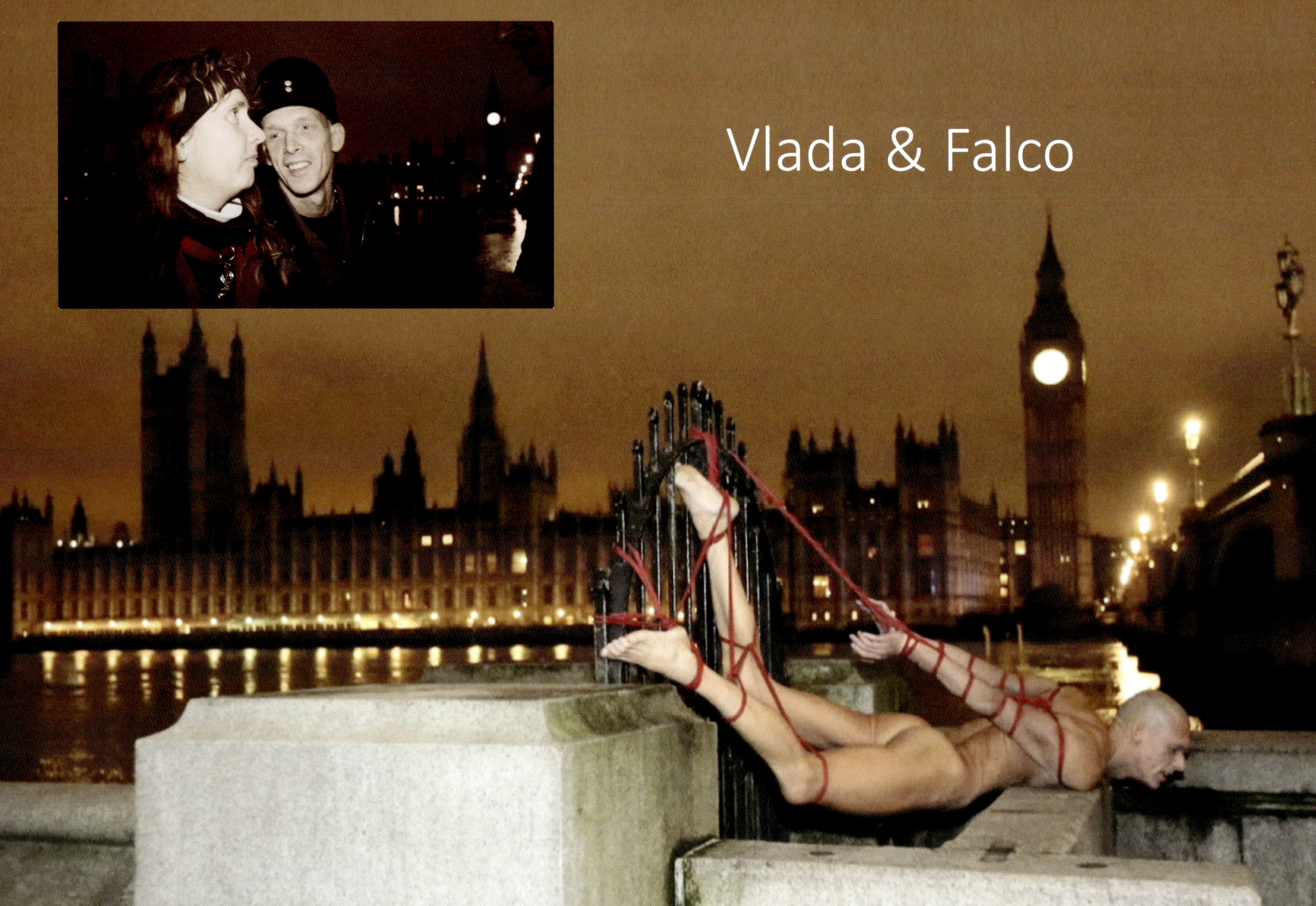

# Vlada & Falco

**The 2012 London bondage festival attracted enthusiasts from around the world including Vlada and Falco from Russia.  One late night in London I went with Jon to accompany them. They choose amazing places to practice their Kinbaku and wanted to do gorilla photoshoots with Vlada tying and taking photographs.**

Vlada:  Because it's a famous place, we make beautiful pictures.  But then this place is already beautiful and together is more beautiful.

Falco:  It's some extreme.  Maybe it's a new style of bondage. It's our style.

Murakawa:  It was very late and very cold.

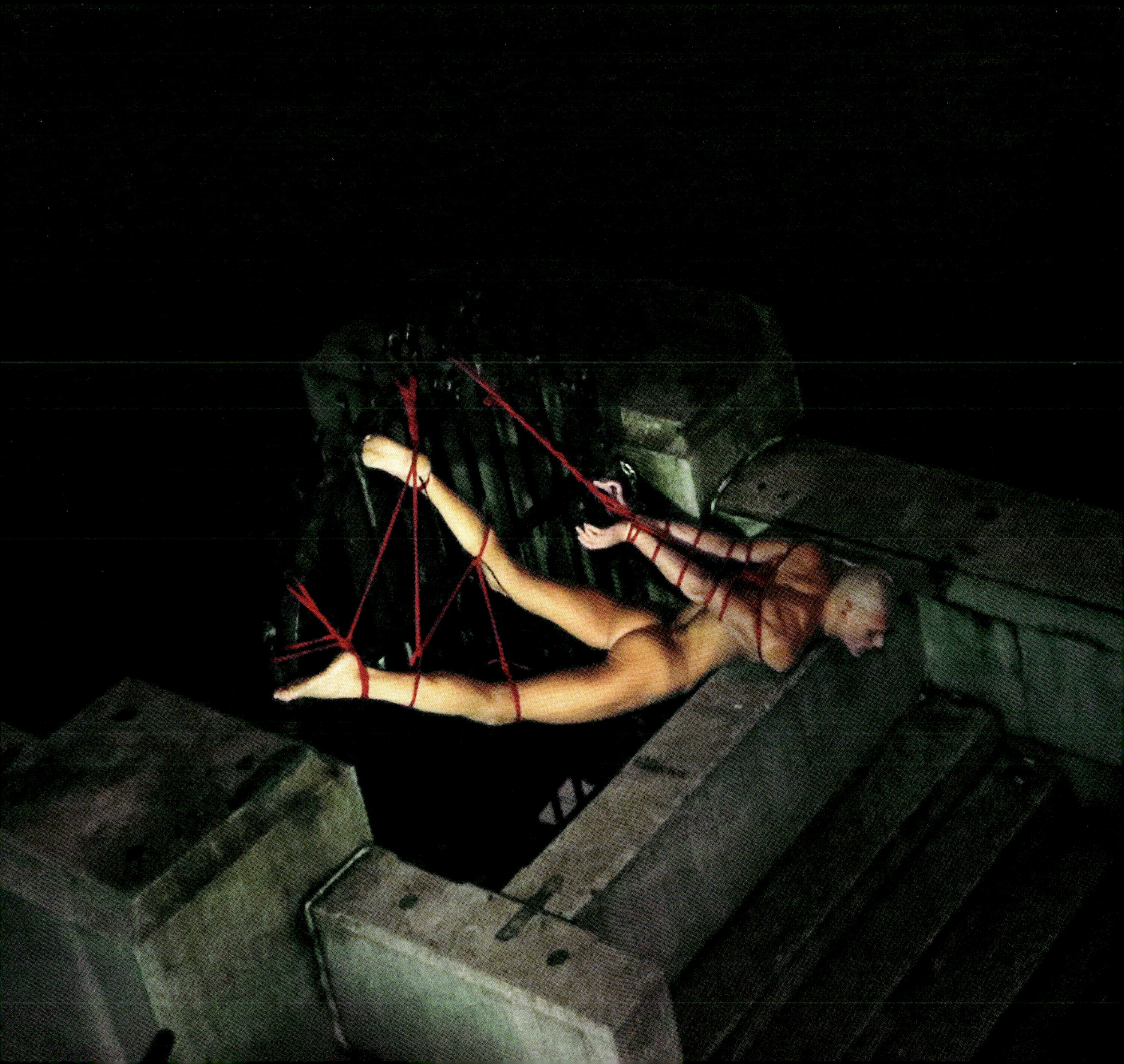

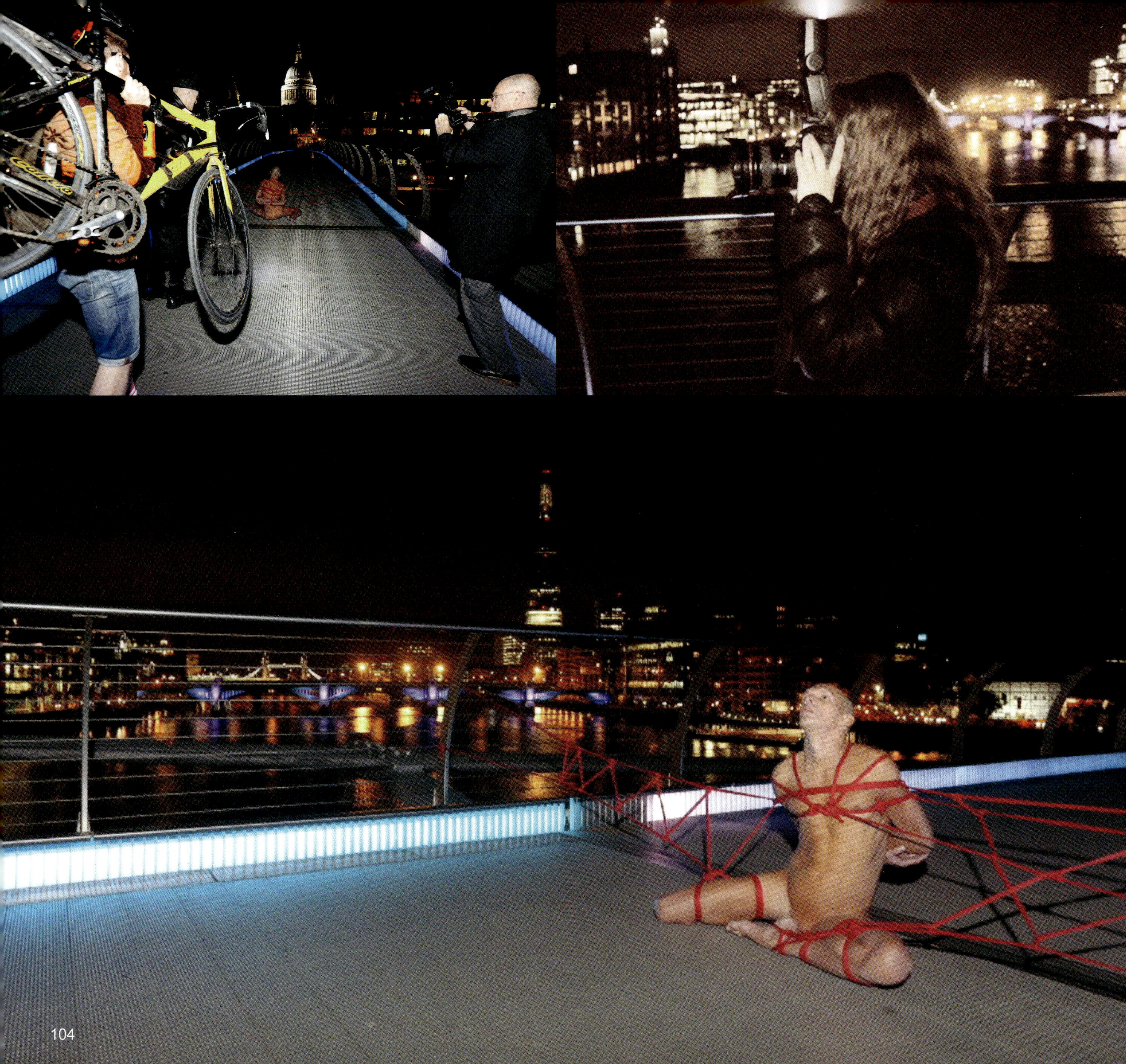

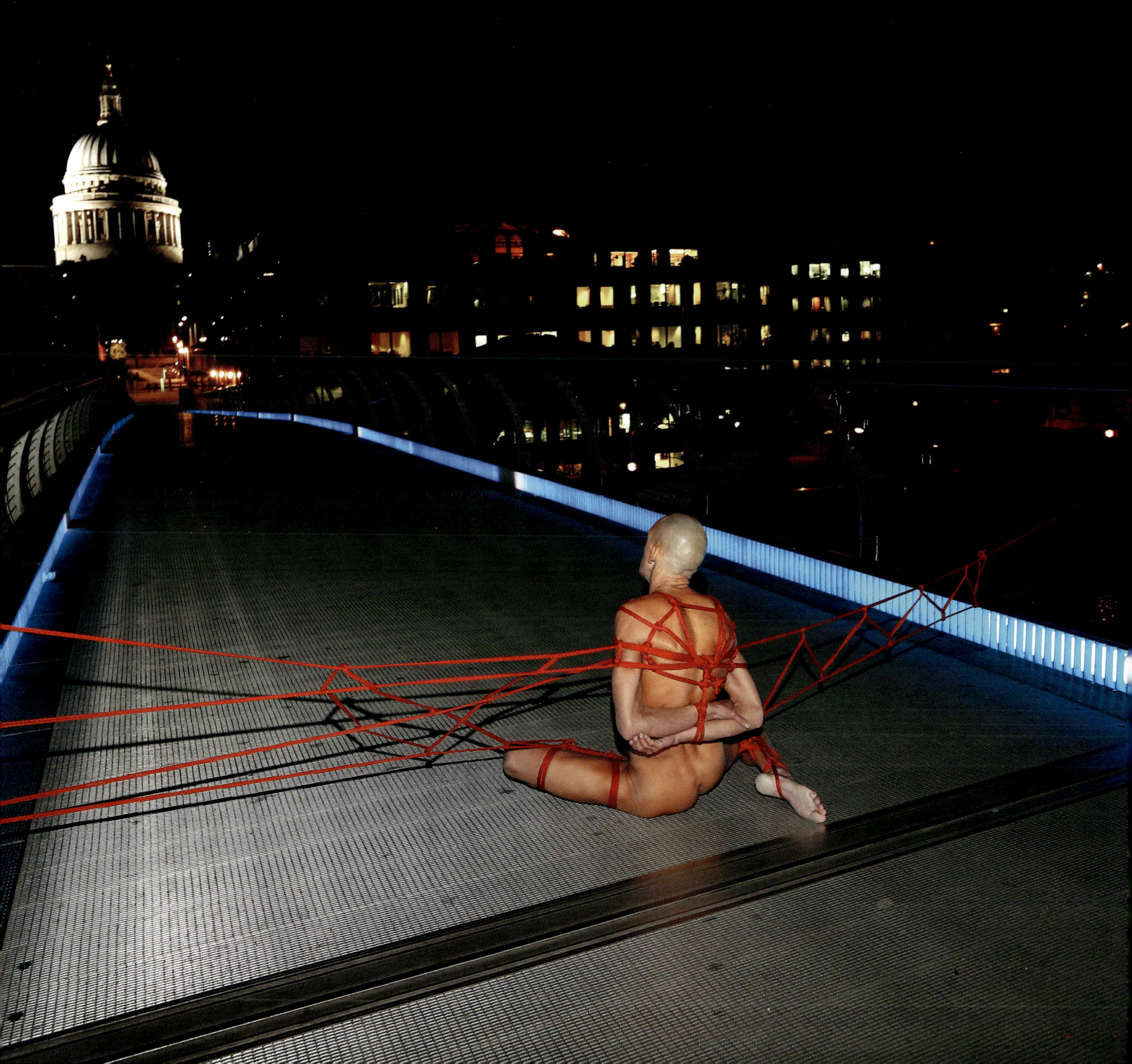

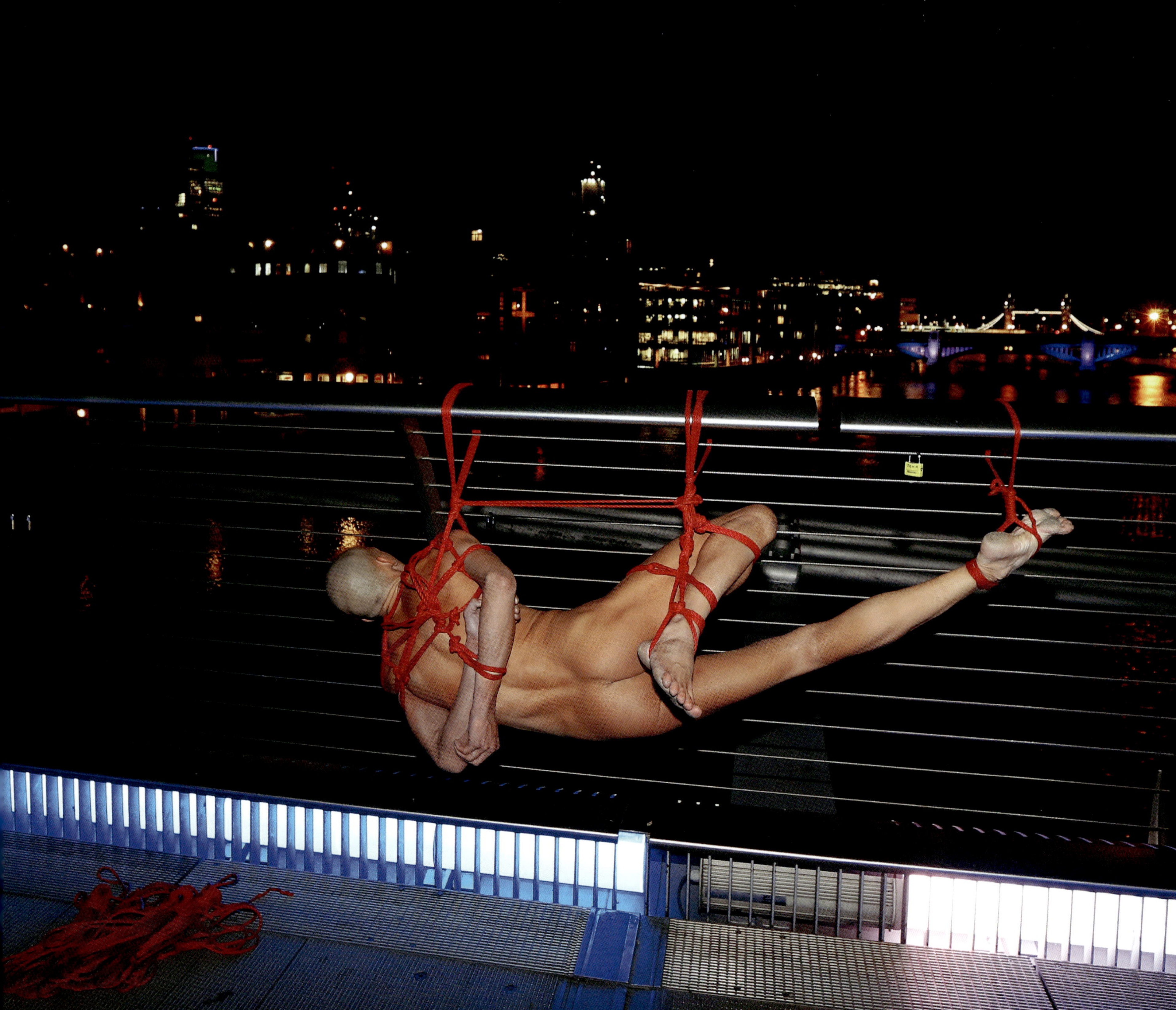

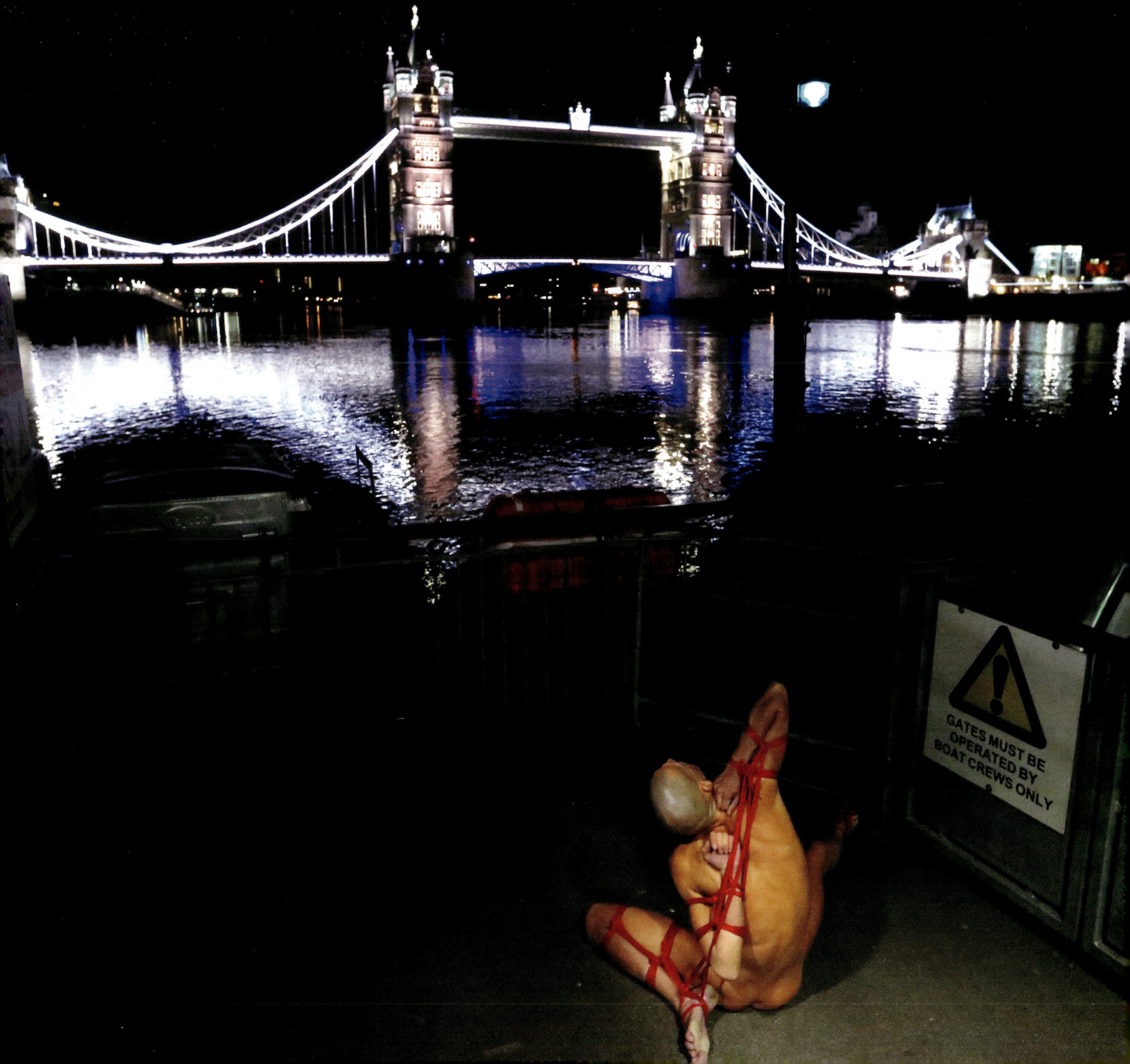
GATES MUST BE
OPERATED BY
BOAT CREWS ONLY

# Amy Morgan & Scarlet Rose

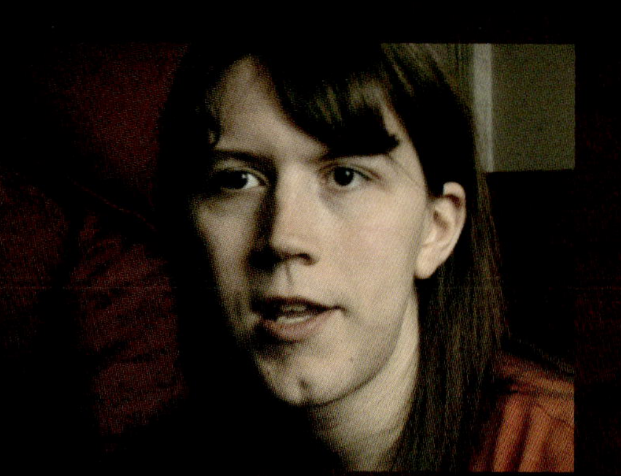

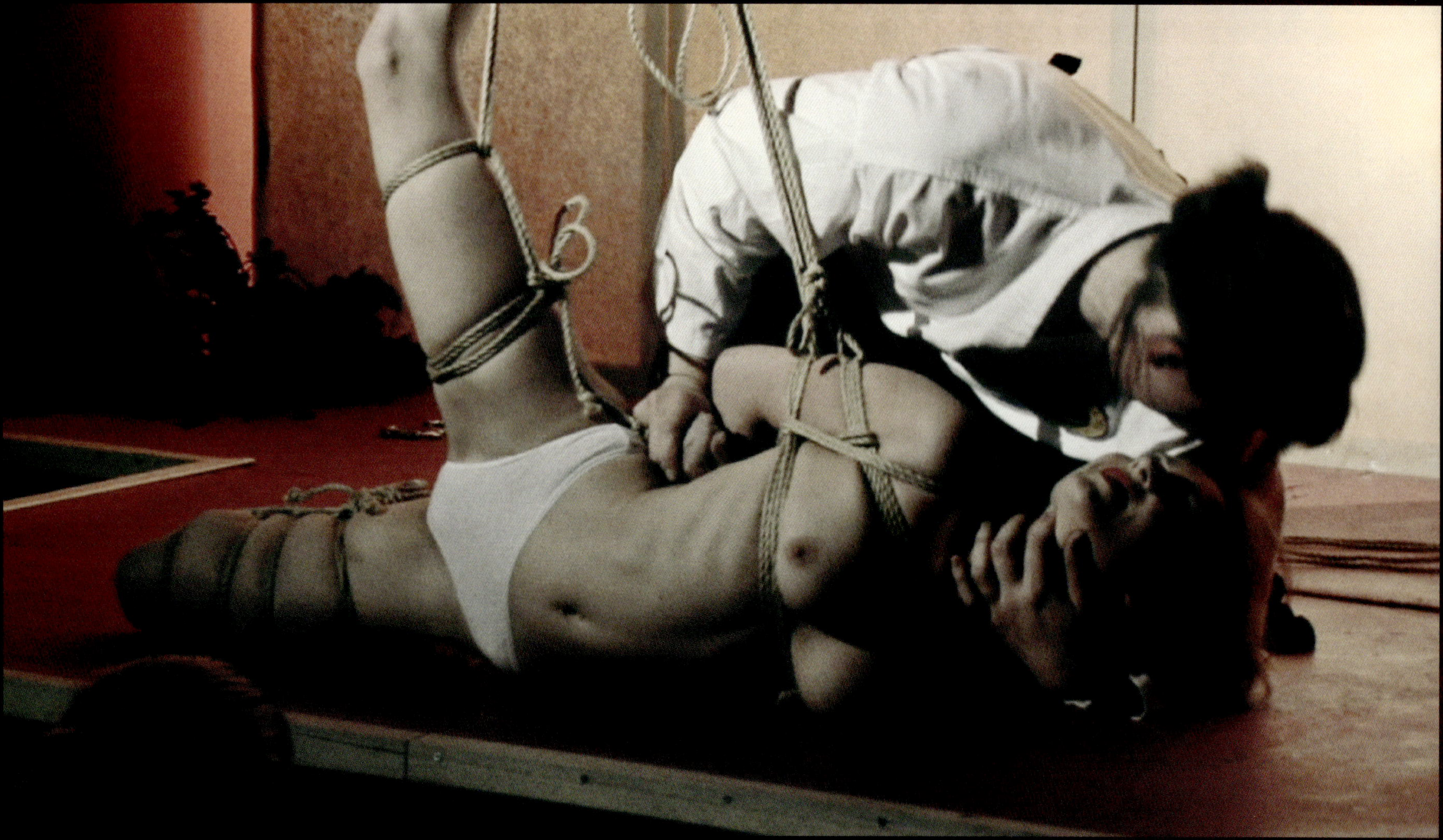

**Like Vlada and Falco, Amy Morgan came to London for the 2012 bondage festival held at the Resistance Gallery.**

Amy Morgan:  Coming here to the London festival was my first time outside of the United States really looking for rope and looking for experiences.  Rope for me is an extra level of intimacy where you're taking string and binding someone and restraining them.  And you have to be really close to them which provides a new level of intimacy.

When I get up on stage I just go with it.  I already know my technique.  It's well practiced  and I just think about the things that I am creating; not just for the audience but for me and the person I am tying.

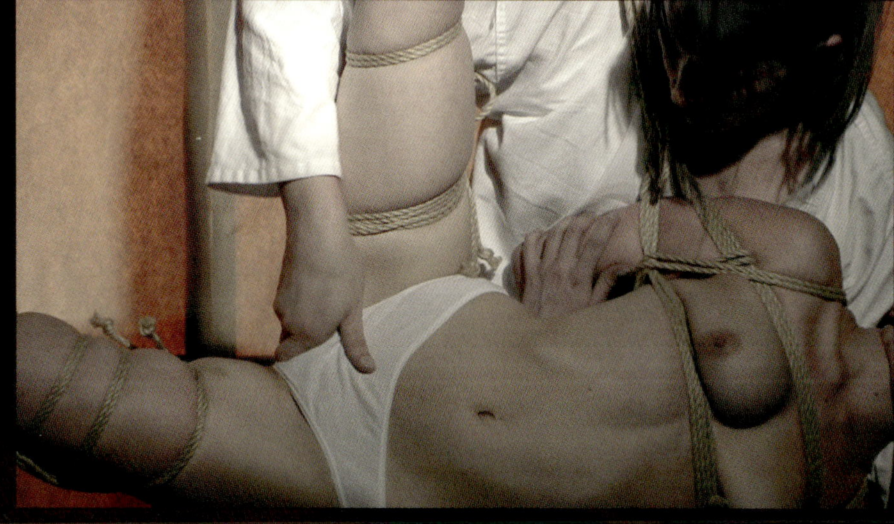

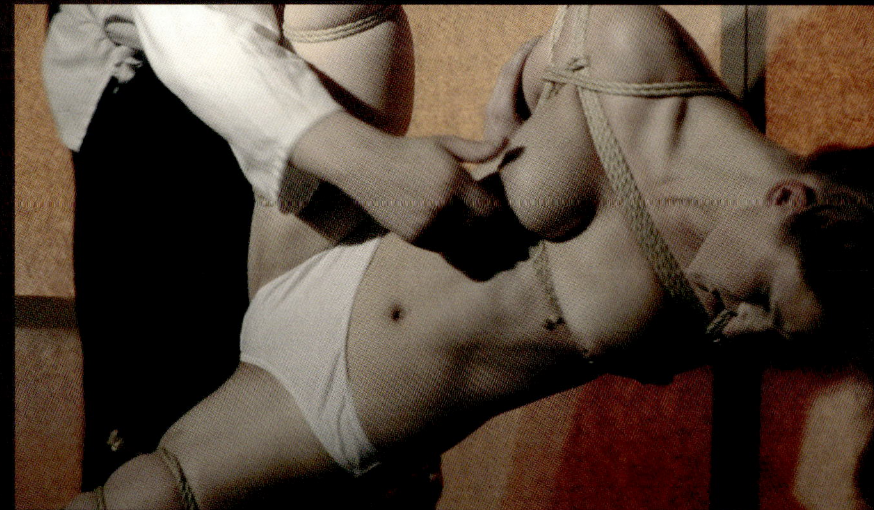

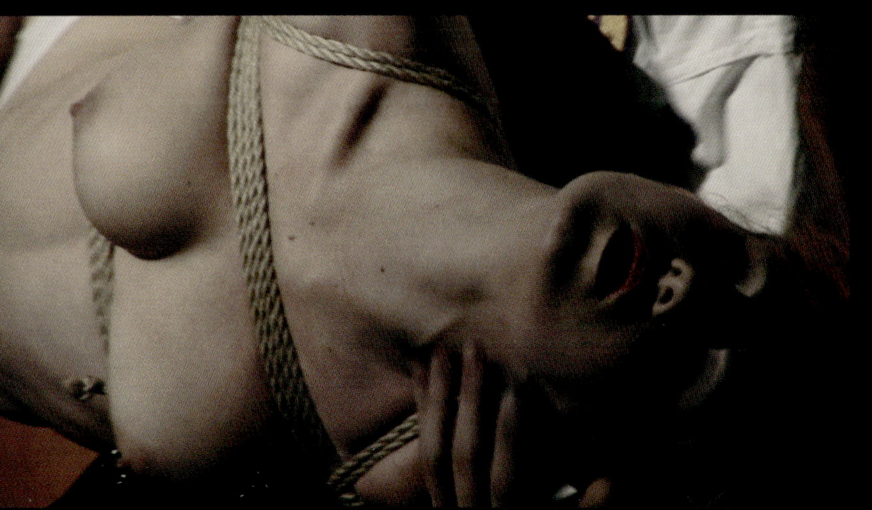

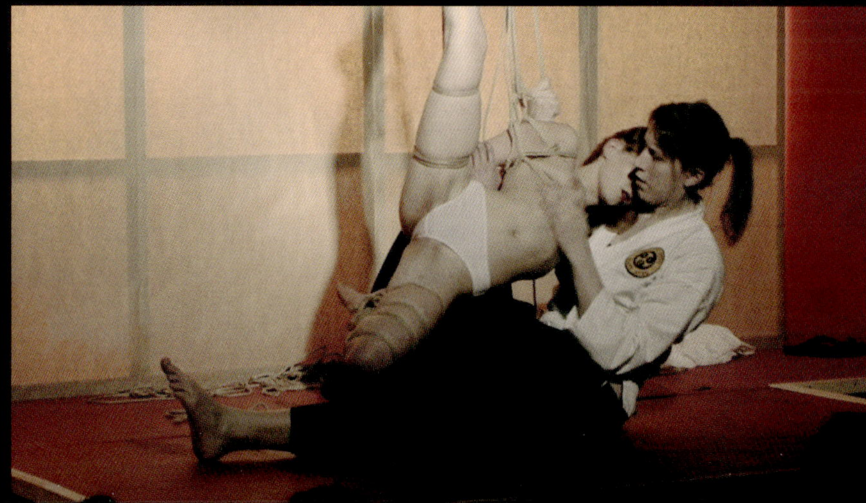

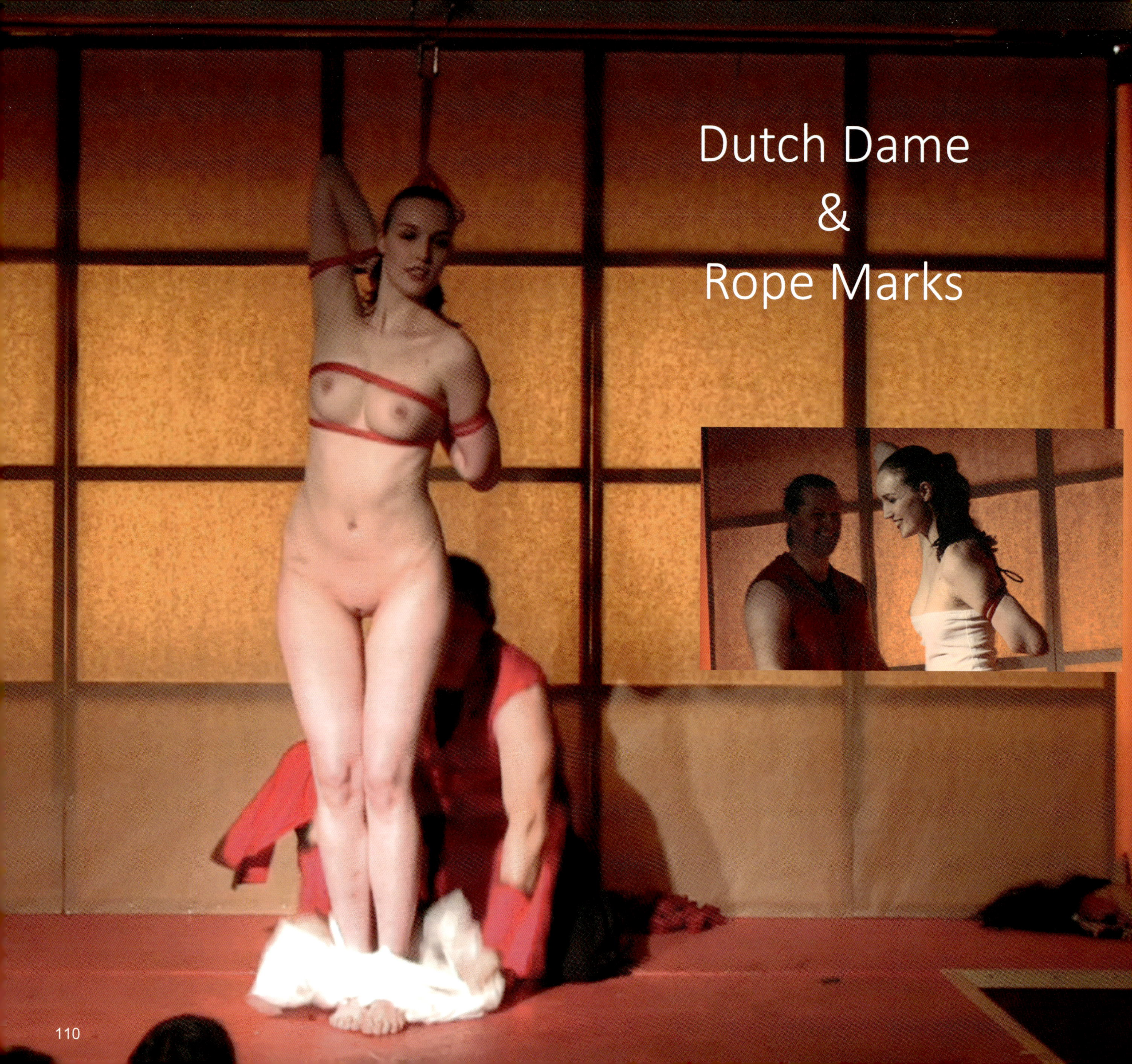

Dutch Dame
&
Rope Marks

**Dutch Dame and Rope Marks
performed at the London festival in
2012 and 2013.**

Amy Morgan:  The performance with
Rope Marks and Dutch Dame was really
fantastic.  When he ripped that dress
off and she was fully nude and exposed,
it was so erotic and utterly different
from the other performances that I had
seen.

The aerobics that she was able to bring
out  were utterly amazing.

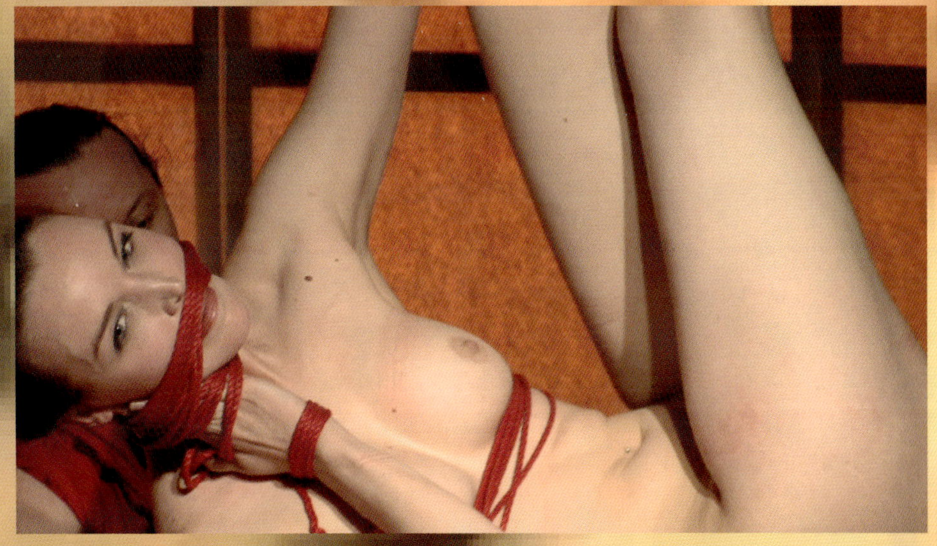

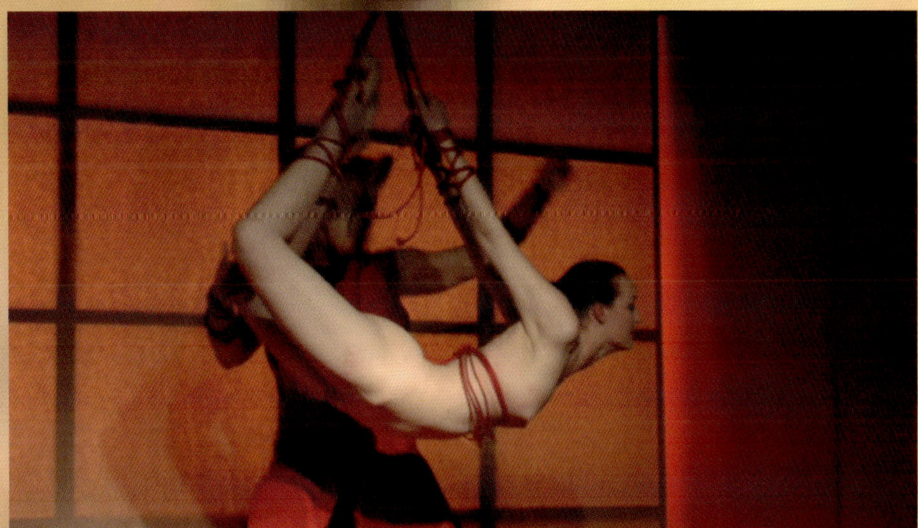

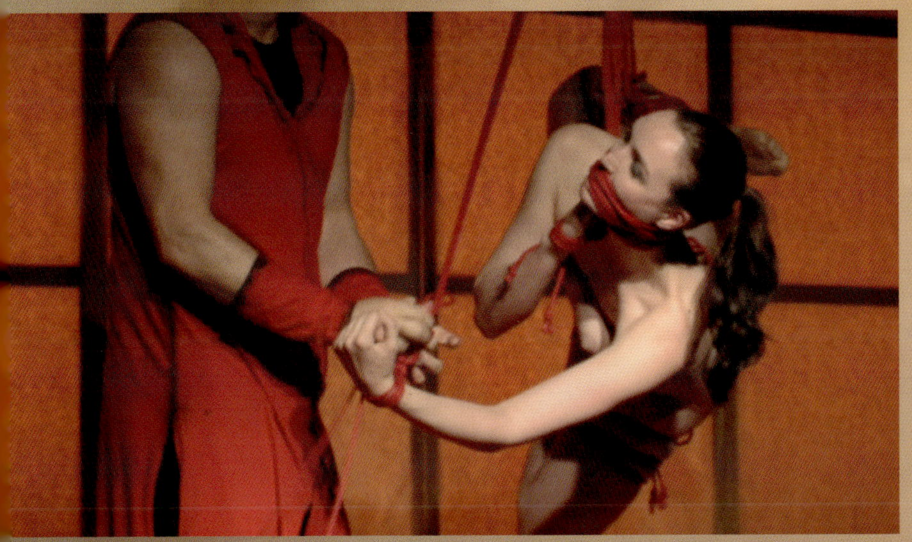

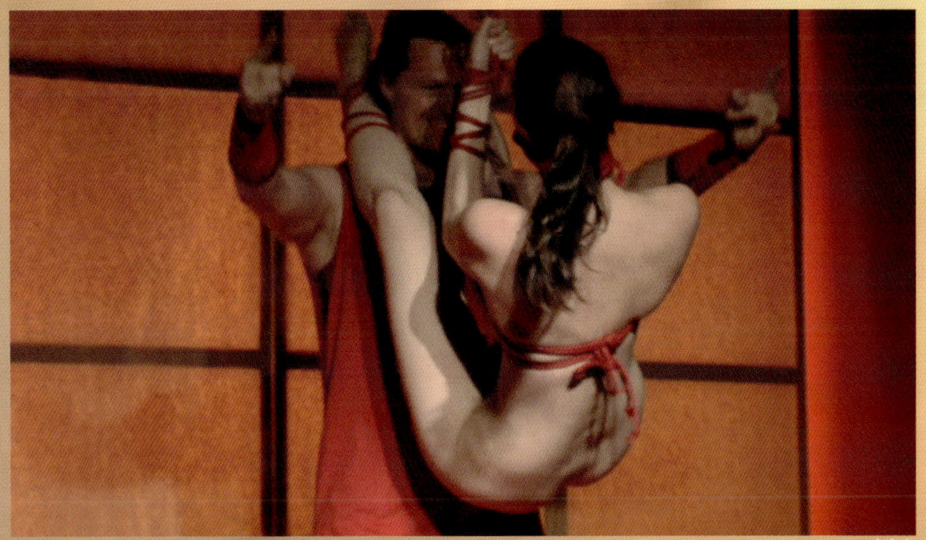

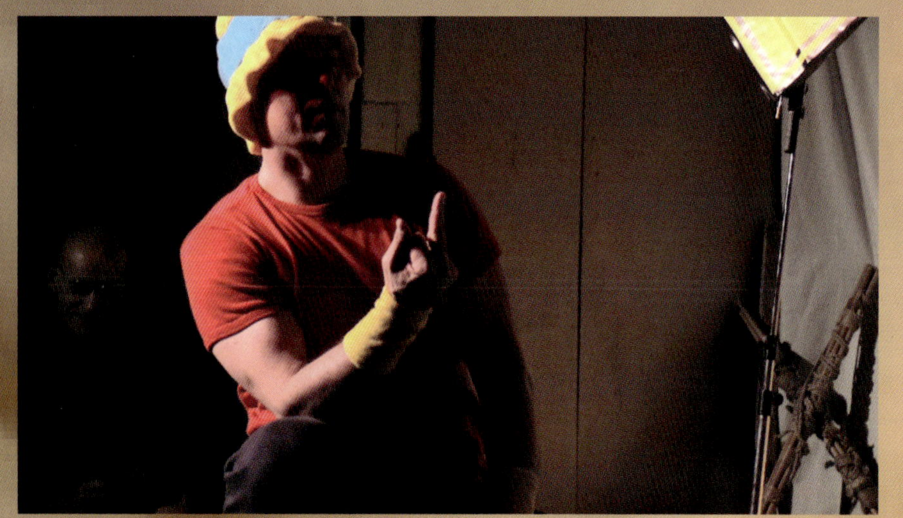
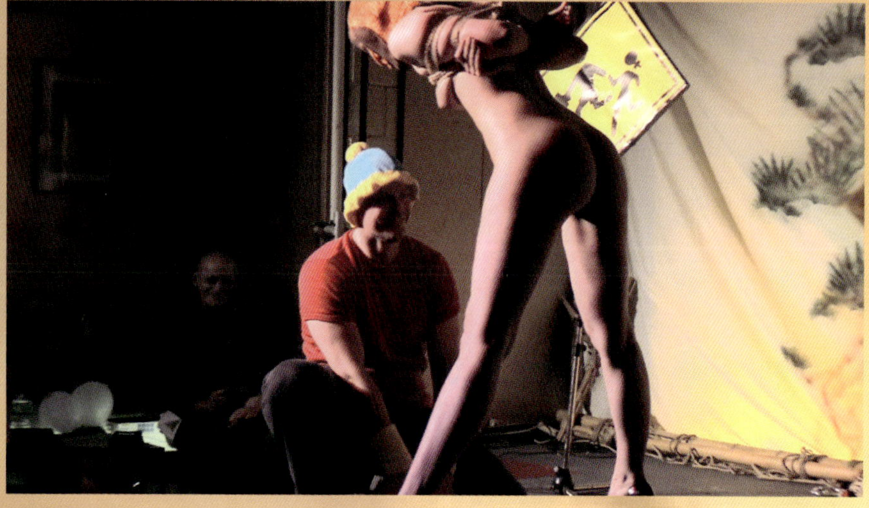

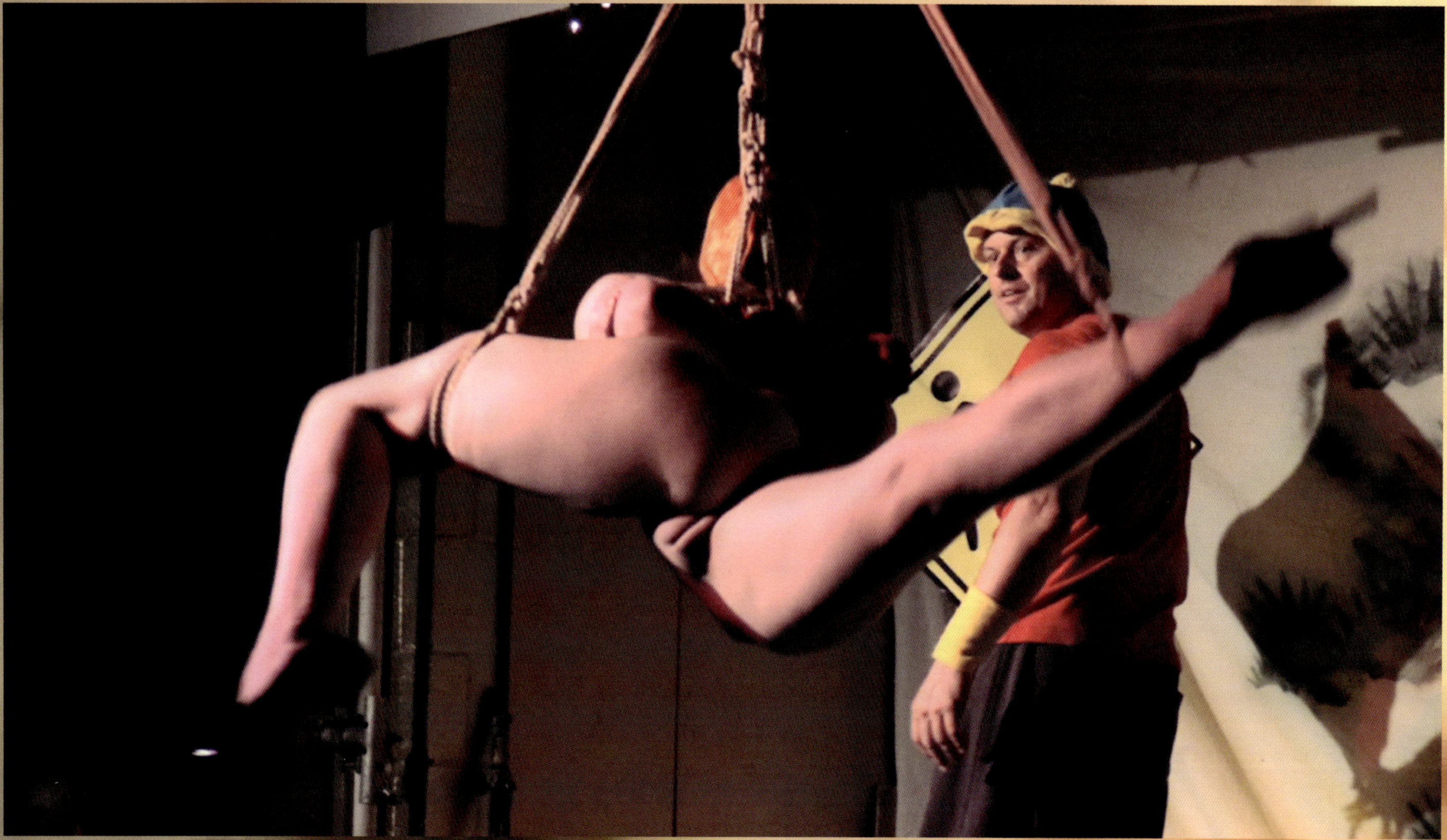

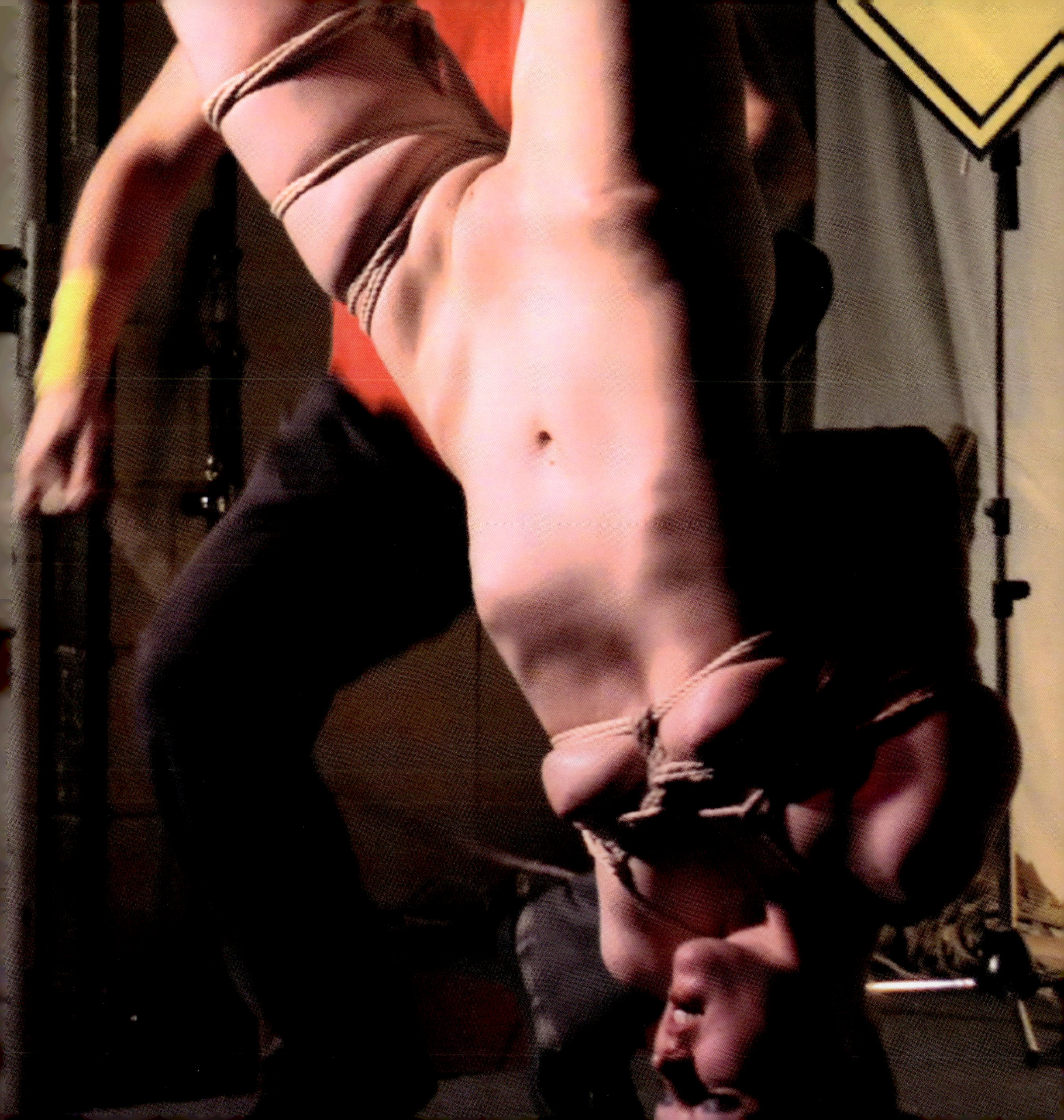

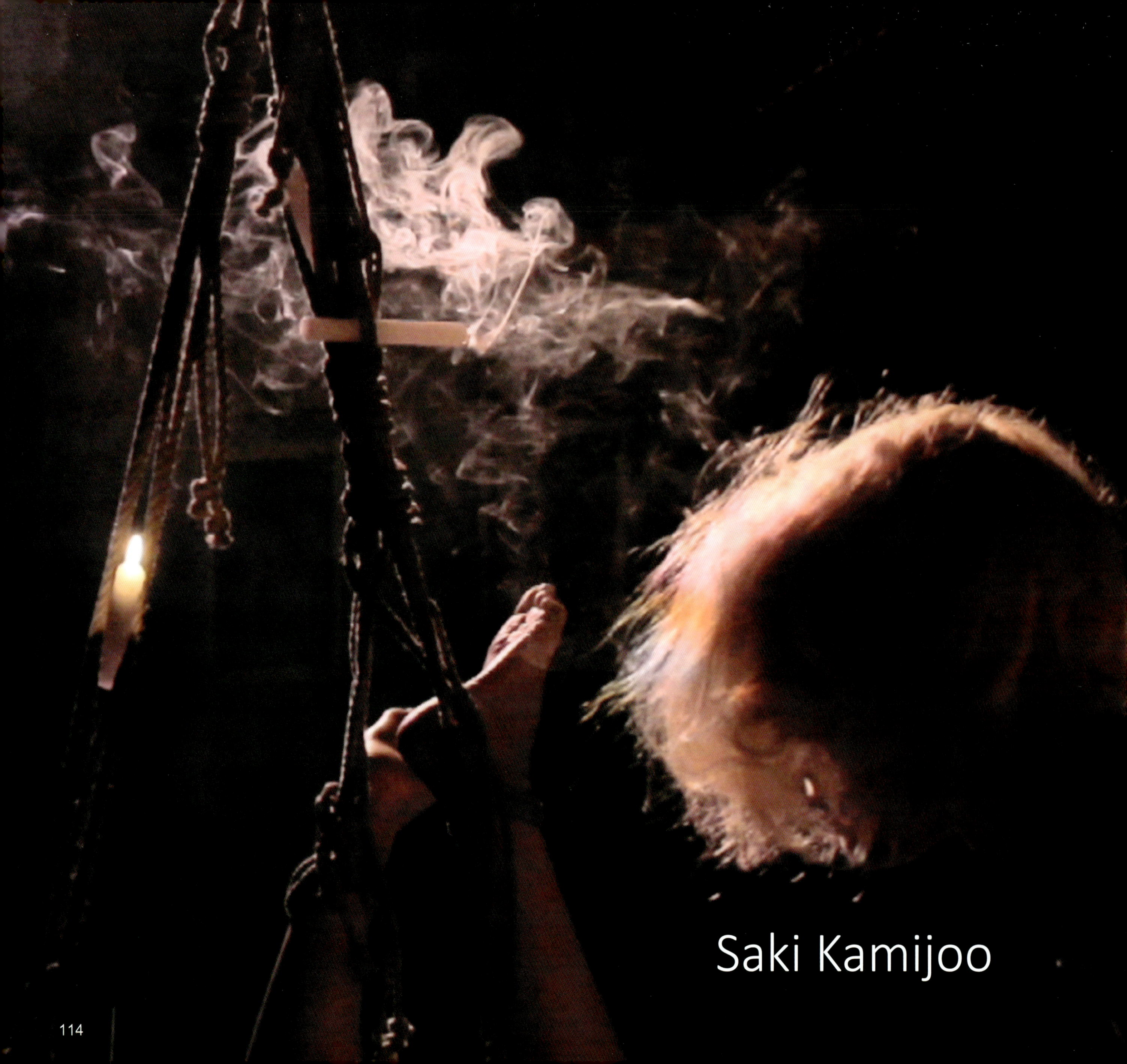
Saki Kamijoo

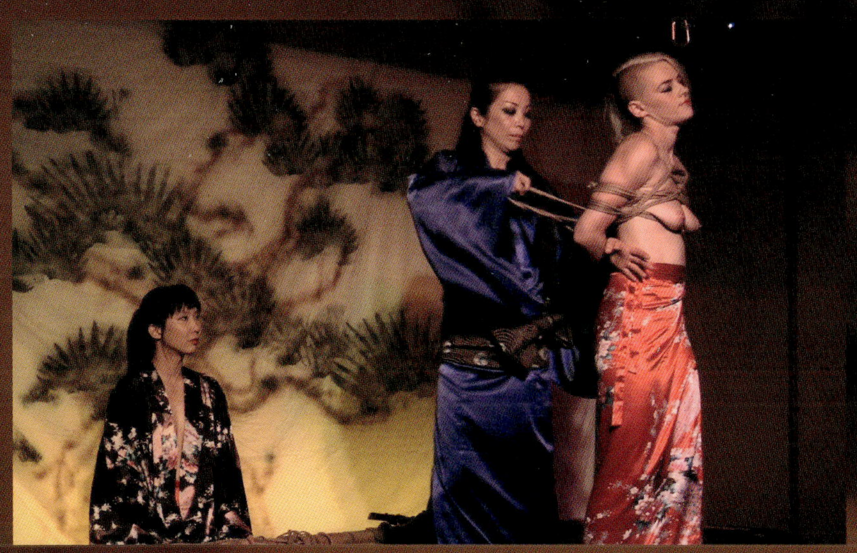 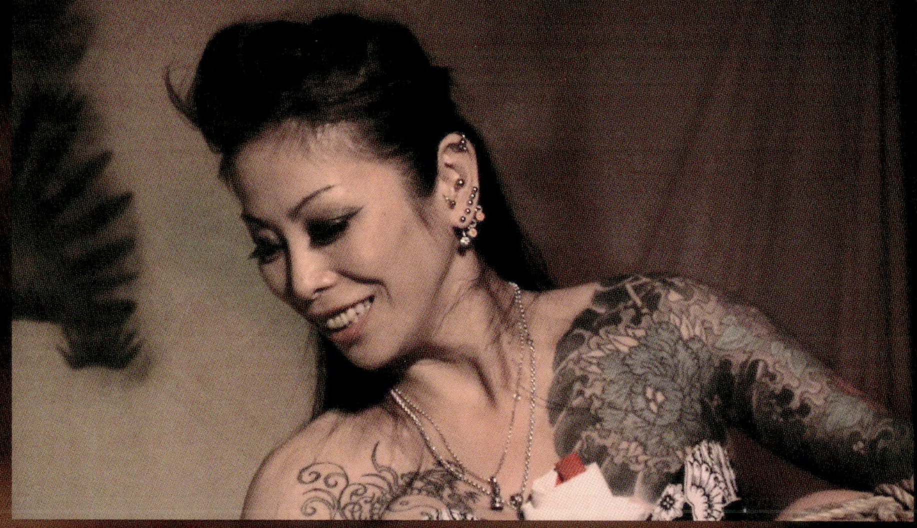

Saki Kamijoo is a well known rope bondage performer from Japan.  In the 2013 London festival she performed with Nancy Wing and Skinny Redhead.

Saki's style is fast and furious with a special way of dominating her models.  Her long leather whip is used with precision, which included extinguishing the candles at the end of the performance.

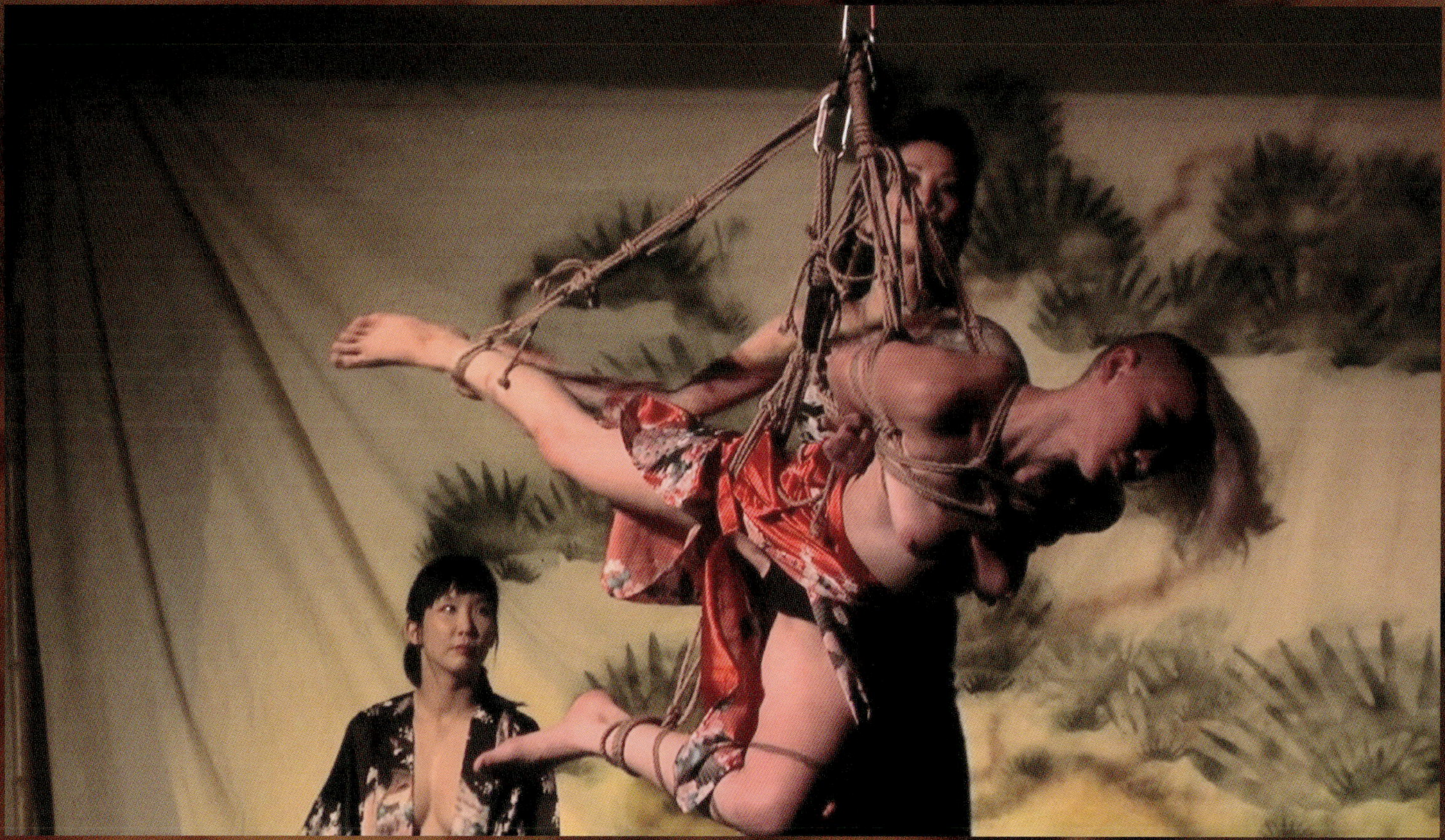

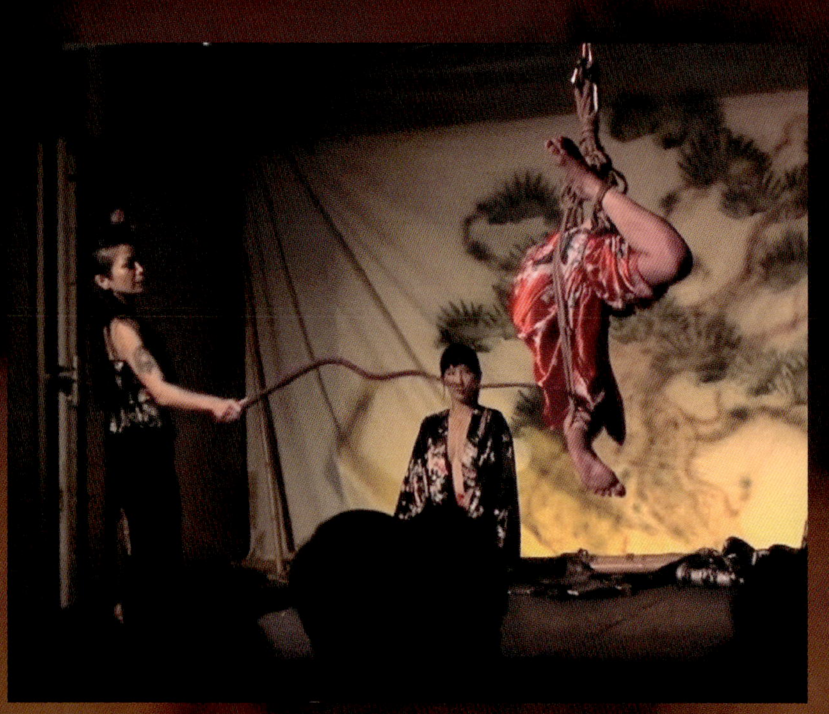
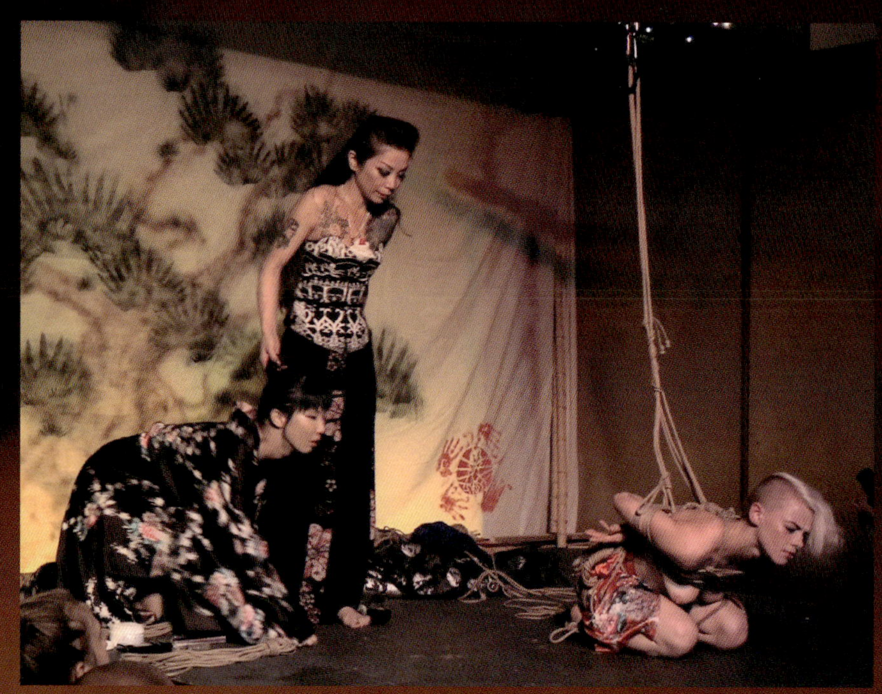

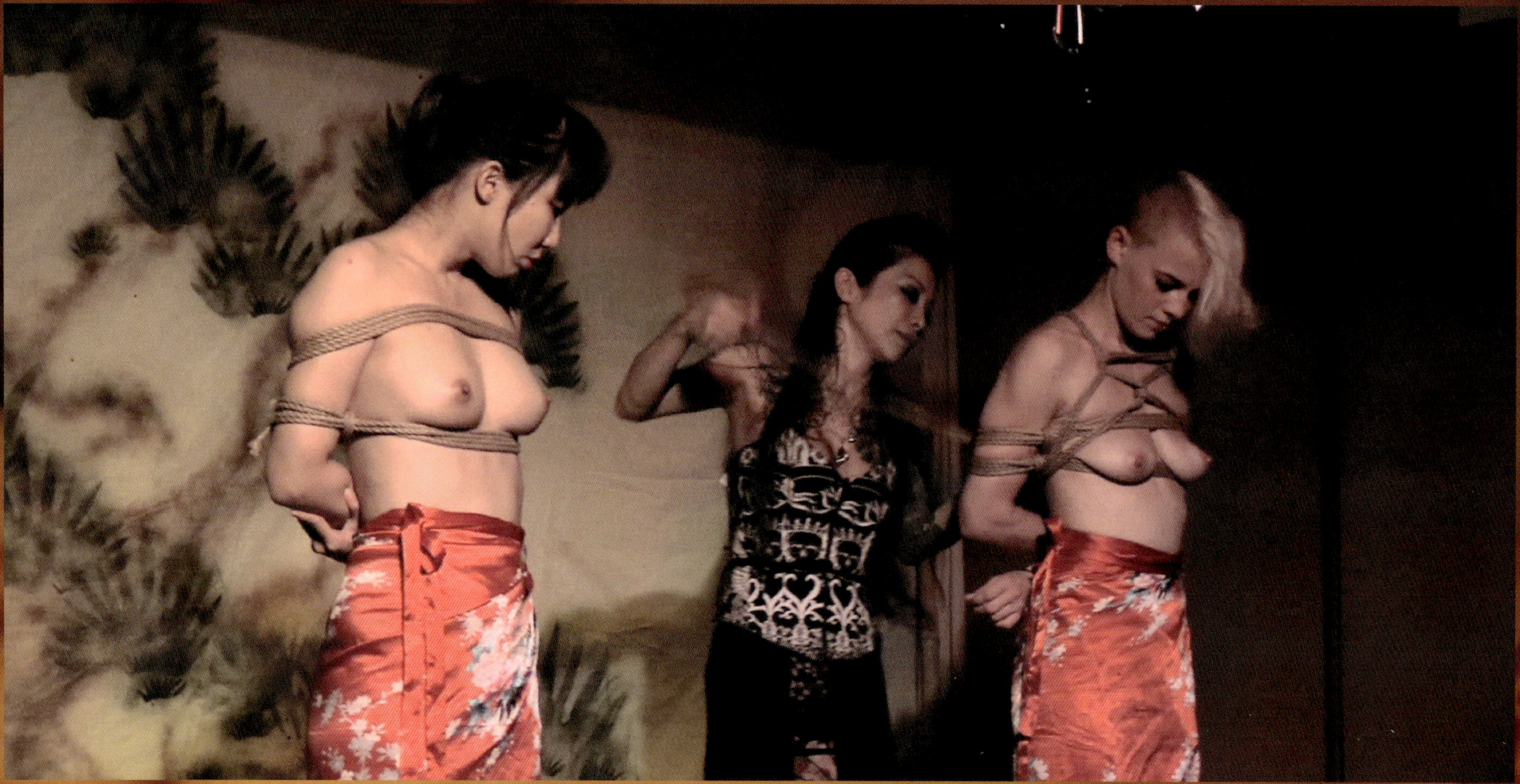

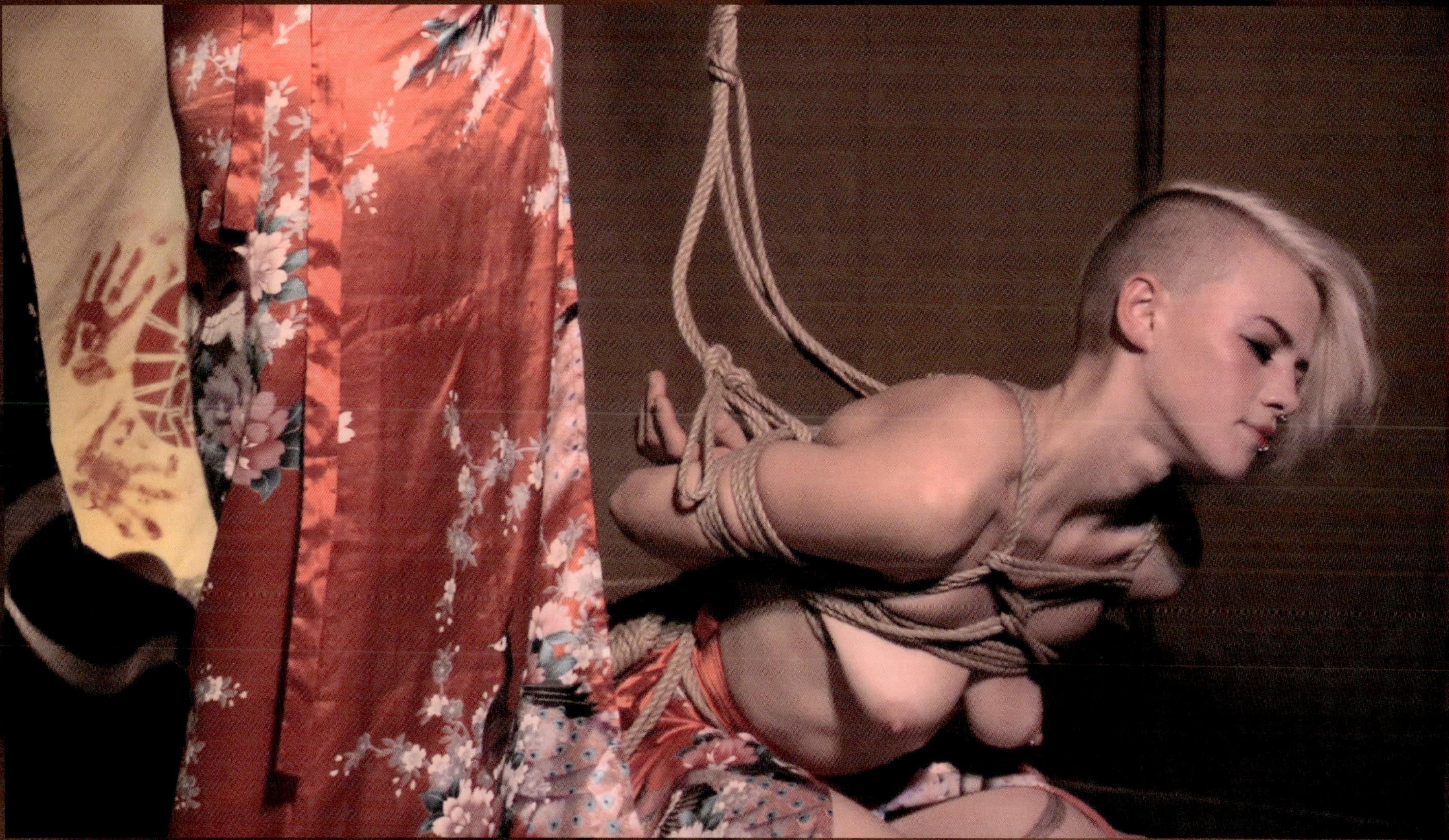

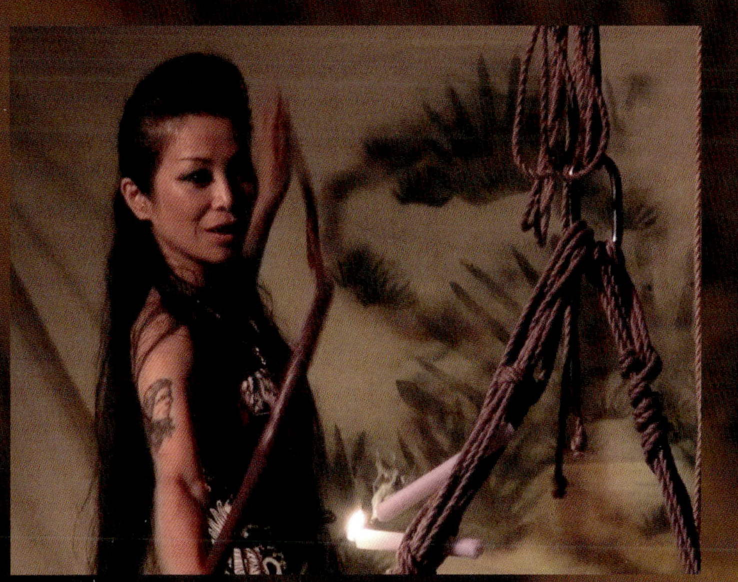

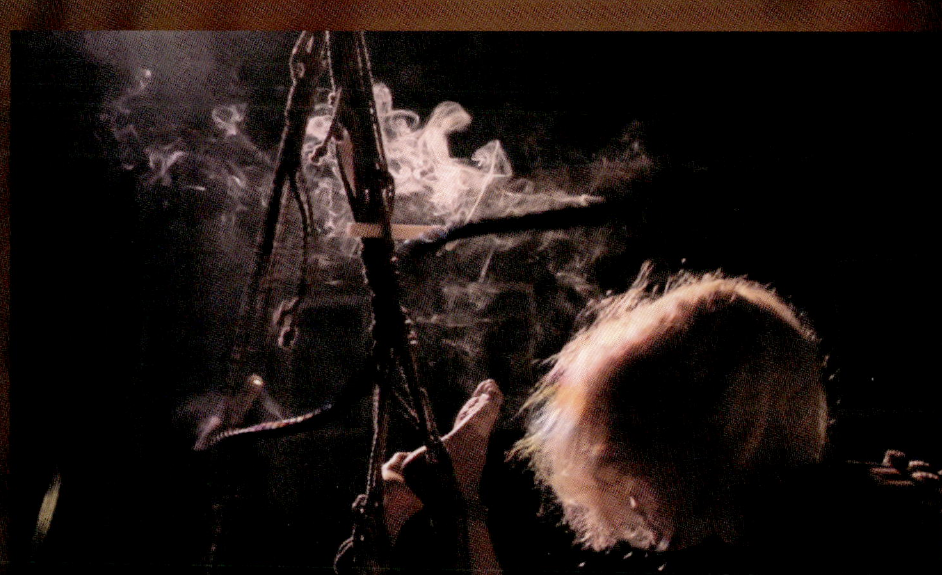

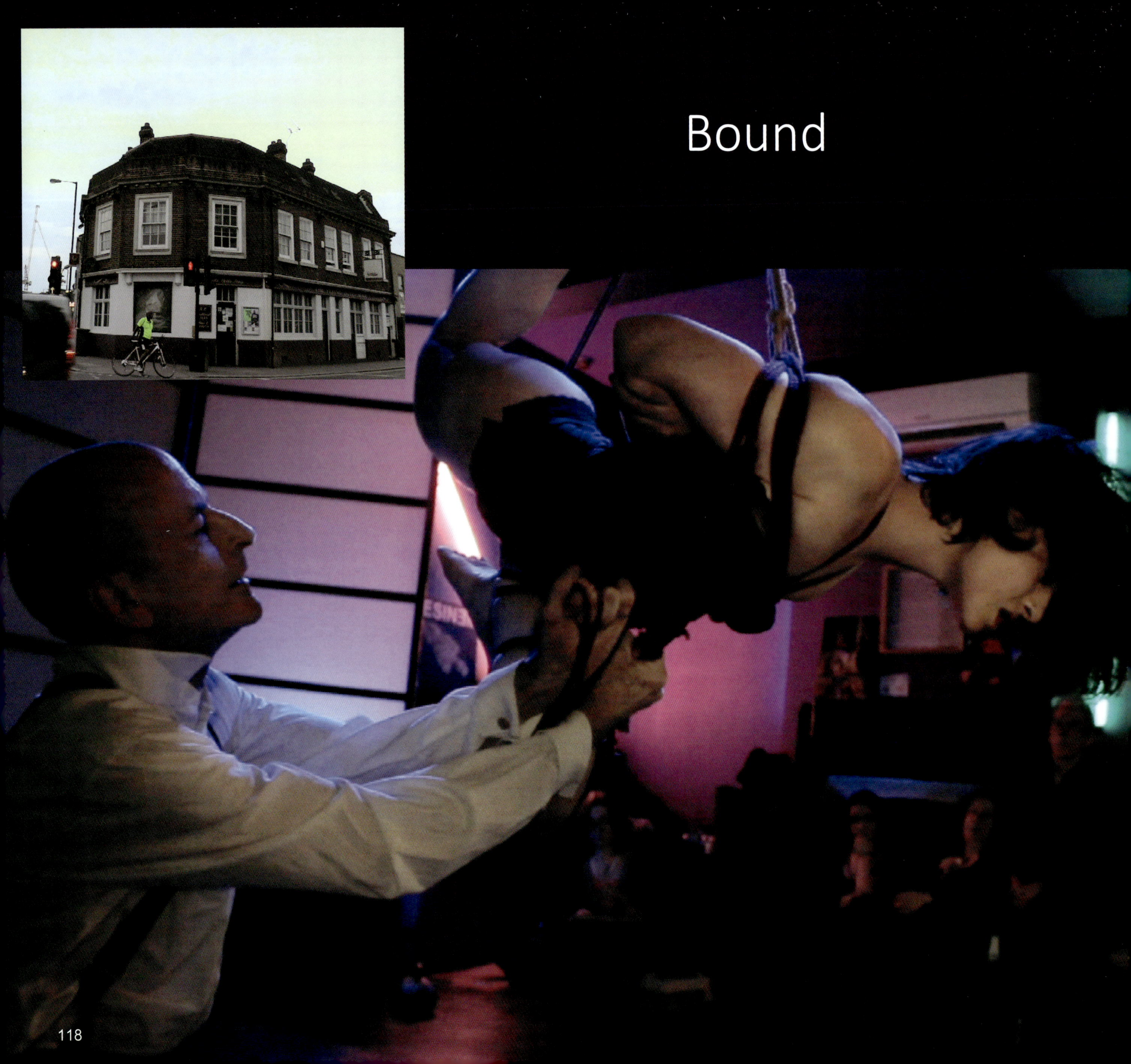

# Bound

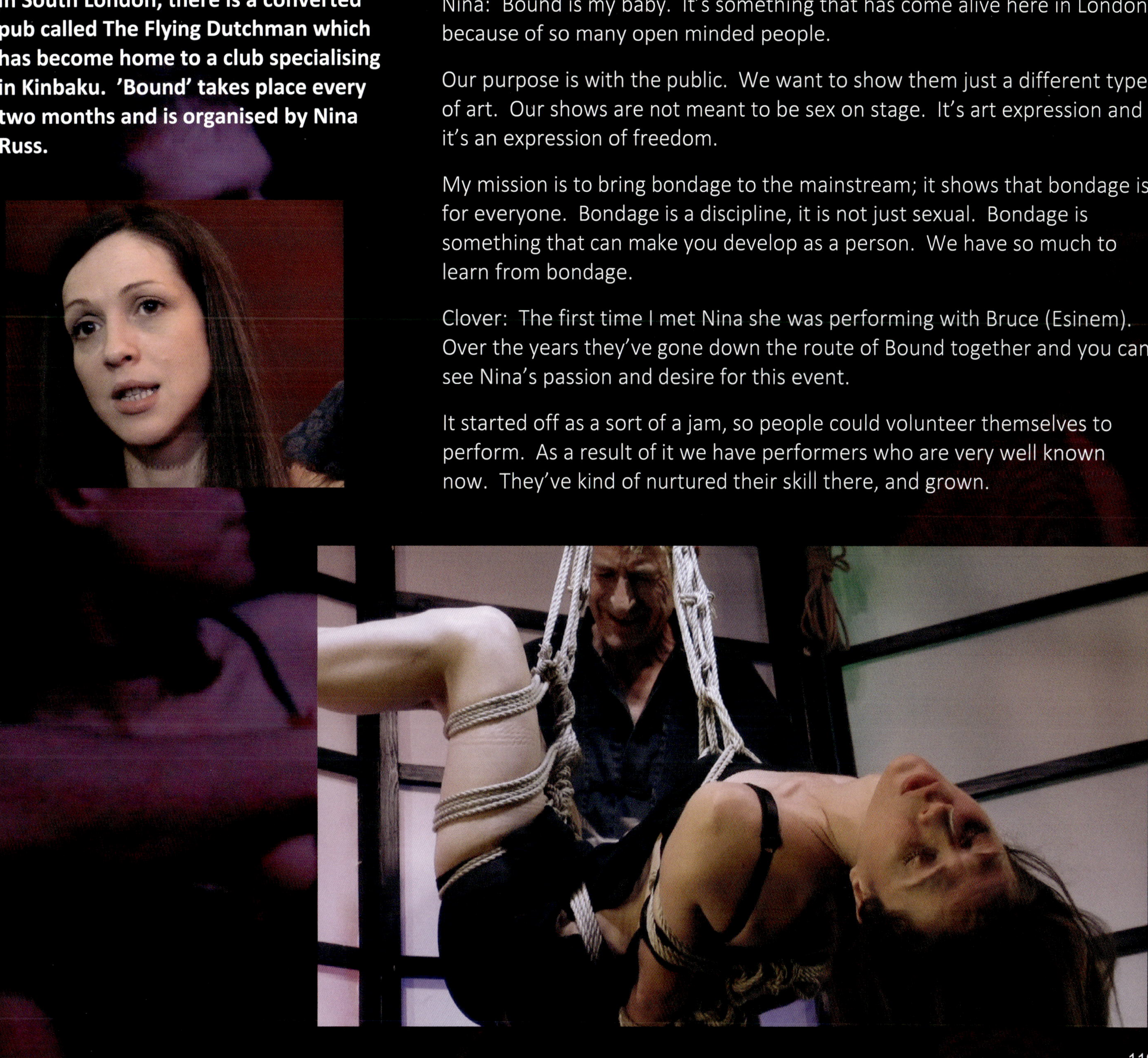

**In South London, there is a converted pub called The Flying Dutchman which has become home to a club specialising in Kinbaku. 'Bound' takes place every two months and is organised by Nina Russ.**

Nina:  Bound is my baby.  It's something that has come alive here in London because of so many open minded people.

Our purpose is with the public.  We want to show them just a different type of art.  Our shows are not meant to be sex on stage.  It's art expression and it's an expression of freedom.

My mission is to bring bondage to the mainstream; it shows that bondage is for everyone.  Bondage is a discipline, it is not just sexual.  Bondage is something that can make you develop as a person.  We have so much to learn from bondage.

Clover:  The first time I met Nina she was performing with Bruce (Esinem).  Over the years they've gone down the route of Bound together and you can see Nina's passion and desire for this event.

It started off as a sort of a jam, so people could volunteer themselves to perform.  As a result of it we have performers who are very well known now.  They've kind of nurtured their skill there, and grown.

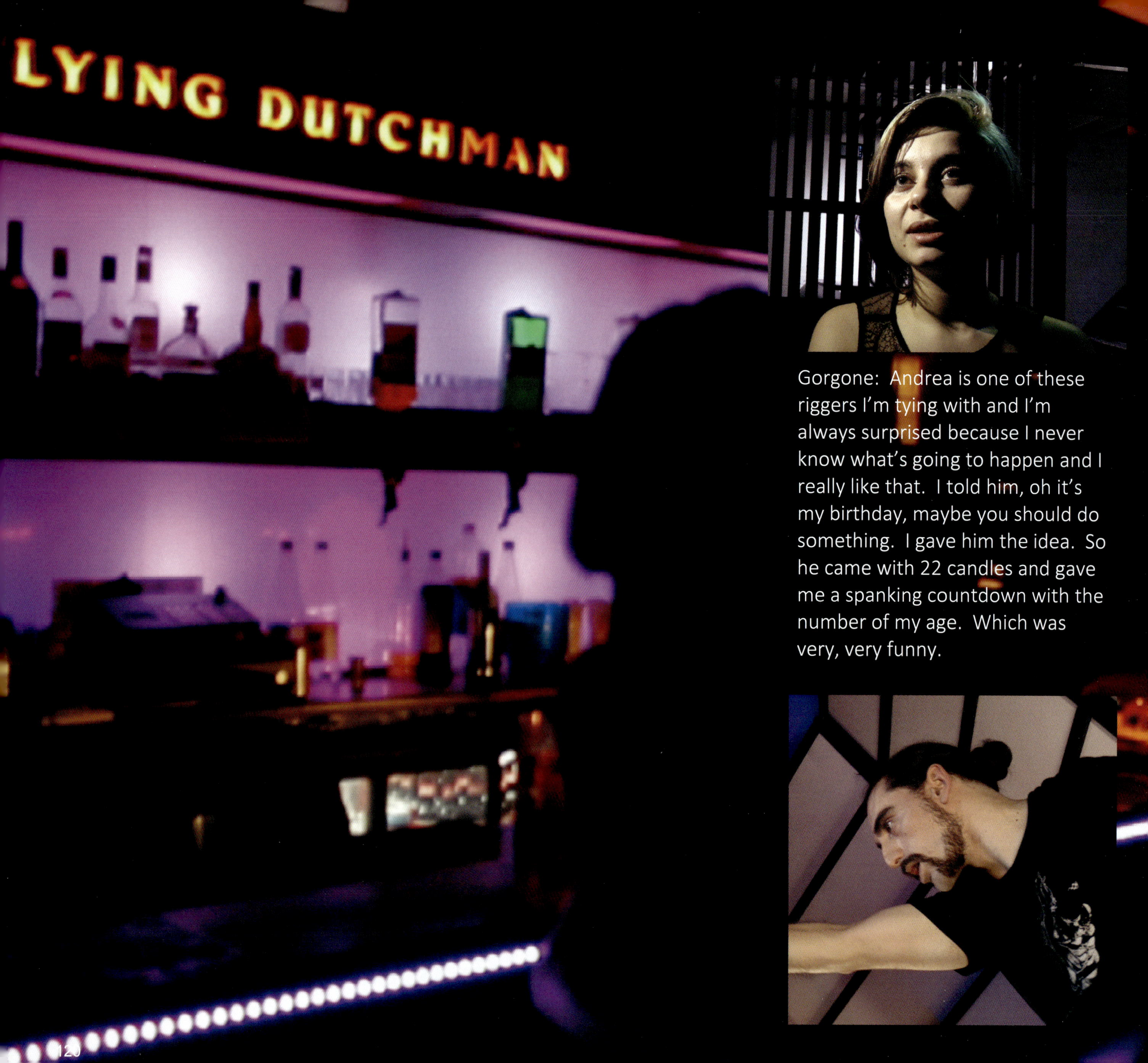



Gorgone: Andrea is one of these riggers I'm tying with and I'm always surprised because I never know what's going to happen and I really like that. I told him, oh it's my birthday, maybe you should do something. I gave him the idea. So he came with 22 candles and gave me a spanking countdown with the number of my age. Which was very, very funny.

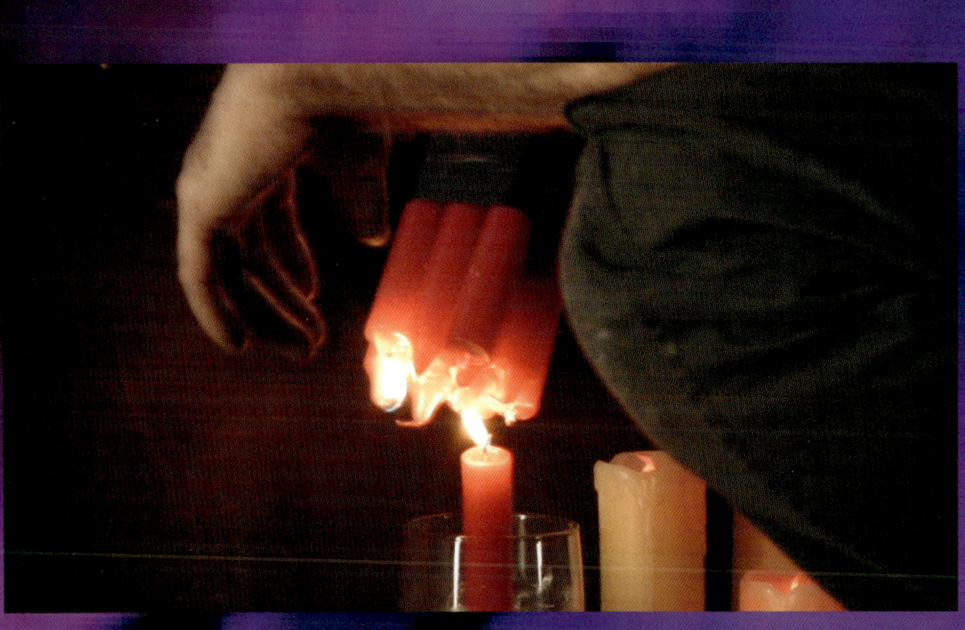

**After Andrea dripped the candle wax, Gorgone called out the number of smacks....**

Gorgone: ... 1, 2, 3, 4 sir, 5, sir ... 14, 15, 16, ...

The show was very special because it was where we really had fun - casual fun.

19, 20, Agh ...

I've never laughed so much during a performance. It was really, really cool, ... 22!

Andrea:  Happy Birthday Gorgone.

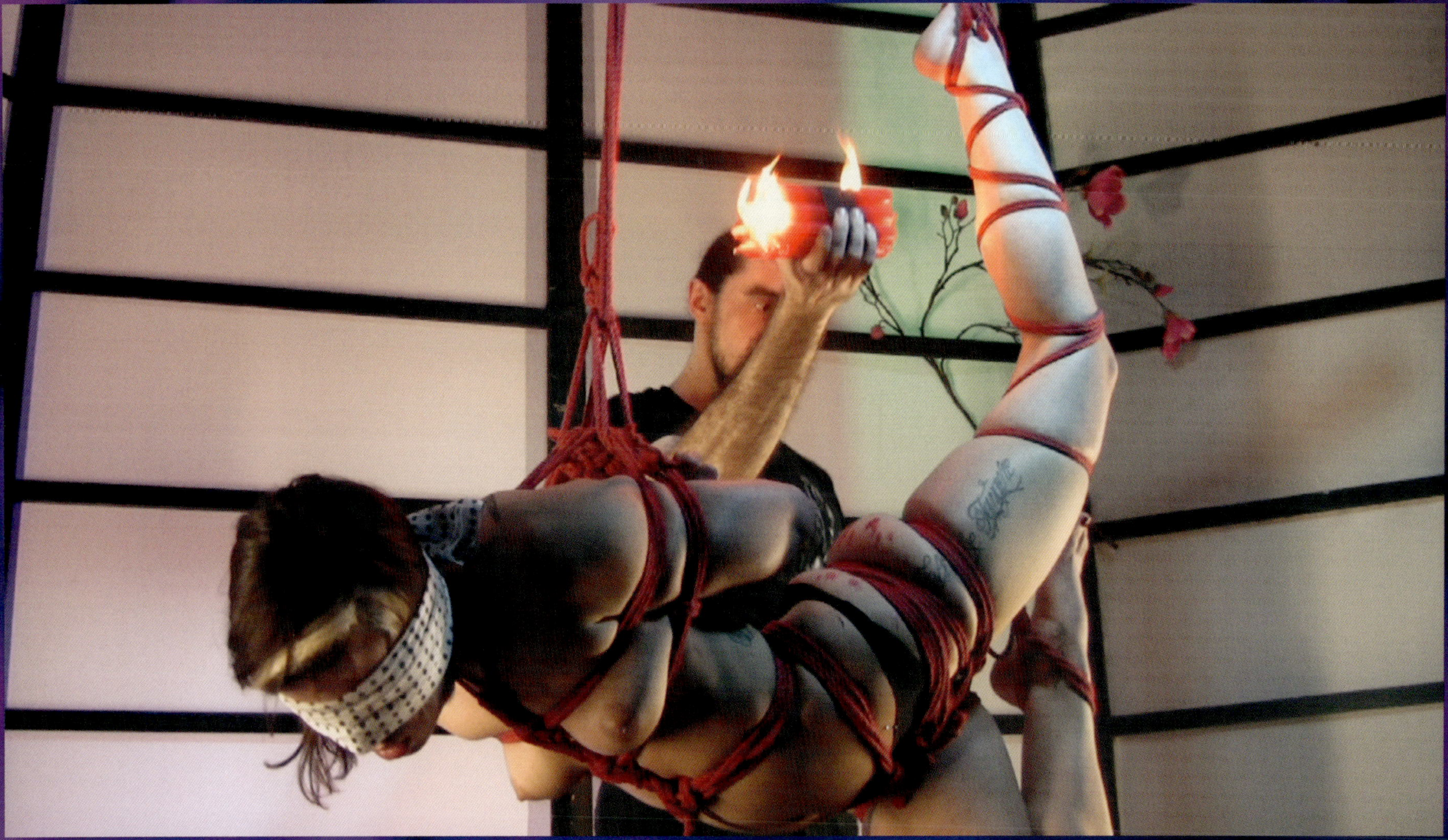

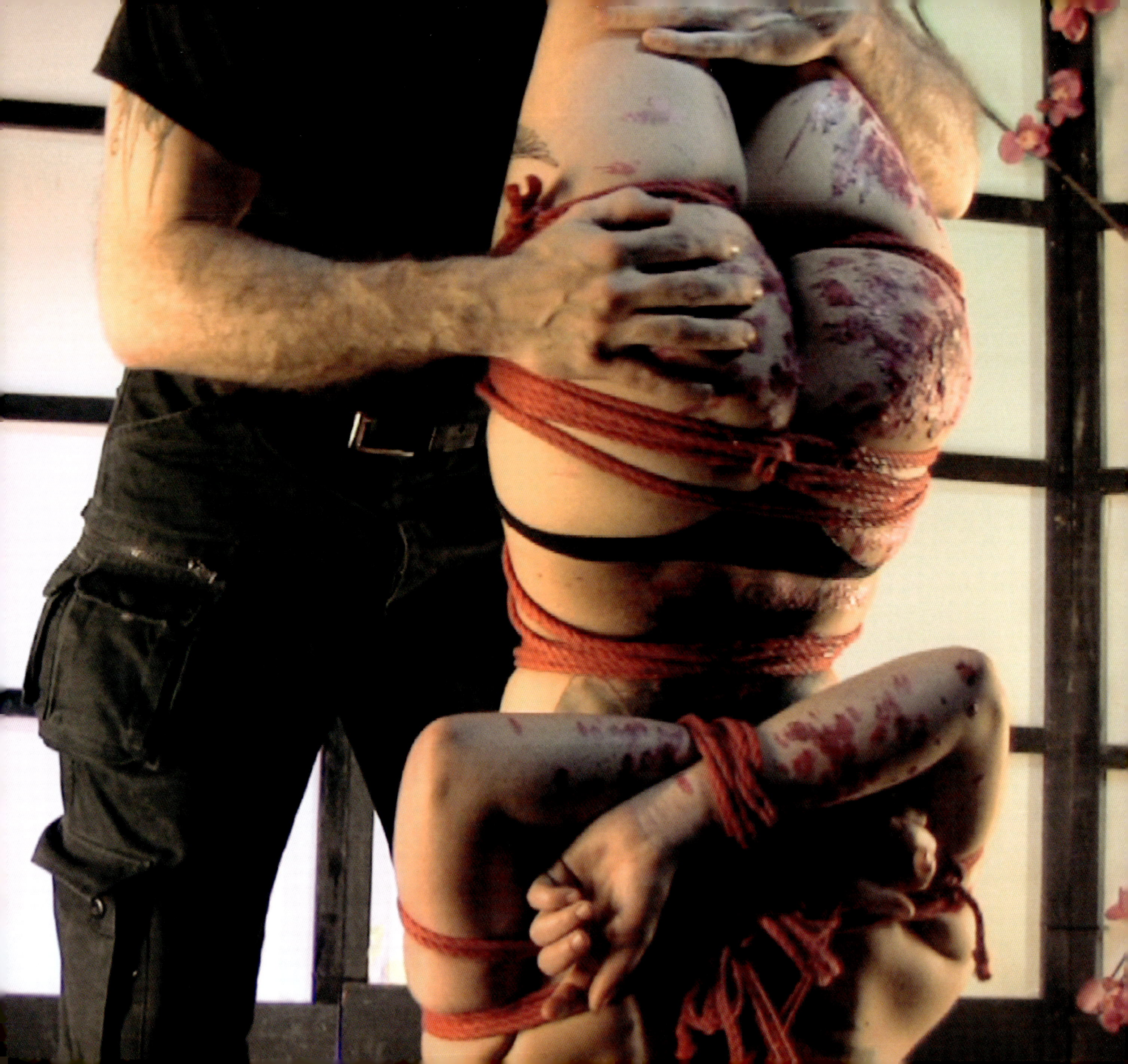

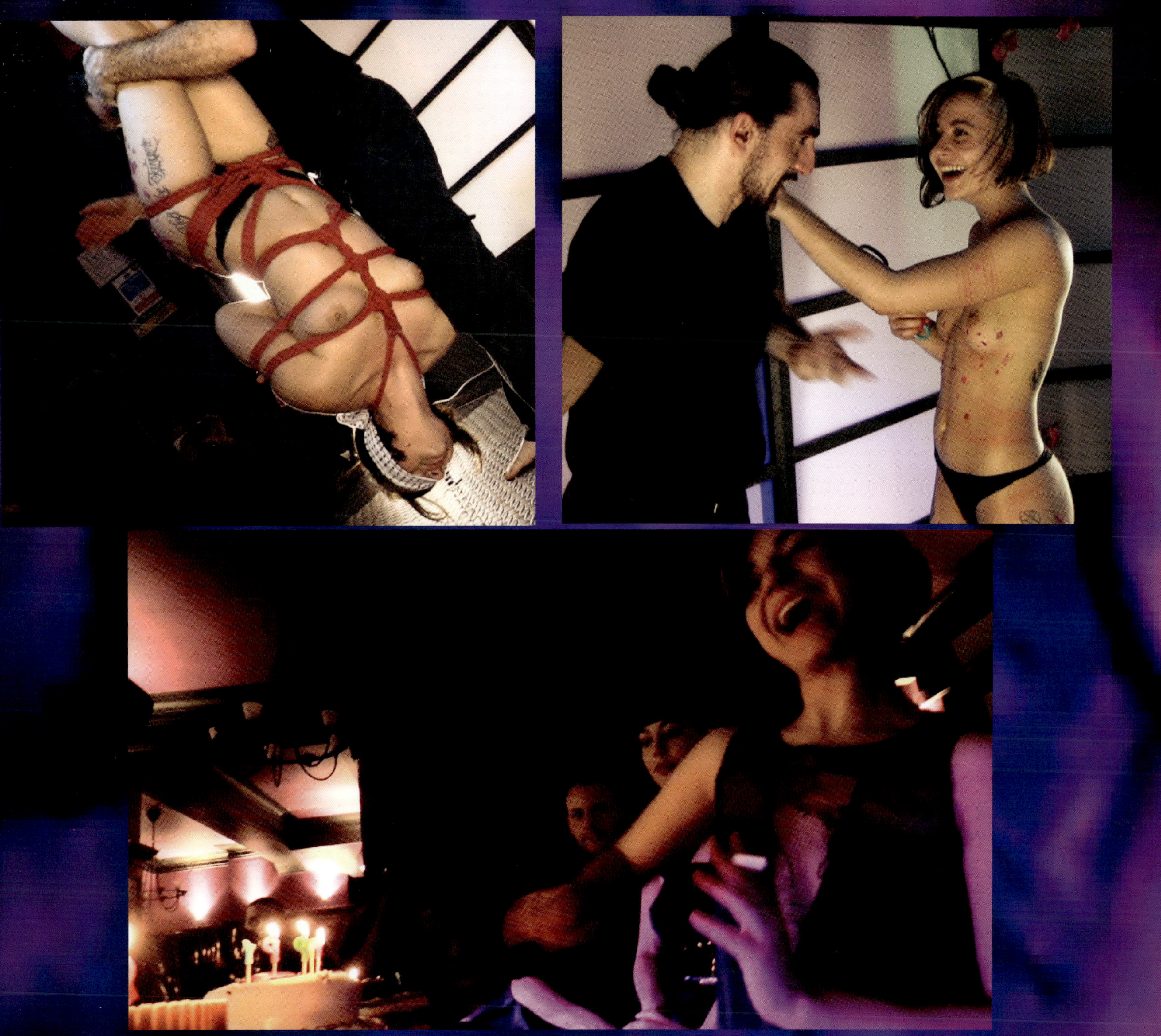

# Chapter 3

## INTIMATE BONDS

Now we see the lighter, intimate and darker sides of Kinbaku and the relationships that are formed when people are emotionally bound.  We reach some surprising conclusions about the pleasure of rope.

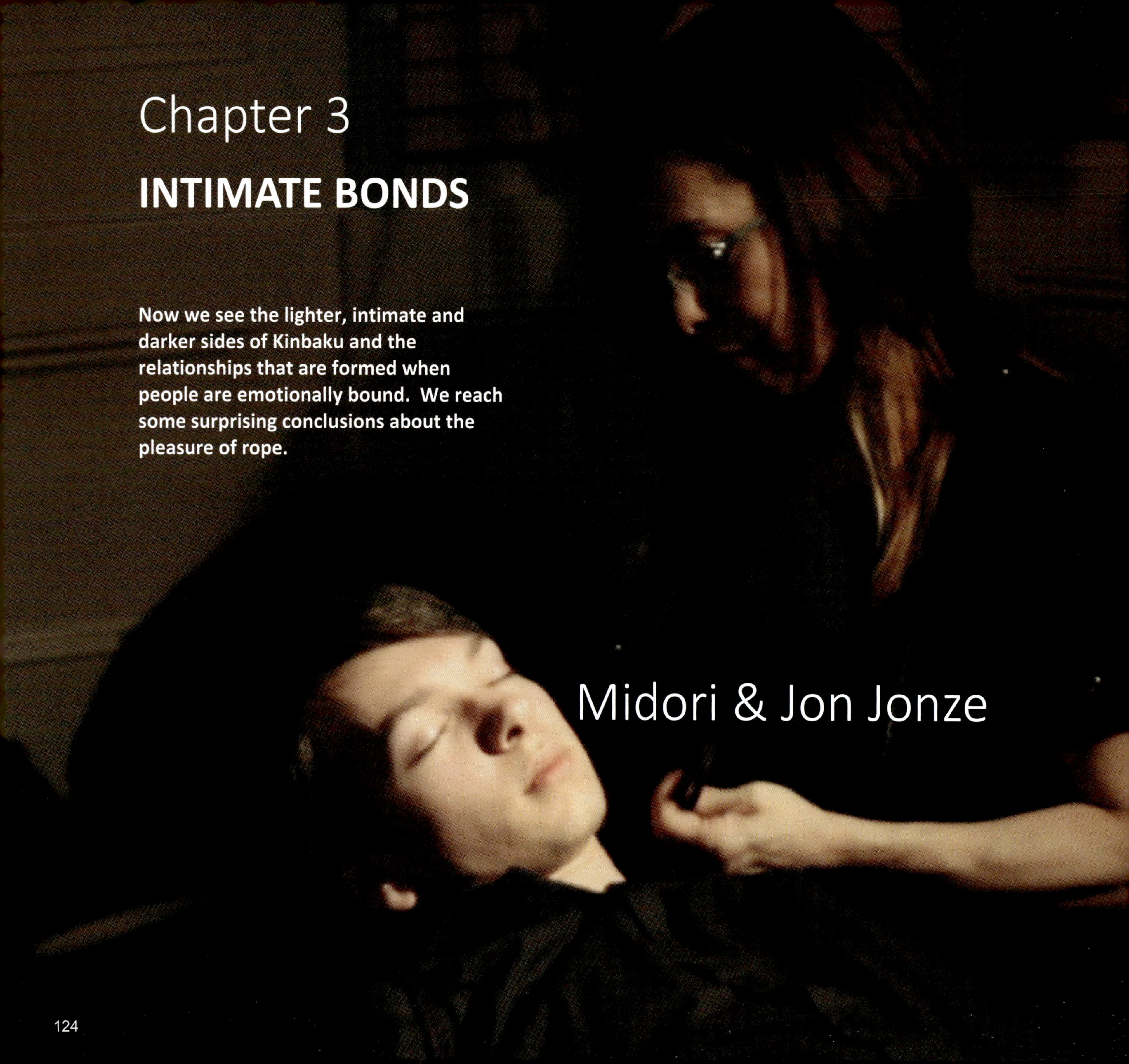

Midori & Jon Jonze

**When Midori came to London, she wanted to show me the more intimate side of bondage and brought Jon to my house.**

Midori: There's a distinct difference between performance and private play.  With performance my objective with my performer is to entertain.  To move, to awe, to even perhaps to frighten the audience at times.

But in private play the scene is entirely different and don't get the two scenarios mistaken.  Private play is all about two people, two souls, two passions, two hungers, coming together, connecting; to dare to find a place of intimacy and authenticity.  To cast aside the fears and self censoring and to take a chance at connecting, even if that's a little scary.

There's a mutuality to it.  I feed off the responses.  My entire being is hyper aroused and hyper sensitive to every sigh, every nuance.  And then taking the rope skills that I know I respond to each feedback, back and forth, back and forth.  Pleasure wrapped in rope.

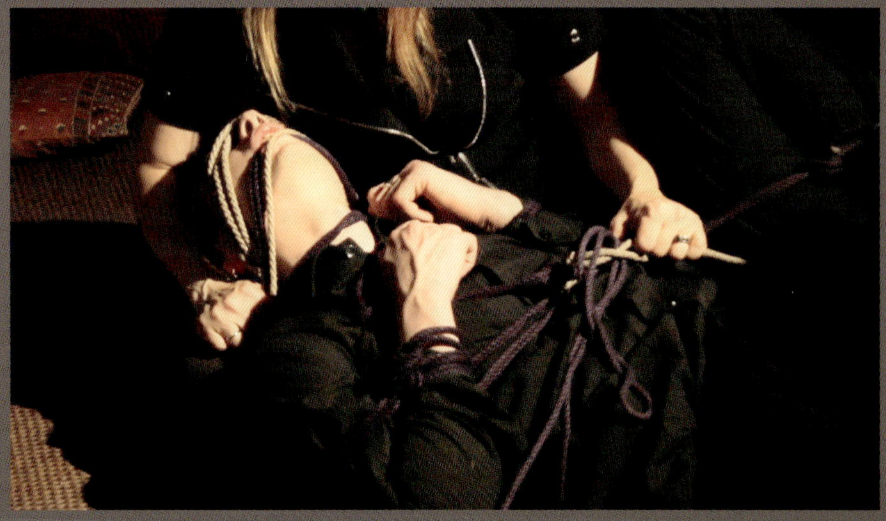

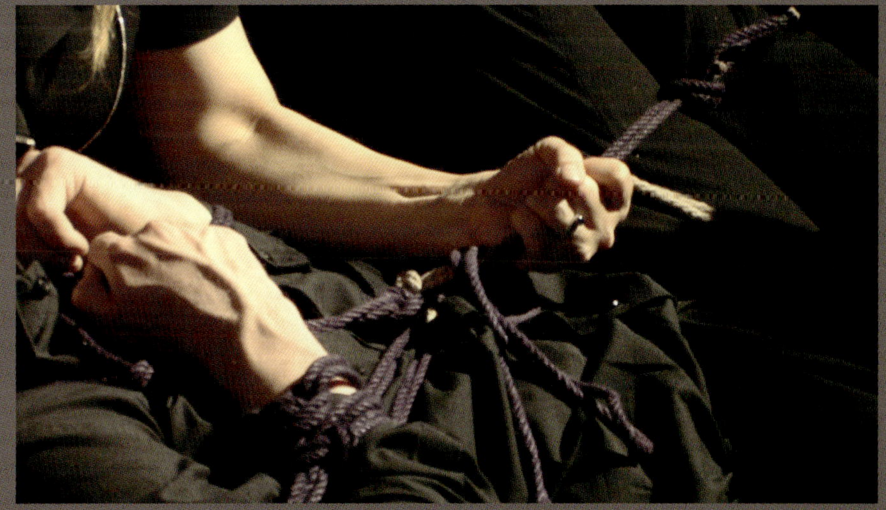

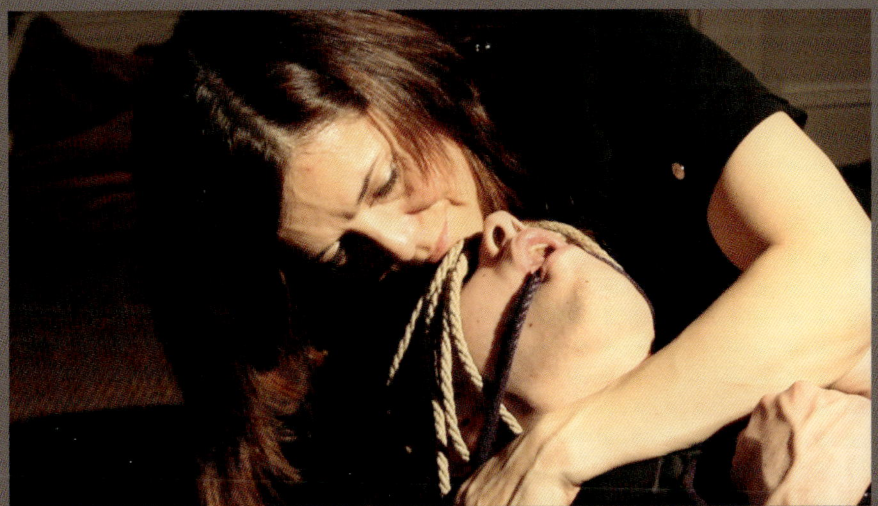

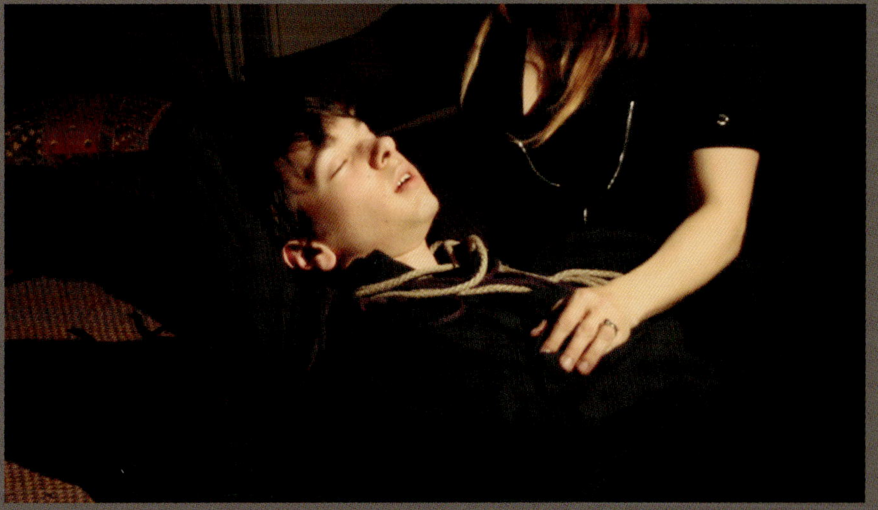

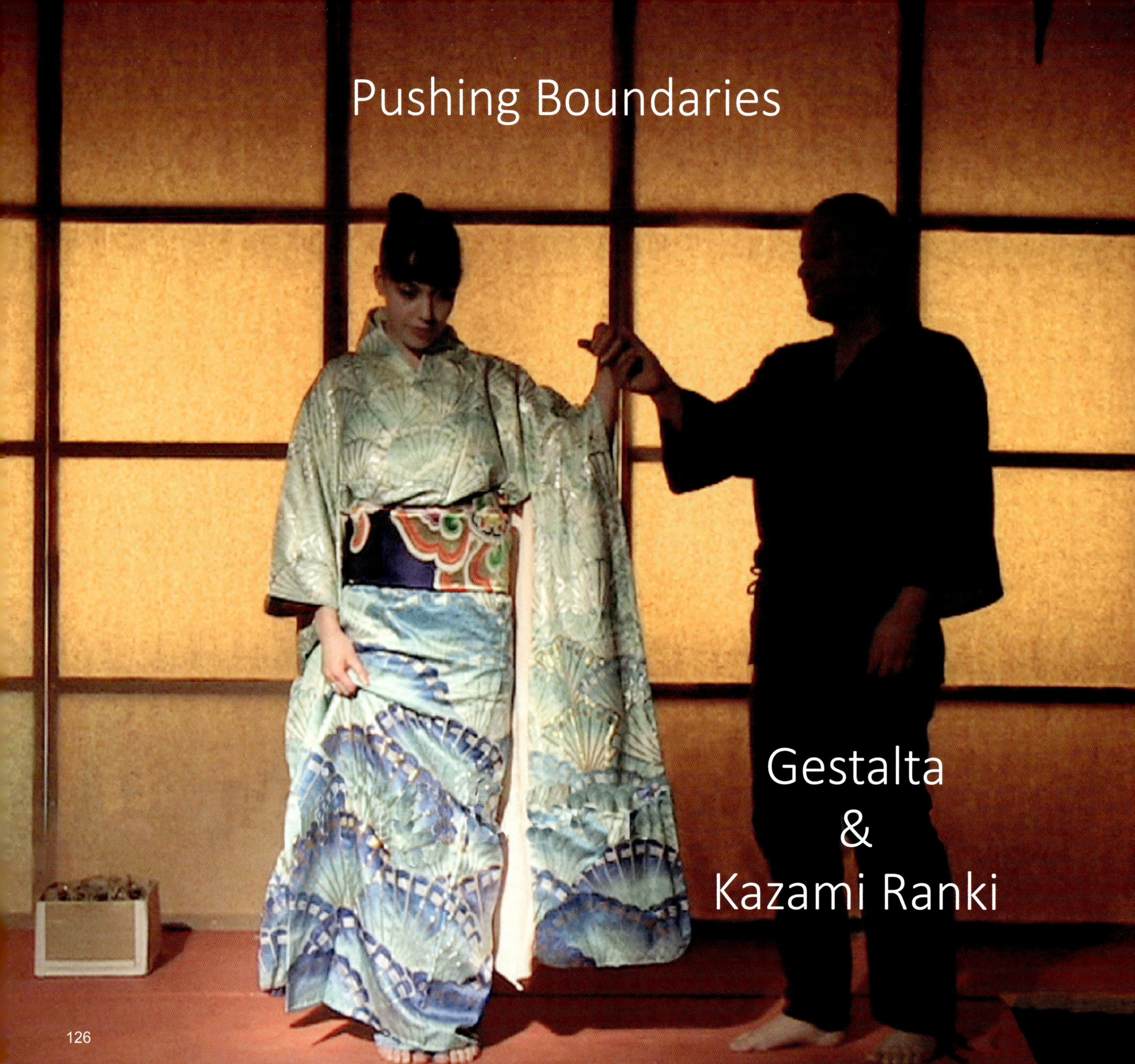
Pushing Boundaries
Gestalta
&
Kazami Ranki
126

Gestalta:  Yeah, this is the last part of the first performance I did with Kazami.  It's the one where we did a breast suspension.

Amy Morgan:  As soon as he started binding her breasts so tightly and wound the rope around her breast I was pleased because I love that kind of stuff.

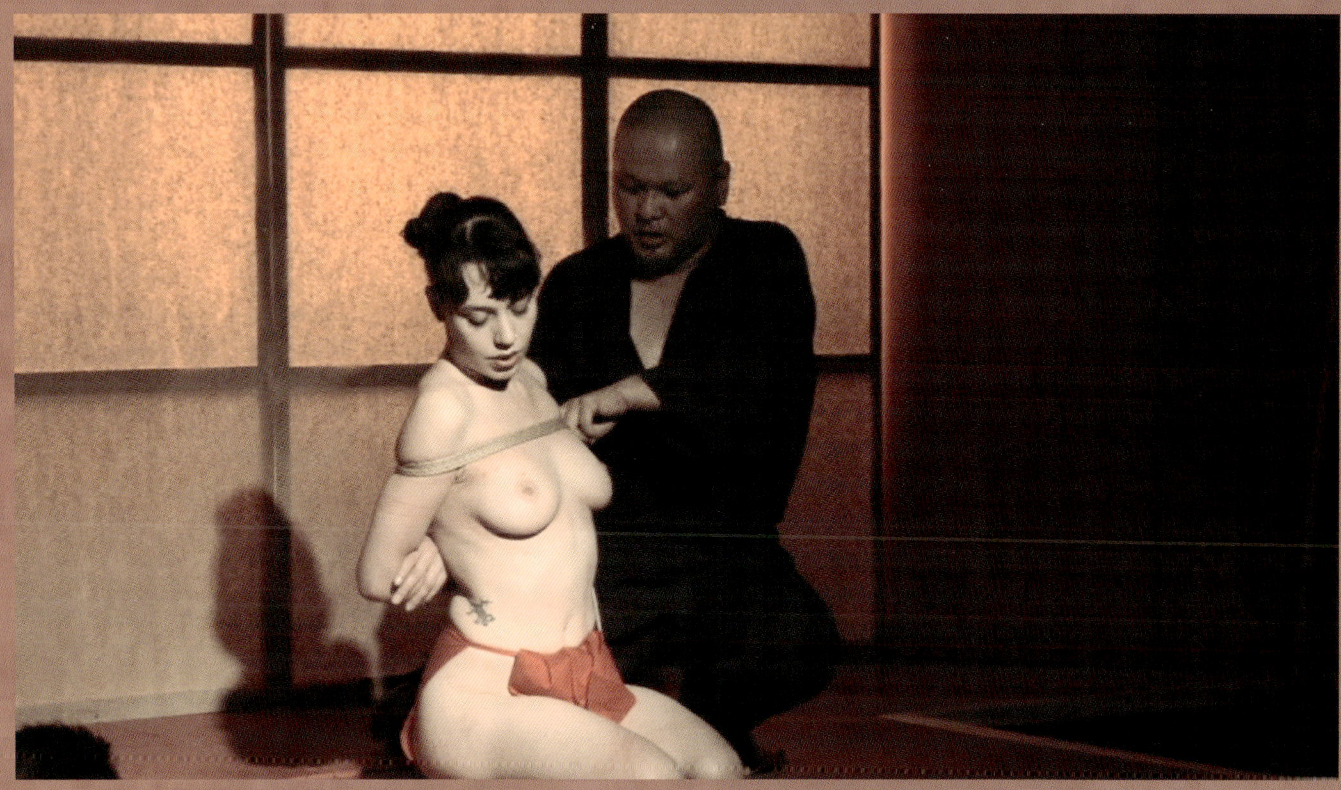

Gestalta:  Oh gosh, there is a lot of weight on them, I didn't realise.  God they've gone red!

Amy:  When he suspended her like that, I was in awe, not just of this display of rope craft but also Gestalta.  Not every woman can take that.

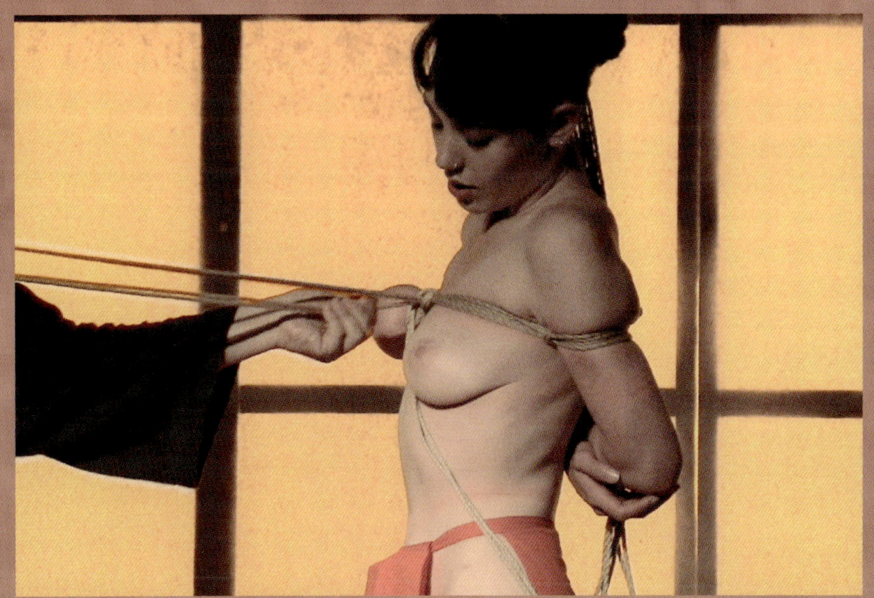

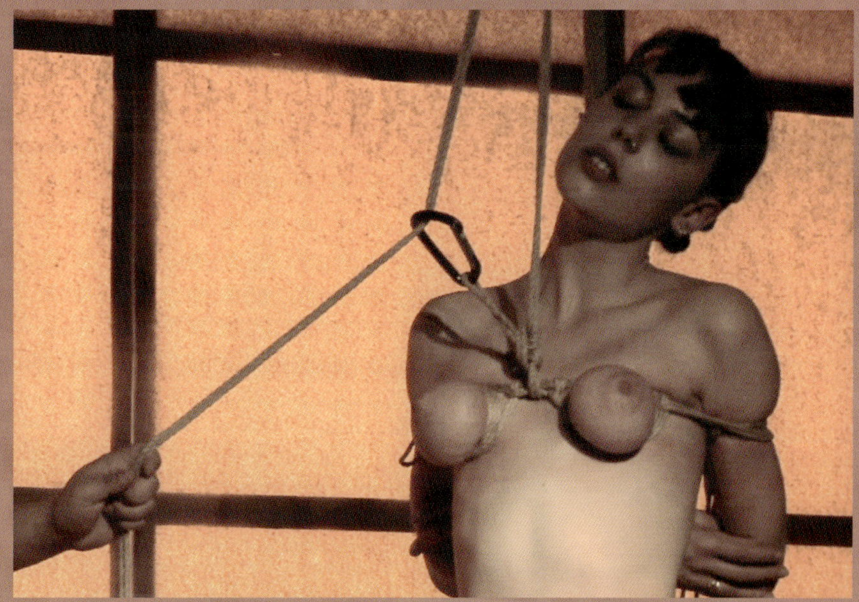

Gestalta:  I remember feeling a bit funny after this one but at the same time it was relatively painless and quite nice really.

I've certainly got a bit of a reputation for being the sort of person who says 'yes' to everything.  I do get a few people asking me if I'm actually unbreakable which I'm sure isn't true.  I just haven't found anything that's been too much yet. Yet!

Amy:  The performance of Gestalta was amazing and Kazami is such an inspiration for me that I want to become one of his students.

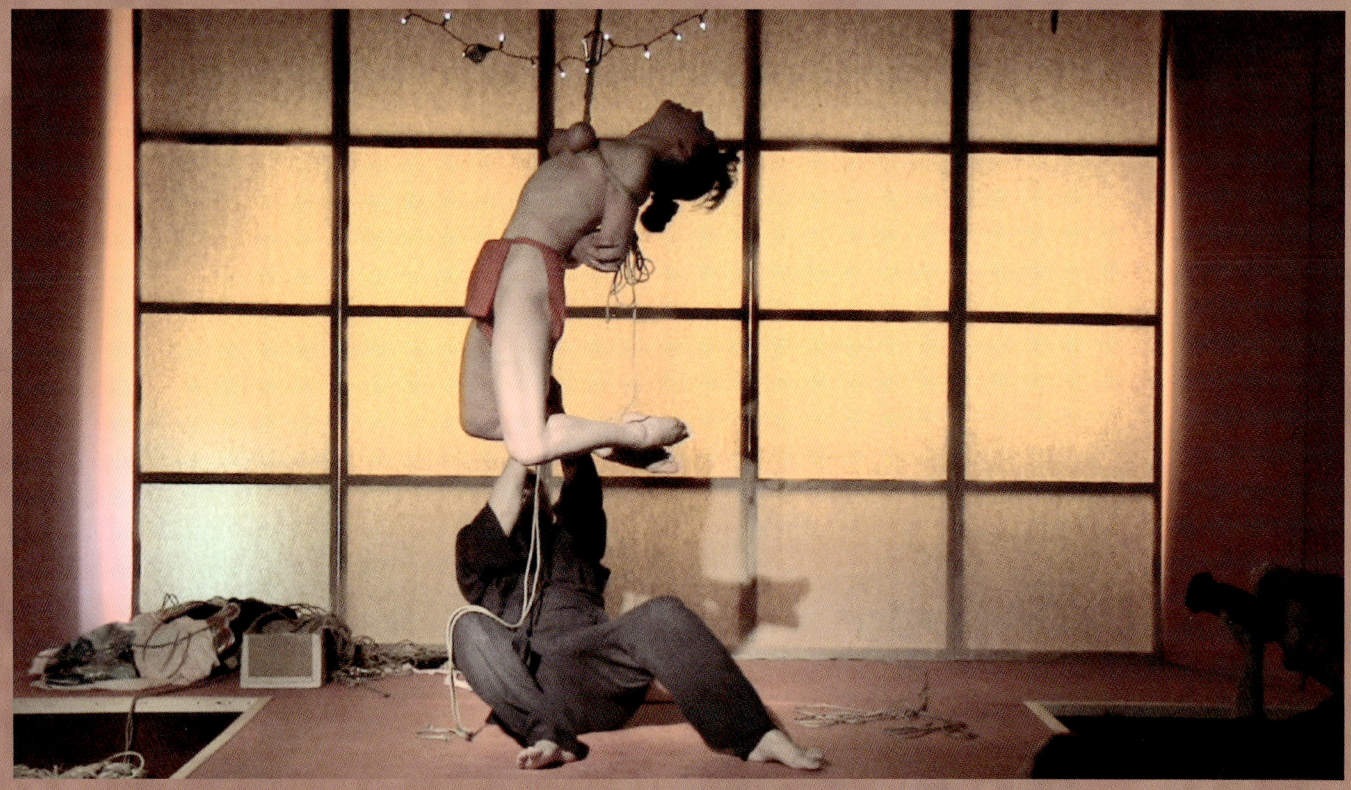

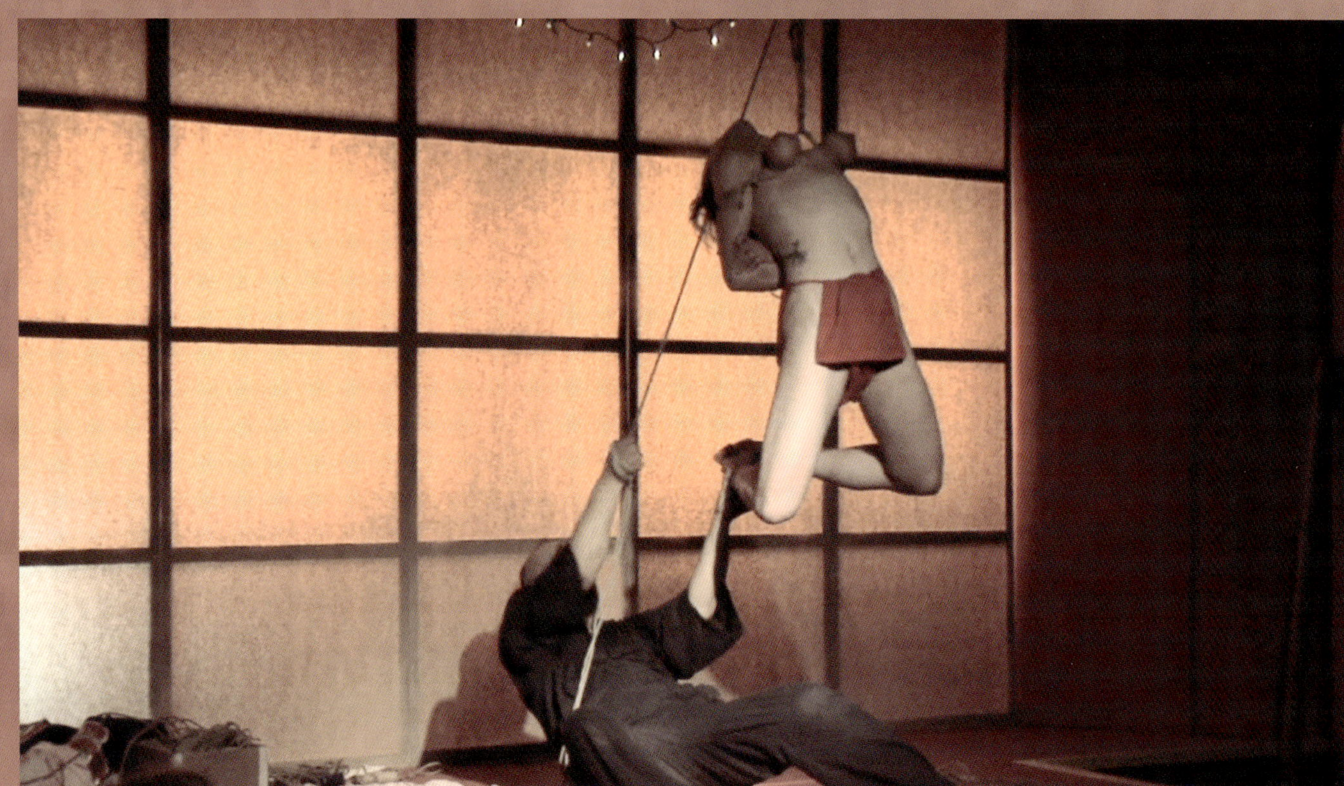

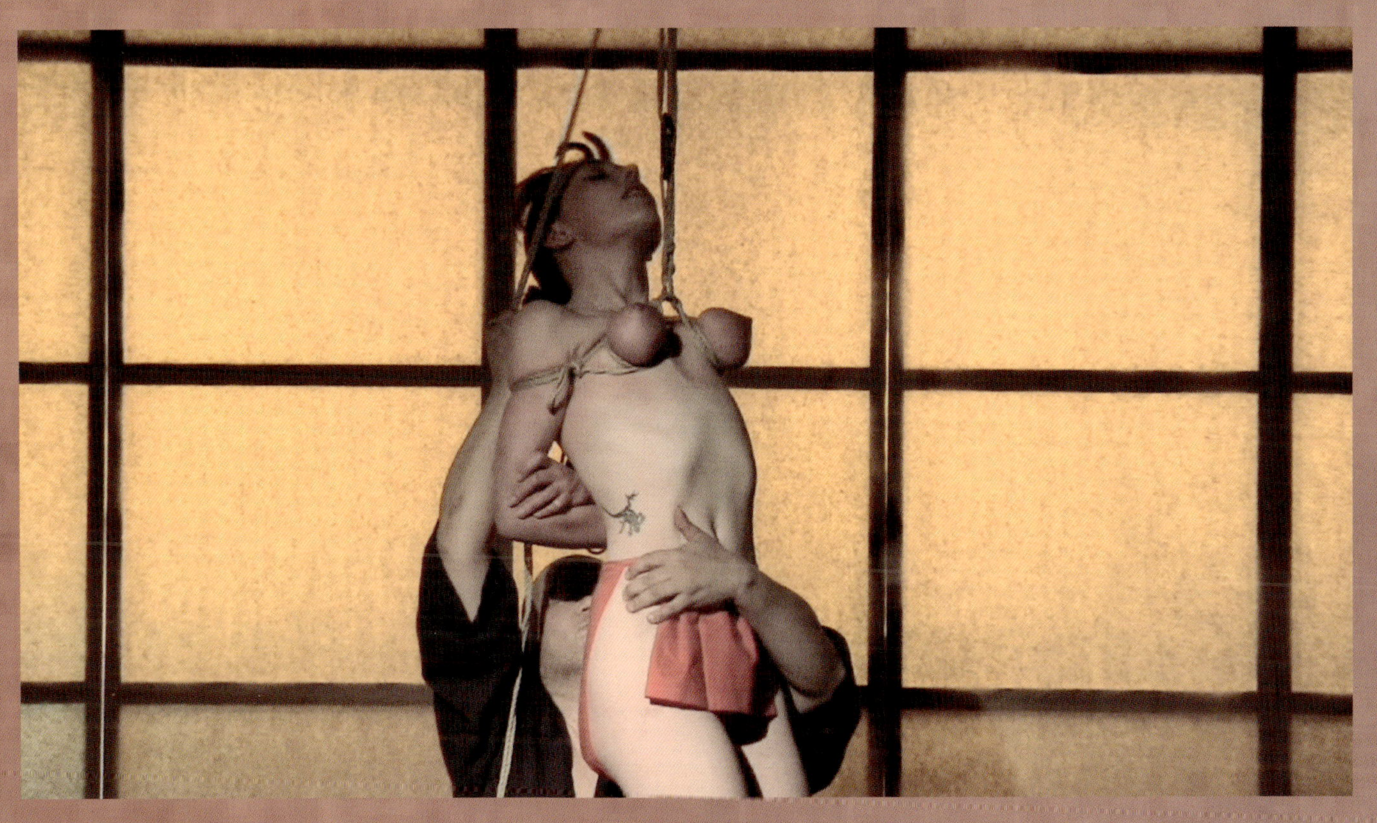

Clover: While it was a great show and looked amazing, I don't want to take that kind of risk with my body. The damage you can do to a breast is quite irreparable. But at the same time you can see that Kazami had some knowledge with this because he used it as part of a chest harness.

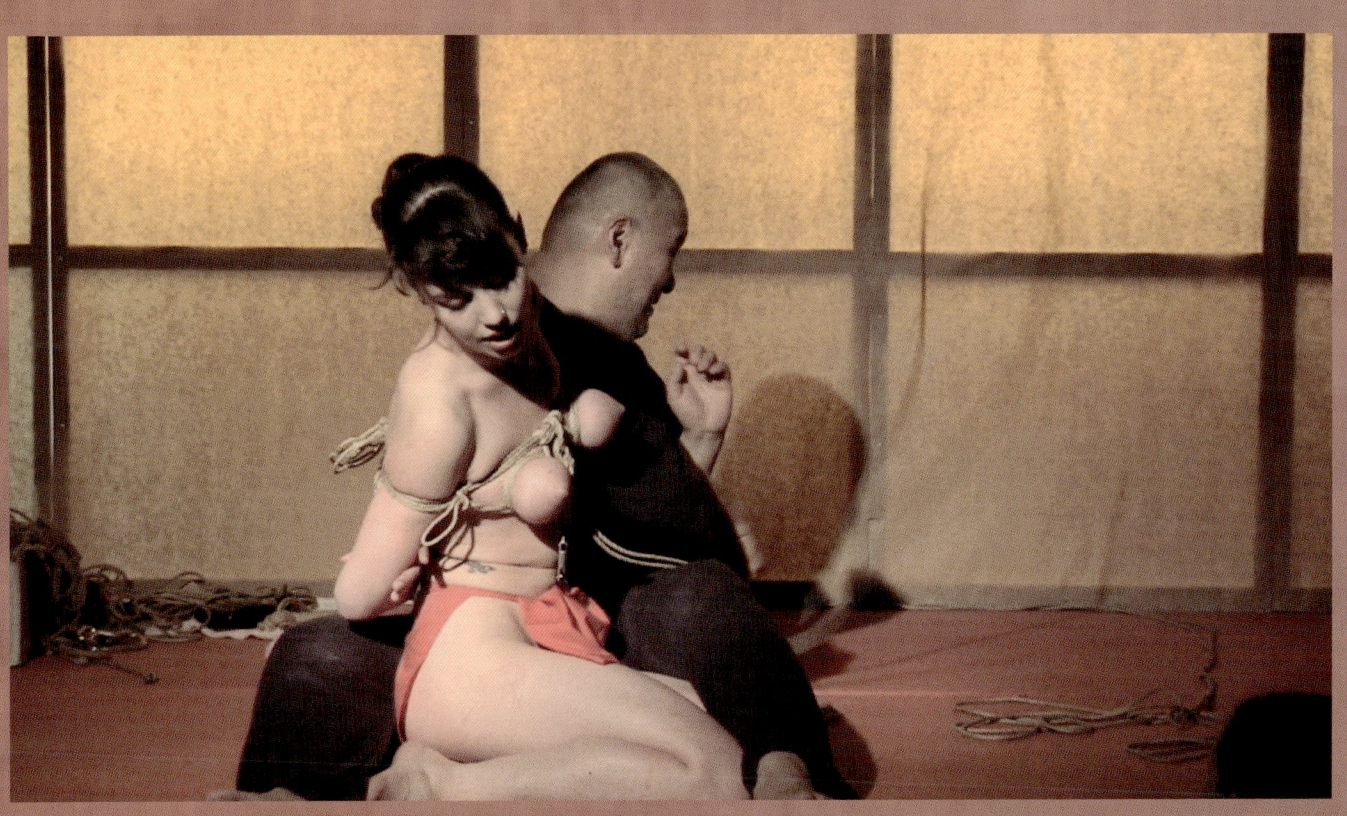

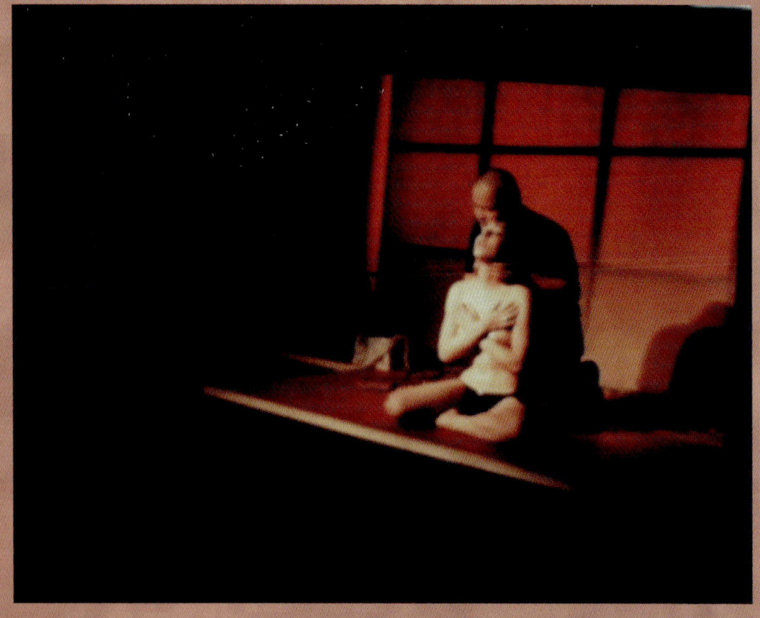

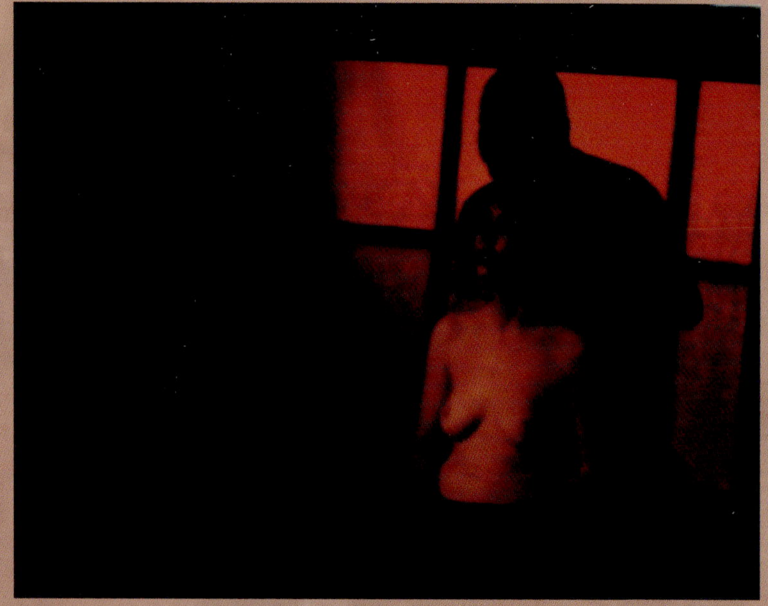

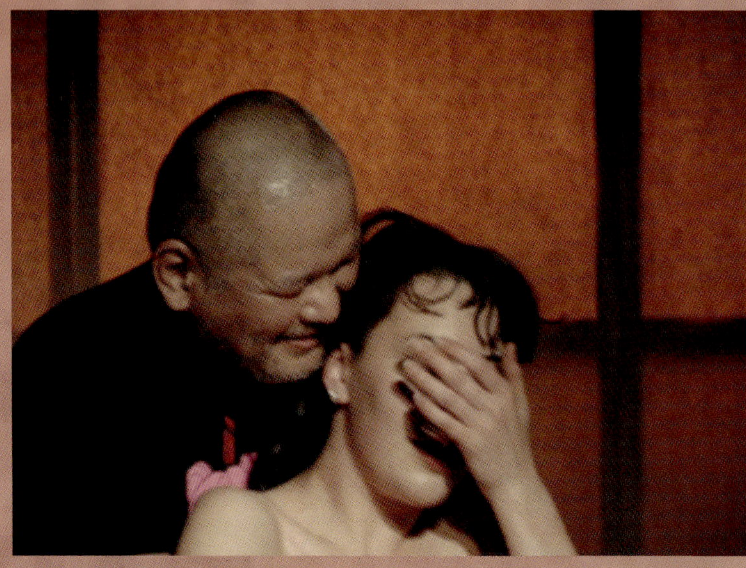

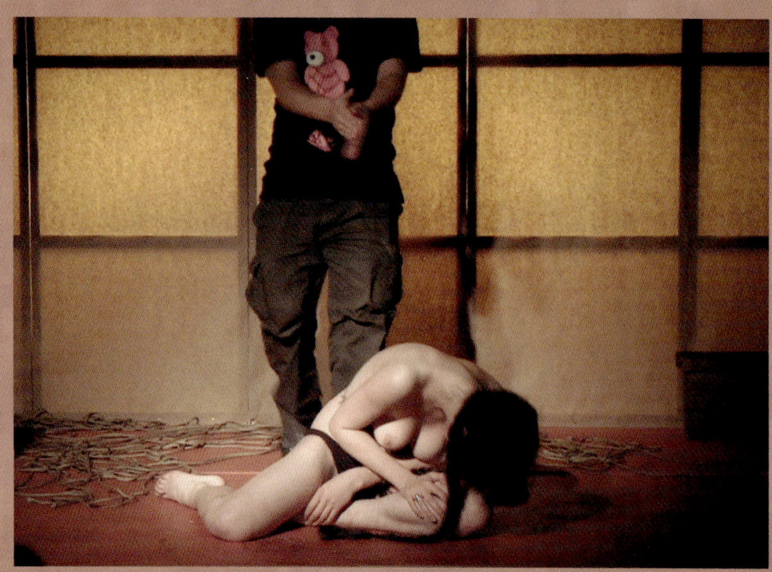

Gestalta:  Certainly when I'm working with Kazami, if he's going to do something a bit different, he will ask me beforehand. And as far as I'm concerned, as soon as I've said 'yes', that's where my control ends.  Obviously I have complete freedom to say 'no' should I want to.  In the second show that I did with Kazami, about five minutes before we went on stage, he told me that we were going to do a blood choke - where you cut off the blood supply to the brain by pressing fingers on the arteries.

**But was Getalta given enough time to weigh up the risks and truly understand what was about to happen?  When Kazami did the blood choke, Gestalta lost conciousness until Kazami brought her round.**

Gestalta:  The biggest shock was when he woke me up.  I felt like an eternity of time had passed.  It was like a near death experience.  I felt… what the hell happened?  I seem to remember that I screamed right at the end of it; but apparently I didn't.

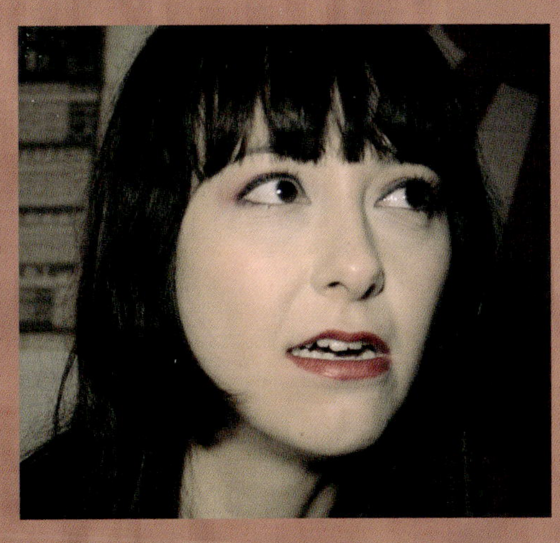

Aizen Kaguya:  Sometimes doing ropes is dangerous.  You can live dangerously doing this.  Once I did a Kinbaku session with a man alone in his house and I was tied up for two hours and a half.  I had a very difficult time with him because he was controlling my breathing for so long.  It was quite a nightmare..

I couldn't breathe.  I started to say to him I cannot breathe and he said 'I know'.  And I was shocked to see his eyes and he knew my feelings.  I realized that it could be very dangerous to do this on my own with someone that I don't know.  My body was shaking and at the end I started to cry so badly.  I was completely panicking in this session.  But he understood what he had done.

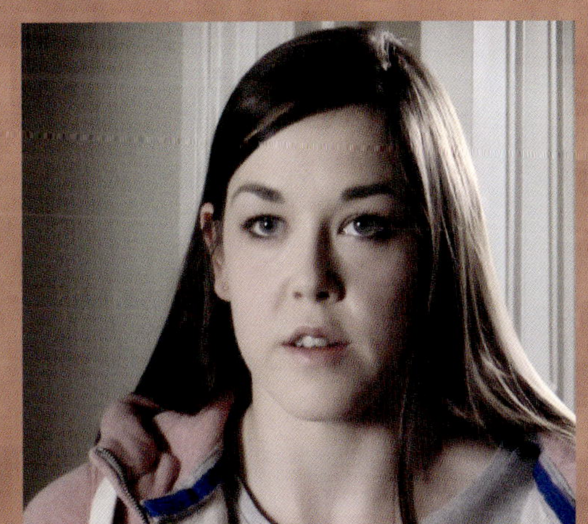

Clover:  I think you need to be able to trust a rigger with your life and if I'm ever considering someone tying me I ask myself that.  If the answer isn't yes, then I won't tie with them because the consequences of something going wrong are unthinkable.

In the rope scene there are some undesirable characters that you may not want to play with or tie with.  There can be people you might refer to as predators who will seek out those who are quite new.

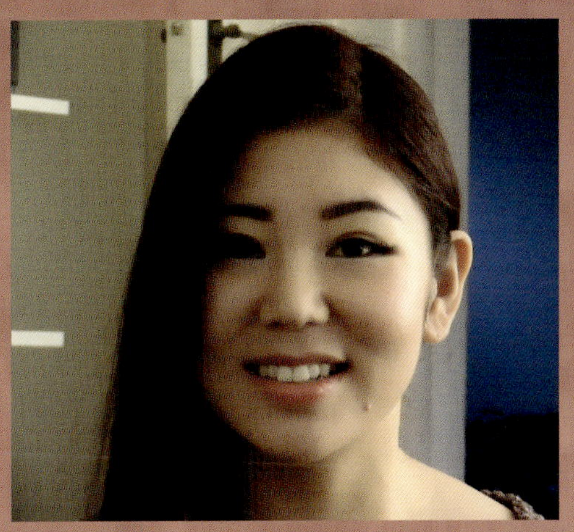

Miumi-U, a Japanese rigger : Rope is not really safe for her.  If you want, you can kill.

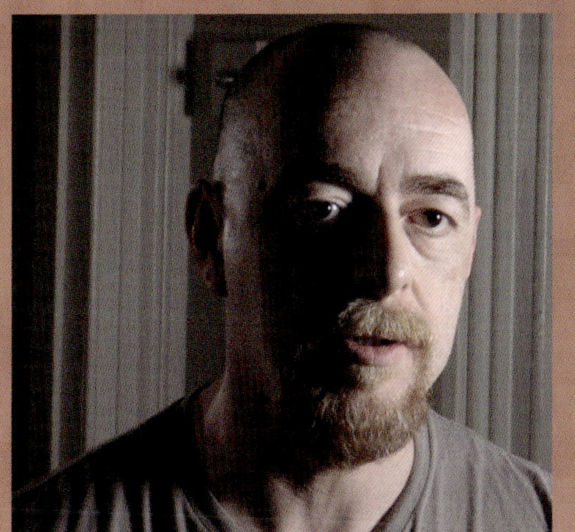

WykD Dave:  You can see how the scene is attractive to people who are predators because there are people who want to be tied up and quite frankly, want to be in a position of vulnerability.

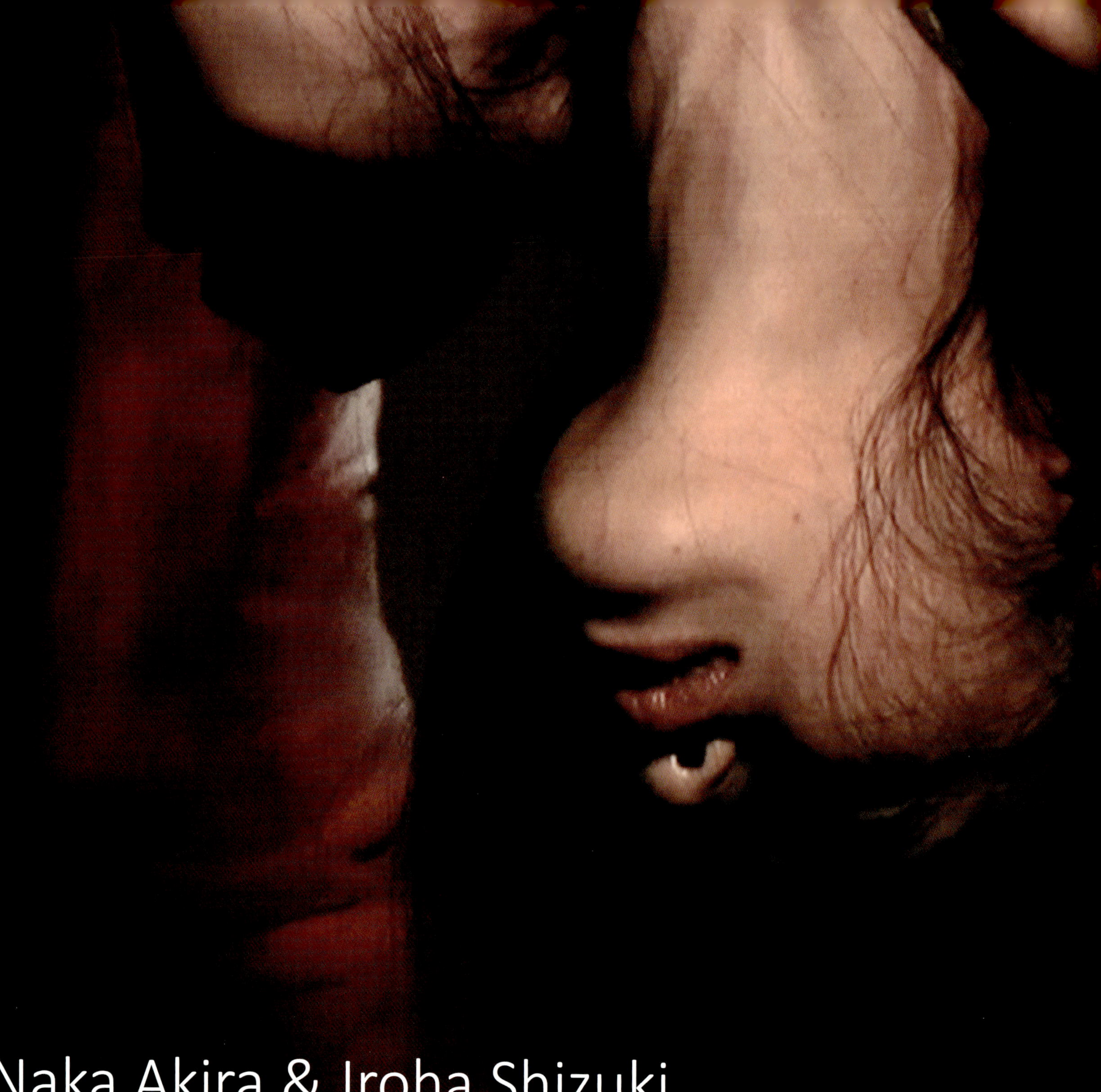

Naka Akira & Iroha Shizuki

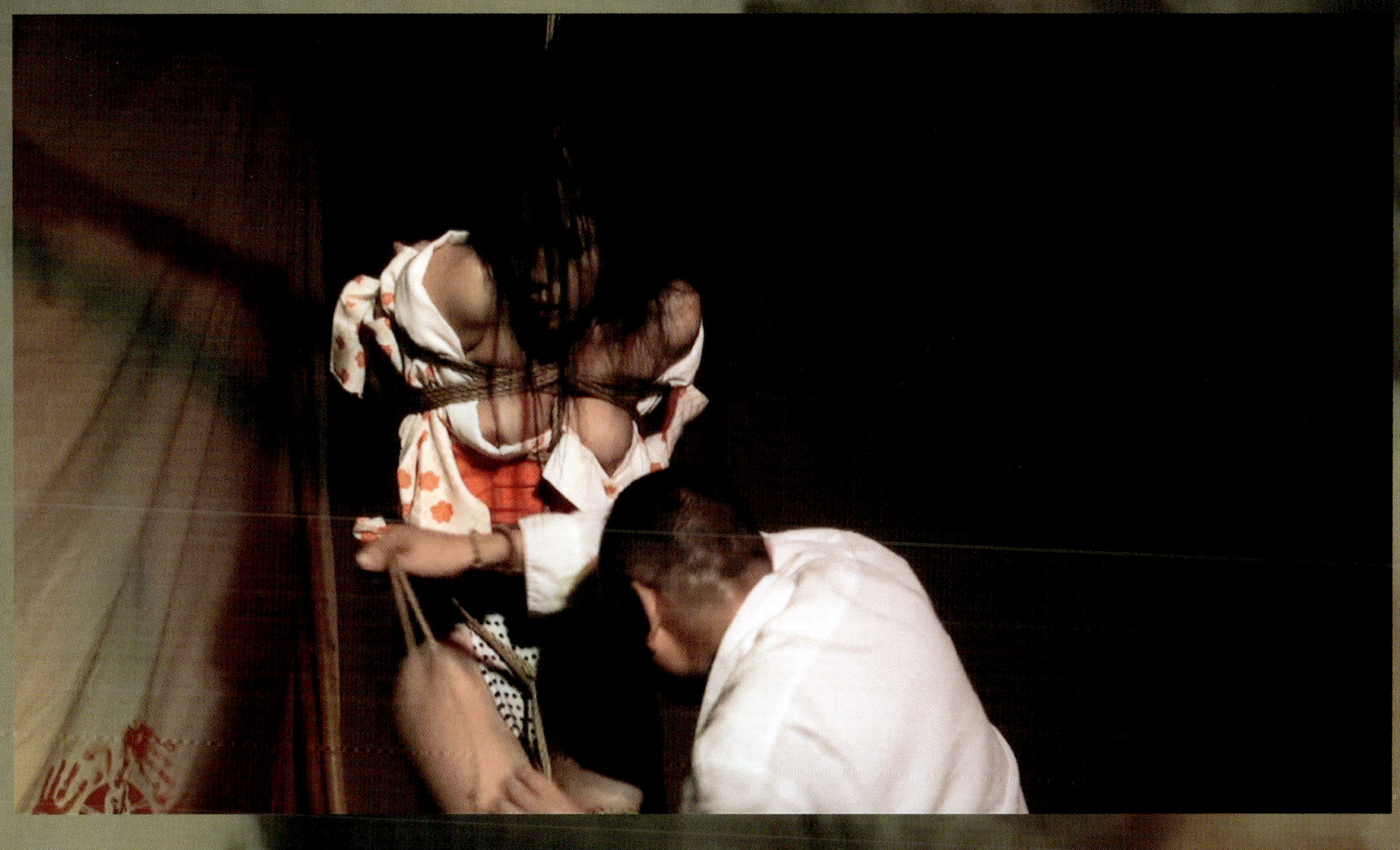

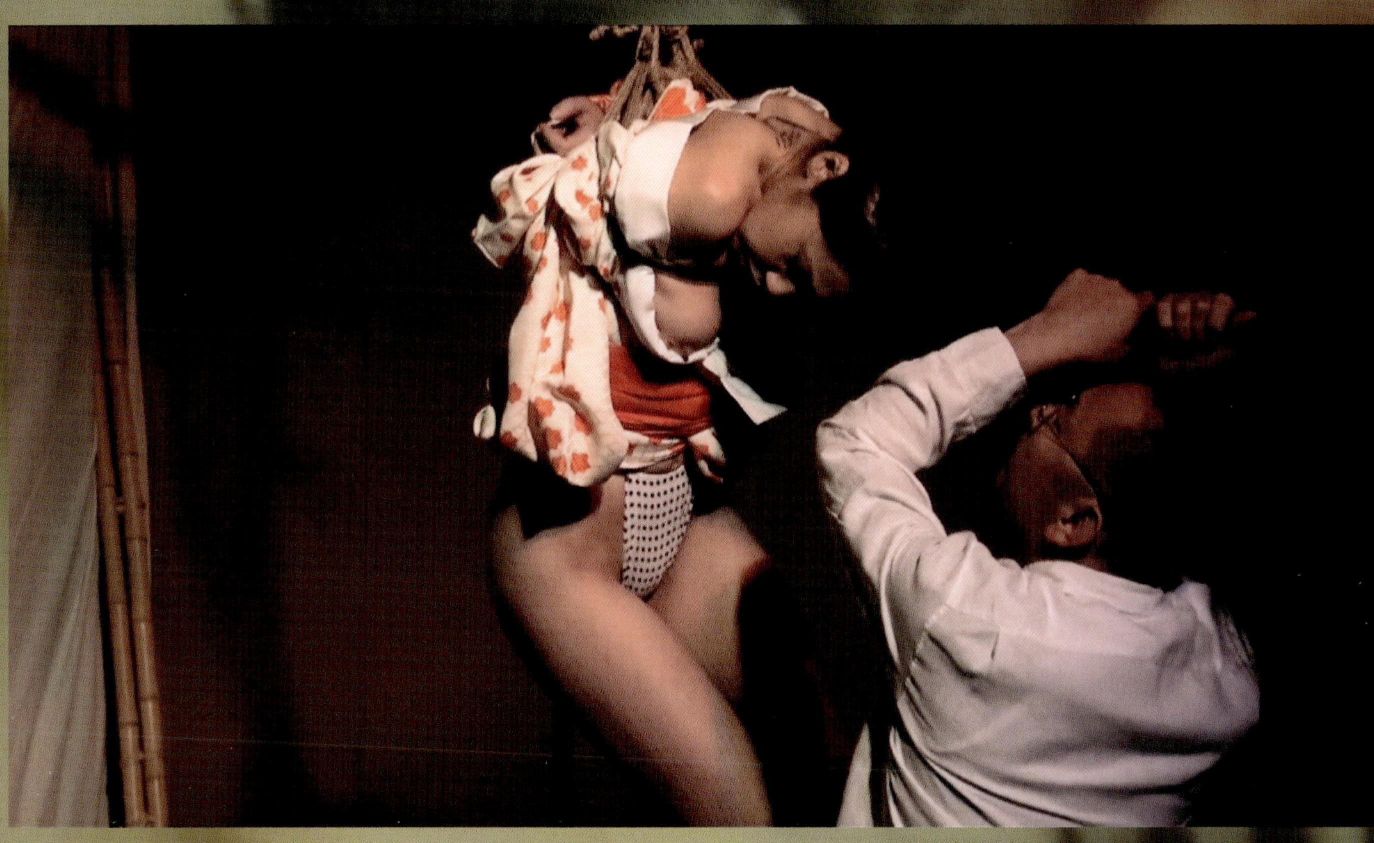

**The intense emotional relationship that  can arise between bondage partners was displayed by a much celebrated couple who headlined the 2013 London rope bondage festival**.

Clover:  Naka Akira has come to London. His influence has really spread across the western world. He has a very unique style: he ties on bamboo.

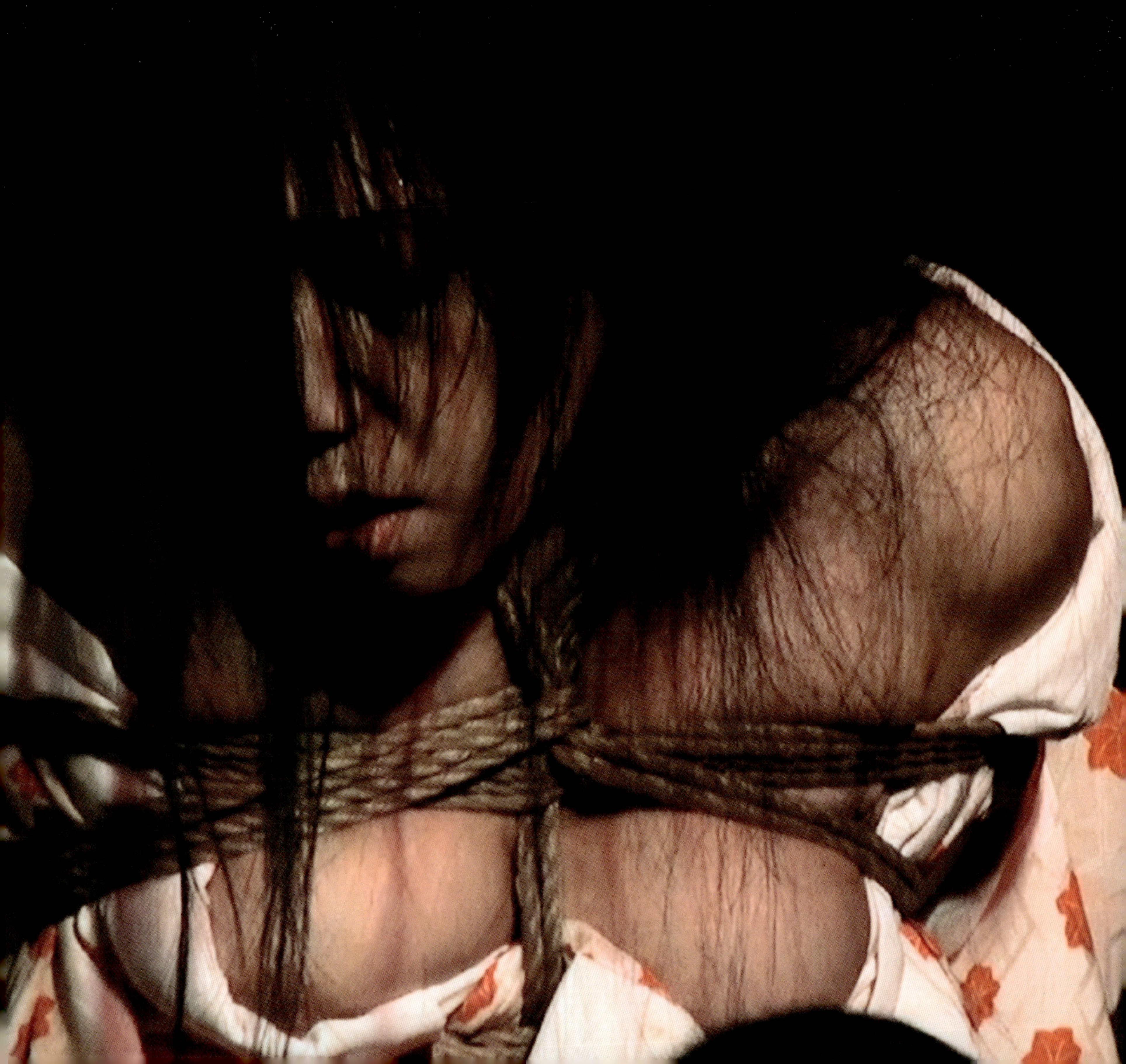

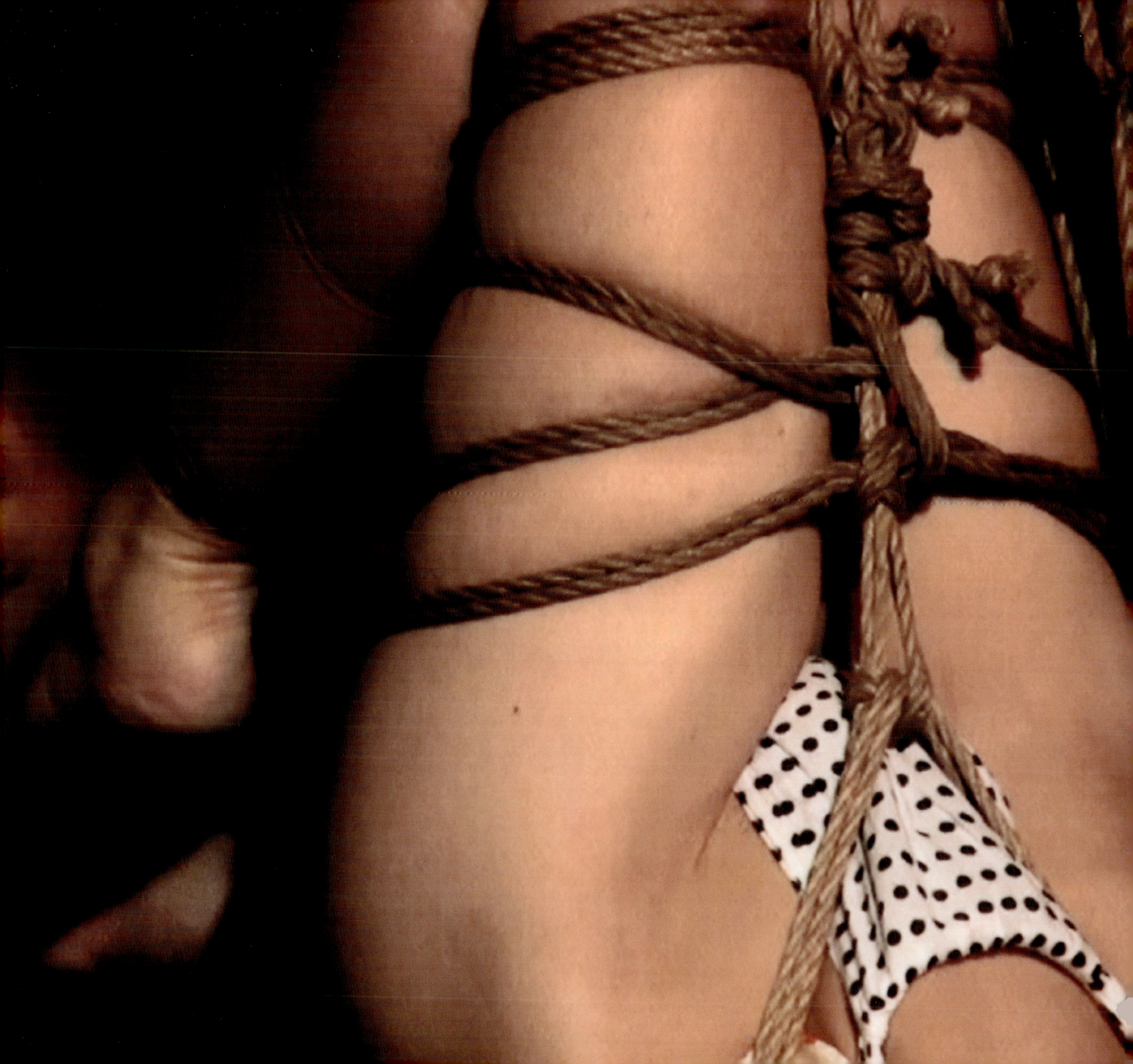

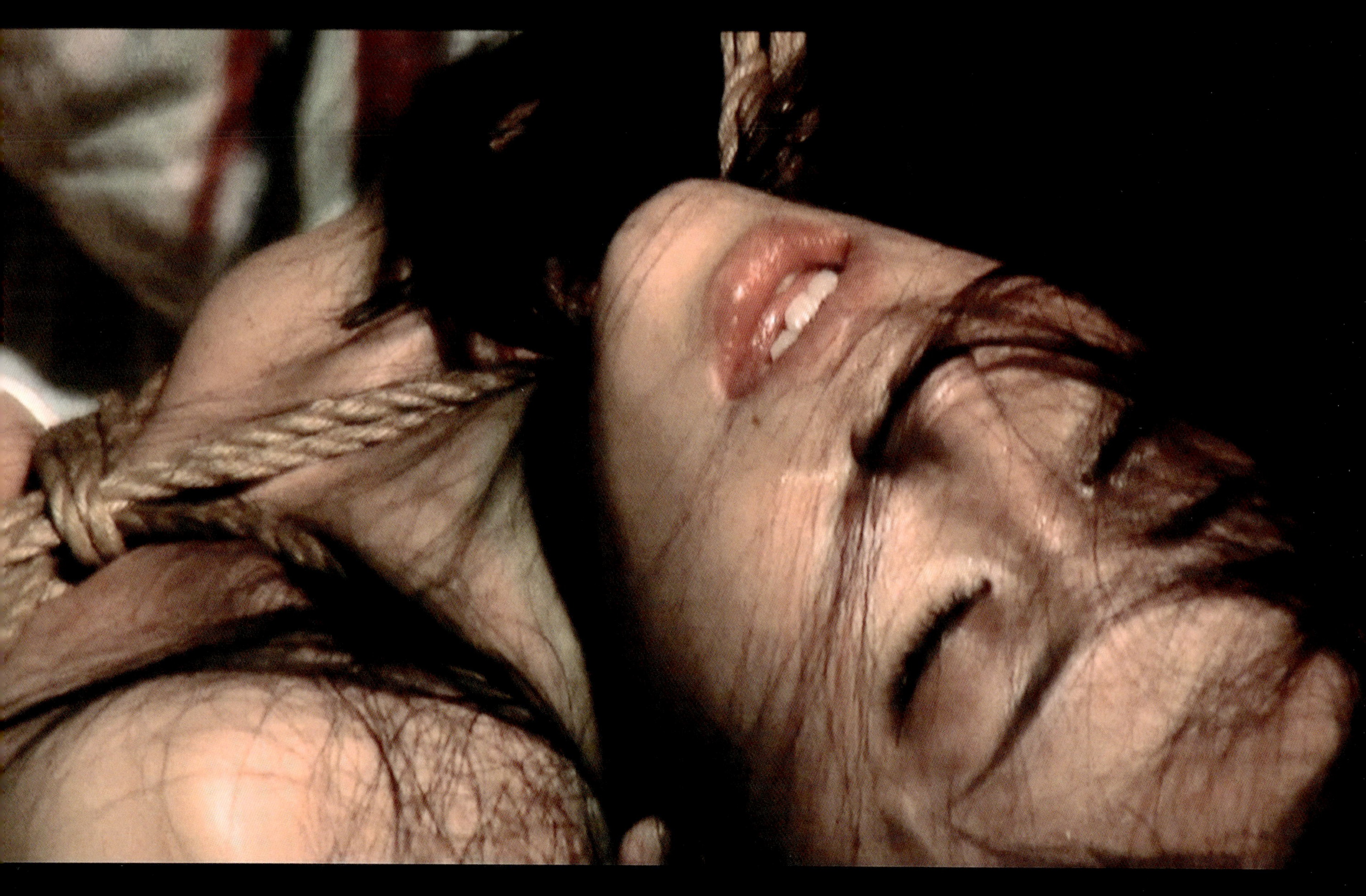

Clover:  One of the key things about Naka Akira's rope bondage is expression.  When he tied with Iroha you can see the expression in her feet, in her hands, in her face, her whole body is screaming with emotion.

His scenes are extremely intense and emotional. When you see it you just can't help but be pulled into it, almost like you are experiencing it yourself.

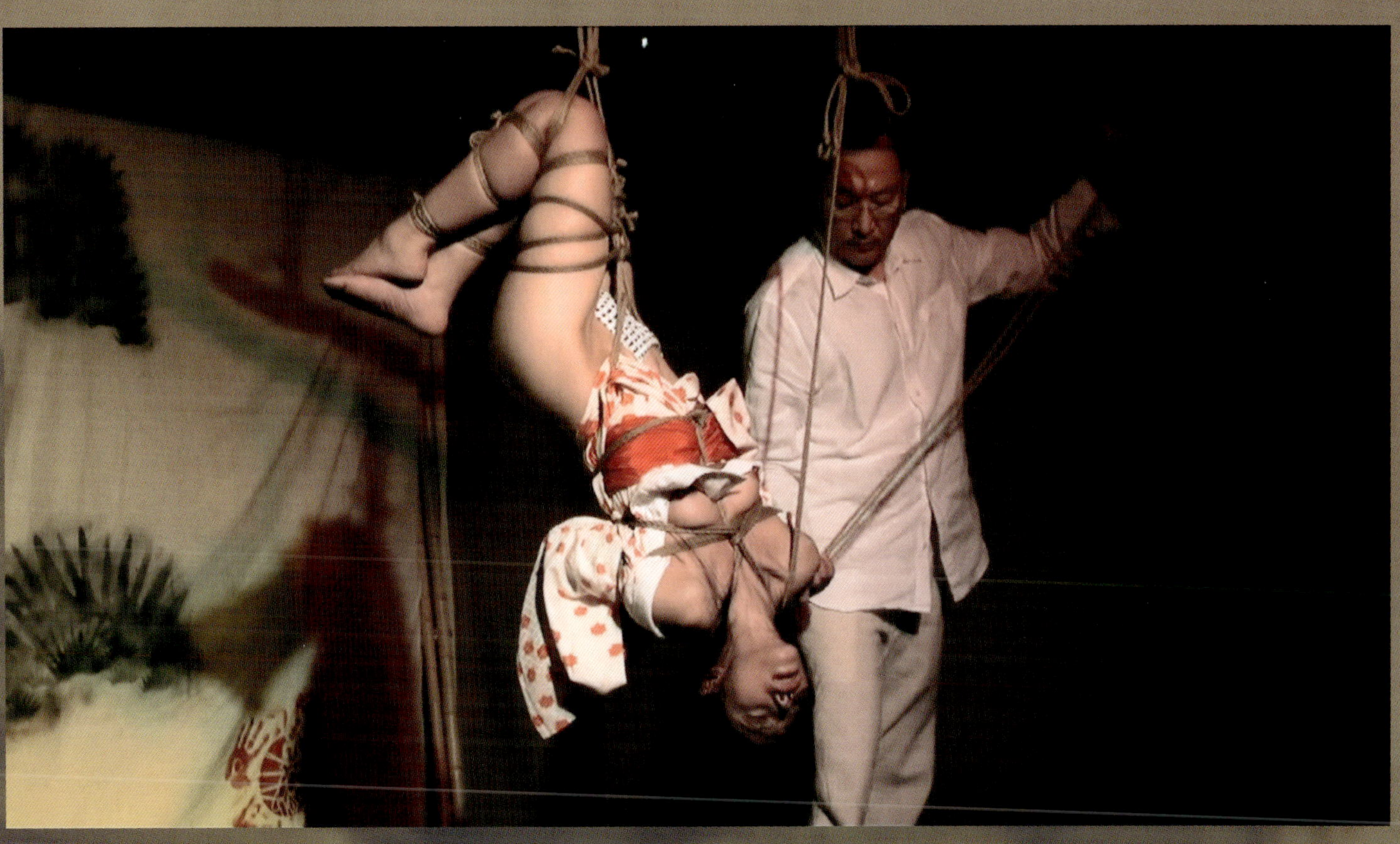

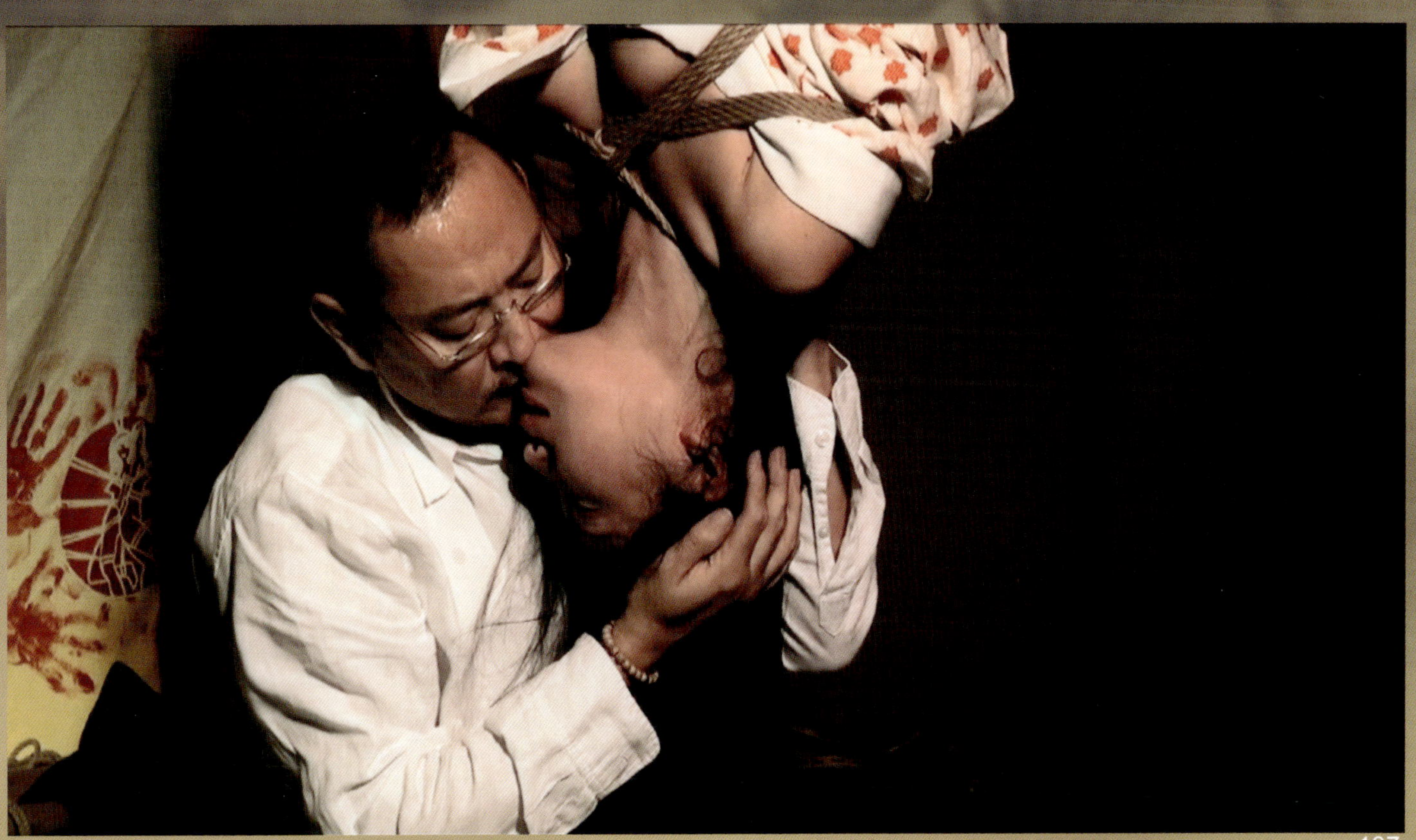

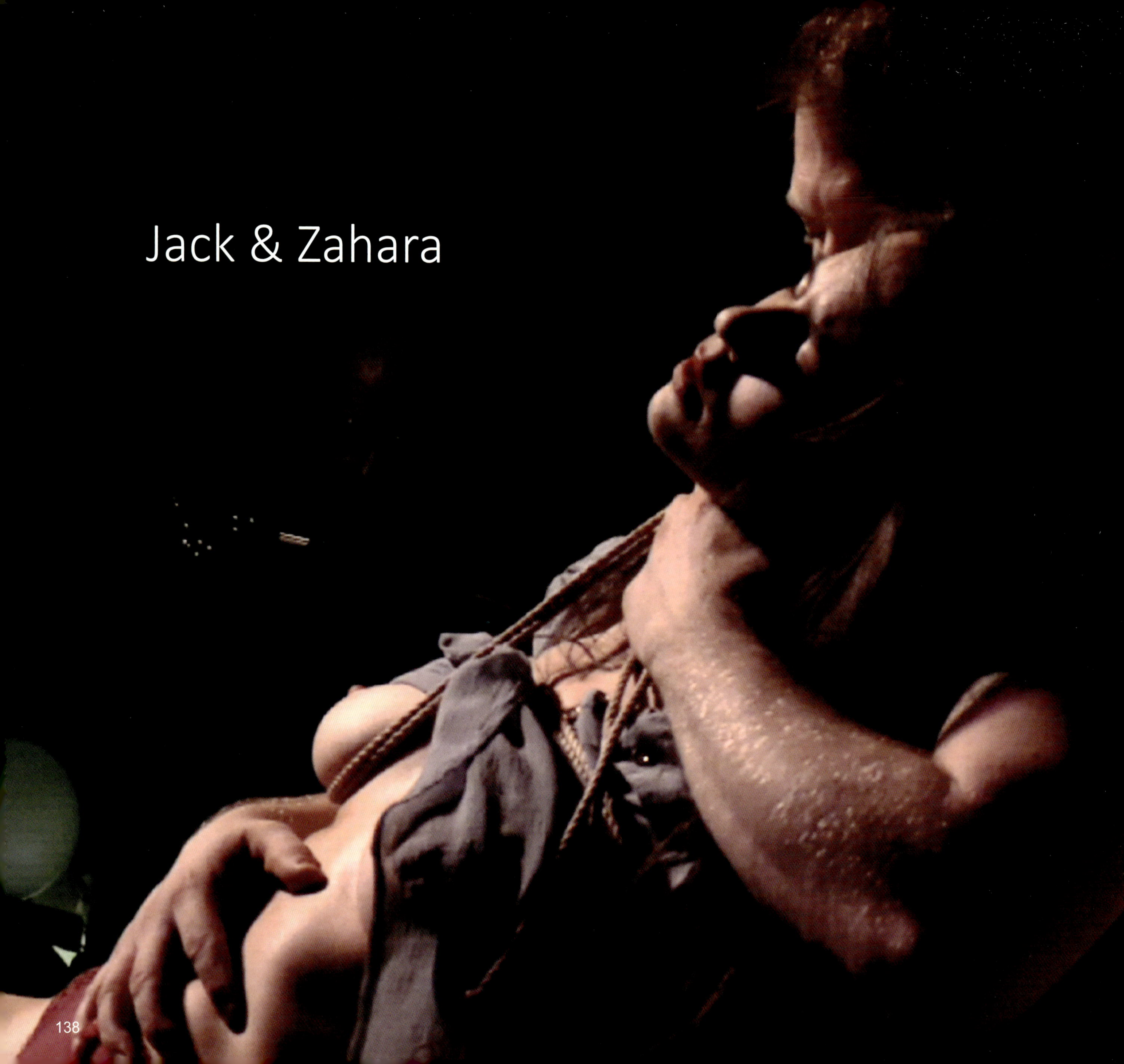

Jack & Zahara

The emotional dynamics of Naka Akira and Iroha Shizuki seem to be mirrored in the stage act of Jack and Zahara who also performed at the 2013 festival.

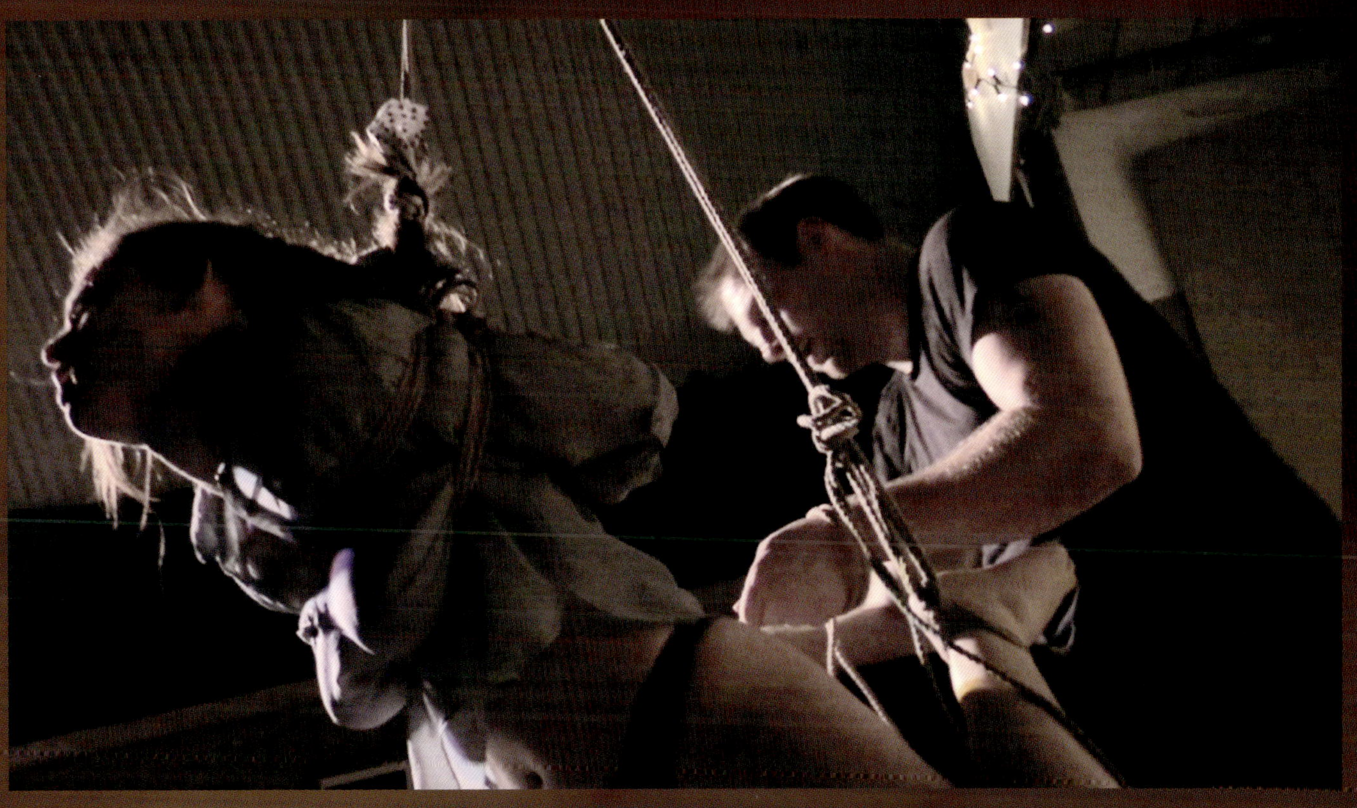

Jack:  I'm deeply humbled by the fact that the way I've achieved what I have is entirely because of Zahara. I couldn't do what I do if she didn't respond the way she responds.

Zahara:  No one else can make me feel the way that he makes me feel.

Yes we're showing people rope but we're also showing everyone how much we love each other.

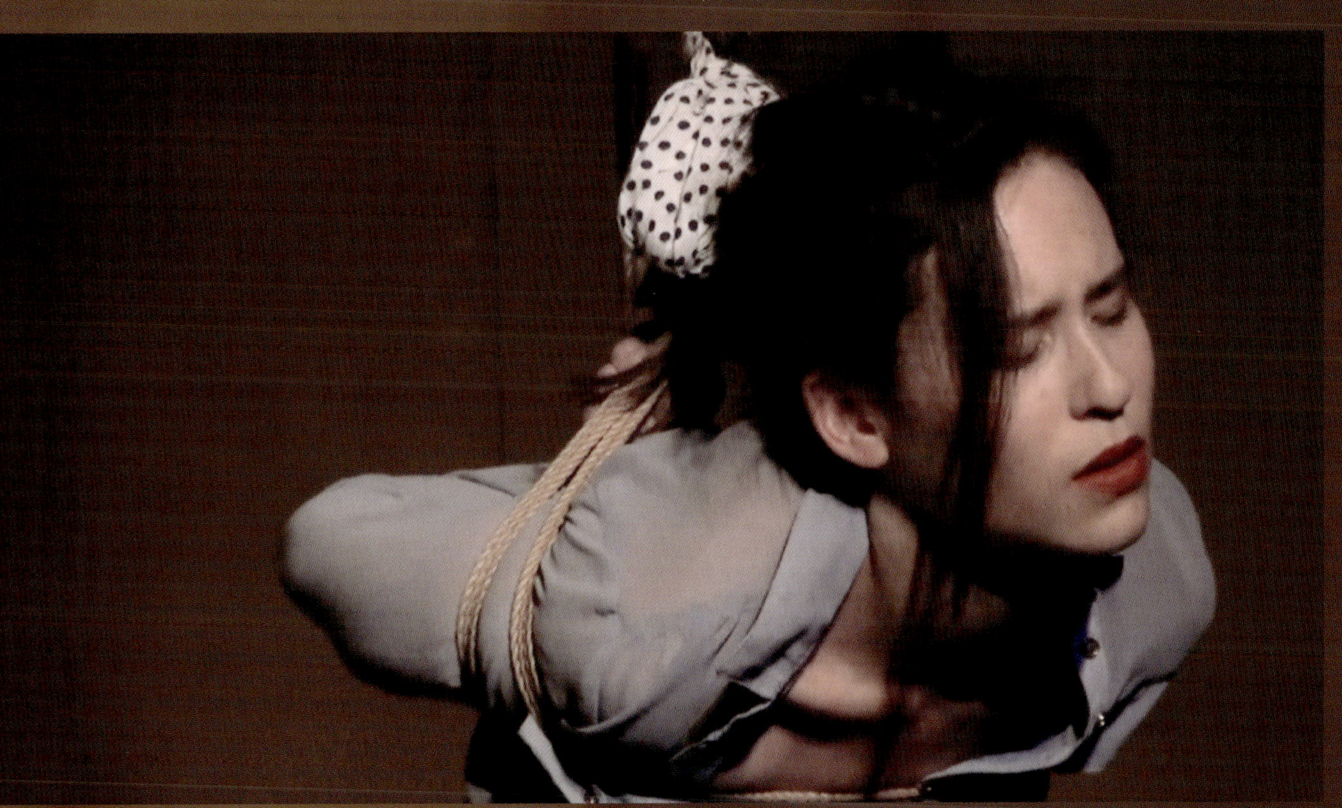

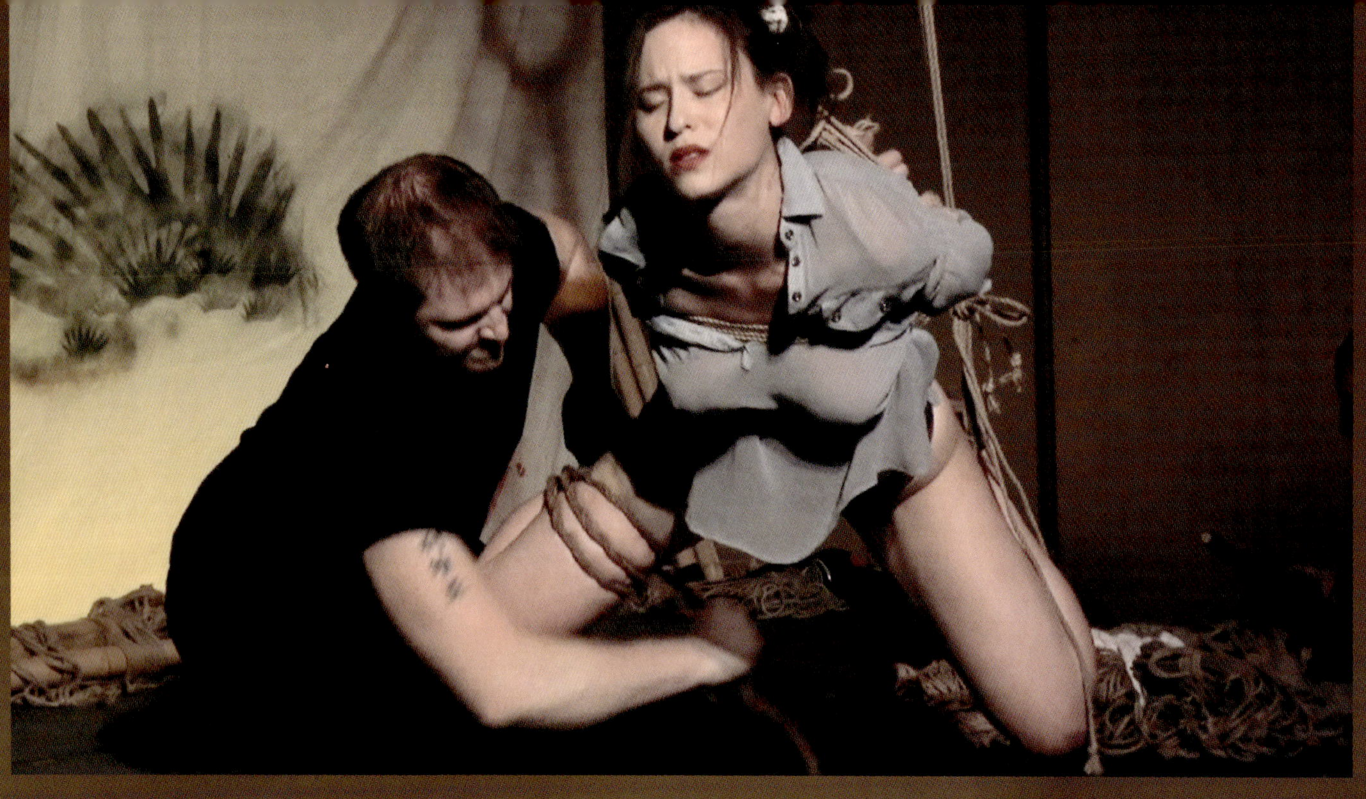

Zahara:  This year is probably the hardest performance we have ever done.

Jack:  We've totally changed our style due to Naka Akira.  We now use a high hands Takate Kote

Zahara:  It opens up your body more, like an arch.

Jack: It also pulls many more emotions out.  For some reason it works for us.

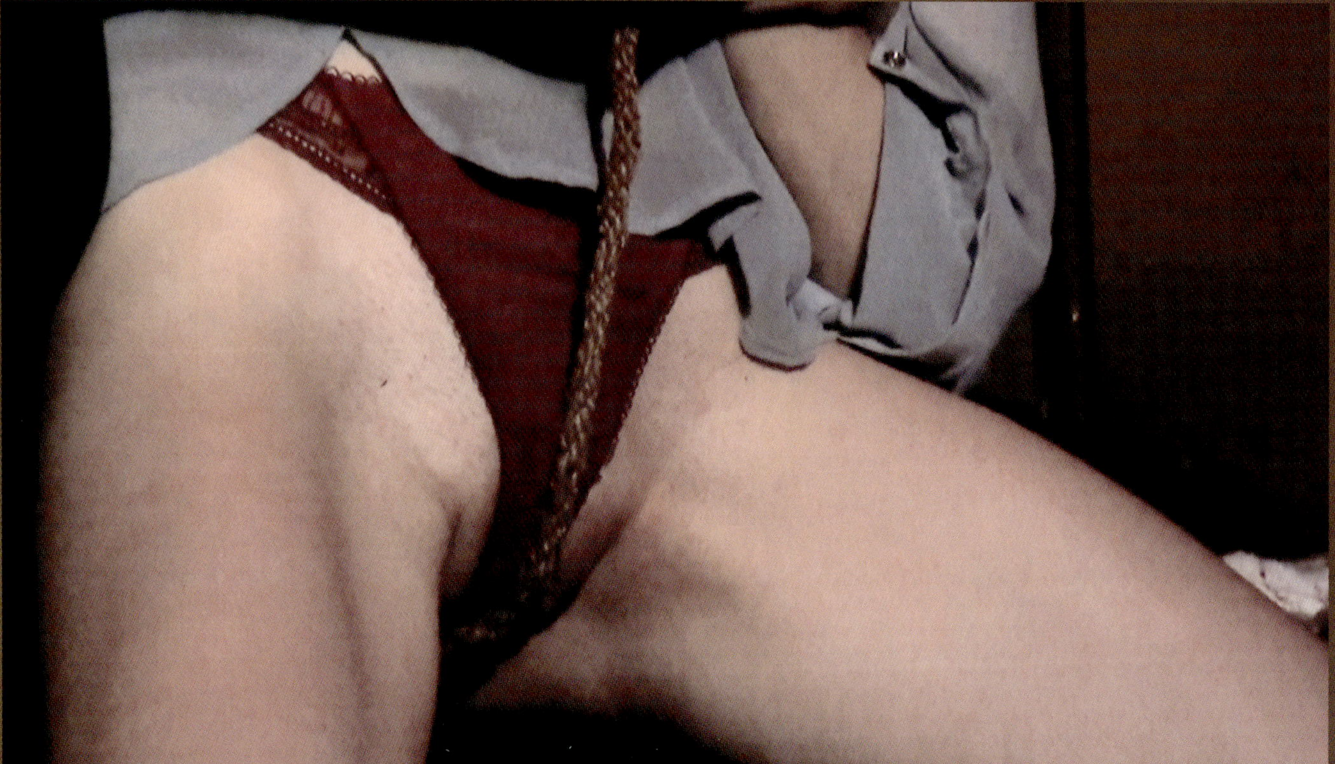

Zahara:  He used lots of coconut rope which is very scratchy, but times a million.

Jack:  The rope is extremely nasty and extremely painful; it's like tying her in barbed wire.

I was particularly mean today.  I like causing a bit of pain.  But even I'm shaking from this performance which was very emotional for us.

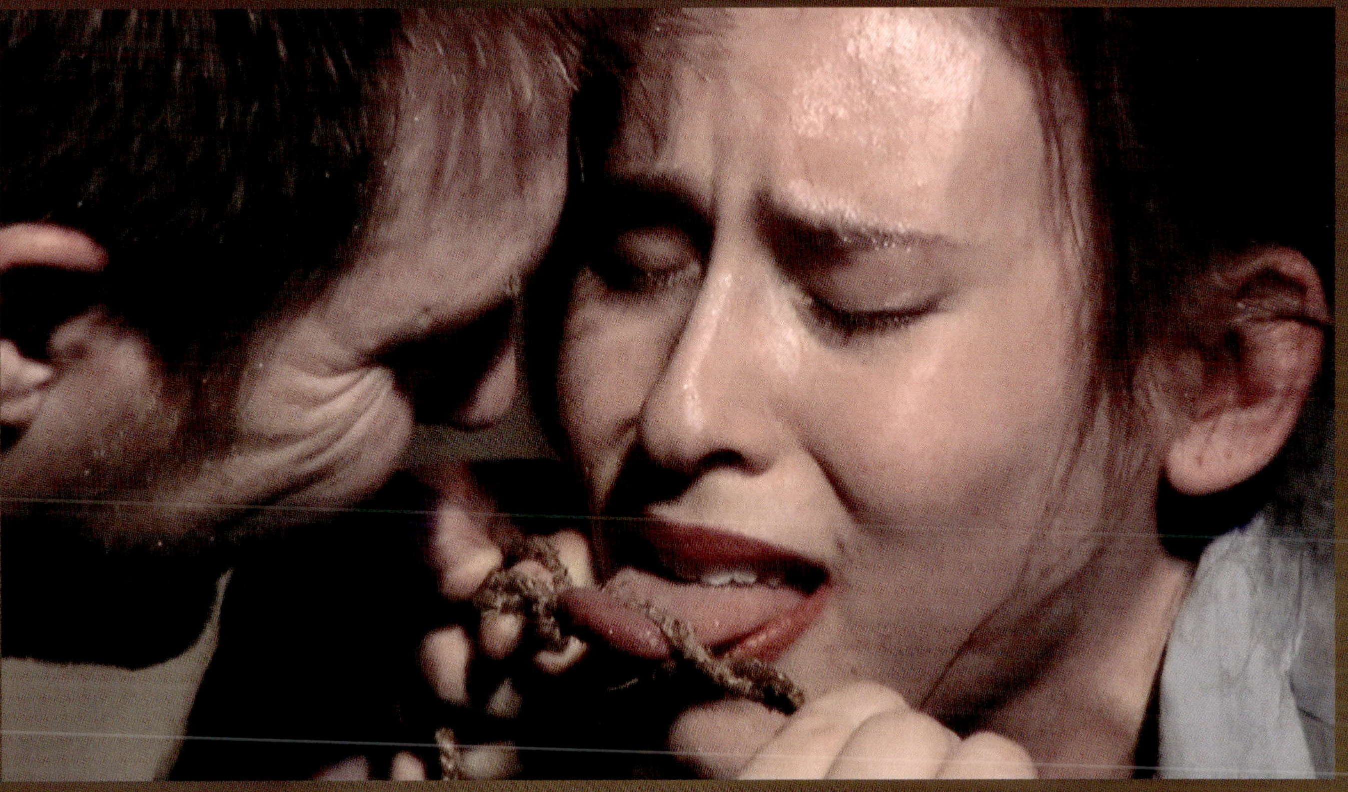

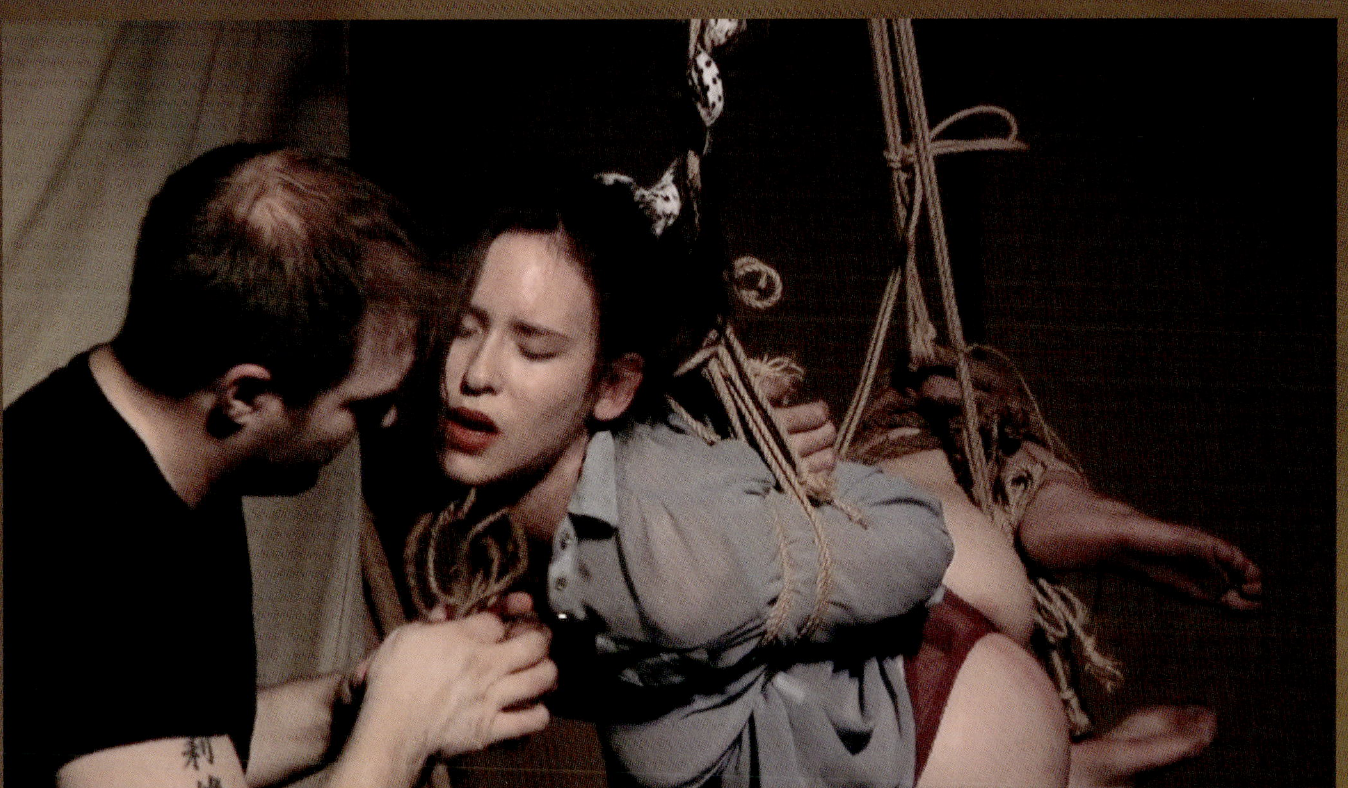

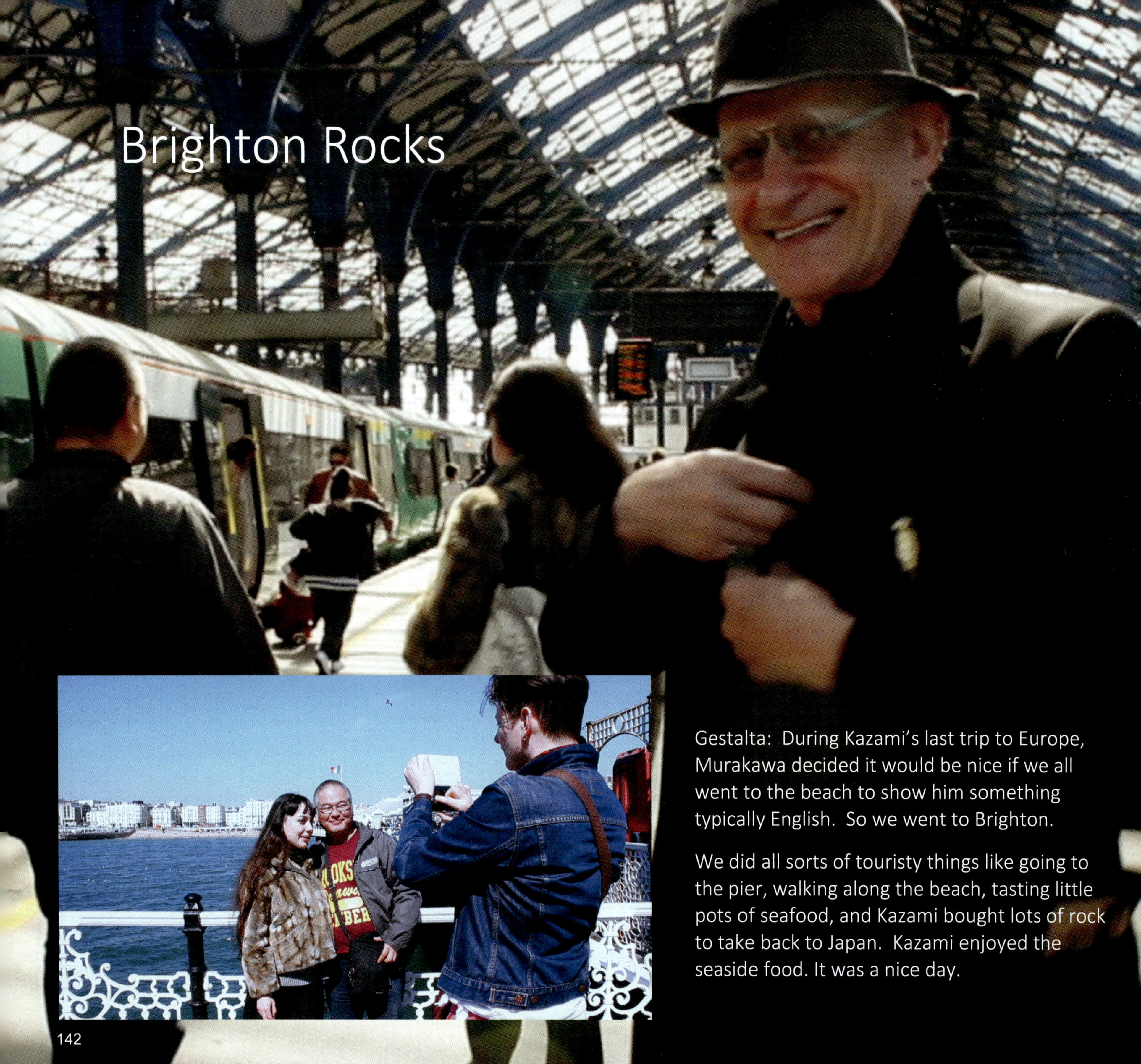


Gestalta:  During Kazami's last trip to Europe, Murakawa decided it would be nice if we all went to the beach to show him something typically English.  So we went to Brighton.

We did all sorts of touristy things like going to the pier, walking along the beach, tasting little pots of seafood, and Kazami bought lots of rock to take back to Japan.  Kazami enjoyed the seaside food. It was a nice day.

Gestalta:  I'm still modelling for Kazami. We've been to Australia to do some workshops and some shows there. The first performance in Australia was one where he finally managed to find a tie that was pretty much at the limit of anything I'd want to go through with rope.  I was in a position where I couldn't breathe and I felt my spine was being compressed and crushed.  It was quite scary really!

We also did a dual performance with Milla Reika and her model Nami which was a lot of fun.  I was tied with Nami with her face two inches from mine and she was making a lot of noise.  In the tie we were hugging while we were suspended and they bull whipped us a little bit. Quite a lot really!

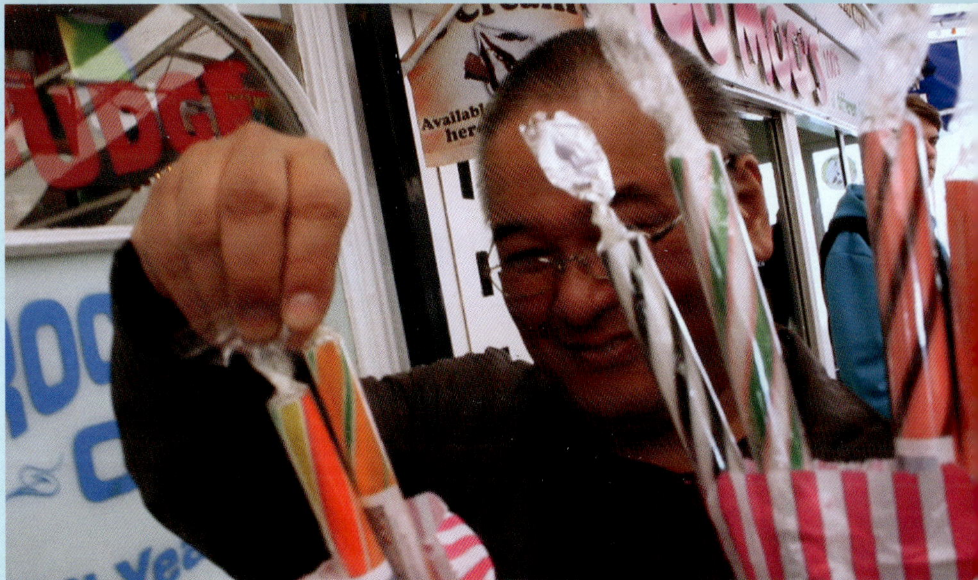

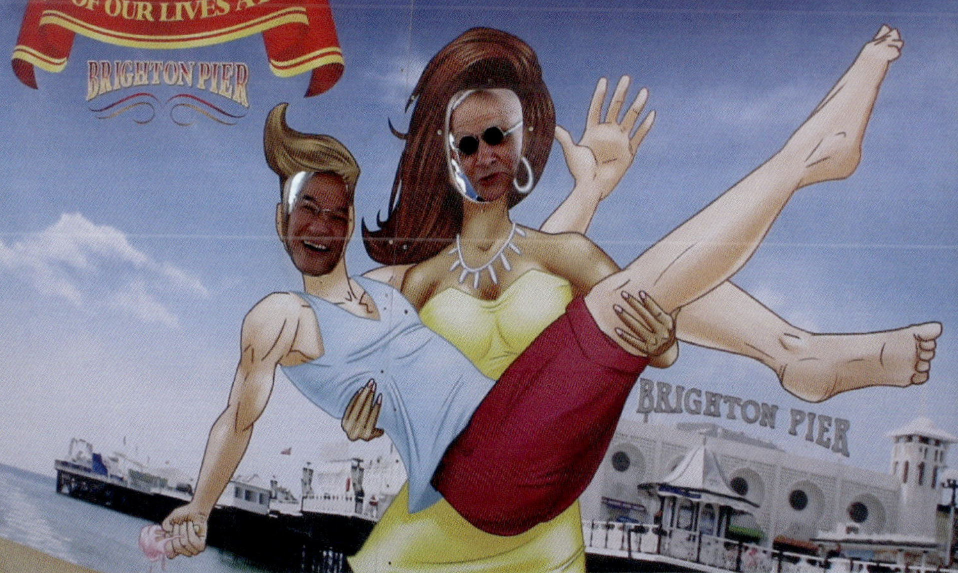


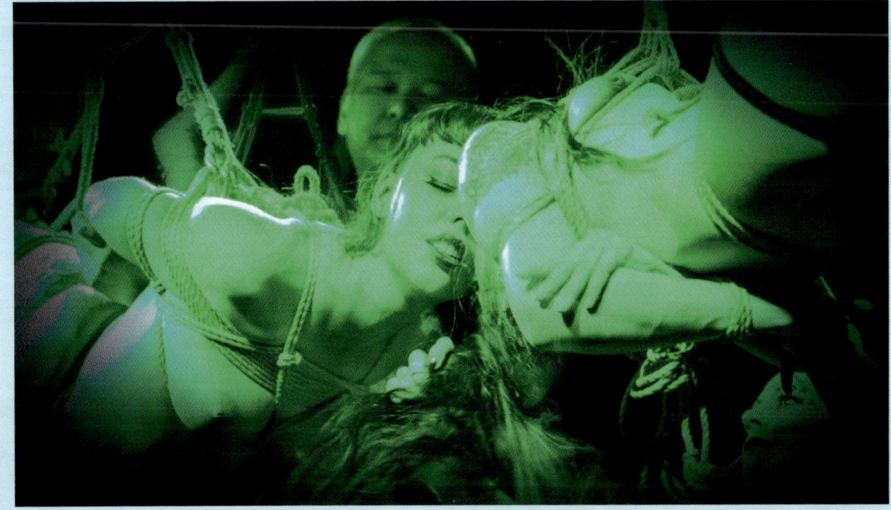

I still have a little scar from that on my leg.  I was put in a situation where I was trying to comfort Nami but at the same time was wanting to laugh, which is what I generally do if I'm in pain.  It's still lots of fun!

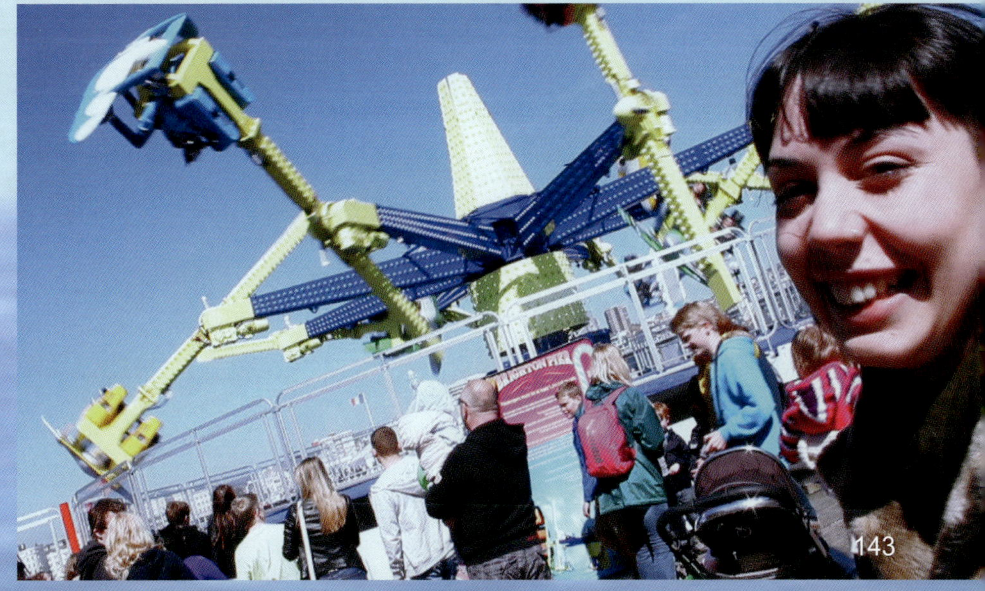

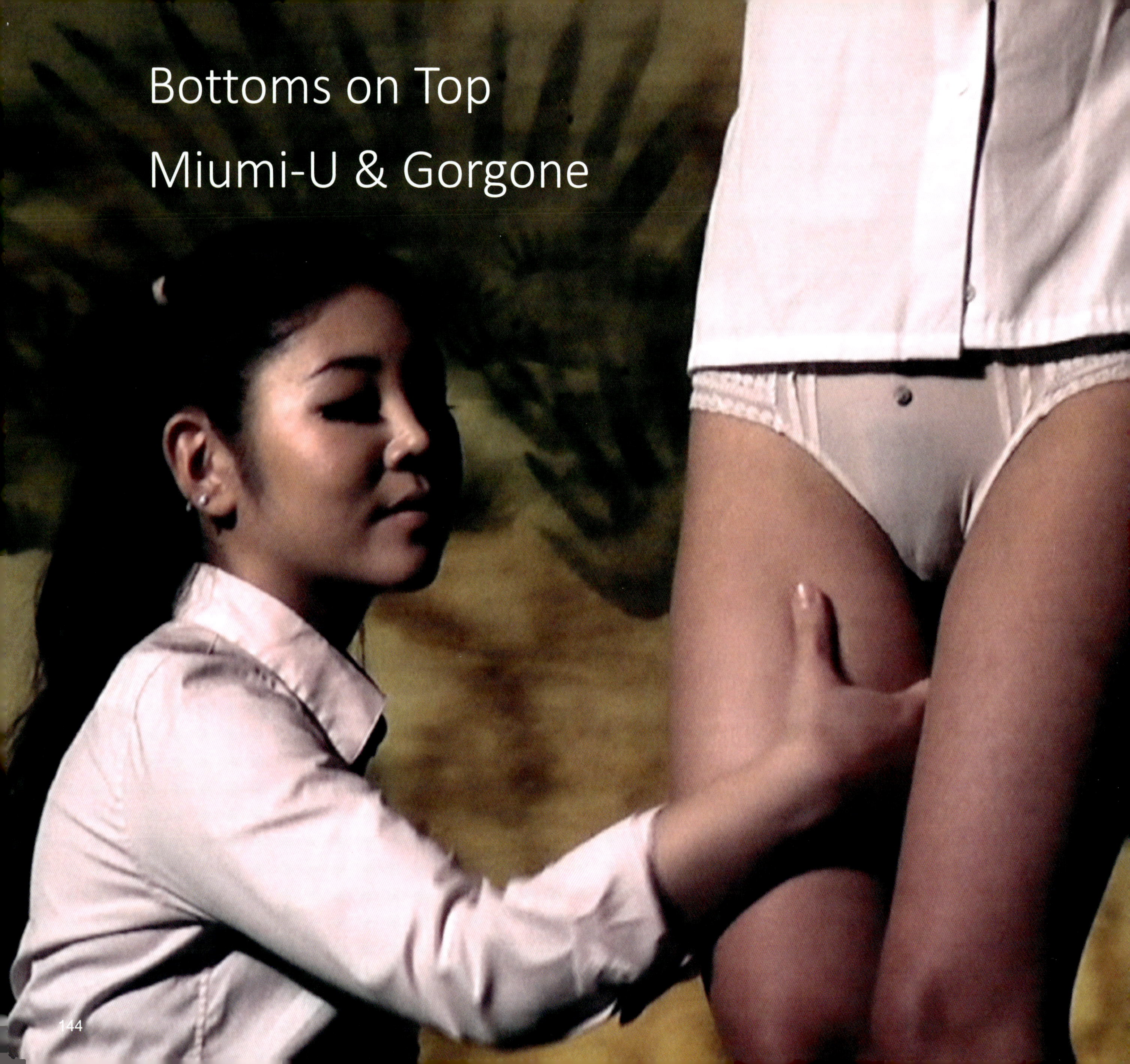
Bottoms on Top
Miumi-U & Gorgone

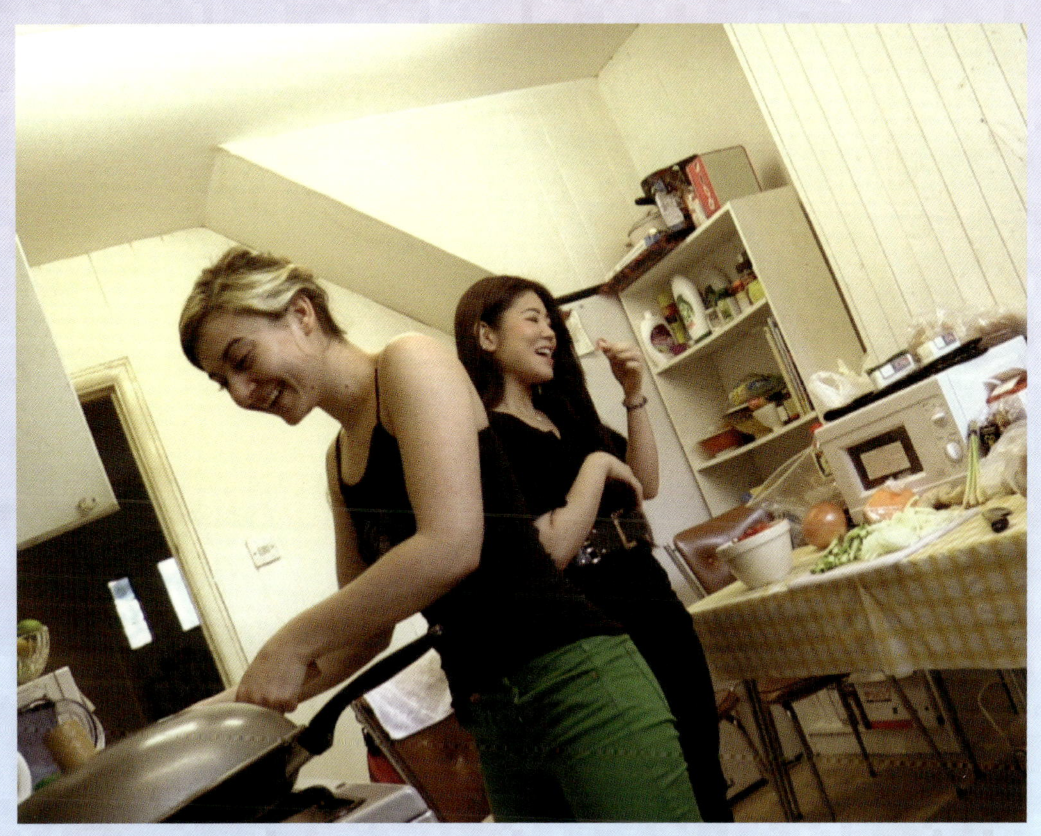

**A more sensual kind of relationship with rope and food was to be found with Miumi-U and Gorgone.  They seem to be feminising Kinbaku.**

Gorgone:  You're very hungry babe?

Miumi-U: I'm starving.

Gorgone:  Miumi-U actually was very challenging for me the first time she tied me because she's very soft; she's extremely delicate.  And the first time Miumi-U tied me I felt like something is wrong.  That's really weird.  Her touch was so different.  The touch of her hands.  The touch of her ropes.  Everything was so different and then I got kind of embraced by her and her ropes.

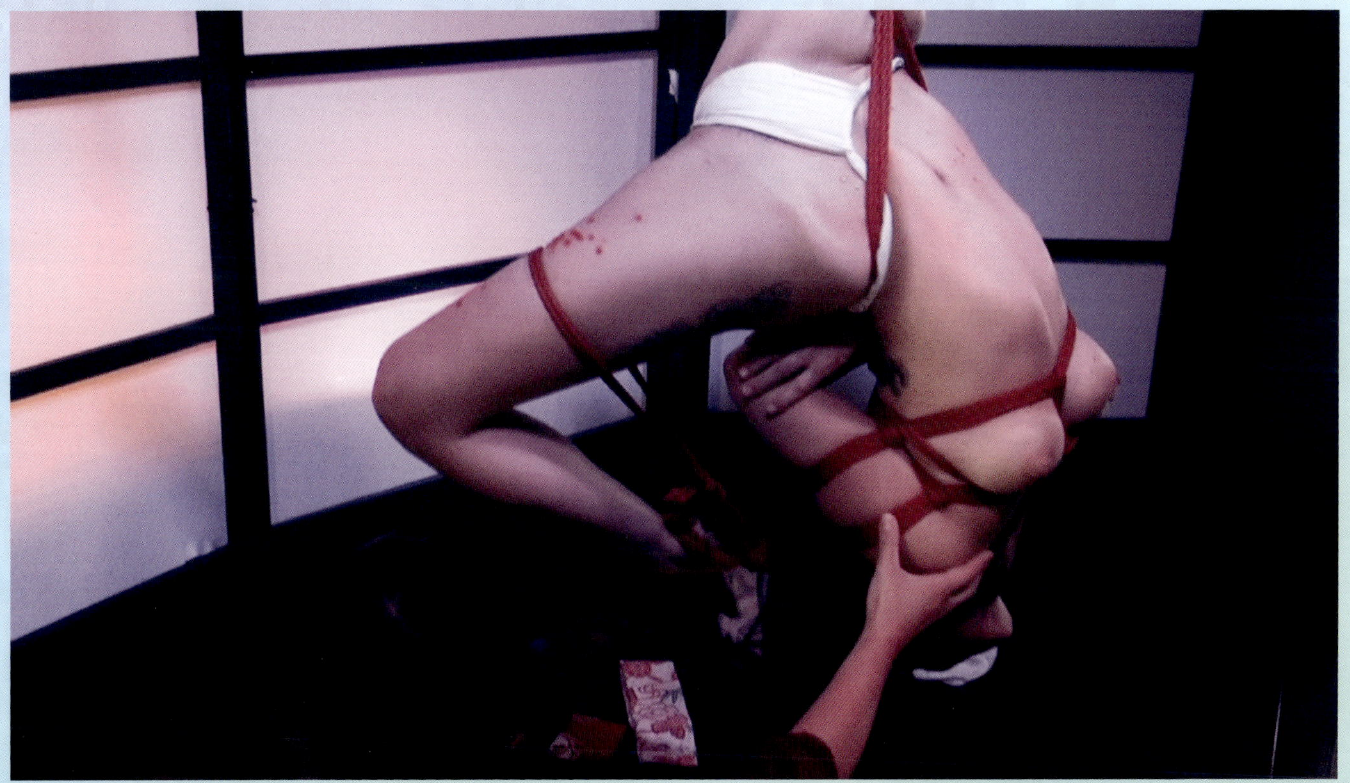

Miumi-U: You can cook and I can tie.

Gorgone:  A very easy connection between tying and cooking is that you are dealing with a given number of ingredients. Then you can combine them, however, and you get different results.  But there are some basic ingredients that you're always going to use, which is like the basics of bondage.

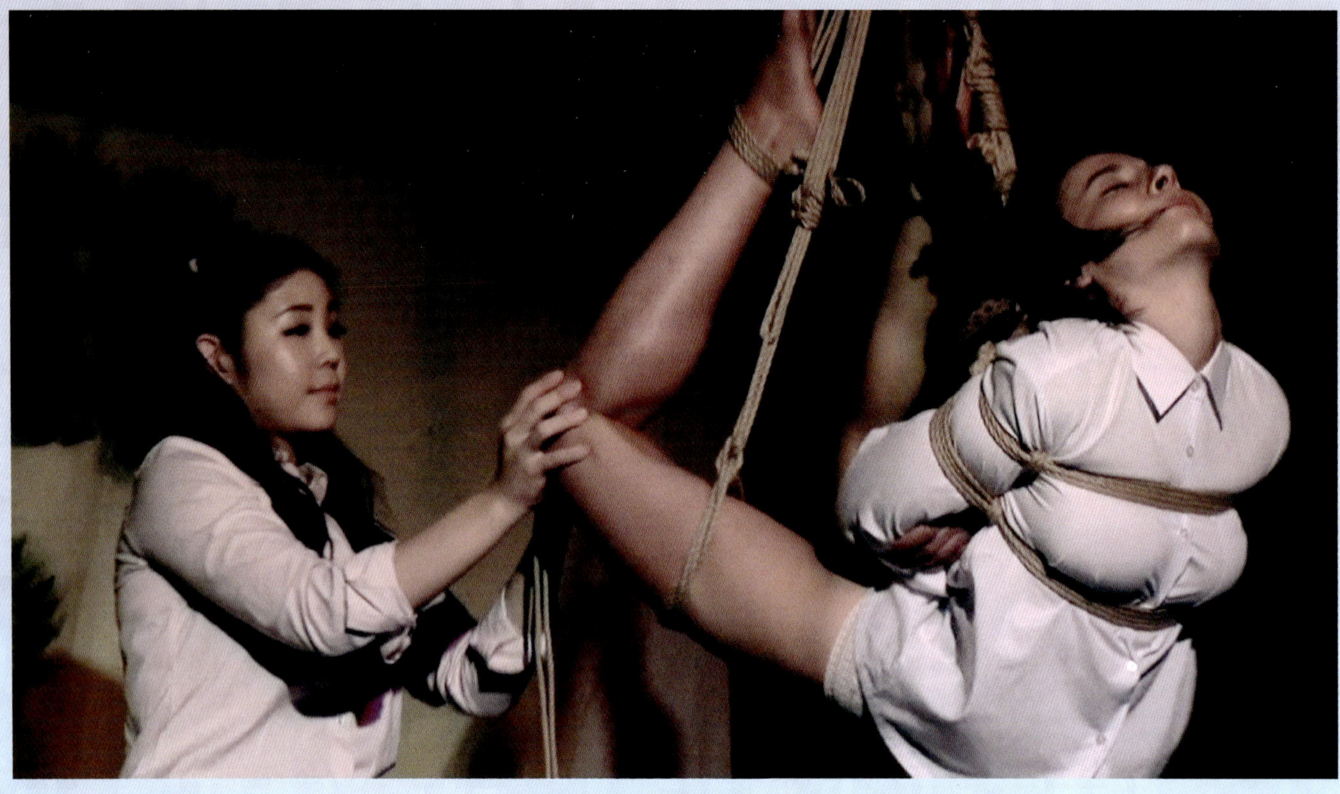

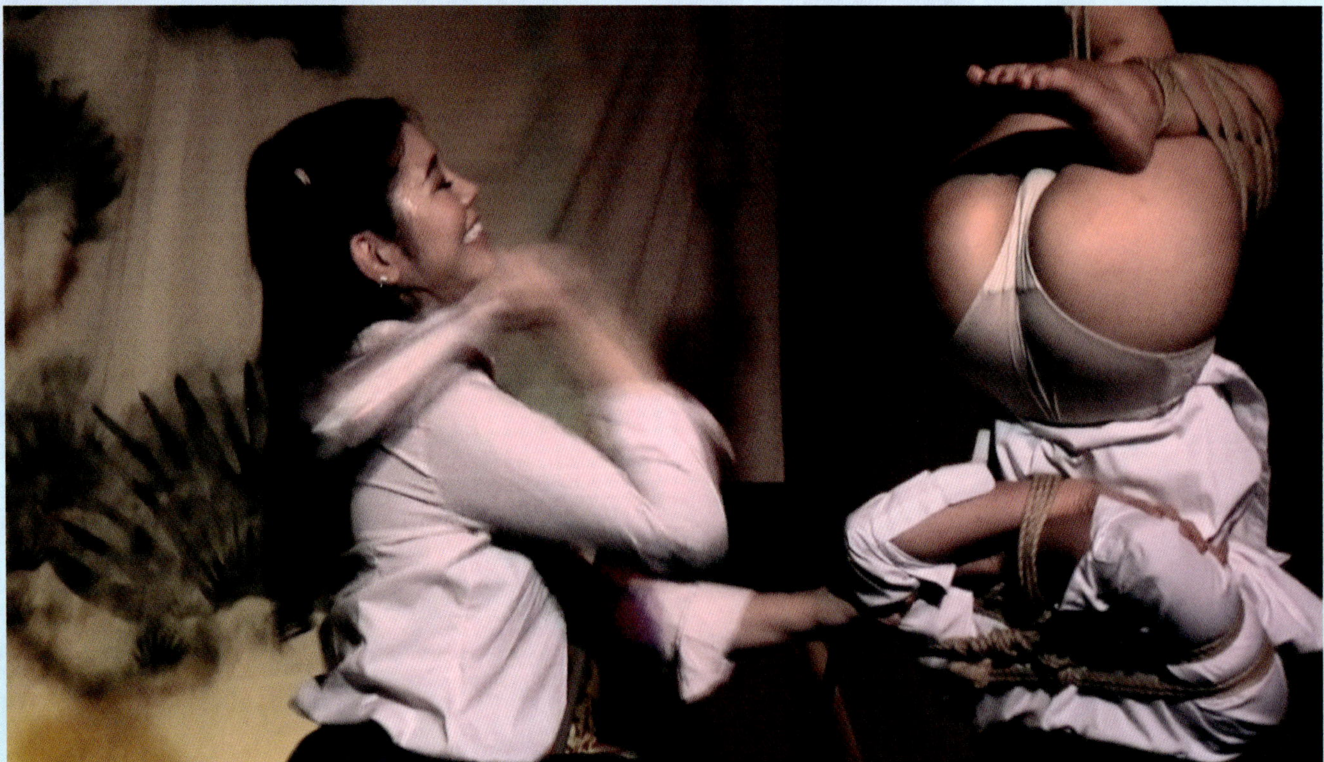

Miumi-U:  I prefer to tie only women.  Men are not my style.  Because not beautiful for me.  I like ladies shape, yes.

Gorgone:  Eating and cooking can be very sensual because you're touching, you're smelling, you're tasting, and it's full of colours.  I like it when it looks beautiful sometimes.  You have to be focused because you don't want to burn something, or you don't want to overcook something.  You have to be quick and reactive; you have to adapt.  Everything that really reminds me of tying.

And cooking can be dangerous!

Miumi-U:  Rope is a kind of conversation for me.  You don't need to speak English.  You don't need to speak Japanese.  And just thinking, and concentrate on her;  yes that's it.

Gorgone: I think your real strength and identity as a rigger, beside your technique that is very good, is that you're very fluid and elegant and delicate and feminine and sexy and I think it makes a very beautiful character.

Miumi-U: Yes, but sometimes you need to be more aggressive, because I want to make it looks like aggressive: you know like strong, the man.

Gorgone: But you whipped me at Bound, with the rope. It was so cute, like you gave me …. one … then checked on me …. second one checked on me and asked if I was OK. It was so cute.

Miumi-U: Oh, I'm so weird.

Gorgone: Even if you're elegant and delicate, you can be so mean, so that's OK!

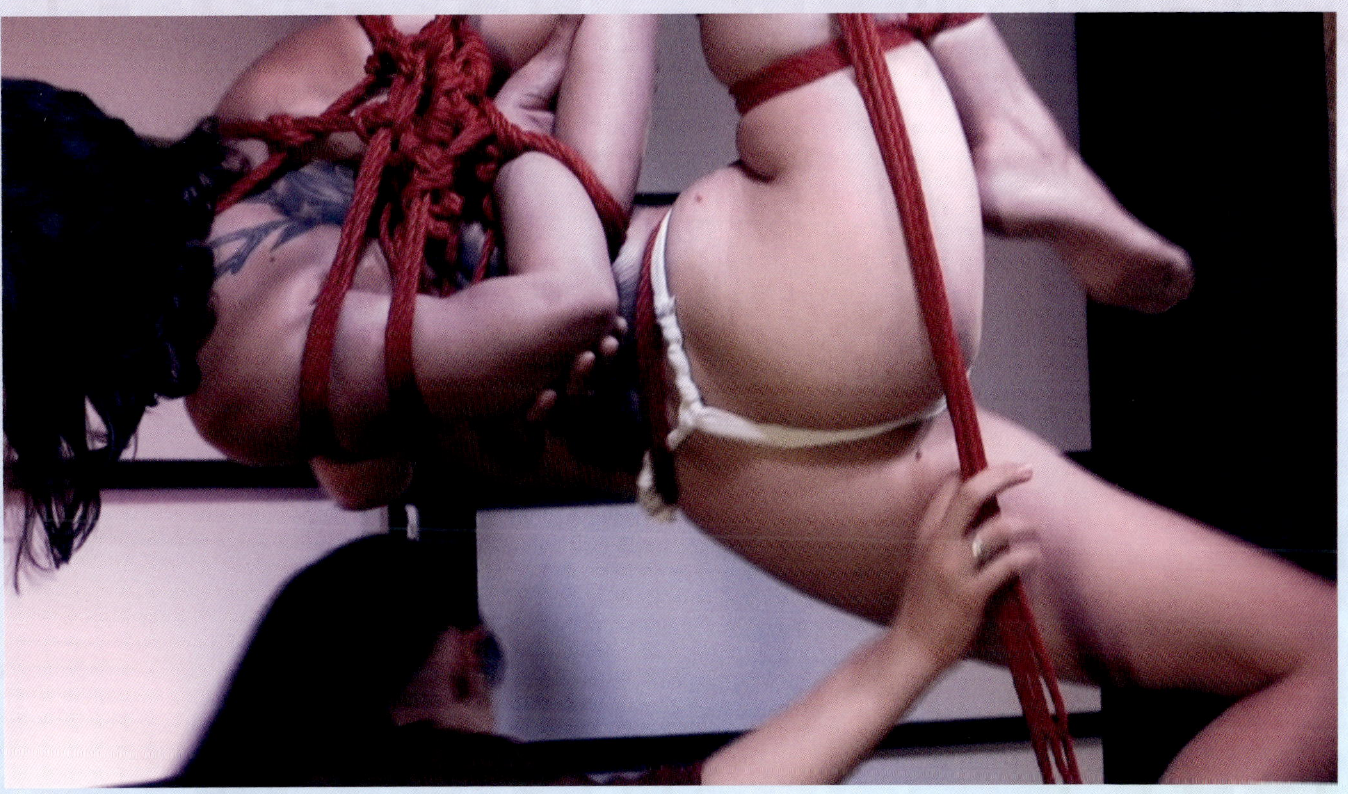

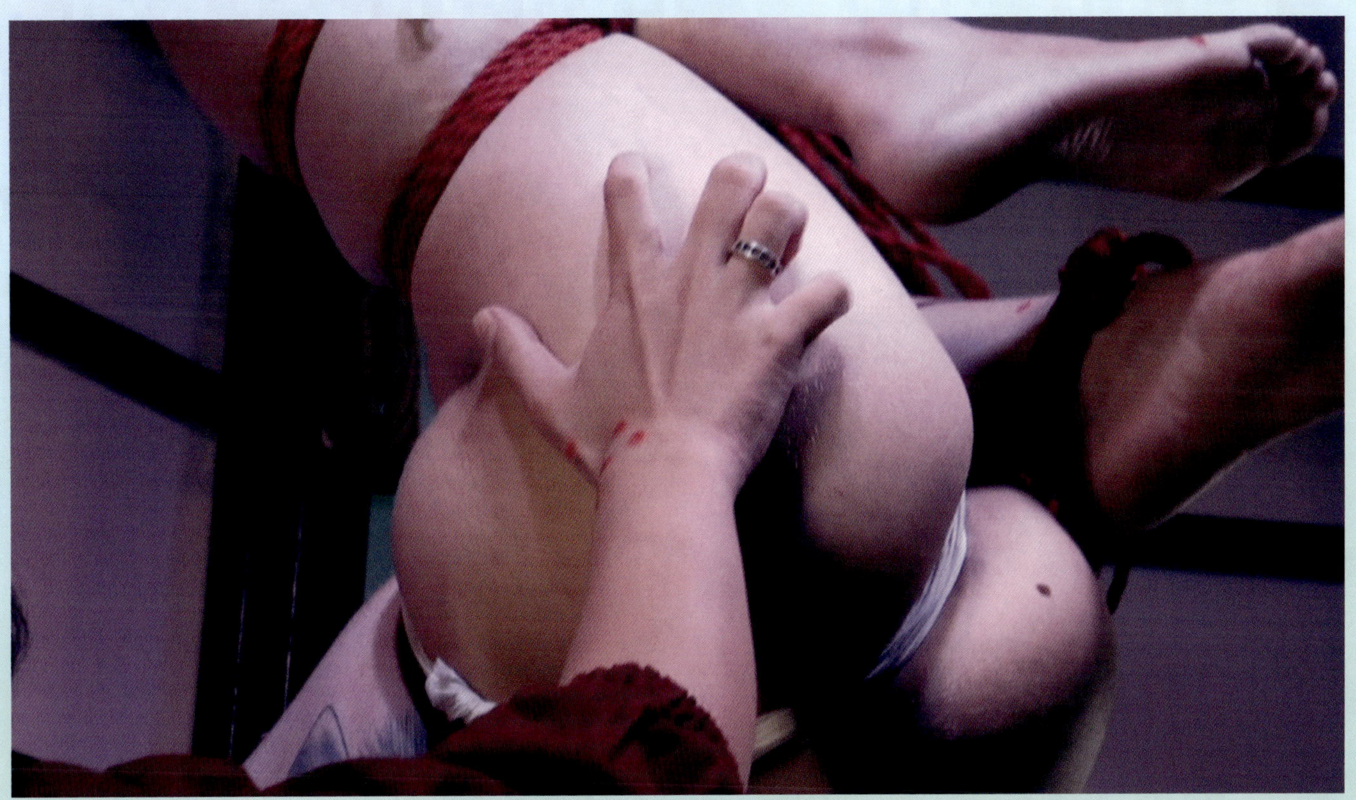

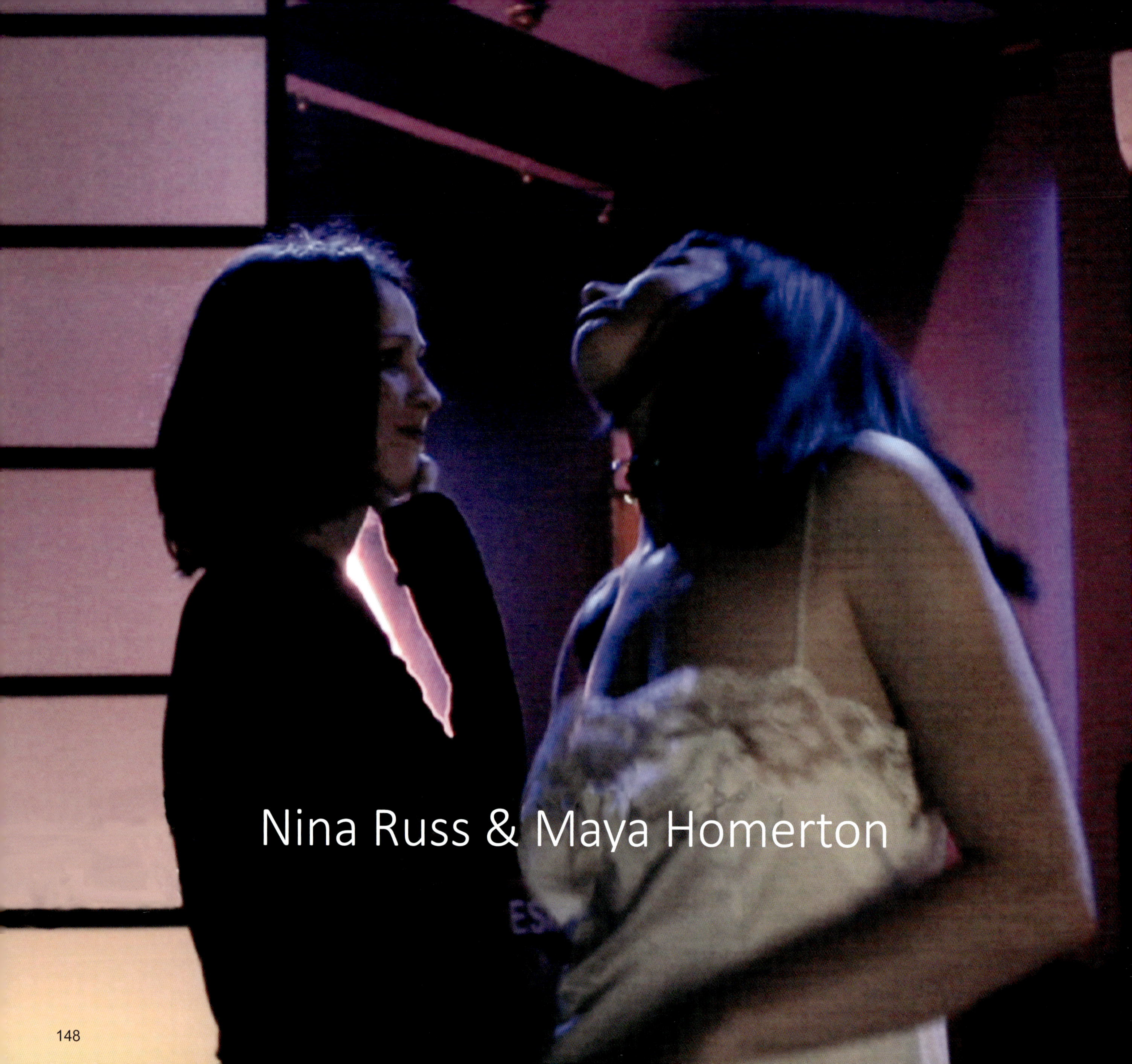

Nina Russ & Maya Homerton

**Nina Russ left Italy to come to live in London.....**

Nina:  The mentality in Italy of the woman tying was almost impossible.  So I've arrived in London and Bruce ( Esinem ) actually gave me the chance to tie and he taught me how to do it and it's been great.

I recommend for everyone to work with one model because you have to know the body.  If you work with ten models, you have to know ten bodies.

Bondage is not comfortable.  I've heard a lot of people who say - you know if bondage is painful it means the rigger is not good.  It's not true.

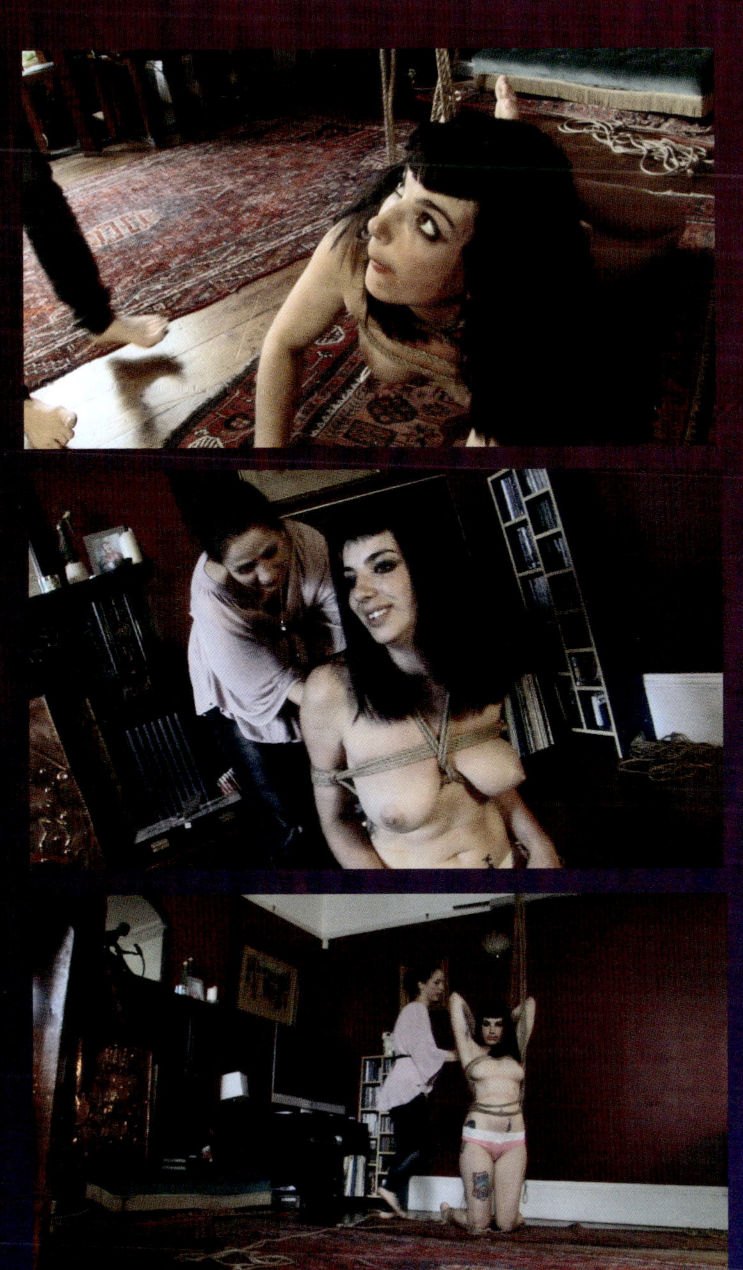

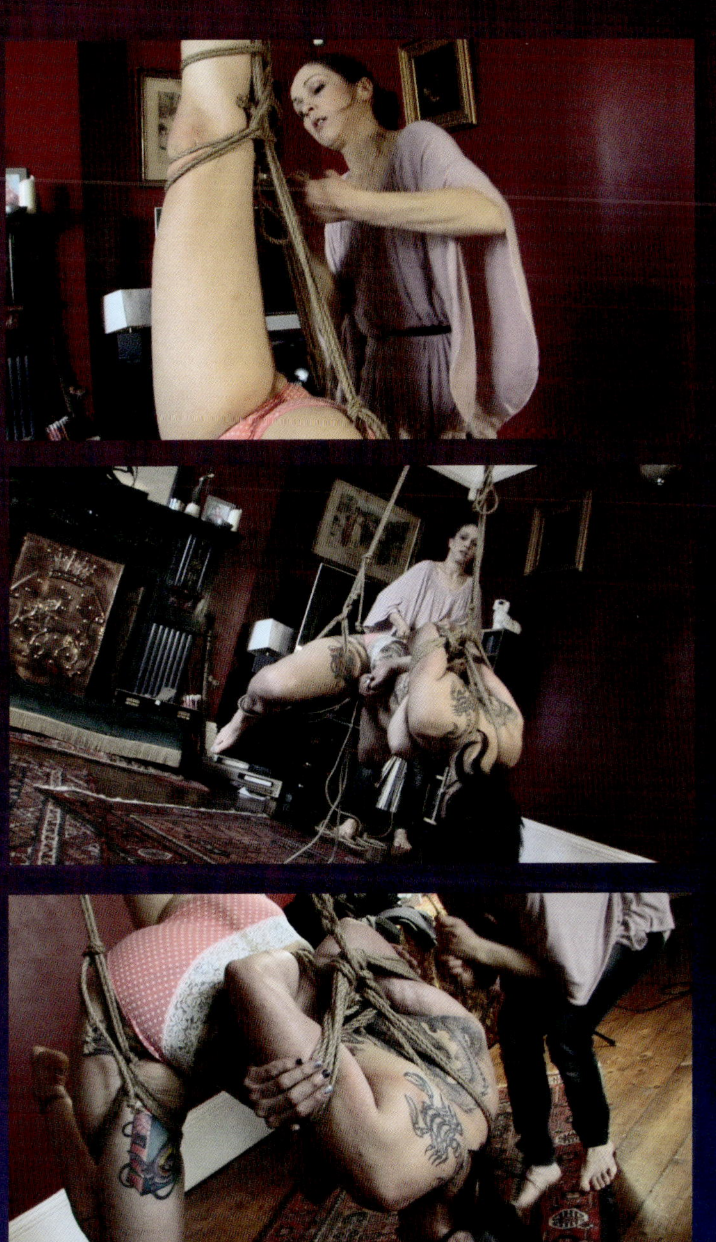

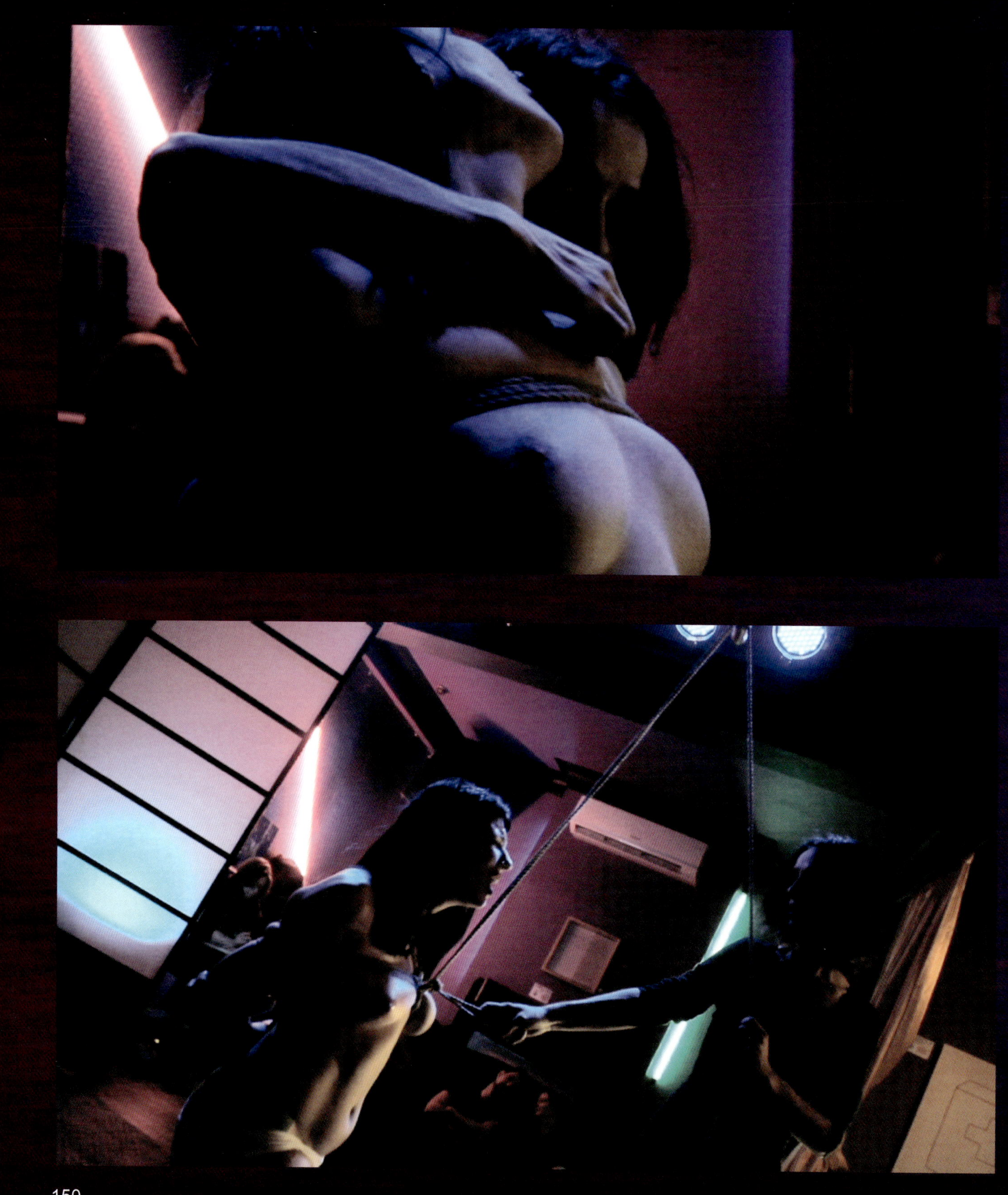

Nina:  You have to personalise everything because every person will react differently to pain for example.

So I've met with Maya and Maya gave me all her trust. She trust me from the first moment and that was great because it gave me the chance to actually experiment more and do things without fear.

Now I treat her a bit like an object.  She's my poor victim.  Well not so poor and not so much a victim!

The bondage has brought balance in my life.  If you're taking the balance to someone, you're actually affecting their brain.  You are controlling that person by having their attention.

It's touching the body to stimulate the brain.

Before going on stage I feel tension.  I feel the energy, And the balance comes exactly here.  You have to keep everything under control.

When you do bondage you cannot pretend to do bondage without knowing your body.

If you do not know what muscles you have in your body, how can you know where to place that rope? If you do not know where nerves are, or how your blood is working, how can you do bondage?  It's dangerous, you cannot.

Because I've discovered the tension in balance, and not just the tension in rope but the tension in general, it has changed me as a person.  It has helped me to grow.

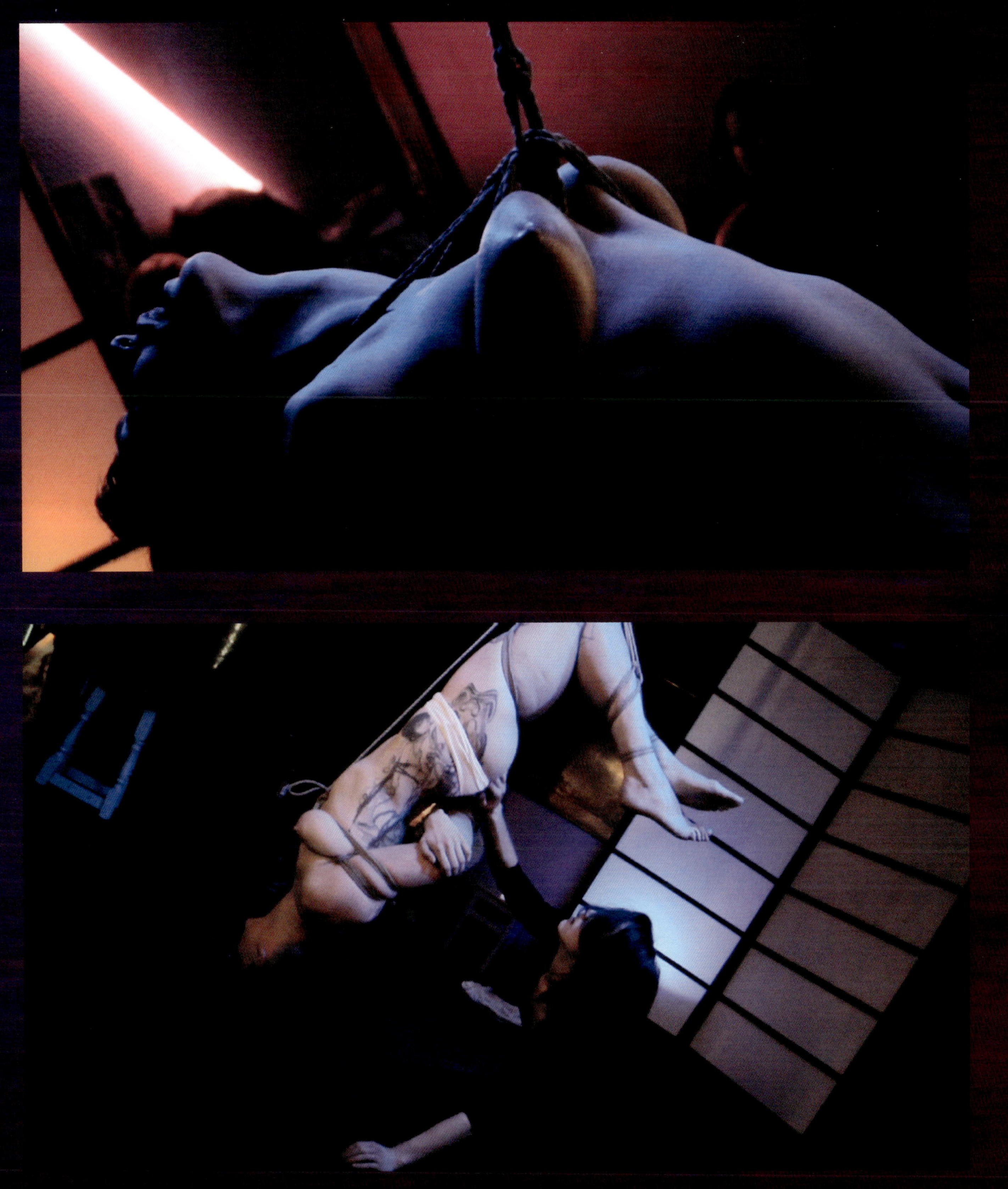

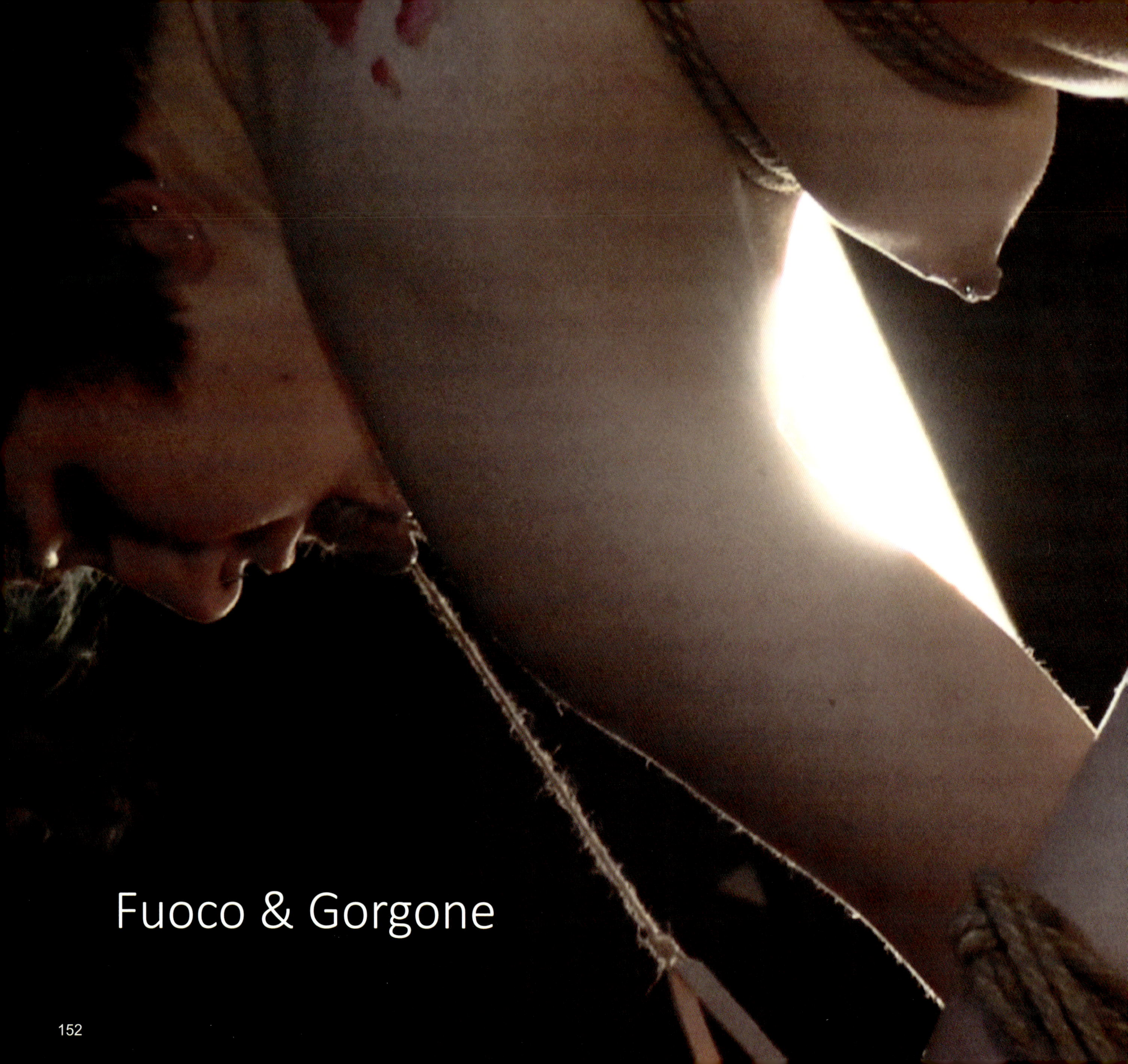

Fuoco & Gorgone

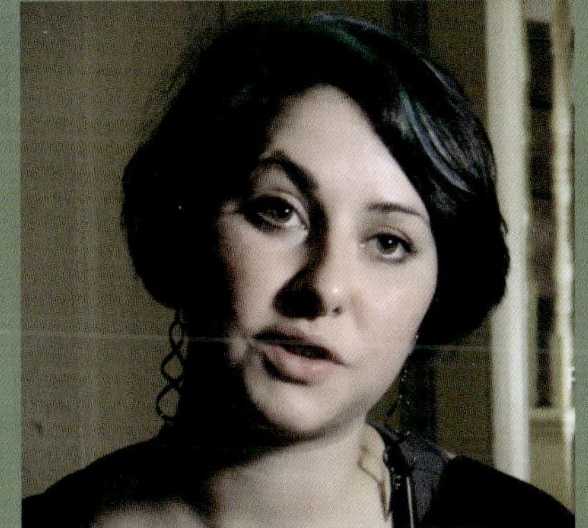

Fuoco:  One of the things that I enjoy about working with riggers who are models in general is that they're very aware of your experience in rope.  So there are lots of riggers who are just riggers and they'll put a rope somewhere and they won't understand that it's painful, or they won't exactly know how it feels.  Gorgone is very, very good at knowing how things feel.

Gorgone:  I like to tie the tongues for example, I do that all the time because I really love it.

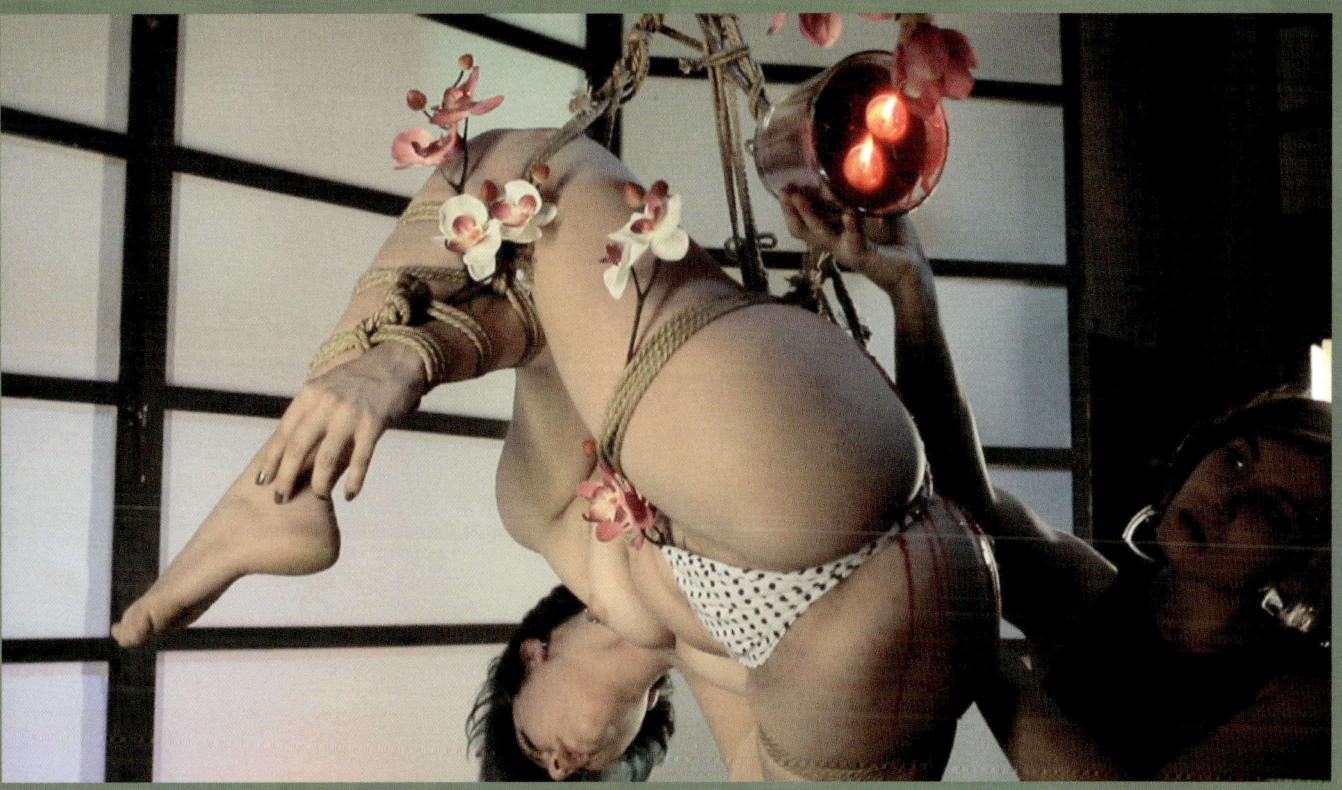

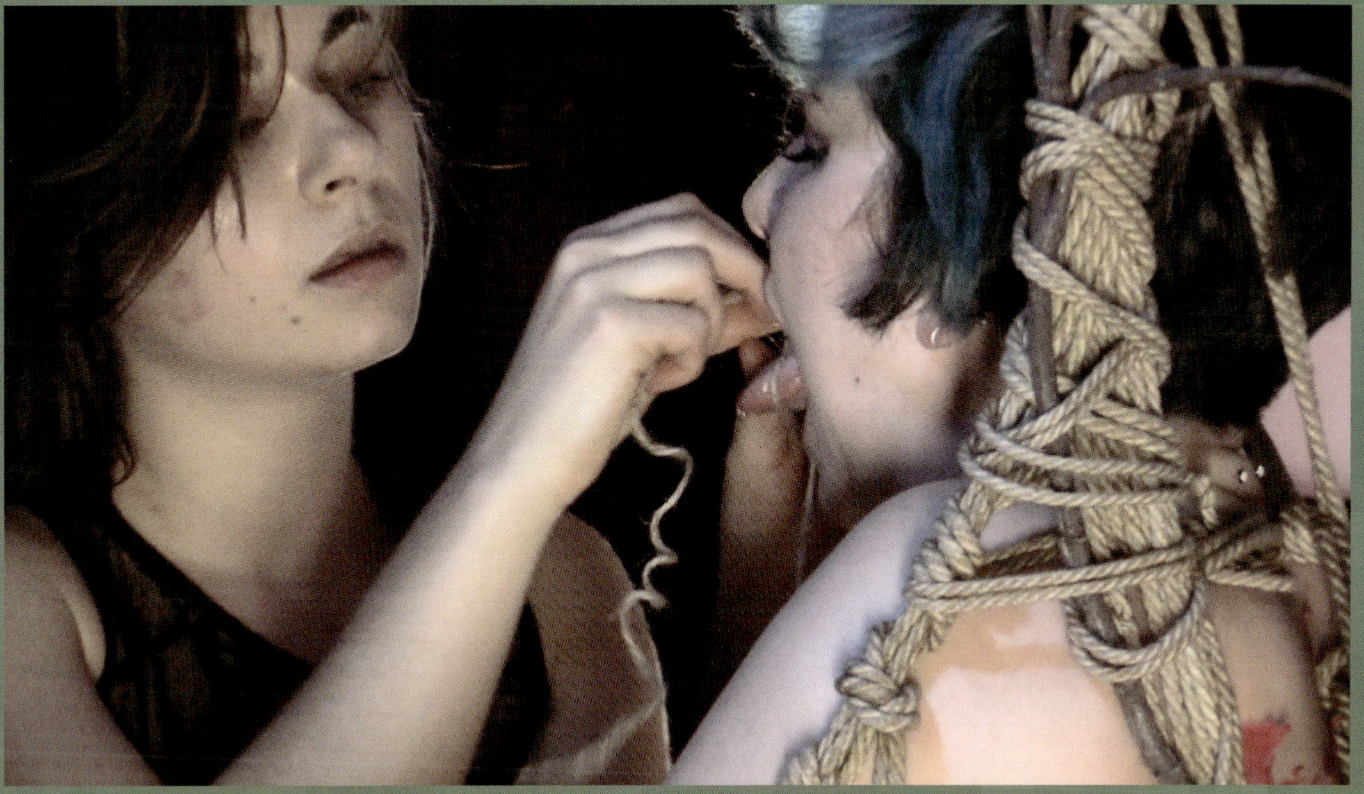

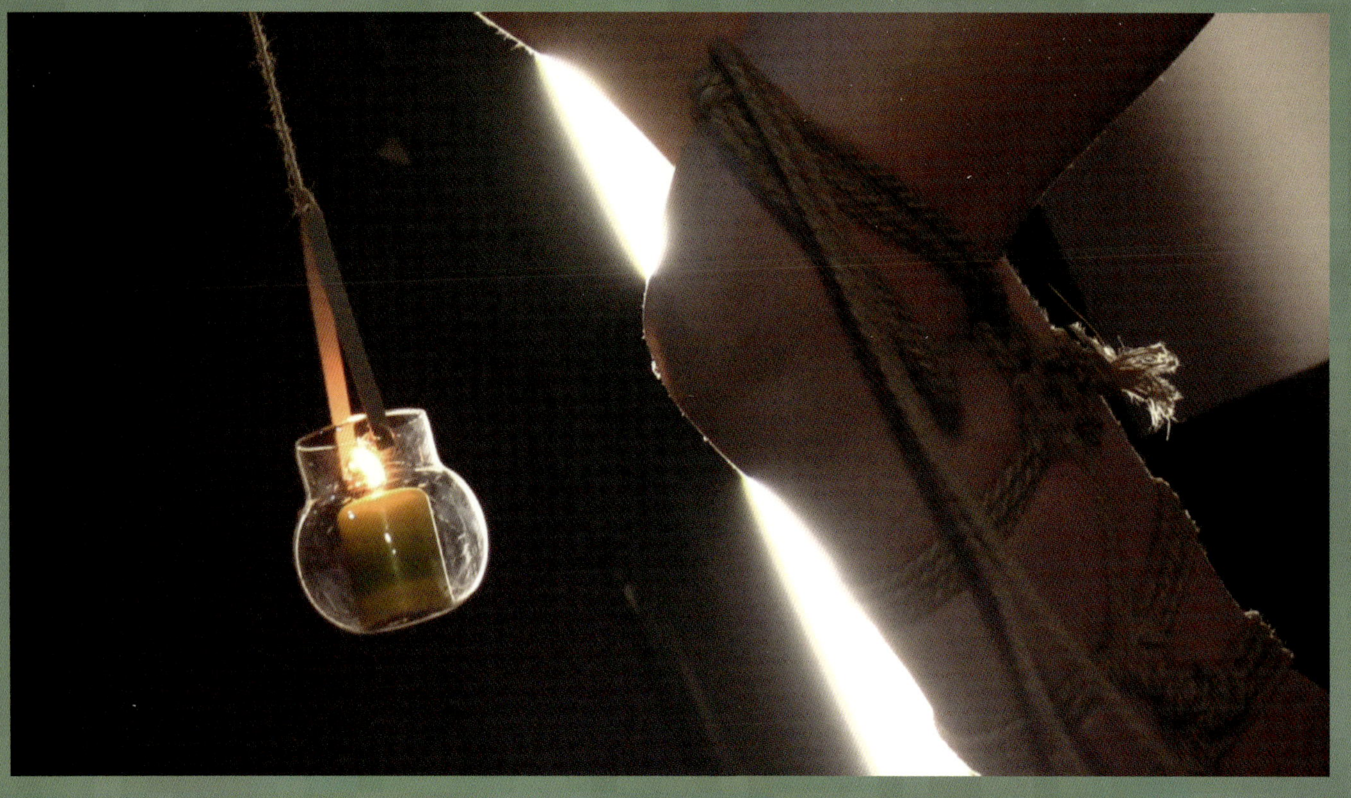

Fuoco: I was told that the tongue tie actually looked kind of brutal but it was not painful at all. It honestly doesn't hurt. Your tongue is quite strong.

It is that normally when you put a clothes pin or a tie of some sort on your tongue you end up drooling. But the nice thing about having a candle on the end of the tongue tie is that it was drying out my tongue. So there was no drool which was really nice!

Gorgone: I really like the intensity, the imagery of the tongue being tied because it's a very sensitive spot. It's very intimate.

Fuoco: I'm actually quite selective about who I tell I do rope, and how I explain it. When I told my mom that I did rope performances, she asked me if I was having sex on stage. I said, no, no, no, that's not what I'm doing!

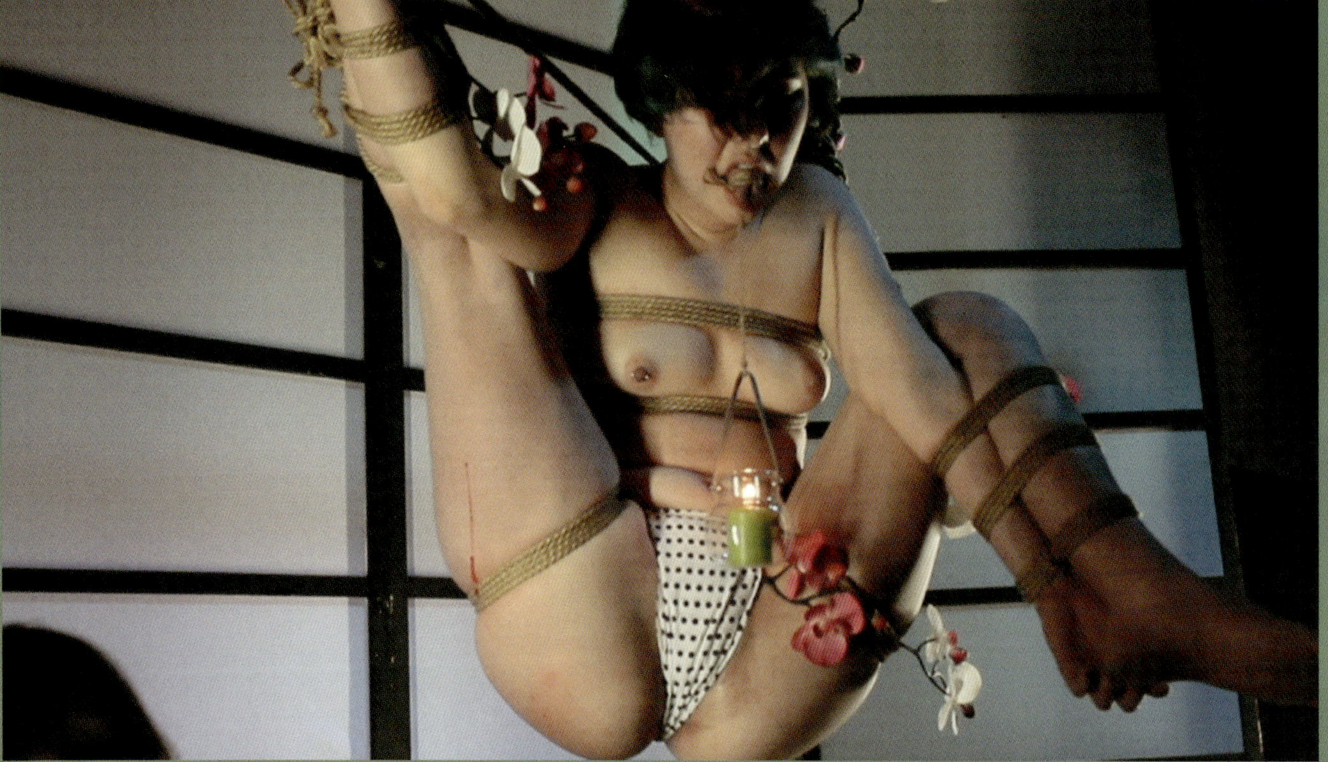

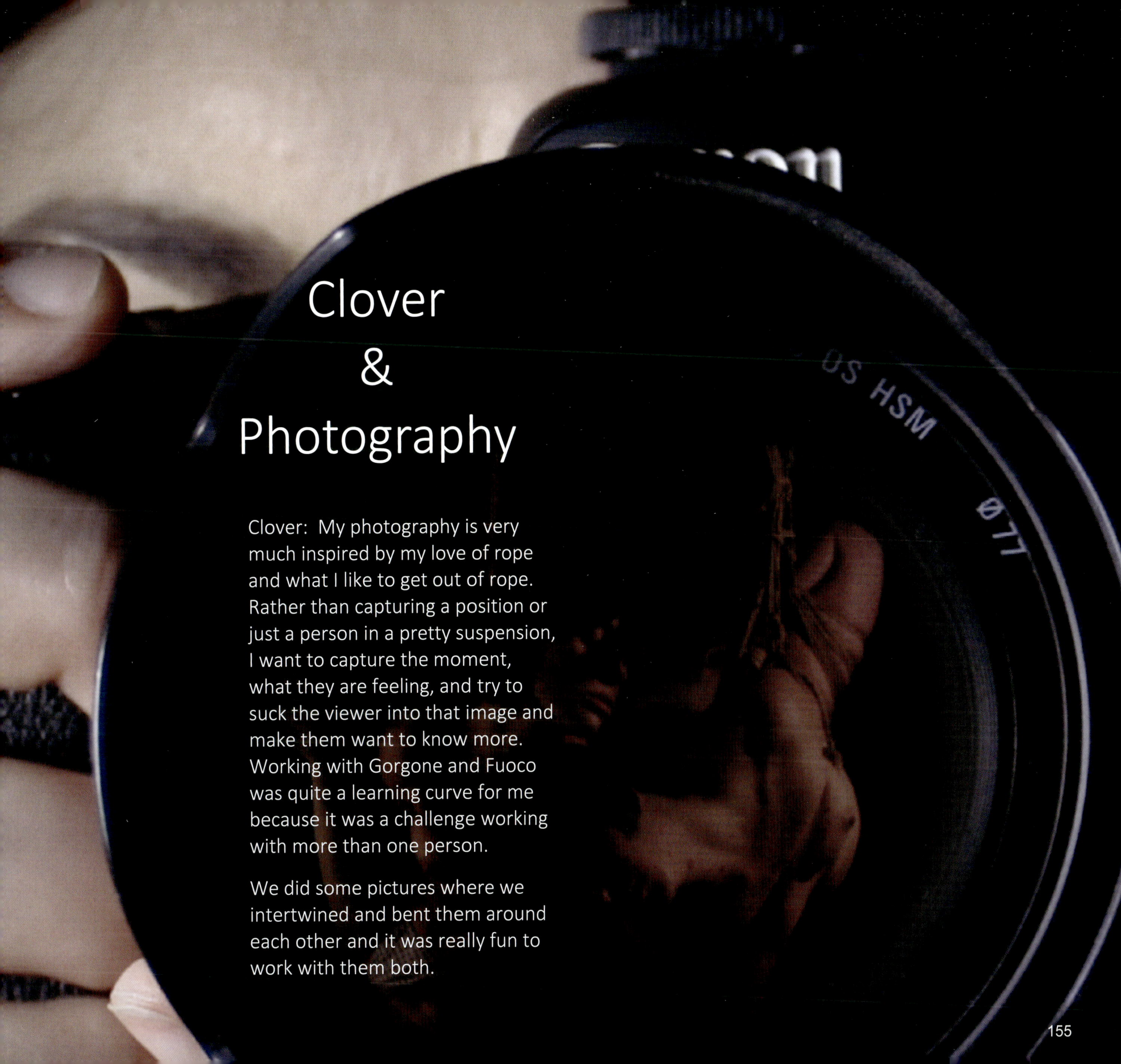

# Clover
# &
# Photography

Clover:  My photography is very much inspired by my love of rope and what I like to get out of rope. Rather than capturing a position or just a person in a pretty suspension, I want to capture the moment, what they are feeling, and try to suck the viewer into that image and make them want to know more. Working with Gorgone and Fuoco was quite a learning curve for me because it was a challenge working with more than one person.

We did some pictures where we intertwined and bent them around each other and it was really fun to work with them both.

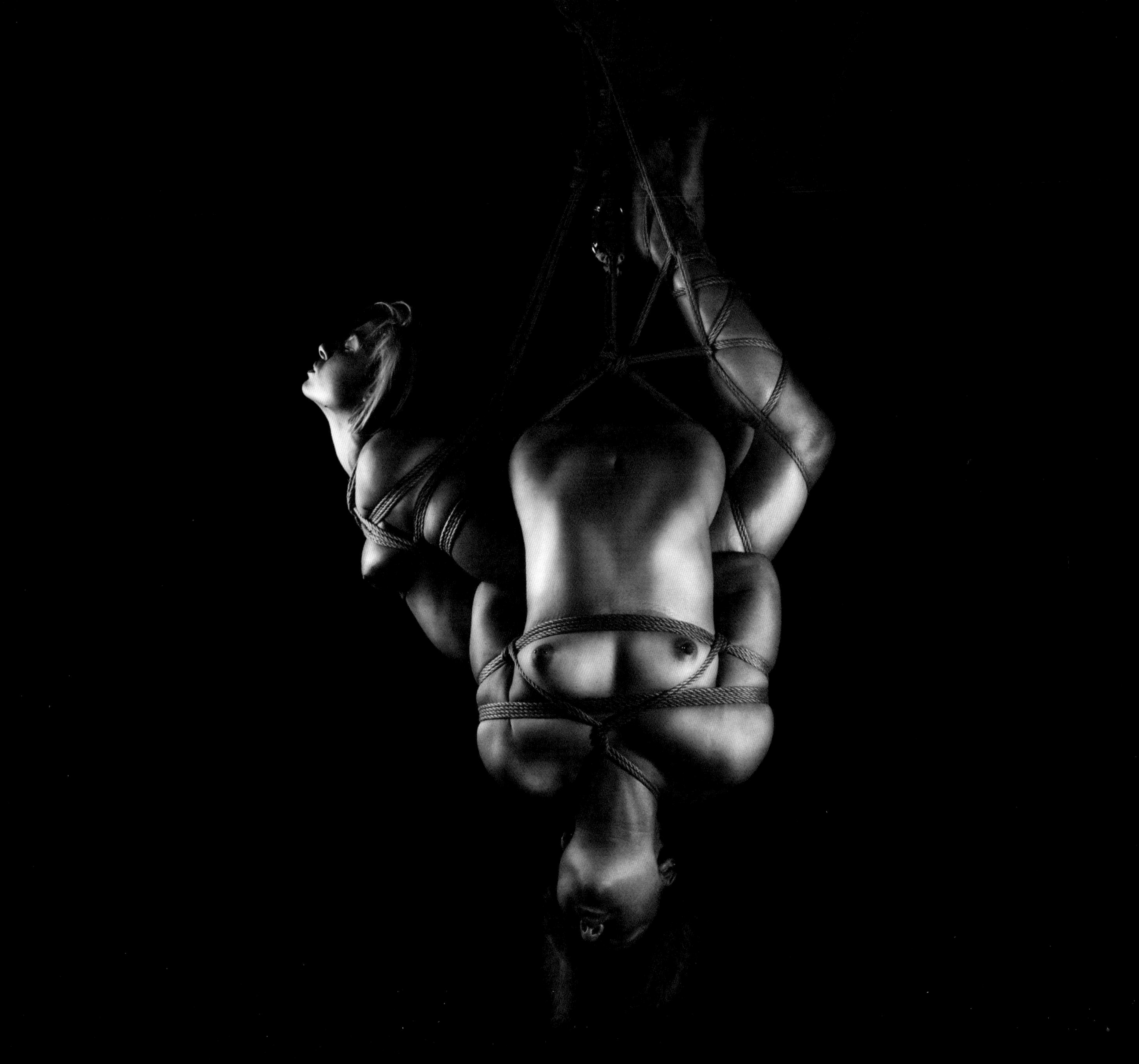

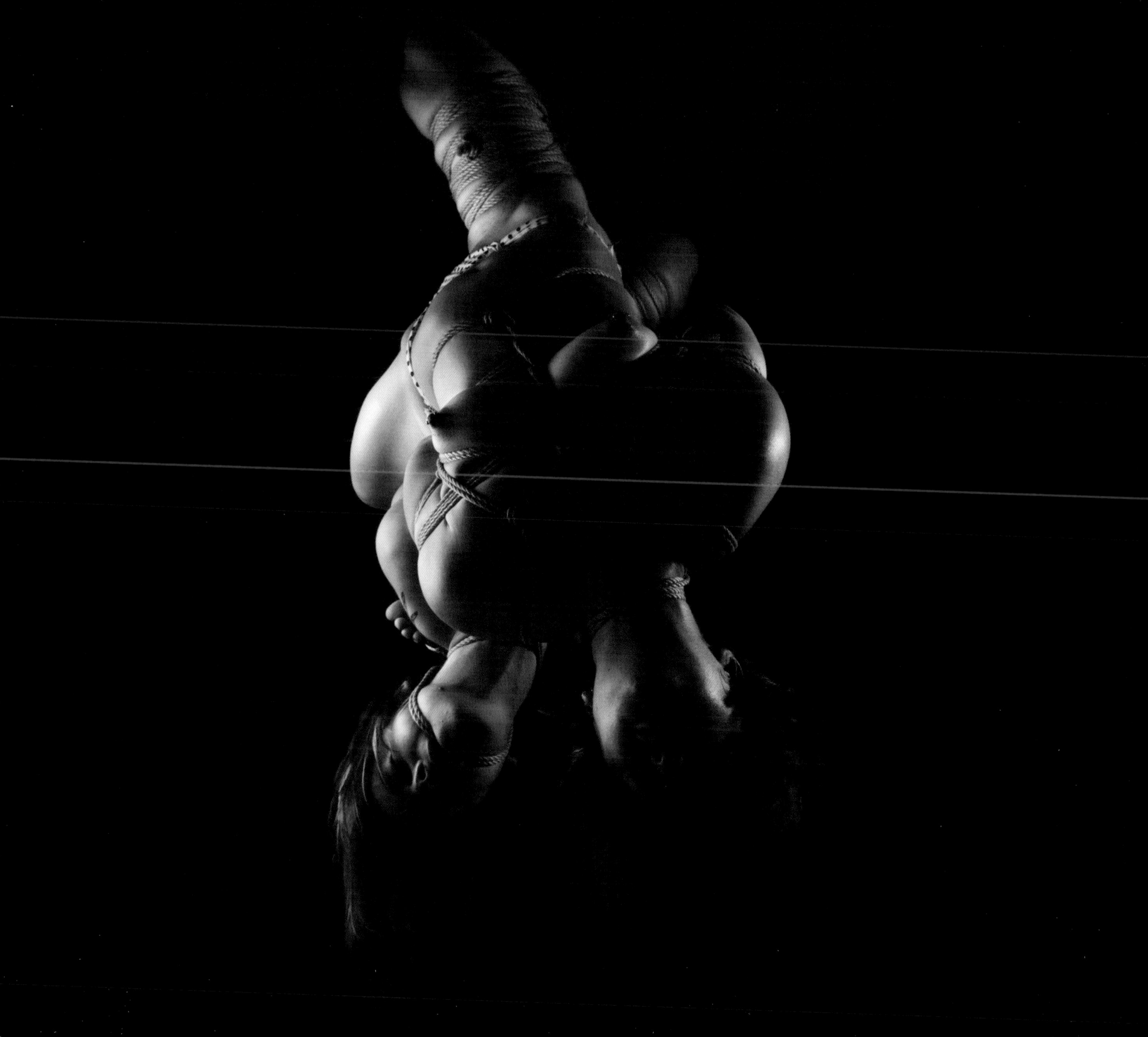

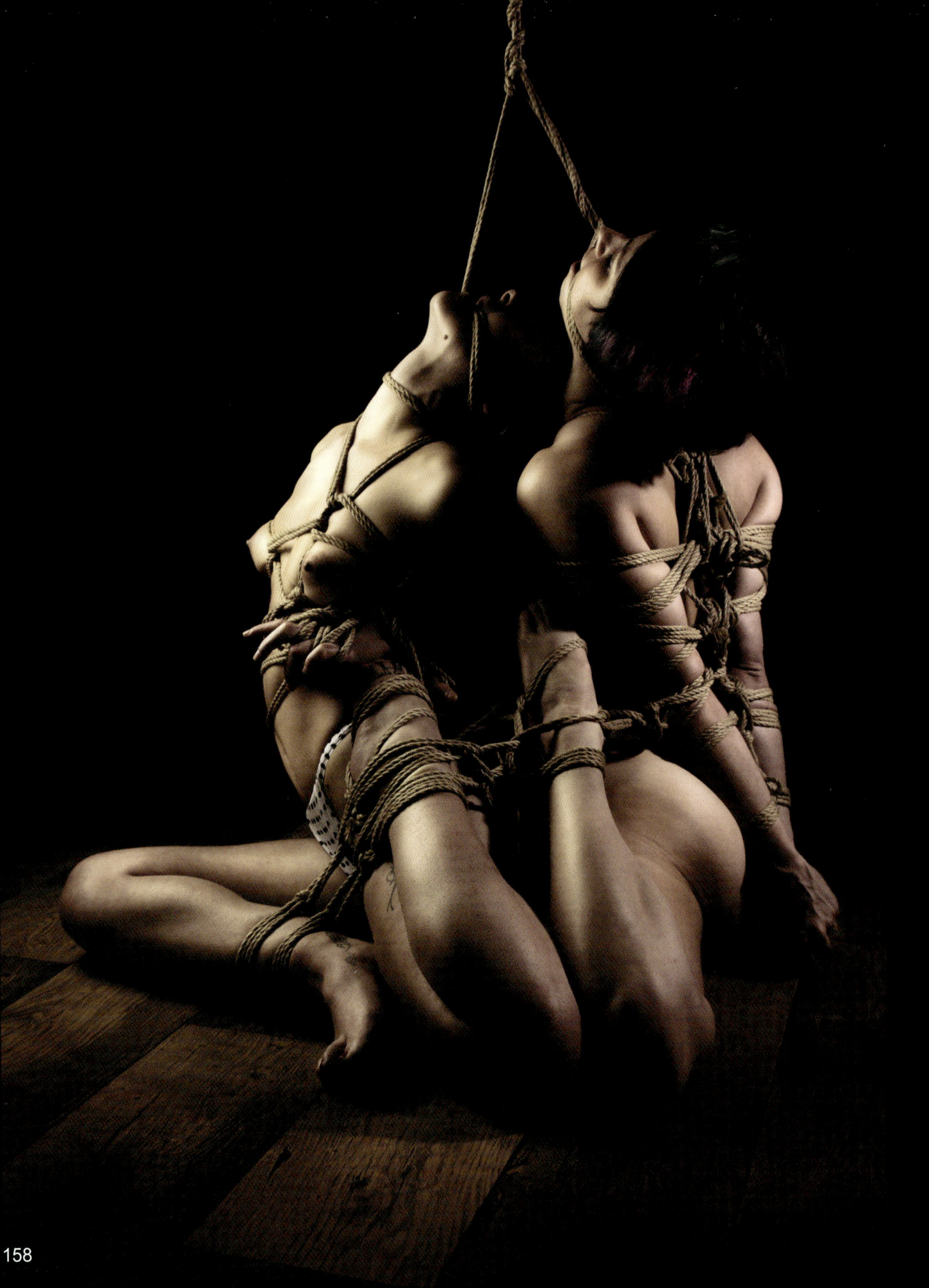

**Gorgone and Fuoco were tied by WykD Dave.**

WykD Dave:  I'd say my role in frankly any photoshoot is to get the best I can out of the models and to use what the model has got.  Every model has something different.

Fuoco:  Yes, that photoshoot was a lot of fun.  Both Gorgone and I are quite flexible and so there were several ties that we did where one or both of us would be saying... 'Bend me further....  Bend me further'. There were several moments when she reached back and grabbed my foot thinking it was hers and went to pull it into a stretch.  It was like  - wait, whose leg do I have?

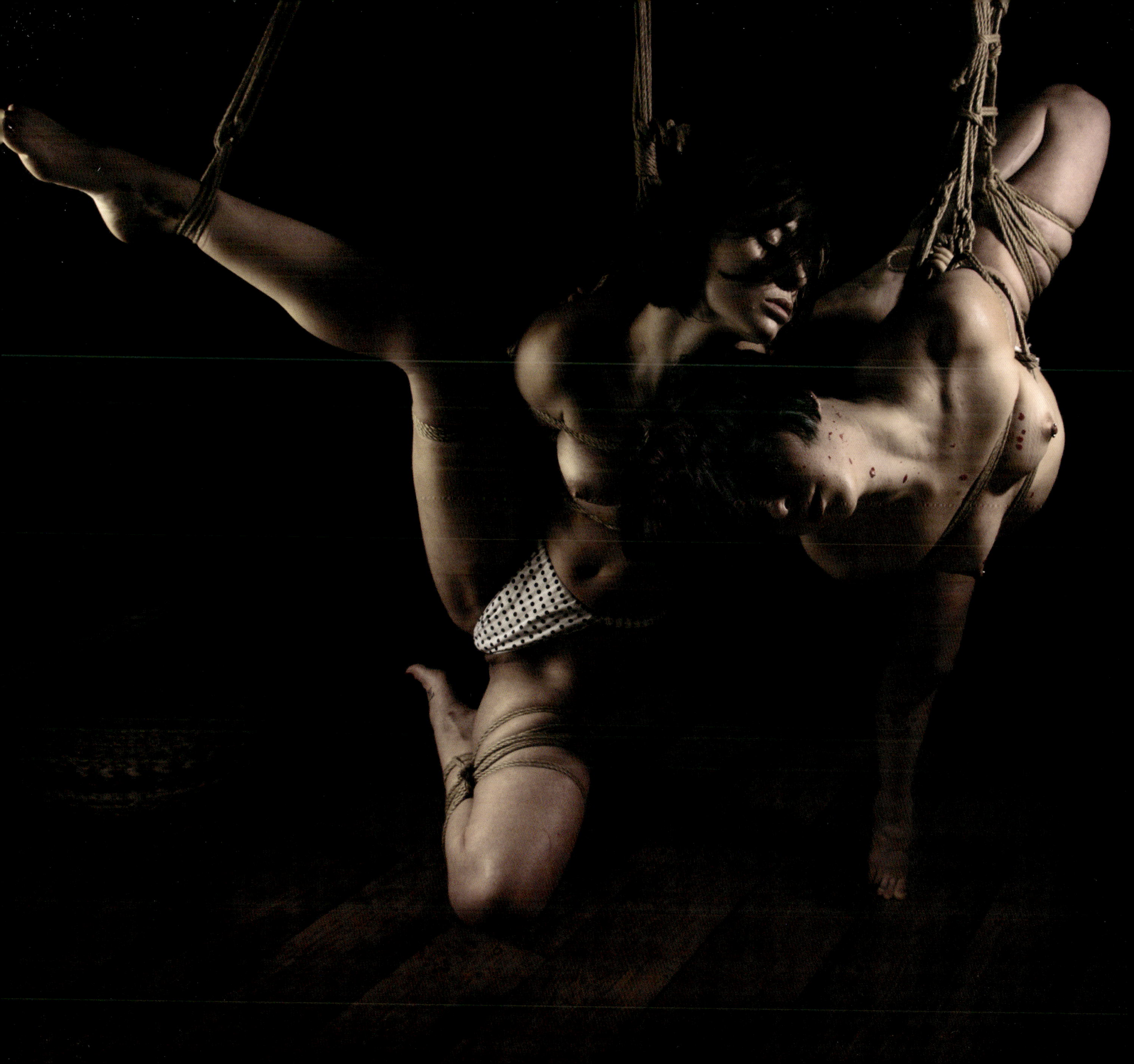

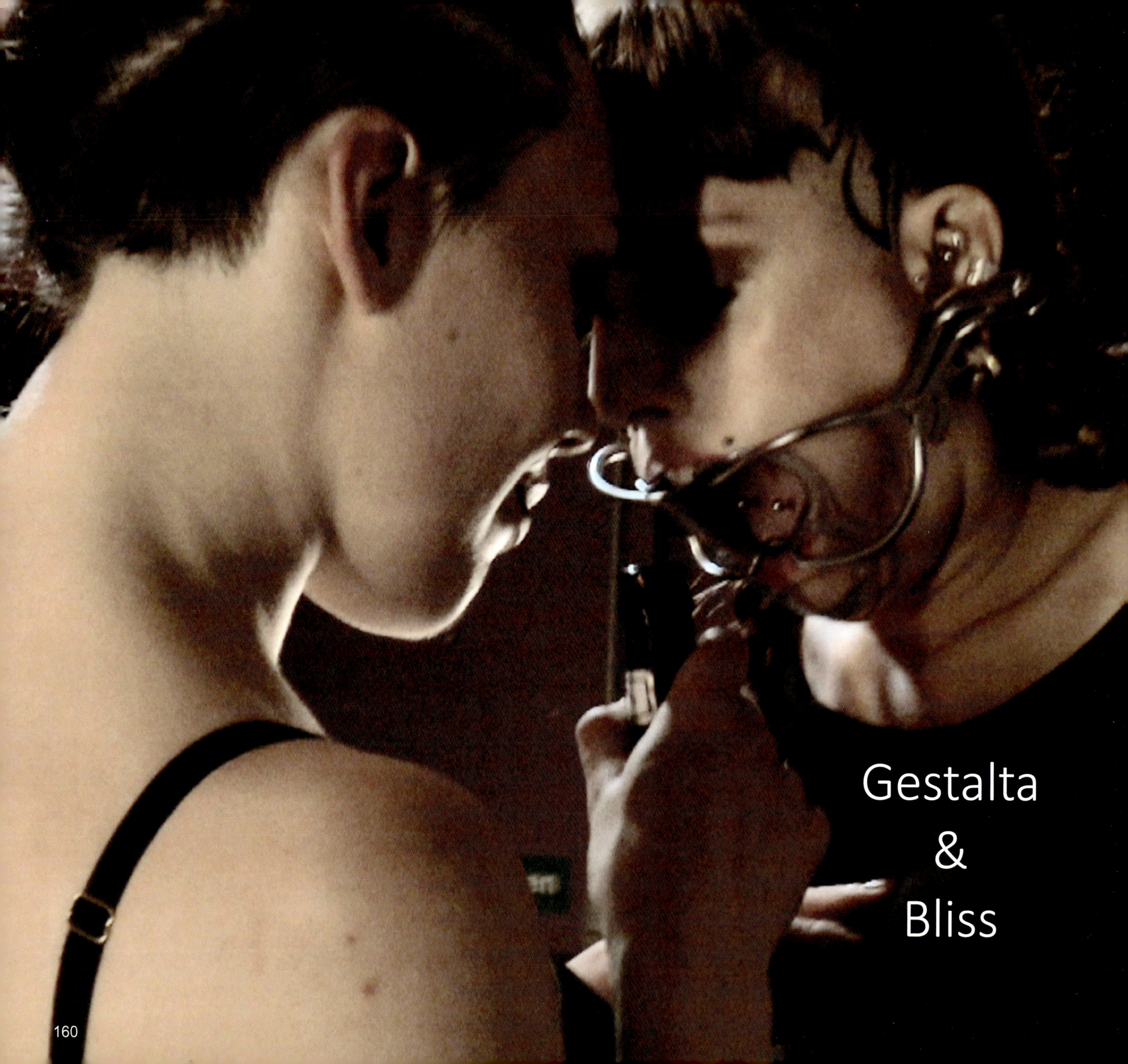

Gestalta
&
Bliss

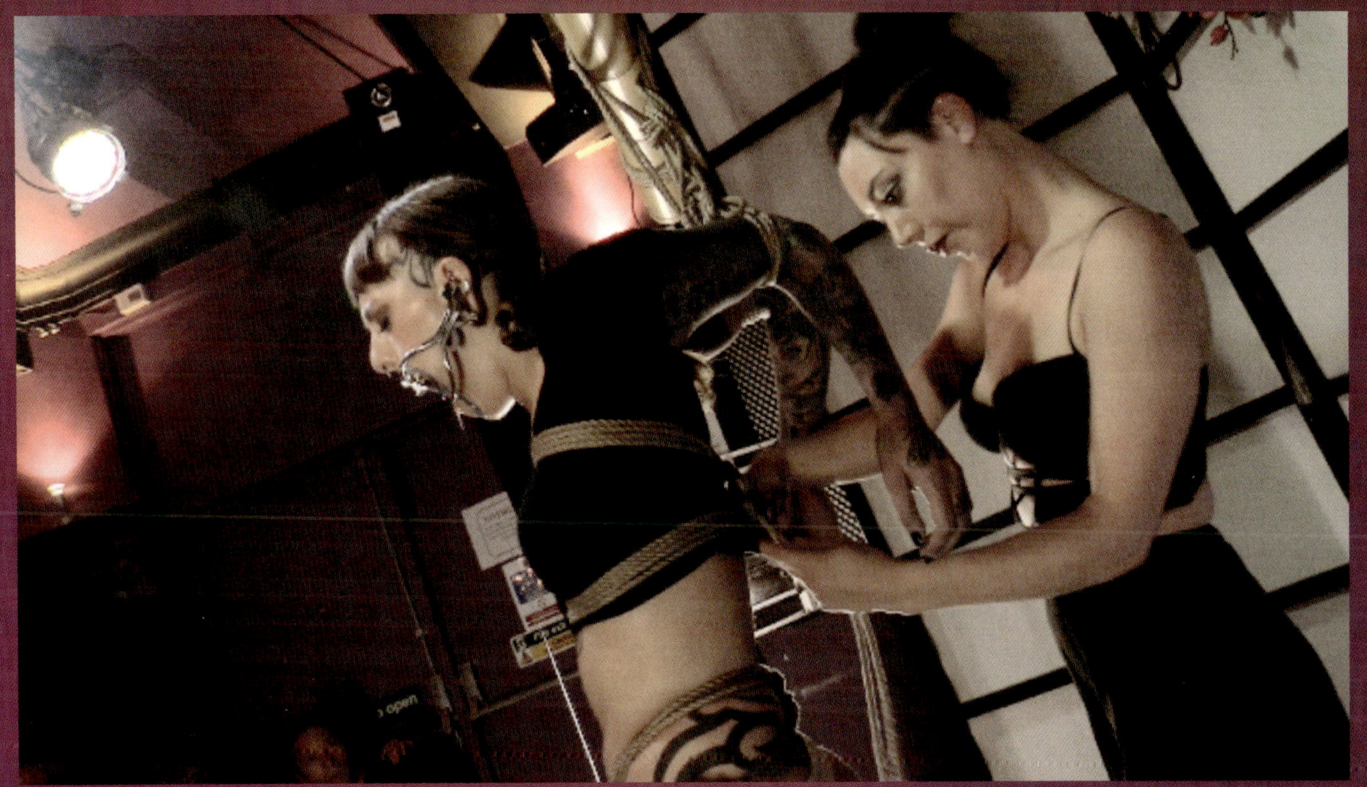

**Gestalta gave her debut performance as a rigger with Bliss as model at Bound in 2014.**

Gestalta:  Ever since I've been modelling I've been tying a tiny bit.  Lately I've been making a very conscious effort to try and do a lot more tying.  I've found that years of modelling has come in handy in that you do pick things up very fast when you've been exposed to it for that long.  I'm getting to the point where I watch everything that the riggers are doing and try to take notes.

I still like rope just as much as I ever have and it seemed like the time to start doing it from a new angle; start experimenting with new forms.

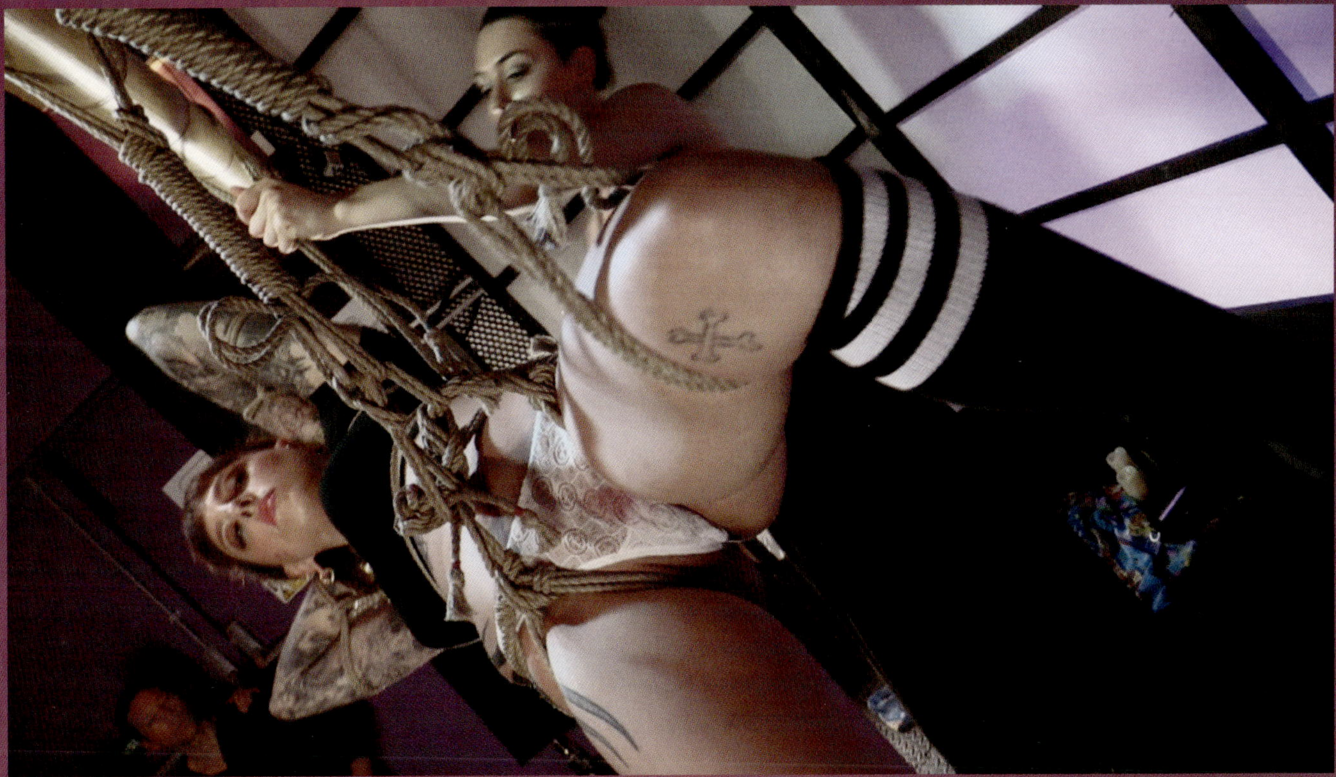

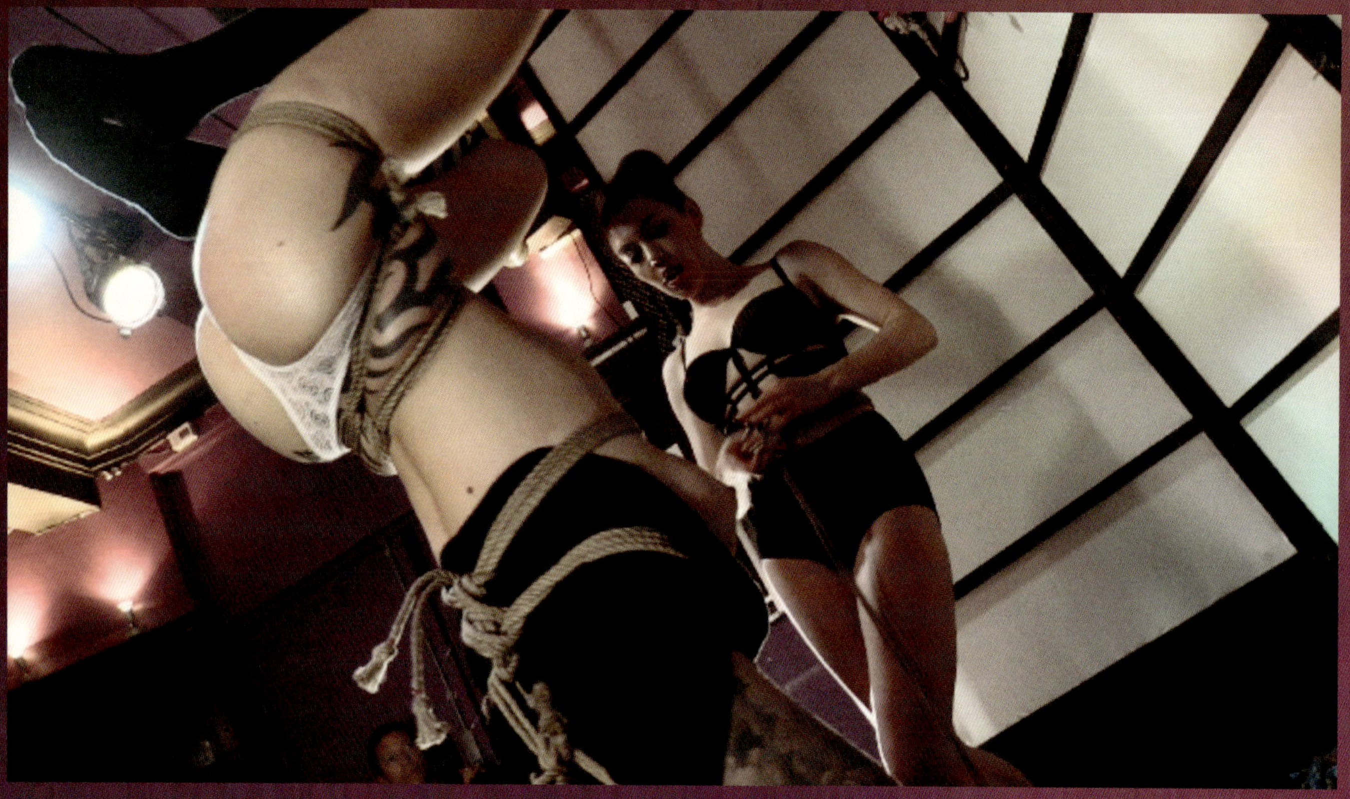

Bliss:  It was really fun. I like it when she tortures me.  And when she slobbers over me and gets me all messy. I am a messy girl.

Gestalta:  Actually, I enjoyed this performance more than any show I enjoyed in ages.

I'm no longer a model.

Bliss:  She's a sexy rigger, really hot, let's do it again!

Gestalta:  Let's do it again!

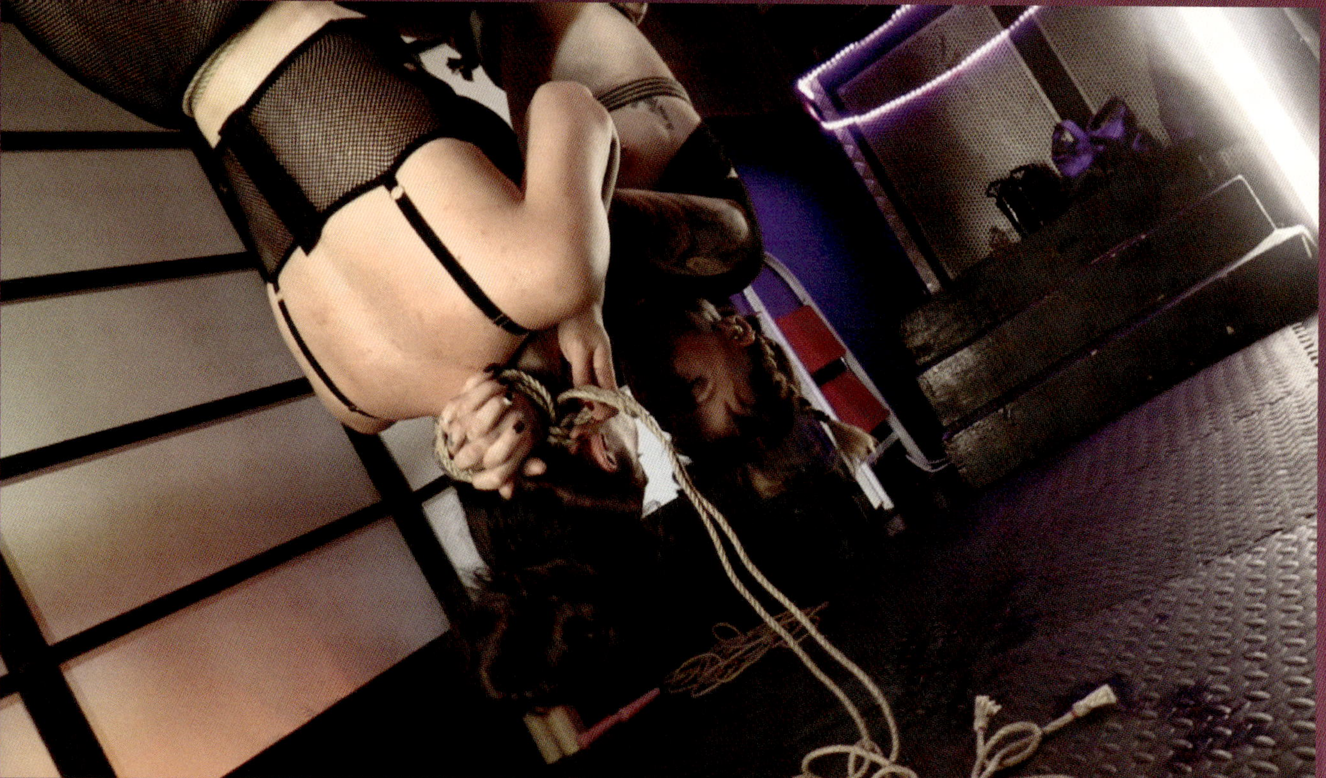

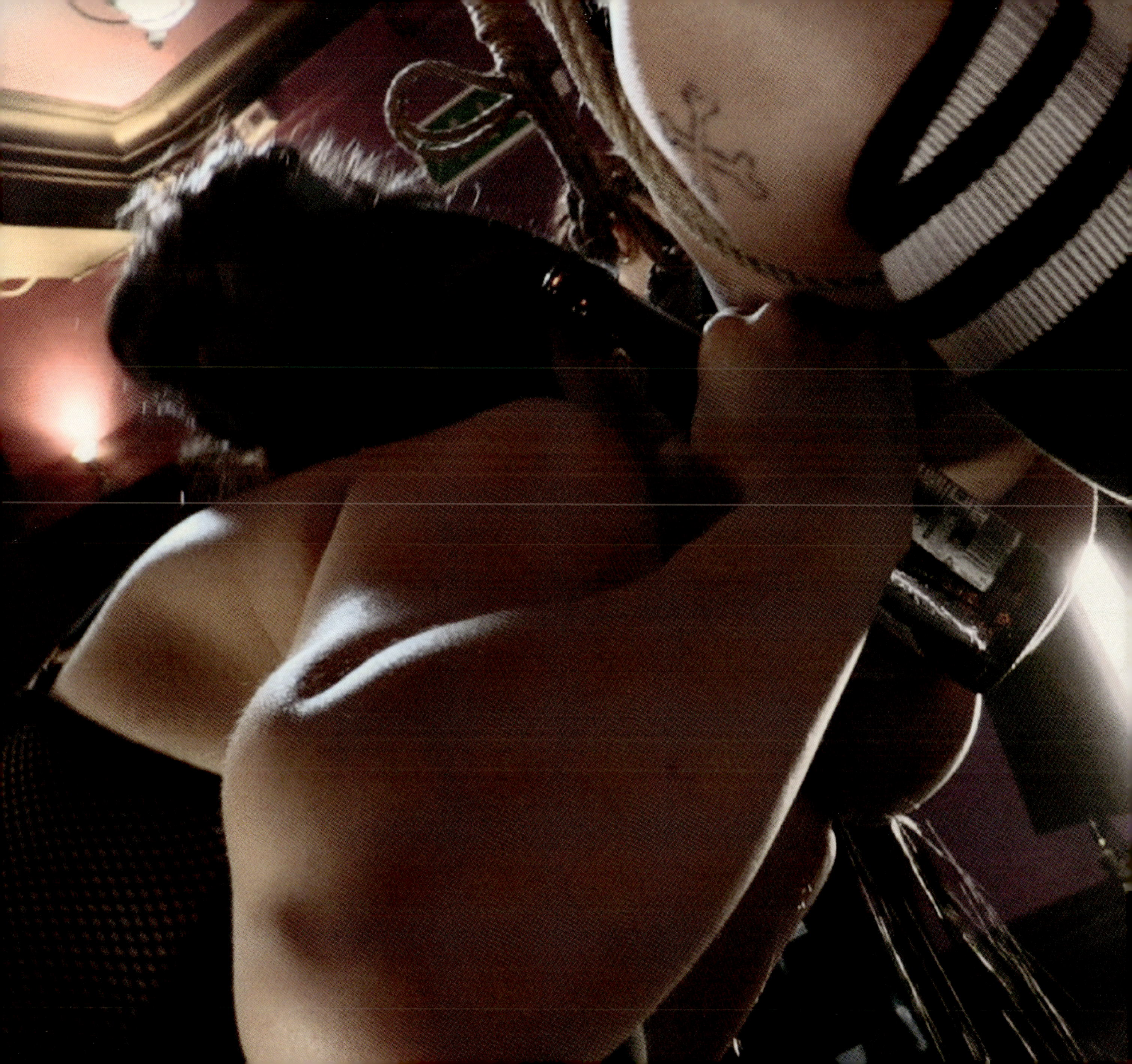

# Loose Ends

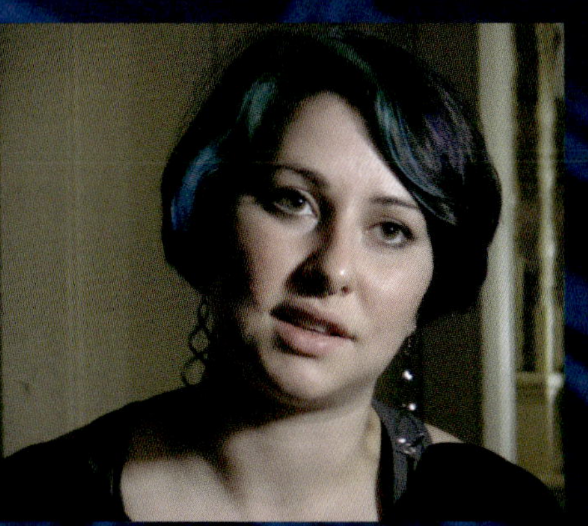

Fuoco:  Women have been disincentivised from pursuing their sexual gratification for years and years and if this is the way you want to pursue it and if this is what gives you good orgasms and great sex, then you should go for it.

Esinem:  I've heard comments from members of the audience... 'Why's she allowing herself to be tied up by that old geezer'!  Yes, for some of them that's the appeal.  I think some of them love the idea of a dirty old man.

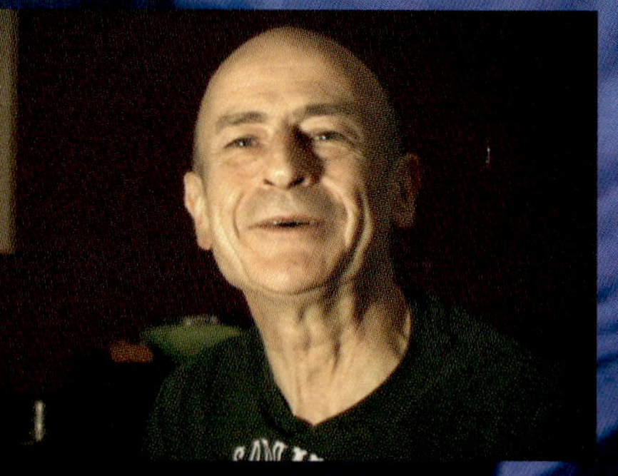

Gestalta:  There are a lot more female riggers in the rope bondage scene, which is something I don't think was around even when the film was first being made. Certainly it wasn't the case when I was first doing rope.

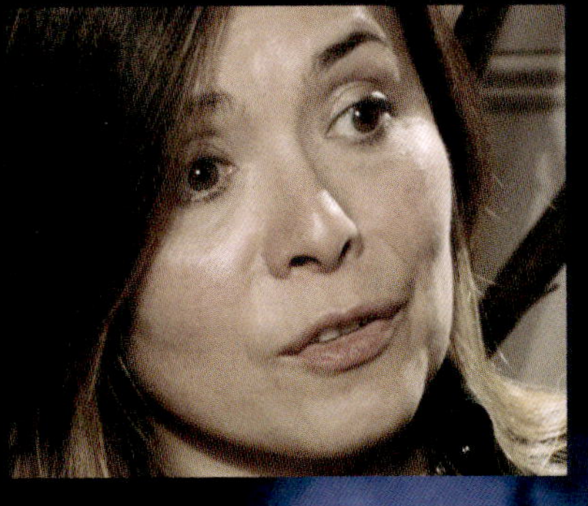

Midori:  If a person is a misogynist, they're going to want to talk, breathe, and have phone conversations as a misogynistic jerk.  If a humanistic guy who celebrates women plays in the same way with rope, he's going to be coming from a place of genuine affection for that person.

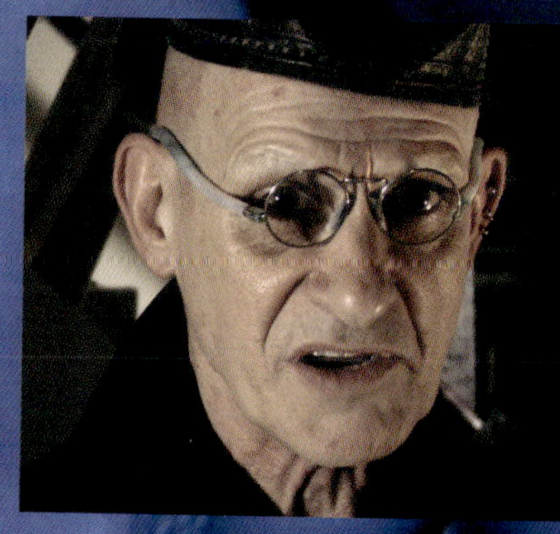

Nawashi Murakawa:  It's a joyous, wonderful art form: it's not something which is to do with sex crime.

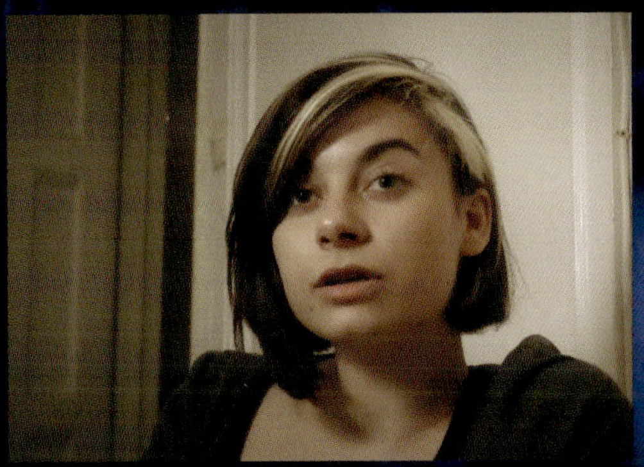

Gorgone:  The only thing that kept if from being mainstream up to now was because it's erotic, it's sensual, it's sexual, and this is still taboo in our cultures.

Clover:  I remember saying to Dave once that we're not kinky anymore because all we do is rope.  I think things just become a part of your life that you forget that actually not everyone else does this.

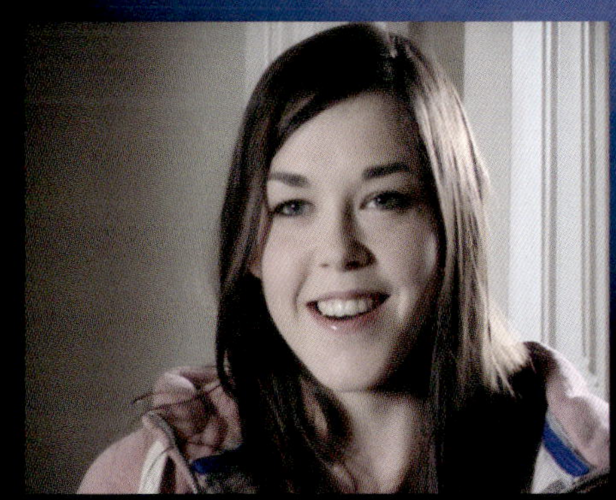

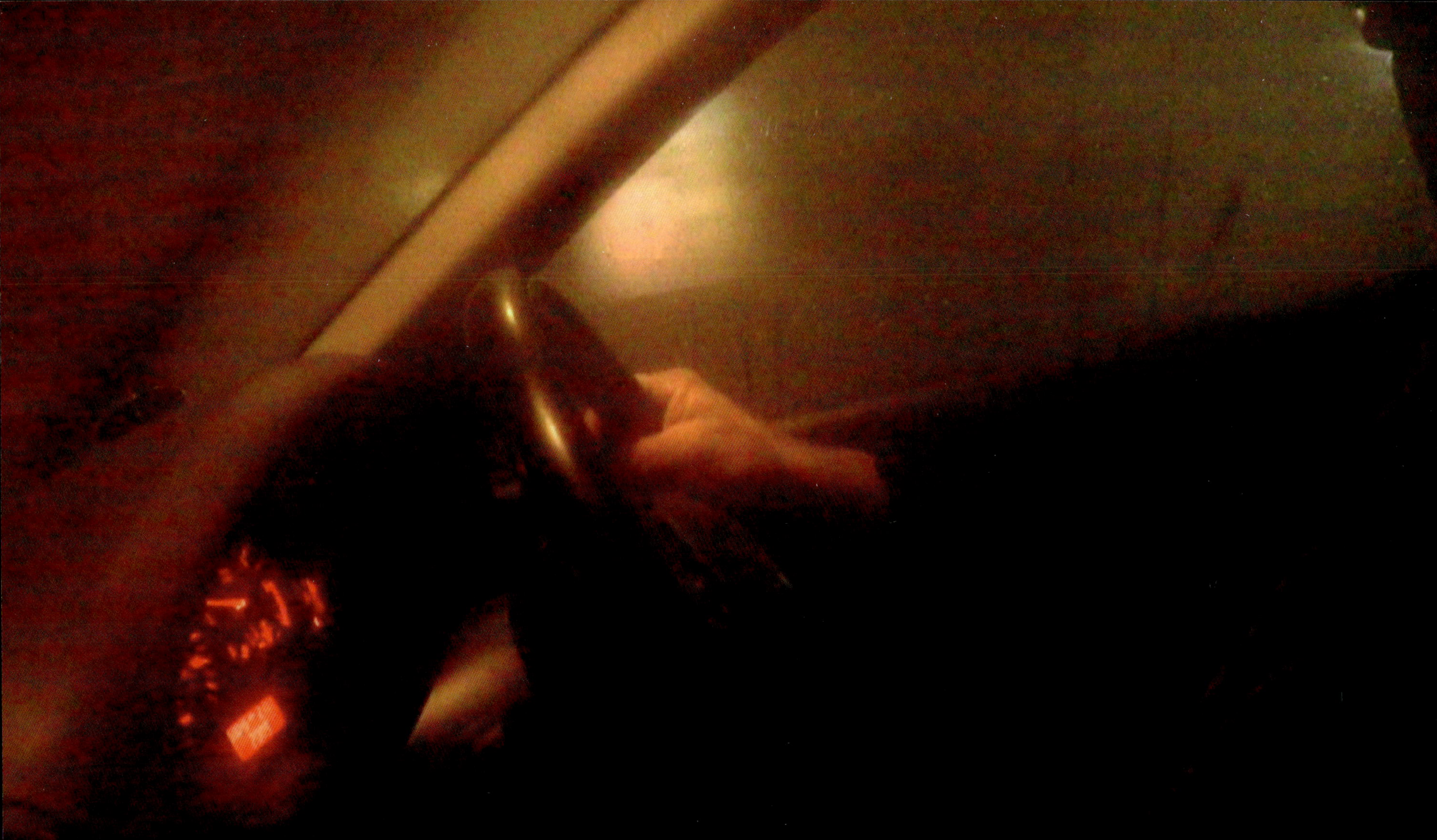

I've come to the end of my four year journey exploring the art of Japanese rope bondage.

What I discovered, I've shared, and it was not what I expected at all.  And I trust that it was not what many of you expected either.

There are, no doubt, some unpleasant characters lurking around the scene, but almost all the people I've met have been generous and free thinking.  Their enjoyment of rope is at the core of their sexual liberation and fulfilment.

I didn't encounter sexism, or issues over gender differences, and absolutely no ageism.

Am I leaving their world for ever?  I hope not.  I've got to know a number of the people in the film and enjoy their company.

Many have been courageous to reveal themselves with honesty and candour, so I can only hope that you've seen a true reflection of their personalities and lives.

I'm flattered to have been warmly welcomed into the Kinbaku community, even without practicing the art form myself……

…. perhaps I should.

# The Pleasure of Rope

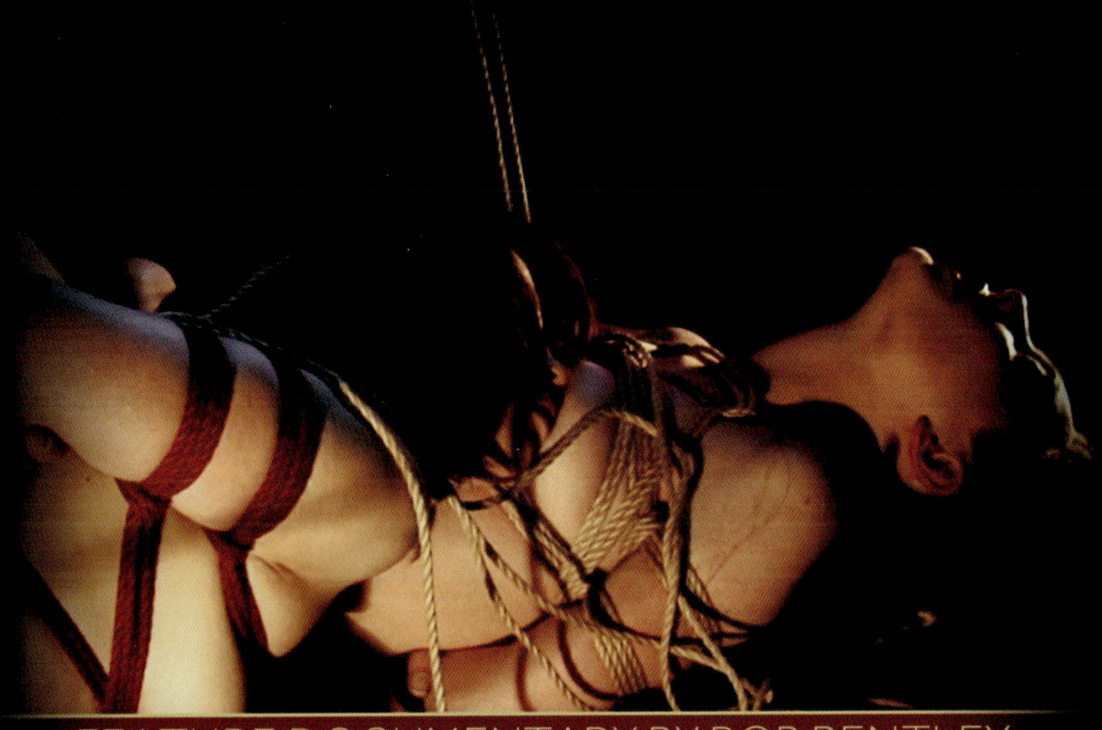

EXPLORING THE JAPANESE ART OF KINBAKU

FEATURE DOCUMENTARY BY BOB BENTLEY

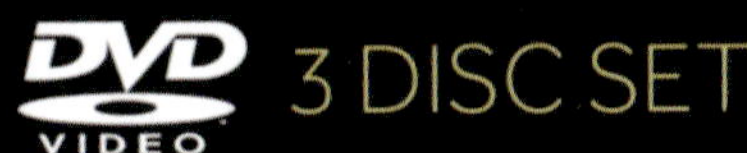

DVD VIDEO · 3 DISC SET

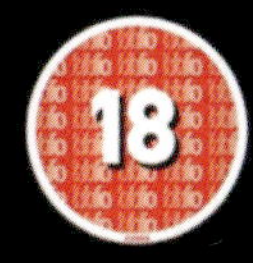

18

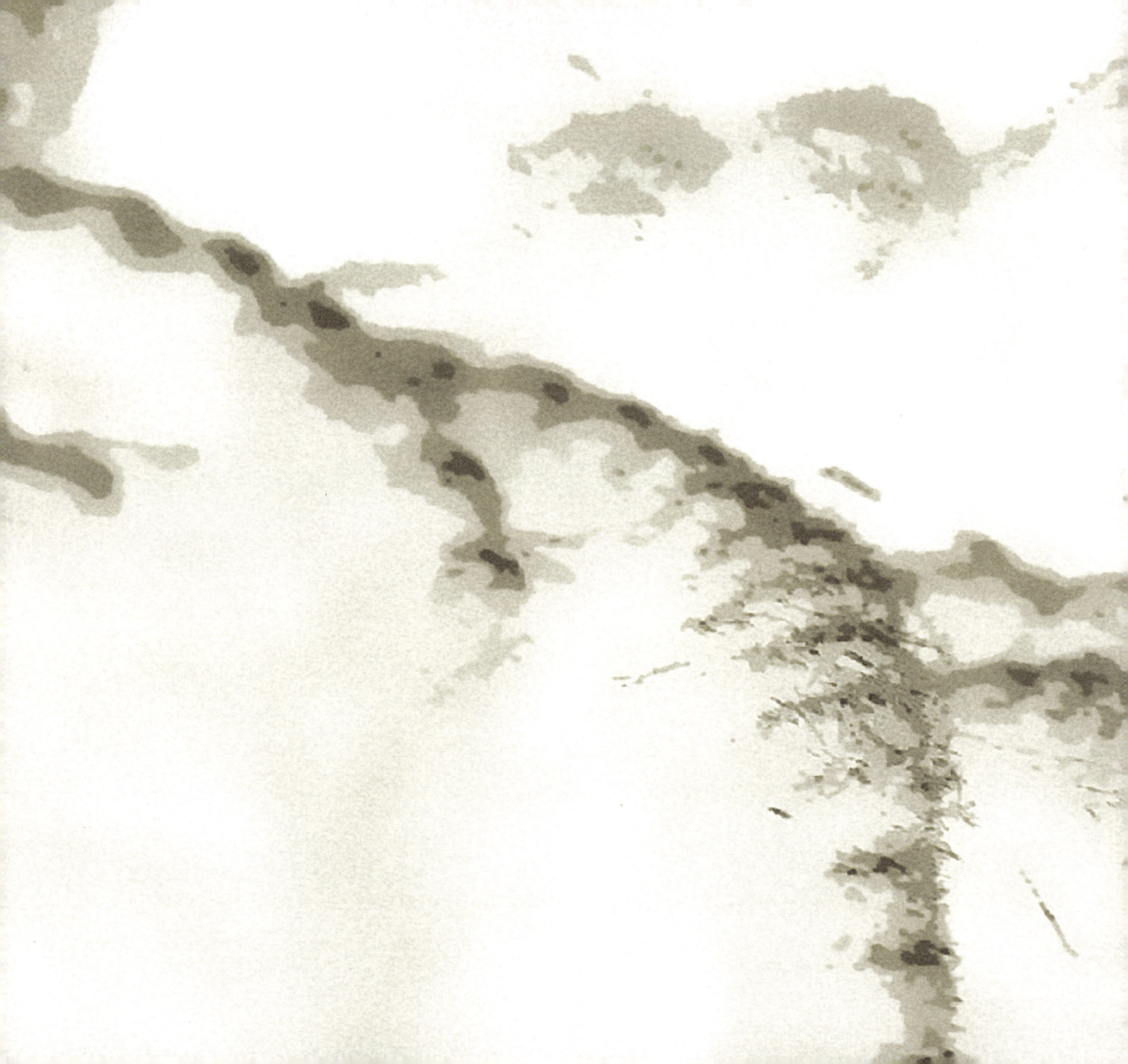